Coalition Politics and Hindu Nationalism

This edited collection examines the emergence of the Bharatiya Janata Party (BJP) in India, and the ways in which its Hindu nationalist agenda has been affected by the constraints of being a dominant member of a coalition government.

Religious influence in contemporary politics offers a fertile ground for political-sociological analysis, especially in societies where religion is a very important source of collective identity. In South Asian societies religion can, and often has, provided legitimacy to both governments and those who oppose them. This book examines the emergence of the BJP and the ways in which its Hindu nationalist agenda has been affected by the constraints of being a dominant member of a coalition government. The collected authors take stock of the party's first full term in power, presiding over the diverse forces of the governing NDA coalition, and the 2004 elections. They assess the BJP's performance in relation to its stated goals, and more specifically how it has fared in a range of policy fields – centre-state relations, foreign policy, defence policies, the 'second generation' of economic reforms, initiatives to curb corruption and the fate of minorities.

Explicitly linking the volume to literature on coalition politics, this book will be of great importance to students and researchers in the fields of comparative politics and South Asian studies and politics.

Katharine Adeney is a Lecturer in Politics at the University of Sheffield. She is author of *Federalism and Ethnic Conflict Regulation in India and Pakistan* (Palgrave, forthcoming) and has published in *Political Studies* and *Commonwealth and Comparative Politics*. **Lawrence Sáez** is a Visiting Fellow at the Centre for International Studies at the London School of Economics. Sáez has published two books: *Federalism Without a Centre* (Sage, 2002) and *Banking Reform in India and China* (Palgrave, 2004).

Routledge advances in South Asian studies

Coalition Politics and Hindu Nationalism

Edited by
Katharine Adeney and Lawrence Sáez

Routledge
Taylor & Francis Group

LONDON AND NEW YORK

First published 2005
by Routledge
2 Park Square, Milton Park, Abingdon, Oxon OX14 4RN

Simultaneously published in the USA and Canada
by Routledge
270 Madison Ave, New York, NY 10016

Routledge is an imprint of the Taylor & Francis Group

© 2005 Editorial matter and selection by Katharine Adeney and
Lawrence Sáez; individual contributions their contributors

Typeset in Baskerville by Wearset Ltd, Boldon, Tyne and Wear
Printed and bound in Great Britain by MPG Books Ltd, Bodmin

British Library Cataloguing in Publication Data
A catalogue record for this book is available from the British Library

Library of Congress Cataloging in Publication Data
A catalog record for this book has been requested

ISBN 0-415-35981-3

To Steve and Joy

Contents

Illustrations

Figures

Map

Tables

Contributors

Katharine Adeney is a Lecturer in Politics at Sheffield University. Her principal research interests include: the countries of South Asia, especially India and Pakistan; ethnic conflict regulation and federal design in Iraq and Afghanistan; national identities; democratisation in South Asia. She is author of *Federalism and Ethnic Conflict Regulation in India and Pakistan* (Palgrave Macmillan, forthcoming) as well as articles in *Political Studies* and *Commonwealth and Comparative Politics*.

James Chiriyankandath is a Principal Lecturer in Politics and International Relations at London Metropolitan University. His research focuses on the politics, international relations and contemporary history of South Asia and the Middle East. His most recent articles are in *Commonwealth and Comparative Politics, Democratization* and *Nationalism and Ethnic Politics*.

Meghnad Desai is a member of the House of Lords, retired Professor of Economics of the LSE and former Director of the Centre for the Study of Global Governance. His research interests include Indian politics and Indian economic problems; socialism and the Labour Party; Chinese economic reform, Marxian economics and poverty. His most recent works are *Nehru's Hero Dilip Kumar in the Life of India* (Roli Books, 2004), *Marx's Revenge* (Verso, 2002) and *Development and Nationhood* (OUP, 2005).

Christophe Jaffrelot is the Director of the Centre D'études et de Recherches Internationalies (CERI) in Paris. His research focuses on theories of nationalism and democracy, the rise of the lower castes and the untouchables in North Indian politics and ethnic conflicts in Pakistan. His publications include *The Hindu Nationalist Movement and Indian Politics* (Hurst, 1996) and *Dr Ambedkar and Untouchability* (Hurst, 2005). He has edited *Pakistan: Nationalism, Without a Nation* (Zed, 2002), *The Sangh Parivar: A Reader* (OUP, 2005) and co-edited (with Thomas Blom Hansen) *BJP – The Compulsions of Politics* (OUP, 1998 and 2001).

Rob Jenkins is a Professor of Political Science at Birkbeck College, University of London. His research focuses on Indian politics and political economy, including work on federalism, electoral politics, Hindu nationalism and social movements. He is the author of *Democratic Politics and Economic Reform in India* (Cambridge University Press, 1999) and co-author (with Anne Marie Goetz) of *Reinventing Accountability: Making Democracy Work for Human Development* (Palgrave Macmillan, 2005).

Apurba Kundu recently returned from a sabbatical year as a Senior Research Fellow at the European Institute for Asian Studies to resume his lectureship in Cybernetics at the University of Bradford. He has been editor of *Comtemporary South Asia* since 1998, and is the author of *Militarism in India: The Army and Civil Society in Consensus* (I.B. Tauris, 1998) as well as articles in *Contemporary South Asia*, *Indian Defence Review* and *Pacific Affairs*.

Marie Lall is a principal researcher in the Education Policy Research Unit, Institute of Education, and visiting lecturer at the School of Oriental and African Studies, University of London. She is also an associate fellow at the Royal Institute of International Affairs (Chatham House). She works on the political economy of India, the Indian Diaspora and Indian education policy. She is the author of *India's Missed Opportunity* (Ashgate, 2001).

James Manor is a Professor of Politics and Director of the Civil Society and Governance Programme at the Institute for Development Studies. His research concentrates on state-society relations, mainly on South Asia. Recent work has focused on civil society and governance and democratic decentralisation in a diversity of systems. He is the editor of (among others) *Decentralization and Democracy in South Asia and West Africa: Participation, Accountability and Performance* (Cambridge University Press, 1998) and *Nehru to the Nineties: The Changing Office of Prime Minister in India* (Hurst, 1994).

Alistair McMillan holds a British Academy Postdoctoral Fellowship, based at Nuffield College, Oxford. His research concentrates on electoral politics and voting behaviour. He is author of *Standing at the Margins: Representation and Electoral Reservation in India* (OUP, 2005).

Subrata Mitra is a Professor of South Asian Politics at the South Asia Institute, Heidelberg University, Germany. His research subjects have concentrated on voting behaviour as well as state and society relations in India. He is the co-author (with V.B. Singh) of *Democracy and Social Change in India: A Cross-sectional Analysis of the National Electorate* (Sage, 1999) and author of *Culture and Rationality: The Politics of Social Change in Post-colonial India* (Sage, 1999) and *The Puzzle of India's Governance: Culture, Context and Comparative Theory* (Routledge, 2005).

Nitya Rao is a Lecturer in Gender and Development at the School of Development Studies, University of East Anglia. Her current research interests include gendered changes in land and agrarian relations, livelihood strategies, equity issues in education policies and delivery mechanisms, gendered access and mobility and social relations within environmental and other people's movements. She is co-editor (with Ines Smyth) of *Partnerships for Girls' Education* (Oxfam, 2005) and has published in the *Journal of Development Studies* and *Economic and Political Weekly*.

Lawrence Sáez is a Visiting Fellow at the Centre for International Studies at the London School of Economics. His research has concentrated on federalism and comparative political economy. He is the author of *Federalism Without a Centre* (Sage, 2002) and *Banking Reform in China and India* (Palgrave Macmillan, 2004).

Gurharpal Singh is Nadir Dinshaw Professor of Inter-Religious Relations at the Department of Theology, University of Birmingham. He has published works on corruption and ethnic conflict in South Asia. His current research concerns globalisation and inter-religious relations, democratisation in South Asia. He is the author of *Ethnic Conflict in India: A Case-study of Punjab* (Macmillan/St Martin's Press, 2000).

Andrew Wyatt is a Lecturer in Politics at the University of Bristol. His research has examined the process of change in the societal, institutional and external dimensions of Indian politics. He is the co-editor (with John Zavos) of *Decentring the Indian Nation* (Frank Cass, 2003) and co-editor (with Vernon Hewitt and John Zavos) of *The Politics of Cultural Mobilization in India* (OUP, 2004), and has published in *Political Studies* and *Asian Survey*.

John Zavos is a Lecturer in South Asian Studies in the School for Arts, Histories and Cultures at the University of Manchester. His research interests are in the relationship between religion and politics in South Asia and in the South Asian diaspora. He has worked extensively on the development of the Hindu nationalist movement and its relationship over time with the Hindu tradition. He is the author of *The Emergence of Hindu Nationalism in India* (OUP, 2000).

Acknowledgements

The idea for producing a volume of this type emerged – as is the case in many brilliant concepts – in a pub after a reception for South Asia scholars at the Foreign and Commonwealth Office (FCO). Gurharpal Singh and James Chiriyankandath, as partners in crime, must take some of the credit for the initiative behind the idea. As editors of this volume we have carried this project to fruition by organising an authors' conference in February 2004 at the Institute of Commonwealth Studies, London.

This edited volume is a collaboration among some of the world's leading scholars and rising stars of South Asian politics. Our work has been made possible by a number of people. First of all, we would like to thank Tim Shaw, the Director of the Institute of Commonwealth Studies, for allowing us to host the authors' conference in his building. Having repeatedly made a nuisance of ourselves, we would also like to thank Emma Butler and Denise Elliott for being so helpful. We also must thank the Society for South Asian Studies and the Political Studies Association for generously providing us with the funds that made the authors' workshop possible.

The contributors to this volume benefited tremendously by the detailed comments and observations made by the participants of the February conference at the Institute of Commonwealth Studies. We especially would like to thank the discussants of the papers: Apratim Barua, Rajat Ganguly, Barbara Harriss-White, Therese O'Toole, Vicky Randall, Rahul Roy-Choudhury, and Kunal Sen (as well as those paper presenters who performed a discussant role). We would like to thank the Electoral Commission of India for permission to reproduce their electoral map. We would also like to thank the two anonymous referees who made suggestions on how to focus the collection, to create the coherent edited volume that you have before you. Finally, our gratitude goes to our editor at Routledge, Heidi Bagtazo, for being so encouraging throughout the whole process, and dispensing invaluable advice.

An enterprise of this sort is always time consuming. Katharine Adeney would like to express her gratitude to Balliol College, Oxford, for providing her with the time as a Junior Research Fellow to organise the conference, write her own chapter and undertake editorial tasks. Lawrence Sáez would like to thank the Centre for International Studies at the London School of Economics for the same. Finally, and most importantly, we want to thank our respective spouses, Steve Vaccarini and Joy Yang, for being so accommodating during this process.

Katharine Adeney and Lawrence Sáez
September 2004

Acronyms and concepts

ABVP	Akhil Bharatiya Vidyarthi Parishad
AIADMK	All India Anna Dravida Munnetra Kazhagam
BJD	Biju Janata Dal
BJP	Bharatiya Janata Party
BMS	Bharatiya Mazdoor Sangh
BSP	Bahujan Samaj Party
BVP	Bharat Vikas Parishad
CPI	Communist Party of India
CPI-ML	Communist Party of India-Marxist Leninist
CPM	Communist Party of India (Marxist)
CTBT	Comprehensive Test Ban Treaty
DMK	Dravida Munnetra Kazhagam
DRI	Deendayal Research Institute
Hindutva	Hinduness
IMF	International Monetary Fund
INC	Indian National Congress
JD (S)	Janata Dal (Secular)
JD (U)	Janata Dal (United)
JP	Janata Party
MDMK	Marumalarchi Dravida Munnetra Kazhagam
MLA	Member of the Legislative Assembly
NCA	Nuclear Command Authority
NCERT	National Council for Educational Research and Training
NCRWC	National Commission to Review the Working of the Constitution
NDA	National Democratic Alliance
NPT	Nuclear Non-Proliferation Treaty
NSAB	National Security Advisory Board
PMK	Pattali Makkal Katchi
RAW	Research and Analysis Wing
RJD	Rashtriya Janata Dal
RLD	Rashtriya Lok Dal
RSS	Rashtriya Swayamsevak Sangh

SAD	Shiromani Akali Dal
SAFTA	South Asian Free Trade Area
Sangh Parivar	Family of Associations
SCs	Scheduled Castes
SJM	*Swadeshi* Jagran Manch
SMP	single-member plurality
SP	Samajwadi Party
STs	Scheduled Tribes
Swadeshi	Indianisation, self reliance, indigenisation
TDP	Telugu Desam Party
TRC	Tamizhaga Rajiv Congress
VHP	Viswa Hindu Parishad
VKA	Vanvasi Kalyan Ashram
WTO	World Trade Organisation

Part I
Theoretical concerns

Introduction

Coalition politics, religious nationalism and public policy: a theoretical examination

Katharine Adeney and Lawrence Sáez

Introduction

The ability of the 24 party National Democratic Alliance (NDA) to govern for the whole of its elected term is one of the most remarkable contemporary events in the history of post-independence politics in India.[1] The 1999 general election in India saw the formation of a multiparty governing coalition led by a political party, the Bharatiya Janata Party (BJP), espousing a Hindu nationalist agenda. This was significant because it was the first national coalition government in India to complete a full five-year term in office. It raised the question as to whether a new pattern in Indian governance was emerging.

The completion of a full term of office by the NDA is also significant because 'Hindu nationalism' as an ideology does not command majority support among the Indian population, although it has been growing in popularity in recent years. One of the key characteristics of Hindu nationalist militancy in India is the presence of overlapping, but highly disciplined, organisations that promote different facets of a unique interpretation of Hindu nationalism called *Hindutva* (Hinduness). Within this framework, the BJP is associated with a network of organisations, often referred collectively as the *Sangh Parivar* (Family of Associations).[2] In this sense, the successful maintenance of a coalition led by an explicitly religious nationalist political party has a direct bearing on the literature on coalition formation and maintenance.

The 1999 NDA coalition was not the first time that Hindu nationalists had come to power in India – they had been elected at state level in the early 1990s and had come to power at national level for 13 days in 1996 – vacating office when it became clear that they could not command a majority in the Lok Sabha (House of the People). They were again elected in the general election of 1998, and formed a government with the aid of 13 parties.

Yet the 1998 coalition proved to be unstable and was toppled a year after its inception, primarily as a result of the defection of a crucial alliance partner from the state of Tamil Nadu. Elections were not held immediately because of the conflict between India and Pakistan over the incursions into Kargil (as discussed in the chapters by Kundu and Chiriyankandath and Wyatt). When elections were finally held in September 1999 the BJP-led coalition, now known as the NDA, was returned to power with an increased majority. Unlike in 1998 it had agreed a common manifesto *before* the elections – *'For a Proud, Prosperous India: An Agenda'* (NDA 1999) (more often referred to as the *'National Agenda for Governance'*).[3] In this book, the authors will show that the stability of the second NDA Government (1999–2004) reinforces some of the theoretical predictions about sustaining the stability of a coalition once in power.

Comparative politics literature and the Indian experience

Within the literature on comparative politics, 'vote pooling' (Horowitz 1991) is understood as a pre-election alliance where political parties agree to cooperate in securing votes by not putting up candidates in a certain constituency against other members of the alliance. Vote pooling had occurred in both the 1998 and the 1999 elections, but after the 1999 elections, as McMillan shows, the expected payoffs of 'seat pooling' (where political parties barter their MPs' support in return for influence and posts in the government) were obfuscated by an expansion of the cabinet. According to Horowitz (1991) – pre-electoral alliances induce moderation because of the requirement to appeal to more than the party's 'natural' constituency of support.

Despite the vote pooling, few observers of the Indian political scene would have predicted the stability of the coalition and that the next general elections would be held in 2004. This was partly because much of the literature on coalition politics assumes that coalition governments are unstable. Lijphart (1984: 81) argues that '[t]here is a very large difference between the durability of minimal winning one-party cabinets and oversized cabinets: the average life of the latter is only about one-third of the former'. In discussing the types of legislative paralysis that accompanies the process of breakdown in democratic regimes, Linz (1978: 66) argued that '[s]uch problems may be more serious and visible in the case of multiparty governing coalitions'. Moreover, in a study of coalition formation in 12 European countries, Laver and Schofield (1991: 154) argued that 'those regimes in which coalitions tend to be more durable are far more likely to have been governed by a single-party majority cabinet or by minimal winning coalitions'. They added that those 'regimes in which coalitions tend to be less durable are far more likely to have been governed by surplus majority or minority cabinets'.

In addition to the general theories predicting the short-lived nature of governing coalitions, coalitions in India before 1999, especially at the national level, were historically unstable. The Janata Party coalition lasted only two years (from 1977–79). The National Front coalition (in power from 1989–91) and the United Front coalition (from 1996–98) both lasted only two years. Finally, as discussed, a BJP-led coalition only lasted one year in power (from 1998–99).

Another assumption that informed predictions about the sustainability of the 1999 NDA coalition is that the political party leading the coalition was a nationalist one. In most of the literature that argues that governing coalitions are weak, the issue of ideological cohesion is an important one in predicting the durability of the coalition. For instance, in his examination of cabinet durability under conditions of a coalition government in a multiparty parliamentary system, Dodd (1976: 20) hypothesised that 'the greater the conflict between parties on the salient ideological or cleavage dimensions, the greater are the *a priori* constraints on bargaining among parties'.

Since nationalist claims are often expressed as a general, two-person, zero sum game, logically, it might be expected that nationalist political parties would have a more difficult time trying to reach a lasting compromise on what are perceived to be 'nationalist' issues with non-nationalist members of the coalition. Rabushka and Shepsle (1972) argue that in ethnically divided societies a democratic system makes it likely that policy positions will harden among the relevant communities – and extremism and violence is more likely. In addition, even Donald Horowitz who focuses on institutional incentives to achieve moderation in ethnically divided societies argues, '[t]here is abundant evidence on all fronts that durable multiethnic parties and coalitions are rare exceptions where ethnic divisions are sharp' (1985: 437).

As the chapters in this book make clear, these two assumptions – namely that coalition governments are more unstable and that nationalists cannot compromise – have not accurately reflected the situation in India for reasons that are discussed below.

Hindu nationalism and public policy

This book sets out to achieve multiple, but complementary goals. One goal is to determine what the effects are of multi-party coalitions on public policy making. This issue has been a perennial topic of interest in the comparative politics literature, notably with William Riker's classic book, *The Theory of Political Coalitions* (1962). Following on Riker's tradition, other authors have explicitly formalised the link between institutionalised processes and the probability of a given type of policy formulation, mostly by weighing the expected utility of entering into a coalition. With the development of a multiparty system at the national level in India, the politics of coalition formation has also become a major topic for Indologists (Singh 1997a; Ram and Gehlot 2000; Patil 2001; Singh, M.P. 2001).

Some recent developments in veto players' theory, notably George Tsebelis's book, *Veto Players* (2002), have attempted to explain variations in policy outcomes beyond the scope of formal institutional settings. Tsebelis focuses on the number of 'veto players' as well as their ideological distance from each other. He argues that 'significant departures from the status quo are impossible when . . . veto players are many – when they have significant ideological distances among them, and when they are internally cohesive' (2002: 2). Therefore, contrary to expectation, policy stability is *increased* by the number of players as well as their ideological distance from each other.

Tsebelis's assumptions are interesting ones for our examination of India. If his argument concerning the number of actors is correct, then the stability of the 24 party NDA looks less like an aberration. Tsebelis's argument that cooperative and competitive strategies coexist inside an alliance – with the partners in the coalition playing a game with variable payoffs – most closely approximates in theory the dynamics of coalition formation in India. Many of the parties within the NDA espouse a secular agenda, and depend on Muslim votes, or covet that community's support such as the Telugu Desam Party (TDP). Therefore, these parties are not natural converts to the Hindu nationalist agenda. In addition, apart from the likelihood of these political parties being opposed to an alliance with the BJP, as many of them are regionally based parties, the question must be asked, how does an alliance with these parties fit with the BJP's unitary conception of the 'Indian nation'?

The answer to why these political parties are willing to enter an alliance with the BJP is provided by the fact that the majority of the parties in India operate in different spatial arenas. Rudolph and Rudolph (1987: 179) attributed 'an emergent bifurcation between support for national and regional parties in parliamentary as well as state assembly elections' to an increasing volatility in regional party voting. The majority of political parties' bases of support are regionally concentrated even if they do not espouse a regional agenda (Manor 1995; Jenkins 1999; Sáez 2002). Therefore in many cases, members of the coalition would not compete directly with one another. Despite India having a multiparty system and a multiparty government continually since 1996, at the state level the picture is rather different. If measured empirically, using standard measures of determining the effective number of parties in a legislature, there appears to be a consolidation towards the emergence of states that are two party systems or two coalition systems (Manor 1995; Yadav and Palshikar 2003; Sridharan 2002), although there are notable multiparty systems; the states of Uttar Pradesh (UP), Bihar, Tamil Nadu, and many northeastern states, being among the most prominent examples (Sáez 2002; CSDS 2003; Chhibber and Nooruddin 2004). The electoral arithmetic allows for alliances with political parties that are not close ideologically, in order to defeat a more electorally dangerous opponent in the local arena, such as the Indian National Congress (INC) (Chhibber and Kollman 2004).

In answer to the second question, 'How does an alliance with regionally based parties fit with the BJP's unitary conception of a Hindu nation?', one answer is that as regionally based political parties are likely to play an increasing role in the future, the BJP cannot afford to ignore them. However, while this is true, as the chapter by Adeney analyses, Hindu nationalist political parties have made alliances with regional parties in the past – the latest alliance is only distinguished by its scale.

One of the aims of this collection is to determine when coalition politics has restrained the BJP. The coalition partners' pragmatic acceptance of an alliance with the BJP has not meant that they accept the Hindu nationalist agenda. Therefore, have the policy differences between the alliance partners operated in the manner proposed by Tsebelis – restraining the BJP and leading to policy stability? The joint manifesto of 1999 was toned down, with the BJP's previous commitment to introduce a Uniform Civil Code, their pledge to build a temple at Ayodhya and their vow to revoke the special status of Kashmir in the constitution, omitted. When in government, partial restraint was seen in relation to minorities as the chapters by Mitra, Lall and Rao demonstrate. Certain policies were withdrawn or overturned such as the decision to make school children sing *Saraswati Vandana*, a Hindu hymn. However, it does not tell the whole story. Other policies were not restrained as shown in Lall's chapter in relation to the National Curriculum Framework. This shows that the BJP was willing to compromise on some issues but not on others. Certain issues were tradable, partly because the BJP was concerned to hold onto office, but others, on the surface, less ground breaking, were not.

The example of the different outcomes between the first, short-lived BJP-led Government and the second NDA Government suggests that we must reassess our understanding of the costs of coalition building and coalition maintenance. First of all, it is important to note that although the history of Indian coalition governments is damming, conversely, the lessons learnt from previous coalition experiences – especially its own effort from 1998–99 – were valuable ones for the BJP. Second, we should approach the role of ideological polarisation from a different angle. In her book, *The Costs of Coalitions* (2002), Carol Mershon challenges the assumption that the costs of coalitions remain invariant across different ideological spectra. Mershon argues that political parties are political actors that not only calculate the cost of their actions, but also seek to change those costs. She argues that these changes in costs explain the differences in coalition longevity. Mershon's analysis is useful because it partially explains why Jayalalitha brought down the first NDA coalition in 1999 – assuming that her costs were low because she would be included in a future INC coalition (however, the INC's electoral prospects were undermined by the conflict in Kargil).

Mershon's analysis is also useful because she discusses how a change in political institutions or a change in the configuration of the policy space could lead to changes in coalition politics. In India, unlike Italy (one of Mershon's principal case studies), the institutional setting has not changed, but the configuration of the policy space arguably has. The 1999–2004 Government was the first time that any political party had led a coalition to complete a full term of office at the national level.[4] This was striking given that the BJP led a campaign that ended with the destruction of the Babri Masjid Mosque in Ayodhya in 1992, one of the most shameful episodes in contemporary Indian history and one whose reverberations continue to be felt in Indian politics today. It cannot be explained merely by the continuing regionalisation of the party system, nor by the BJP's new found competence in running a coalition.

The BJP's aim, as discussed elsewhere by Jaffrelot (1996) and also by Hewitt (2000) is a long-term one. In their view, the BJP has succeeded in changing the terms of discourse in relation to minorities. Therefore, one possibility in explaining coalition stability from 1999–2004 is that the coalition was stable because the BJP's ideas have become more 'acceptable'. This is a point hinted at in Mitra's chapter. This is a different outcome to the one posited above in the discussion of Tsebelis – that the BJP has moderated to secure compromise and that the ideological distance between the coalition partners has led to stability in policy outcomes. If this argument is accepted then the stability of the coalition is explainable by the fact that the political parties have drawn *closer together* (although the more extreme commitments of the BJP remain anathema to its coalition partners).

The importance of religious nationalism to coalition sustainability

The process of public policy making is an important facet of the comparative literature on public administration. However, the effect that nationalist ideologies have on coalition formation is just as important. On one level it could be assumed that there would be no difference between nationalist ideologies and any other ideological differences that would make coalition formation more or less difficult. On another level, nationalism is often portrayed as a general, two-person, zero-sum game. If the latter position is accepted then the ability of nationalist political parties to compromise and form coalitions is reduced or excluded entirely. We contend that the latter view of nationalist discourse is a limited one. Even in a two-person game, conflicts are rarely zero-sum in their entirety because the interests of the players are opposed in some respects but are complementary in others. It is with this in mind that consociational democracy theorists, such as Lijphart, start from the premise that political parties representing different 'ethnic' communities can (and often do) form grand coalitions and that compromise is possible. Indeed, the grand coalition requirement of consociational democracy, including representatives from the various ethnic groups within the polity in the executive, is deliberately premised on securing *more than* a minimum winning coalition in the interests of societal stability (Lijphart 1977). In addition, the academic debate concerning the design of electoral systems for divided societies proceeds from the assumption that coalition governments are possible depending on the institutional arrangements for electing a government. That the specialists on this subject disagree as to the specific electoral mechanism to achieve compromise does not detract from its possibility (Lijphart 1990; Horowitz 1991; Reynolds *et al.* 1997; Evans and O'Leary 2000; Reilly 2001).

Yet the weakness of consociational theory has always been that it works best when it is not needed (Barry 1975). Therefore, is there a limit placed on the ability of nationalist political parties to compromise? The success of multiethnic democracies, such as Switzerland, Belgium, Canada, and indeed, India, is testament to the fact that compromises can and do occur. This is because, as eloquently summed up by Stockwell, those who assume that ethnic groups cannot share power, erroneously assume that ethnic groups share 'identical ethnic preference functions; ethnic groups are in disagreement on all issues; and alternatives are viewed according to a perpetual frame common to all ethnic group members' (2003: 13). The great ethnic diversity of India and its multiple cross cutting cleavages (Manor 1996) specifically undermines the notion of a unified 'ethnicity' or 'nationalism' and therefore makes compromise more likely.

One important question remains unanswered. While there is nothing inherent in nationalism that makes coalition formation with a nationalist political party more difficult than with a party espousing any other ideological cleavage, is there anything specifically about *religious* nationalism that justifies the concerns about coalition formation and maintenance? Is religious nationalism driven by a different sort of nationalist ideological compass that makes evaluations of policy making in this setting appear deceptively simple?

It *is* harder to compromise on religious identity than it is to compromise on linguistic identity (e.g. it is possible to speak/learn multiple languages in a way that it is not possible to espouse multiple religions). In addition, adherence to a religious identity prescribes a whole way of life, and often a moral compass to determine actions. However, this tells us little about coalition formation and maintenance. Most religions are internally heterogeneous (as is the case with Hinduism) and therefore there is nothing inherently connected to religious nationalism *per se* that either prohibits or encourages coalition formation or compromise. More closely connected to coalition politics, Lijphart's work on consociational democracy and grand coalition information specifically concerned religious political parties especially in the case of the Netherlands (1977: 83–5), although there were other cleavages in the societies he discussed.

Returning to India, Hinduism has traditionally been viewed as a tolerant religion, accommodative of a plurality of views. It is often contrasted to monotheistic religions, such as Islam and Christianity, which seek to expand their membership through conversion. This 'toleration' would be favourable to coalition maintenance. Yet, as said, religions are internally heterogeneous. Hinduism is not as tolerant as it is often portrayed. Although it does not seek to proselytise, this is not extended to peoples of the Sikh, Buddhist or Jain faith that are viewed by many Hindus to be lapsed Hindus.[5]

In addition, the Indian subcontinent has witnessed some appalling acts of violence, and Hindus have often (although not always) been the protagonists in these incidents. Some might also argue that the structure of Hinduism itself lends itself to intolerance and violence, based as it is on the coercive caste system. It is perhaps in this sense that some authors have equated Hindu nationalism as a variant of fascism (Harriss-White 2003). The compromises that the BJP have been willing to make are less palatable to its traditional foot soldiers, the Rashtriya Swayamsevak Sangh (RSS), a phenomenon that is discussed in part by Manor and Zavos in this volume.

However, it *is* the case that Hinduism can accept a plurality of beliefs. As discussed in the chapter by Desai, Hinduism is 'neither unitary nor indeed unifying'. To achieve its aims, as highlighted in Desai's chapter, the BJP had to secure the support of the lower castes, and thus moderate its agenda. It is precisely because Hinduism is so diverse that the appeal of political Hinduism is so weak. In this sense, a movement seeking to revive Hinduism in the national discourse would have to tone down a programme to appeal to a wide audience, or to attract coalition partners. This is exactly what has happened in India, and indeed, as analysed in the chapters by Adeney, Zavos and Desai, Hindu Nationalists have been willing to compromise on their agenda in the past. That they were willing to do so to secure government power is therefore not surprising. In contrast, the INC was slower to reach this conclusion despite the regionalisation of the polity – perceiving that its 'secular' programme would have a wider appeal and that it would not require coalition partners to come to power. The INC has now accepted the fallacy of this argument – to its benefit in the 2004 elections. But it is important to reiterate that the diversity within the Hindu religion, while extreme, is not unique to Hinduism. This diversity exists in differing degrees within religions such as Islam and Christianity.

Conclusion

In sum, this book aims to make several contributions to the study of Indian politics as well as to the subfield of comparative politics. Nevertheless, it is important to note that the subject matter covered in this book is highly controversial and open to misinterpretation. Many scholars of Indian politics feel passionate about the type of politics that the BJP represents. For better or worse, it is quite easy to categorise Hindu nationalism, as represented by the BJP, in highly favourable or unfavourable terms. This reality makes an academic evaluation of the performance of the NDA coalition extremely challenging. We have determined that one way of linking the relationship between coalition politics and Hindu nationalism to policy outcomes is to have some form of formal assessment. Namely, we are interested in finding out what the NDA promised in contrast to what they delivered, and as such the manifesto commitments provide the basis of many of the chapters in this volume. We think that this approach provides an important empirical dimension to the study of Hindu nationalism and reduces the normative judgements inevitably involved in such a project.

In addition, our aim is to link outcomes (or non-outcomes) either with the constraints of coalition politics, the constraints of exogenous factors or the Hindu nationalist ideological agenda. As some of the authors in the volume will highlight, some policy outcomes (or non-outcomes) may only be explainable by global pressures or other exogenous factors. The chapters by Chiriyankandath and Wyatt, Jenkins and Kundu highlight the importance of the external dimension. In evaluating policy outcomes (or non-outcomes), the contributors to this volume have been explicit in terms of determining what concrete processes help explain these outcomes (or non-outcomes).

Therefore, we propose that there are four likely processes by which public policy making under conditions of a minority governing coalition (such as the NDA) can be evaluated:

- The BJP and coalition partners are both compatible on a given policy issue, so their agenda is the same.
- The BJP is not fully satisfied with a given outcome (or non-outcome), but coalition partners force the issue.
- The coalition partners are not fully satisfied with a given outcome (or non-outcome), but the BJP forges ahead anyway.
- Neither coalition partners nor the BJP are satisfied by a given outcome (or non-outcome), but external pressures (such as global pressures) force an outcome.

Obviously other equally valid methods of analysing the performance of the BJP-led NDA coalition are possible.[6] However, we think that these four options will provide a loose, yet parsimonious framework within which to evaluate the performance of the BJP-led coalition from 1999 through 2004. We hope that this framework will not be unduly burdensome on the reader.

Although the authors of this volume were motivated by an effort to evaluate the performance of the BJP-led coalition while in office, since the project was conceived general elections were held which resulted in the BJP coalition being replaced by another coalition led by the INC. The prospect of the 2004 general election in India weighed heavily as this volume was being drafted, particularly when the contributors to this book met in London in February 2004.[7] It is fair to say that most of the contributors to this volume at the time of the conference in February 2004 operated under the assumption that a BJP victory was likely, although James Manor rightly reminded us that state level results determine national elections and pointed to a number of states in which the BJP or their allies could do much worse than predicted. This indeed proved to be the case. While surprising, this intriguing turn of events help us provide a specific timeline to the public policy initiatives that were carried out by the NDA from 1999 until 2004.

Finally, our book aims to make a contribution to the study of Indian politics, largely by comparing different types of administration. In the context of India, the comparison can be made between a government led by a Hindu nationalist party versus one that is led by a non-Hindu nationalist party or coalition. Although this book is not meant to be a history of policy making, nor of different governments in India, some contributors to this volume have found it helpful to make these comparisons. We also think that readers who are familiar with the peculiarities of policy making in India will do the same. In some cases, the contributors have found it necessary to highlight how the BJP coalition has differed or, in some respects, been the same to previous administrations. For analytical constraints, however, none of the chapters will undertake a systematic time comparison of the NDA coalition with those governments that came before. Nevertheless, we anticipate that those readers who are well informed about political development in India will make these evaluations independently.

Notes

1 The 24 members of the NDA coalition included 22 formal members of the alliance and two parties that supported the NDA from outside. The formal members of the NDA included the BJP, Indian National Lok Dal Jammu and Kashmir National Conference, Shiromani Akali Dal (SAD), Biju Janata Dal (BJD), Shiv Sena, Sikkim Democratic Front, Haryana Vikas Party, Lok Jana Shakti Party, Rashtriya Lok Dal, Akhil Bhartiya Lok Tantrik Congress, Marumalarchi Dravida Munnetra Kazhagam (MDMK), Dravida Munnetra Kazhagam (DMK), Pattali Makkal Katchi (PMK), Tamizhaga Rajiv Congress (TRC), Manipur State Congress Party, Kerala Congress (Mani), Janata Dal (United) (JD (U)), Samata Party, Anna MGR, Indian Federal Democratic Party, Janata Party (JP). The parliamentary parties that supported the NDA alliance from the outside were the Telugu Desam Party (TDP) and the All India Trinamool Congress (the latter later joined the Government). This information was collected from the BJP Parliamentary Party Office in Delhi. We wish to thank Rehka Saxena for obtaining this information.

2 Broadly, the *Sangh Parivar* includes three frontline groups, the Rashtriya Swayamsevak Sangh (RSS, National Organisation of Volunteers), the Vishwa Hindu Parishad (VHP, World Hindu Council), and an associated student organisation called the Akhil Bharatiya Vidyarthi Parishad (ABVP, All India Student's Council). As some of the contributors to this volume will show, the Hindu nationalist agenda is also pushed forth by ancillary organisations that are not commonly associated with religious fundamentalist groups, such as labour unions, think tanks or rural development organisations. For instance, the *Sangh Parivar* includes a very prominent trade union, the Bharatiya Mazdoor Sangh (BMS, Indian Workers Union), which at times has been active in voicing its opposition to foreign economic linkages. Likewise, RSS affiliates such as the Seva Vibhag (SV, Service Department), the Bharat Vikas Parishad (BVP) and the Vanvasi Kalyan Ashram (VKA) are non-governmental organisations that have been active in working with India's tribal communities. Finally, the Vidhya Bhararti (VB, Indian Enlightenment) are a network of schools. The Deendayal Research Institute (DRI) has undertaken research work on rural development.

3 The text of the 1998 BJP Election Manifesto *'Vote for a Stable Government and an Able Prime Minister'* is available at www.bjp.org. Likewise, the full text of the 1999 NDA coalition manifesto *'For a Proud, Prosperous India: An Agenda'* is also available from the same website. In preparation for the 2004 general election, the NDA released another manifesto, *'An Agenda for Development, Good Governance, Peace and Harmony'*. The text of this manifesto is also available from the BJP website. Unless otherwise specified, the authors of this book will be making direct references to the 1999 NDA manifesto.

4 The BJP first formed part of a governing coalition government at the state level in 1995 when it allied itself to the Shiv Sena in the state of Maharashtra. That same year, the BJP was able to form a government in the state of Gujarat.

5 This is discussed in relation to the Sikhs of the Punjab in Adeney's chapter.

6 Rob Jenkins' contribution to this volume explicitly struggles with this question.

7 A conference, entitled 'Coalition politics and Hindu nationalism in India', was held at the Institute of Commonwealth Studies, London, from 21–22 February 2004. Preliminary drafts of the essays in this volume were presented at the conference.

1 The BJP coalition

Partisanship and power-sharing in government

Alistair McMillan

Introduction

The political science literature on coalition formation in parliamentary systems has tended to focus on two elements of governmental power: office seeking and policy direction. These two elements clearly overlap – a particular government portfolio tends to bring with it responsibility for a particular policy area. Office-driven models tend to focus on the quantitative distribution of a fixed amount of governmental benefits. Policy-driven models have focused on how coalition membership is determined by, and influences, ideological position. As Terrence Cook (2002: 4) summarises, theory suggests that a party leader should seek a coalition which is '(1) winning, (2) minimally so, (3) able to cover median policy space, (4) ideologically connected and closed, and (5) expected to pay off partners by the proportionality rule'. These central tenets of coalition theory have provided a basis for an extensive empirical literature that has examined their applicability to European parliamentary systems.[1] This applied analysis has emphasised a number of (interconnected) conditions which are key to understanding the formation and durability of coalitions within particular states; including the institutional structure, the nature of the party system which has evolved, and the ideological context in which political parties operate.

The approach taken in this chapter owes much to Bruce Bueno de Mesquita's *Strategy, Risk and Personality in Coalition Politics: The Case of India* (1975). Drawing on formal models of coalition politics and building upon Riker's *The Theory of Political Coalitions* (1962), Bueno de Mesquita sought to apply formal theory to a complex real world situation. In doing so, he was forced to relax many of the assumptions used to derive formal analytical models. He highlighted the areas in which such models are deficient, while providing an empirical focus lacking in purely descriptive accounts. Two insights provided by Bueno de Mesquita are particularly important for any applied study of coalition behaviour. The first is the analysis of coalitions over time, rather than interpreting behaviour as a one-shot game: 'the assumption that a participant's behaviour in one coalition has a direct bearing on that participant's future influence and future access to new coalitions' (1975: 1). This approach brings out differences in strategic behaviour over time, with attitudes to risk and inter-temporal discounting crucial to outcomes. It is operationalised with reference to the relative 'need for achievement' of political actors, and through the optimality of mixed strategies of co-operation/defection in negotiations over redistributive benefits. The second insight emphasised in Bueno de Mesquita's work is the changing strategic context over the life of a coalition. Rather than simply analysing coalition formation, coalition theory must also address the strategic incentives in maintaining or terminating coalitions in the light of the developing political context. While these insights introduce formidable complications for formal modelling of coalition behaviour, they enable a more realistic interpretation of the incentives facing political actors over a series of interactions.

In examining the NDA coalition, this chapter follows on from Bueno de Mesquita. The focus is slightly different, looking at government formation at the national rather than state level, which restricts the number of cases to two: the coalitions formed following the Lok Sabha general elections in 1998 and 1999. This means that the empirical depth is much shallower, but the attempt to describe coalition behaviour in the light of theoretical analysis, and the focus that this gives to more contextual description, is shared.

The institutional context

The central institutional aspects of the Indian political system impinging on coalition formation and durability include the electoral system, the role of the President (and state governors) in government formation, and the relationship between parliament and the government. The impact of the electoral system is examined below, and related to the broader context of the party system. The institutional influence of the President (and state governors) over coalition formation centres on the role of selecting which party leaders are invited to form governments. Where a party emerges from an election with an overall majority this is a straightforward task, but in the case of a hung parliament it can be more controversial. The expectation is that the largest party will be given the opportunity to show it can form a working majority, and this should give the largest party an advantage in attracting potential coalition partners, given that they can claim to have a greater sway over potential patronage and power. In the aftermath of the 1996 Lok Sabha elections, there was some confusion over who the President should invite to form the government. The largest party, the BJP, was eventually invited to form a government by the President, and did so as a minority administration for 13 days before being forced to accept that it could not gain majority support. In 1998, the new President, Narayanan, acted more circumspectly, requiring evidence that any prospective government could win a vote of no-confidence. This change meant that the largest party had less influence as a *formateur* of a working coalition.[2]

The change in the interpretation of the President's role in coalition government formation illustrates the contingent effect of institutions. Where the constitutional position is not clearly laid down there remains room for personal interpretation. As such, coalition formation takes place within an institutional context which is open to manipulation. Tsebelis (1990: Ch. 4) notes that institutional design cannot always be seen as an exogenous factor, but that actors can seek to change the rules and structures which govern political interactions. In the Indian case, it is clear that the choice of President or state governor can play an important part in future handling of government formation, and while they are supposed to act impartially, some are more impartial than others. Influence over appointment or election to these positions can be used to increase actors' expectations of favourable outcomes. At a wider level, the endogeneity of the constitutional structure can be brought into the interpretation of coalition politics. The BJP has been vocal in its criticism of the operation of the Constitution, and established a National Commission to Review the Working of the Constitution (NCRWC) in 2000. Although the outcome of this exercise was a bureaucratic and intellectually incoherent muddle, it showed that the rules of the political game were not simply taken as given, but that the government was interested in changing the institutional structure.[3]

Less controversially, but with much more political impact, the Constitution was amended in order to persist with the restrictions on a full delimitation of Lok Sabha constituencies (see McMillan 2000, 2001a, 2001b). Starting in the mid-1970s, the practice of delimitation – adjusting the allocation of Lok Sabha seats between states and changing the boundaries of the constituencies in order to try to reduce the disparities in population across parliamentary seats – was postponed. This postponement was intended to lapse after the 2001 Census, when a full delimitation was to take place. According to the rules of Article 81 of the Constitution of India, such delimitation would have had a significant impact in the distribution of seats across the states. This would have had an impact on the outcome of general elections, with an increased representation of the northern Hindi-belt states, which have seen higher than average population growth over the last 30 years. It would clearly have been advantageous for the BJP to let a full delimitation take place under the original constitutional guidelines. However, presumably under pressure from representatives of those who would have lost out under any redistribution of seats, the Government pressed through the Constitution (Eighty-Fourth) Amendment Act in 2001 (GoI 2002a).[4] This restricted future delimitation to *intra*-state reallocation of seats, and maintained the number of seats allocated to each state at the existing level. A measure (the lapse of the delimitation postponement) which would have, by default, given the BJP a large potential electoral advantage was not allowed to be sustained. The *status quo* was reimposed through further constitutional amendment. This indicates that, in the current political context, the interests of regional balance and coalition partnership are sufficient to block institutional reform which could benefit the largest party.[5]

The Indian parliamentary system of government invests executive power in a Cabinet and Council of Ministers, who have to have the support of a majority of the members of the Lok Sabha. Legislation is mainly instigated by the government. As a federal system, government functions are divided between the national and state levels (Part XI of the Constitution). In practice, parliament has a very limited role in scrutinising government legislation and administration, and much of government policy is implemented through Presidential decree. Under the governmental system developed under INC domination in the post-Independence period, the Prime Minister provides a strong personal and centralised focus for the administration, and institutions such as the Planning Commission control much executive policy direction at a step removed from Cabinet control. As such, the formal mechanisms for Cabinet government are weakened, and instead power is centralised on the Prime Minister and otherwise diffused through a variety of executive agencies and Ministries, with limited scope for Parliamentary influence.

While the Lok Sabha and Rajya Sabha have extensive formal authority over the passage of legislation, in practice parliament has provided only a weak institutional check on governments. According to Hardgrave and Kochanek (1993: 81), MPs 'are indifferent to executive abuse of the system, ignore poor drafting of legislation, and provide minimal scrutiny of the budget'. In the absence of a powerful system of parliamentary committees, there are few significant legislative roles available outside the executive. One important position is that of Lok Sabha Speaker, because of the duties surrounding the timetabling of government business and, increasingly important since the passing of the Anti-defection Act, in determining the legitimacy of defections and party splits. The Speaker is chosen by the Lok Sabha, and is expected to play a non-partisan role in looking after the conduct of the House. However, the government has an interest in the Speaker being sympathetic to the passage of government business.

In terms of the impact of the system of parliamentary government on coalition formation and maintenance, the Indian system is largely centred on the office of the Prime Minister, who controls the formal and informal routes through which patronage is exercised and policy direction given. Ministerial positions offer competency over particular areas of government functions, although such competency has to be contested with state governments and other executive agencies. Policy is usually developed through bilateral negotiations between ministers and the Prime Minister, rather than collectively in Cabinet, although this varies across policy issues and ministerial portfolios. In effect, the executive structure plays an important part in the allocation of portfolios among coalition partners.

Under what Rajni Kothari and others labelled as the 'Congress System' (Kothari 1964) relations between the national and state governments were largely controlled through the internal structures of a centralised INC. Under a one party dominant system, the partisan interests of the INC were served through a centralised system of spending, largely controlled by the Finance and Planning Commissions, and an aggressive policy of intervention in state politics, often leading to the imposition of direct rule from New Delhi. As INC hegemony waned, the formal federal structure became more firmly entrenched. This has led to a greater degree of autonomy for state governments, although the system is still heavily centralised (see Austin 1999: Ch. 30). This has meant that state governments still benefit from friendly relations with the central government, but there is less direct interference, and formal structures and Supreme Court intervention have enabled state governments run by opponents of the central government to cohabit with more comfort.

The single-member plurality electoral system (SMP) used for elections to the Lok Sabha and the Vidhan Sabhas (the state parliaments) has a fundamental influence on the votes received by a party and the number of seats won. As a majoritarian – rather than proportional – system, it means that small fluctuations in the number of votes won can lead to large differences in terms of parliamentary seats. While the practical impact of this method of voting is often expected to promote two-party systems, this tends to be due to a misunderstanding of the properties of such a system and its operation in the United States and United Kingdom. Duverger's Law, which associates such electoral systems with two-party systems, suggests that voters will focus on the two strongest parties, since there is only one possible winner (1963). However, this effect is restricted to the constituency level of voting, and says little about the overall aggregation of seats. Further, even at the constituency level there are reasons why voter co-ordination on the two leading candidates in a constituency will be imperfect, in particular a lack of accurate information about which candidates are in a potentially winning situation.[6] As such, while a strong party performance can provide a focus for voter co-ordination on party candidates across constituencies, the overall impact of Duvergian influences is weak. In particular, parties with strong constituency or regional-based support can benefit from the disproportional returns inherent in the SMP system.

For much of the post-Independence period, the INC was able to exploit the SMP system to change a minority of the vote into a majority of seats. Opposition to the INC tended to be divided between a number of alternative parties, mainly with a regionally confined support base. The decline of the INC exposed the fractured nature of the electoral arena, particularly when seen from a national perspective (Sridharan 2002). This enabled a large number of political parties to win seats in the Lok Sabha. Moreover, in situations where no one party has an overall majority of seats, it has created a situation where there are a large number of potential governing coalitions.

While Duverger's analysis tended to focus on tactical voting, with voters opting not to vote for their first preference in favour of a candidate who is in a position to win a seat, an alternative method for concentrating votes on potentially winning candidates is through electoral alliances. Two (or more) otherwise competing parties may agree to withdraw candidates in certain seats in order to focus support on candidates from one party or the other. The success of an electoral alliance depends on satisfactory negotiations over which party will contest each constituency and the transferability of the votes of supporters of one party to an alliance partner. Such arrangements are particularly attractive in non-proportional systems such as SMP, whereby small increases in the number of votes can lead to much larger returns in terms of seats. Electoral alliances have been widespread in Indian politics (see Sridharan 2002: 497–501), and a key element behind the success of the BJP in transforming votes into parliamentary seats in the 1998 and 1999 Lok Sabha elections. Electoral alliances do not necessarily translate into government coalition partnerships. However, they do indicate some strategic or ideological commonality which suggests a working relationship can be carried through into government, and as such provide important reputational information as to which parties are likely to join together in government coalitions.

The weak federal character of the Indian Constitution has been reinforced by the emergent electoral federalism, bolstered by more interventionist rulings of the Supreme Court. This has focussed electoral competition at the state level. As Yogendra Yadav (1999: 2399) suggests, '[n]ow people vote in the parliamentary election as if they are choosing a state government'. The interaction between state- and national-level electoral influences and coalition formation is the focus of Andrew Wyatt's (1999) analysis of politics in Uttar Pradesh in the late 1990s. Wyatt notes the dynamism of electoral alliances, varying across an electoral cycle that is broken by both Lok Sabha and Vidhan Sabha elections. Given that in most states these two elections do not coincide (following the de-linking of national and state elections in the early 1970s), there tends to be a perpetual readjustment reflecting the different strategies used to approach each election. This complicates the analysis of coalition politics in two particular ways; first by changing the temporal range of party interests, and then by adding an additional layer of incumbency/opposition factors. The first effect reinforces the importance of short- and long-term influences on party strategies. As Wyatt (1999: 13) suggests, 'we can see the BSP and the SP sacrificing immediate payoffs in the hope that eliminating other parties will enhance their future share of post-election spoils'. The second effect can change the nature of pay-offs when considered only at one level. Tsebelis (1990: 9), in his model of nested games, describes a 'logic of apparently sub-optimal choice', noting that 'an optimal altern- ative in one arena (or game) will not necessarily be optimal with respect to the entire network of arenas in which the actor is involved'. Viewing coalition negotiations at the national level as the outcome of a series of nested games provides analytical clarity, as well as reinforcing the seg- mented nature of electoral competition across the whole country.

Electoral alliances and coalition formation

An attempt to locate coalition analysis within the broader context of party systems is presented by Lawrence Dodd (1976). Dodd examines the dur- ability of coalition governments, looking at the conditions which enable stable coalition governments to exist. He accepts that minimum winning coalitions are more likely to endure than either over- or under-sized groupings, but suggests three intervening factors relating to the structure of party competition: the degree of cleavage conflict, fractionalisation and stability. The degree of cleavage conflict influences the extent to which parties are willing to bargain over coalition membership,[7] while instability and fractionalisation affect the certainty of information and hence the likelihood of a satisfactory (or stable) outcome (1976: Ch. 3). In the Indian context, Wyatt (1999: 10–11) uses Dodd's analysis to explain the failure of parties in Uttar Pradesh to form apparently mutually beneficial electoral alliances and government coalitions. He suggests that parties appealing to antagonistic caste constituencies (the BSP and SP) have added constraints on their ability to form coalitions imposed, when these would be unpopular among their core support group.

Dodd's approach reflects a tendency to circularity in much of the party system literature, whereby the outcome of the party negotiation is a reflection of the structure of the party system, which in turn is deter- mined by the nature of party negotiations. This is different to the endo- geneity issue raised by Bueno de Mesquita, whereby trade-offs between long- and short-term preferences influence the success of coalition bar- gaining (see Browne *et al.* 1984: 173–4). However, Dodd's approach does highlight the issue of voter attitudes to coalition membership, and the associated costs/benefits in terms of core party support. Further, if broad party system associations are exchanged for party specific vari- ables, such as the nature of party organisation and the vote base of a party, then a clearer set of party systemic variables can be used to examine the relationship between parties and coalition strategy. Such an approach is developed by Gregory Luebbert, who stressed the variety of conflicting goals faced by party leaders when entering negotiations over coalition formation:

These goals include the desire to retain the leadership, to maintain party unity, to participate in a government, to participate in a majority government, to preserve policy preferences, to see the preferences enacted as public policy. . . . From this perspective, the leaders' task is to insist on preferences that are sufficiently focused that they generate the widest possible support within the party, but sufficiently vague and opaque that they do not engage in government formation the disagreements that are a constant feature of any party.

(1986: 46)

This allows Luebbert to model coalition preferences in relation to 'party profiles', which are defined by a party's support base, ideology and organisational structure. Primarily concerned with maintaining this party profile, a leader will face a trade-off between the benefits from government participation and the need to protect their own position and party identity.

Luebbert's conceptualisation of coalition bargaining provides a countervailing explanation to models which suggest that ideological coherence will be a characteristic of coalition governments. Indeed, he suggested that '[i]t follows from their concern to maintain their distinctiveness that party leaders will, all other things being equal, prefer cooperation with a party whose preferences are tangential to cooperation with a party whose preferences are convergent' (1986: 64). In competitive party systems, the tension between compromising identity and government participation will enable an open bargaining process and encourage parties with tangential or even conflicting policy preferences to join together. Such coalitions are likely to be characterised by multiple veto options, with minimum member majorities following vague or segmented policy options.

Minimal winning coalition theory has suggested that successful coalitions are likely to be made up of the smallest number of parties needed to consolidate a government majority. Such a prediction is based on the assumption that this will allow each party's share of the benefits of government incumbency to be maximised. The threshold of support required for a Lok Sabha majority required by any prospective government is roughly 273 seats.[8] The NDA Governments in 1998 and 1999 were based largely, but not exclusively, on the successful electoral alliances which the BJP constructed in the aftermath of its failure to form a government after the 1996 elections. In 1998, the BJP-led alliance failed to win a majority of seats, and was forced to negotiate with a number of opposition parties in order to win the vote of confidence. The BJP secured the support of the TDP, Haryana Lok Dal and Arunachal Congress, and eventually won a vote of confidence with 274 votes. In 1999, the NDA secured a majority of seats, and the post-election negotiations were used to garner the support of some minor parties[9] which consolidated their parliamentary strength.

Events in 1998 support the theory that minimal winning coalitions will form, while in 1999 it appears that the government formation was slightly larger than absolutely necessary to secure power. However, the position is complicated by two factors; the coherence of the BJP-led alliance as a unitary voting block, and the role of parties who voted for the formation of the NDA Government, but refused to take office. These two factors suggest that arguments related to ideological cohesiveness have limited applicability to the Indian case, and that this in turn weakens the strength of any expectation of strict conformity to the concept of the minimal winning coalition.

The alliances with which the BJP fought the 1998 and 1999 elections were formed mainly as part of a strategy of pragmatic co-operation, whereby ideological distinctiveness was traded for the benefits from co-ordination under the SMP electoral system. While some alliance partnerships had some historical and ideological resonance, most were the outcome of a willingness to gang together against a common enemy. The BJP had fought previous elections alongside the Shiv Sena, sharing a common agenda of Hindu assertiveness; and in the Punjab, the Jana Sangh (a forerunner of the BJP) and the Akali Dal had reached accommodations in previous elections. In states such as West Bengal, Tamil Nadu, Orissa and Karnataka, the BJP forged alliances with a combination of regional parties and break-away factions of the Congress and Janata Dal. Alliance building enabled the BJP to extend its influence not only in terms of regional reach, but allowed it to tap into previously hostile social bases of support (Heath 1999).

In some cases these pragmatic alliances proved extremely successful. Electoral gains, however, did not necessarily mean that the BJP and allies would share a common government agenda. Indeed, regional breakaways from INC or the Janata Dal shared many ideological similarities with their former partners in INC, United Front and National Front governments. In a political system characterised by instability and political defection, little weight could be given to any *a priori* assumption that a successful electoral alliance would translate into coherent government coalition.

Any attempt to characterise Indian political parties into a coherent ideological schema, and identify any median political position/space is fraught with difficulty. Whereas Western political systems have tended to be characterised along a left–right ideological spectrum, this is much harder to apply to an Indian context where class, caste and communal identities tend to cross-cut each other, and these aspects vary across a regionally segmented polity. In its heyday the INC could easily claim to occupy a median policy space, but in the 1990s the party's institutional centrism, devalued secularism, and association with economic liberalisation made it difficult to position the party in any ideological spectrum.[10] The BJP's upper-caste support base and association with *Hindutva*, situating it at the extreme of a communal political spectrum, was tempered by a vague commitment to a *swadeshi* (Indianisation) economic policy and regional autonomy (notably a commitment to restrict the use of President's Rule in state politics). Fitting the multiplicity of regional parties into any ideological spectrum is problematic, since manifesto commitments tend to be vague or non-existent.

Discussing ideological proximity in alliance partnerships reveals the lack of any clear barriers to electoral or government co-operation. The Communist Party of India (Marxist) (CPM) has attempted to maintain its ideological distinctiveness and refused to participate in coalitions containing the BJP, which goes back to the earlier era when it stood aside from any state government formation containing the Jana Sangh or Swatantra Party (Bueno de Mesquita 1975: 59). However, it did support the National Front government of V.P. Singh, which also had the outside support of the BJP, and the United Front government supported by the INC.[11] There appears to be only one degree of separation between communists and communalists: the TDP fought the 1998 election in alliance with the CPM, and in 1999 with the BJP.

Given that the BJP-led alliance in 1998 and 1999 was not an ideologically coherent block, why did no other government formation occur? There were negotiations in 1998 over the possibilities of a government either led by, or supported by, the INC; as had happened after 1996 and in 1990. In terms of ideological space, the INC can be seen to be closer to any median political space than the BJP. Theory would, therefore, suggest that the INC plus the remnants of the United Front (and other minor parties) could have formed an alternative government.

As *formateurs* of a potential government in 1998, the BJP had an advantage. The INC had performed very poorly in the election, winning only one more seat than in 1996, whereas the BJP had increased both its vote share and the number of seats won (despite contesting fewer seats). The INC had also failed to gather together any significant electoral partners, with only ramshackle arrangements with Laloo Prasad's Rashtriya Janata Dal (RJD), aside from the longstanding alliance in Kerala. This led to uncertainty over whether the INC could deliver any future electoral gains. More importantly, in terms of the nested games of state political situations, the INC was often the major opponent of its potential national allies. For instance, in Kerala and West Bengal, the INC was the primary threat to the Left Front; in Andhra Pradesh it was the opponent of the TDP; in Orissa, it was the main opposition to the BJD. Finally, the INC had shown itself to be an unreliable partner in previous coalition governments. It frequently sought to undermine any non-INC government, and forced the resignation of the United Front's first and second Prime Ministers: H.D. Deve Gowda (1996–97) and I.K. Gujral (1997–98).

As Luebbert (1986) has described, in competitive party systems the coalition preferences of party leaders are not necessarily driven by ideological proximity, but rather by the desire to retain control of their party organisation and maintain their distinctiveness with respect to their core

support. For leaders of parties which had broken away from the INC –
such as the Trinamul Congress, Tamil Maanila Congress (Moopanar), or
(in 1999) the Nationalist Congress Party – this presented a conflict, in that
association with the former party would weaken their attempt to present a
new 'Congress' identity in a state. A similar consideration was faced by the
offshoots and remnants of the Janata Dal, which had largely been forged
through an anti-INC agenda. For a party such as the TDP, which fought
the 1998 elections in opposition to both the INC (the traditional and
strongest opponent), and the BJP (which had a small support base within
Andhra Pradesh), the prospect of some sort of accommodation with the
BJP was more attractive than that of the INC. This was despite the concern
that association with the BJP could alienate some sections of the TDP
support base, most prominently Muslim voters.

The case of the TDP also illustrates the second aspect of coalition
formation which makes the Indian context distinctive, which is a tendency
for parties to support governments but not participate in the formation of
cabinets. Most theories of coalition formation presume that the benefits of
participation will come in the form of policy influence and governmental
patronage, yet the federal and diffuse nature of the Indian political system
and electoral behaviour mean that parties are often willing to support a
government in New Delhi, but not accept ministerial posts. Minority governments, whereby the government coalition formed a sub-set of a
broader parliamentary coalition – with some parties supporting the
government while taking no ministerial posts – have become increasingly
prevalent.[12] These governments have tended to be short-lived, which fits in
with the expectations of most coalition theorists.

The study of the formation of the NDA Governments of 1998 and 1999
show that, while theoretical predictions of minimal winning and ideologically coherent coalitions are ideals, in practice there are countervailing
pressures and constraints which require consideration. First, as Luebbert
(1986) suggested, in a competitive party system, the need to preserve distinctive party identities may lead to parties associating with partners who
are not ideologically close. Second, in a segmented polity, where national
elections can be seen as the outcome of numerous regional contests, it is
often necessary to examine the component outcomes as an amalgamation
of smaller interactions, rather than simply at the aggregate level. This
approach chimes with Tsebelis's theory of nested games (1990). Both of
these factors tend to weaken any expectations of ideological coherence in
national coalition formations, and emphasise the varying strategic context
in which parties are competing.

The institutional context has clearly influenced the outcome of coalition formation, through the operation of the electoral system, the nature
of the over-lapping federal responsibilities of national and state governments, and the role of the President in government formation and dissolution. In turn, this influences the preferences of party leaders over

coalition membership. Support from 'outside' indicates that parties feel that the gains from accepting a ministerial role from the national government are outweighed by the freedom given by some ideological or programme distance. As Laver and Schofield (1990: 105) note, government participation can lead to 'tainting', whereby the association with unpopular policies can harm future electoral performance. In the Indian context, parties primarily concerned with the control of state governments have been willing to forgo the direct patronage of central government and maintain a distance from policy decisions at the national level in order to consolidate their state-wise support base.

Government participation and portfolio allocation

This section focuses on the way in which the BJP-led NDA Governments have distributed ministerial portfolios at the moment of government formation. The dominant position of the BJP in the Lok Sabha after the 1998 and 1999 elections, both as the largest party and because of its electoral alliances with most of the parties which supported it, meant that it was able to control the distribution of ministerial posts. Atal Behari Vajpayee, was presented as the Prime Ministerial candidate in both campaigns, and held the post from 1998 until the NDA's electoral defeat in 2004. As Prime Minister, Vajpayee was in charge of distributing portfolios between the BJP and supporting parties.

A core assumption of coalition theory is that parties benefit from being in government, because:

> not only do the psychological rewards of wielding power accrue to the party elite and its backbenchers, but also the party is in a position to use the power of the state to reward its friends and punish its enemies.
> (Browne and Franklin 1973: 453)

The way in which government power and patronage is shared between the members of a government coalition has important consequences both for the cohesiveness of the government, and the policy direction which it adopts. Two competing models of portfolio allocation have been developed, one which suggests that government offices will be distributed proportionately between coalition partners, and one which predicts that the distribution will reflect the bargaining power of each of the partners (Laver and Schofield 1990: Ch. 7).[13] Additional consideration can be given to the nature of particular portfolios; their relative importance and relation to particular policy areas.

Whereas some descriptions of coalition governments see cabinet and coalition membership as coterminous (e.g. Dodd 1976), the Indian situation is complicated by the willingness of some parties (such as the TDP) to support the NDA Government, yet refuse to accept office. Other parties, such as the Lok Dal shared this caution, while leaders such as Mamata Banerjee swung between accepting office and remaining apart over the course of the parliaments. For the TDP, rejection of government office was partly offset by the selection of one of their party members (namely G.M.C. Balayogi) as Speaker of the Lok Sabha.[14]

This section focuses on the distribution of portfolios among those members of the BJP-led coalition who did take an active role in government. In the initial allocation of portfolios, following the 1998 elections, 22 Cabinet ministers were appointed, and a further 21 Ministers of State[15] (Table 1.1).

Out of the cabinet posts listed in Table 1.1, half were occupied by members of the BJP, well *under* their proportion of the Lok Sabha representation of the NDA. Looking at the Council of Ministers, this imbalance is slightly redressed, with 14 out of the 21 Ministers outside the Cabinet being from the BJP. The allocation of cabinet and ministerial posts is roughly in accordance to the size of the membership of the governing coalition, although the picture is slightly distorted because the All India Anna Dravida Munnetra Kazhagam (AIADMK) leader, Jayalalitha, negotiated on behalf of the group of parties (including the PMK, MDMK, TRC and JP) elected from Tamil Nadu.

Key ministries in the government, notably the Ministry of External

Table 1.1 Allocation of government portfolios between parties, 1998

	Seats	% seats	Cabinet	% cabinet	CoM	% CoM
BJP	183	72.05	11	50.00	25	58.14
AIADMK	18	7.09	1	4.55	3	6.98
Samata Party	13	5.12	2	9.09	2	4.65
Shiv Sena	6	2.36	1	4.55	1	2.33
BJD	9	3.54	2	9.09	3	6.98
SAD	8	3.15	1	4.55	2	4.65
Lok Shakti	3	1.18	1	4.55	1	2.33
HVP	1	0.39	–	–	–	–
PMK	4	1.57	1	4.55	2	4.65
MDMK	3	1.18	–	–	–	–
TRC	1	0.39	1	4.55	1	2.33
Arunachal Congress	2	0.79	–	–	1	2.33
JP	1	0.39	–	–	–	–
Maneka Gandhi	1	0.39	–	–	1	2.33
Buta Singh	1	0.39	1	4.55	1	2.33
Total	254	100	22	100	43	100

Sources: Election Commission of India (1998); Keesing's *Record of World Events* (1998). For a full list of the BJP-led government majority see Arora (2000 Table 7). Parties and independents which formed post-electoral arrangements with the BJP, but did not receive government posts have been excluded. The nominated members representing Anglo-Indians have been included, adding one seat to the BJP and one to the Samata Party.

Affairs and Ministry of Finance, were controlled by the members of the BJP.[16] Other ministerial appointments can be seen to have fitted the particular interests of the particular parties within the coalition. The BJP retained control of the Ministry of Human Resource Development (encompassing the Department of Education and Department of Culture) and the Ministry of Information and Broadcasting, portfolios which were central to the party's concern with the promotion of a cultural agenda in line with the *Hindutva* ideology. Where possible, alliance partners were allocated portfolios which tied in with the interests of the parties or states which they represented. Jayalalitha's concern about her own personal situation – she was facing legal charges of corruption – was served by the appointment of Thambi Durai, a prominent AIADMK leader, to the Law, Justice and Company Affairs portfolio. Naveen Patnaik's control of the Ministries of Mines and Steel reflected the particular interests of Orissa politics.

As well as party balance, in 1998, the Prime Minister had to consider other aspects of regional, communal and political balance. The distribution of ministries reflected the general distribution of the coalition across the country, although Tamil Nadu and Bihar were over-represented because of the importance of the AIADMK and Samata Party to the coalition; and West Bengal and Haryana were not represented because the Trinamul Congress and Lok Dal's decision to support the Government from outside. The BJP claimed to have given adequate representation to the Scheduled Castes (SCs) and Scheduled Tribes (STs), and appointed some non-Hindu Ministers.

In 1998 and 1999 the Government representation of coalition partners tended to be balanced with the appointment of BJP members from matching states; and Cabinet members from alliance parties were always chaperoned by a Minister of State from the BJP. This meant that, even when the BJP was a subordinate partner in a state alliance, it could often claim that the state had one BJP Minister, and ensure that coalition partners were not able to dominate any one area of policy.

Table 1.2 repeats the analysis of Table 1.1 for the 1999 NDA government. The allocation of portfolios is much closer to proportionality in 1999 than 1998.

In 1999 the BJP was in a stronger position, and this was reflected in a greater share of government portfolios. The Janata Dal (U)/Samata combine was over-represented in the 1999 NDA Cabinet, a consequence of the incorporation of Sharad Yadav and Ram Vilas Paswan into the NDA coalition. The 1999 Council of Ministers was much larger than that of 1998, with 69 Ministers appointed, compared to 43 in 1998. The size of the Government continued to grow; by 2002 the Cabinet had grown to 32 Ministers, and the Council of Ministers to 77.

Table 1.2 Allocation of government portfolios between parties, 1999

	Seats	% seats	Cabinet	% cabinet	CoM	% CoM
BJP	183	67.53	15	57.69	46	66.67
JD(U)/Samata	22	8.12	4	15.38	6	8.70
Shiv Sena	15	5.54	2	7.69	3	4.35
DMK	12	4.43	2	7.69	3	4.35
BJD	10	3.69	1	3.85	2	2.90
Trinamul Congress	8	2.95	1	3.85	2	2.90
MDMK	4	1.48	–	–	2	2.90
PMK	5	1.85	–	–	2	2.90
MADMK	1	0.37	–	–	–	–
SAD	2	0.74	–	–	–	–
ABLTC	2	0.74	–	–	–	–
HVC	1	0.37	–	–	–	–
KNC	4	1.48	–	–	1	1.45
MSCP	1	0.37	–	–	–	–
Ram Jethmalani	–	–	1	3.85	1	1.45
Maneka Gandhi	1	0.37	–	–	1	1.45
Total	271	100	26	100	69	100

Sources: Election Commission of India (1999); Keesing's *Record of World Events* (1999). Parties and independents which formed post-electoral arrangements with the BJP, but did not receive government posts have been excluded. The nominated members representing Anglo-Indians have been included, adding one seat to the BJP and one to the Samata Party.

Coalition durability and government performance

When Harold Macmillan was asked what caused the greatest difficulties in his period as UK Prime Minister, he replied 'Events dear boy, events'. A similar viewpoint, developed within the political science literature, has been proposed by Browne *et al.* (1984), who suggest that coalition durability has to be seen as a consequence of shocks to the political system which change the bargaining situation within a coalition government. Browne *et al.* challenge theories of coalition duration which solely rely on the strength of the formative structure of coalitions, principally those suggesting that outsized or undersized coalitions, or the ideologically incoherent, will be less stable.

There have been numerous political shocks to the BJP-led coalition since 1998. The testing of nuclear weapons, a border conflict with Pakistan and communal riots in Gujarat are some of the most striking. This section looks at how the NDA adjusted to political events since 1998, and whether an 'events' analysis sheds any new light upon the durability of the coalition. A non-systematic review of cabinet reshuffles[17] suggests that the Prime Minister was sensitive to the policy direction of the NDA Government and the demands of the BJP organisation and the broader interests of the *Sangh Parivar*. The non-BJP members of the NDA Government were sensitive to any developments in policy which they saw as undermining their decision to participate in the alliance. However, the key events tended to be tied to the electoral fortunes of the different elements of the coalition, which were taken as indicators of the relative strengths of the BJP and its allies.

An early example of coalition partners' muscle was the forced roll-back of budget measures to increase the price of fertilisers, forced on the NDA Government by the Akali Dal and AIADMK. In October 1998, an attempt to promote a *Hindutva* agenda by the Human Resource Development Minister Murli Manohar Joshi at an Education Conference was quashed after the protests of non-BJP Government members. In contrast, the explosion of a nuclear bomb, carried out without cabinet consultation in May 1998, provoked grumblings but no resignations. In March 2000 the BJP's allies forced the BJP leadership at the centre to stop a move by the (BJP) Gujarat Government to lift the ban on government employees participating in the activities of the RSS. After provocative statements by the Prime Minister on the Ayodhya issue in December 2000, he was forced to re-emphasise the Government's commitment to the National Agenda for Governance. The leader of the DMK, Karunanidhi, threatened that the party would quit the NDA if the commitments of the National Agenda for Governance were violated (Venkatesan 2000).

There was a divide among the parties supporting the BJP over the use of Article 356, which enables the national government to dismiss state governments in certain situations. The BJP had argued against the (mis-)use of Article 356 in its 1998 election manifesto, but there was pressure from the AIADMK, Samata Party and Trinamul Congress to topple state governments led by their chief opponents. However, such intervention was opposed by other coalition supporters in power in their states, notably the Akali Dal and the TDP, who were worried that it would be destabilising. The BJP eventually bowed to pressure in October 1998, announcing President's Rule in Bihar, but the attempt was rebuffed by President Narayanan, who felt there were insufficient reasons and a danger that it would be unconstitutional. A second attempt in February 1999 was stymied by INC opposition in the Rajya Sabha. The BJP's vacillations over the use of Article 356 show that the compulsions of coalition politics did not all pull in the same way. For some state parties the short-term benefits to be gained from the imposition of central authority outweighed the destabilising effects this had on centre-state relations. For other parties in the coalition, both short-term and long-term interests were served by governmental restraint in the use of Article 356.[18]

Other shifts in policy were indicated by changes in portfolio allocation within the NDA Government. In 2001 the BJP emphasised its shift away from *swadeshi* to a more pro-liberalisation agenda through the appointment of Arun Shourie (BJP) as Minister for Disinvestment. This reshuffle saw Sharad Yadav and Ram Vilas Paswan (both JDU) moved out of the Ministries of Civil Aviation and Communications to Labour and Coal and Mines respectively. Both were known to oppose the disinvestment programme.

NDA Government reshuffles also occurred as a reaction to the internal politics of BJP-partners. Ram Jethmalani, Minister for Law, Justice and Company Affairs was forced to resign in July 2000, after becoming embroiled in controversy over the possible prosecution of the Shiv Sena leader, Bal Thackeray. In August 2002 Suresh Prabhu (Shiv Sena), the Power Minister, was forced to relinquish his position allegedly because he had annoyed Thackeray. Mamata Banerjee was also forced to assert her leadership, vetoing appointments offered to other members of the Trinamul Congress (first to Ajit Panja, then Sudip Bandhopadhyay, in 2003). In May 2001 the Samata Party threatened to leave the NDA, when BJP's MLAs helped bring down the Samata government in Manipur. This highlighted the difficulty of reconciling competing state parties with the broader interests of the national coalition.

Reshuffles were also used to react to political and organisational adjustments within the BJP. In December 1998, the NDA Cabinet was expanded to include three new BJP Ministers (Jaswant Singh appointed Foreign Minister; Jagmohan as Communications Minister; Pramod Mahajan as Minister of Information and Broadcasting). This move was seen as reinforcing the moderate wing of the party, in the aftermath of poor results in state assembly elections. A constant tension between the Advani/RSS and Vajpayee/moderate wings of the party were seen to swing in Advani's favour with his appointment as Deputy Prime Minister in June 2002, and with the transfer of the Personnel department from Prime Minister to Home Minister in January 2003. Moreover, the appointment of Swami Chinmayanand (BJP) as Minister of State in the Home Ministry in May 2003 was seen as a sop to the VHP, an organisation with which he had close contacts.

Preparations for upcoming state assembly elections were a source of ministerial manoeuvres, with BJP ministers relieved of ministerial posts to take up party positions, or members from particular states promoted to increase their profile. In a reshuffle in January 2003 – only involving BJP members – Pramod Mahajan left the Cabinet in order to take up the post of BJP General Secretary and plan for the state assembly elections in Rajasthan, Madhya Pradesh, Delhi and Mizoram, while Arun Jaitly re-entered the Cabinet after running the electoral campaign in Gujarat. Following the state assembly elections in 2000, Nitish Kumar, from the Samata Party, left the NDA Government in an attempt to form a state government in Bihar, but was returned as Agriculture Minister when the attempt failed. The run-up to state assembly elections in Uttar Pradesh saw the Rashtriya Lok Dal (RLD)'s Ajit Singh brought into the NDA Government, in order to consolidate his alliance with the BJP; and swiftly demoted again in May 2003 when his support was less important than reaching out to the BSP in Uttar Pradesh.

Misconduct by members of the NDA Government was an additional trigger for reshuffles and rebalancing among the coalition partners. In April 1998, after R. Muthiah, from the AIADMK, was arraigned on charges of assets disproportionate to his known sources of income, Jayalalitha protested that other members of the NDA Government (including Buta Singh, Ramakrishna Hegde and Ram Jethmalani) were also involved in criminal cases. Buta Singh was forced to relinquish his position when the Supreme Court announced that he faced prosecution (over alleged involvement in a parliamentary bribe scandal to gain support in a 1993 vote of confidence for P.V. Narasimha Rao). The *Tehelka.com* scandal in March 2001 led to the resignation of George Fernandes, although after a very short period of penance he returned as Defence Minister. Minister of State for Finance Ginjee Ramachandran, from the MDMK, was forced to resign after the arrest of his personal assistant in a case of alleged bribery in May 2003.

Mamata Banerjee, leader of the Trinamul Congress, used the acceptance or resignation of portfolios to signal her party's distance from the BJP, according to the prevailing electoral climate. In November 1998, when the NDA Government's fortunes were suffering due to a sudden increase in inflation and the party's poor performance in the autumn 1998 assembly elections, she resigned from the Co-ordination Committee of the NDA. Later, during the run up to the 2001 state assembly elections in West Bengal, Mamata resigned from the NDA Government, and temporarily ended up forming an alliance with the INC. However, when this failed to dislodge the ruling Left Front government in West Bengal, Mamata returned to the NDA, and again rejoined the cabinet in September 2003 as Minister without Portfolio.

This section has attempted to examine the changing balance of the NDA Governments. The re-allocation of portfolios among members of the governing coalition, and their impact on the direction and exercise of policy suggests that there was a constant adjustment to the changing fortunes of the different elements of the coalition. These adjustments reflected both inter-party balancing and intra-party factors. Looked at in terms of the 'events' approach, suggested by Browne *et al.*, there were clearly 'shocks' to the political system that led to adjustments in the relationship between coalition partners. However, the most important factor was the changing electoral climate, which was highlighted by the series of state assembly elections interrupting the national electoral cycle. It was the electoral success of the INC in the November 1998 state assembly elections which precipitated the exit of the AIADMK from the NDA Government, causing its fall. Ironically, it was the BJP's electoral success in the same states five years later, which led to the early dissolution of the Lok Sabha; this time from a position of strength. As such, an 'events' approach offers little other than extra contextual detail: the key variables in coalition durability appear to be the strength of the government coalition when initially formed, and expectations of future electoral prospects.

Conclusion

The analysis of coalition formation suggests that expectations of minimal-winning and ideological coherent coalitions, in which all supporting parties co-operate in the distribution of government patronage and formation of policy, are not necessarily going to be realised. This is due to the competitive electoral federalism which characterises modern Indian politics. In a competitive party system, party leaders may seek to maintain a distinctive identity by forming coalitions with parties appealing to a divergent, rather than coherent, ideological support base. In a segmented party system, apparently illogical coalition groupings at the aggregate level may occur because of rational strategic decisions within smaller political arenas. It is argued that the institutional context of a SMP electoral system and a federal system of government has fostered such outcomes. These factors have provided countervailing tendencies which have worked against the formation of coalitions built upon ideologically coherent policy programmes. Similar considerations have allowed regional parties to offer support to central government coalitions, while resisting the benefits that accrue from the acceptance of ministerial offices.

In terms of the distribution of portfolios among those parties which agreed to work alongside the BJP at the centre the evidence suggests that larger parties tended to gain more posts; conforming to the theoretical expectation that portfolio distribution will be proportionate to size. This process was made somewhat easier through the decision of some supporters of the coalition to remain outside the government, foregoing any direct ministerial reward. There were significant qualitative differences between the type of cabinet or departmental responsibility shared between coalition partners. The BJP held the most important portfolios, thereby directing the general shape of government policy. Coalition partners tended to accept ministries representing sectional interests, particularly those dealing with functions important to their party or state.

The ability of coalition members to exert influence over national policy has varied over the duration of NDA Governments. While coalition policy documents – such as the 1998 BJP's *Vote for a Stable Government and an Able Prime Minister* (1998) and the 1999 National Democratic Alliance manifesto – set out a general and public framework for policy direction, in practice the effective constraints on government appeared to be predominantly determined by the electoral context. Within the structure of electoral federalism this worked at both the national and the state level, depending on the perception that the benefits of participation at the centre were compatible with maintaining a competitive edge at the state level. This led to a complex series of re-adjustments and re-alignments.

Given the relentless backdrop of state assembly elections, how did Prime Minister Vajpayee manage to maintain a relatively stable coalition up to 2004? In general, the structure of party competition at the state level remained stable, and the national coalition between the BJP and regional parties was sustained by its foundation in state-wise electoral alliances against a common enemy (the INC). Even though parties, such as the TDP, were concerned that their association with the BJP came with a risk of ideological and electoral tainting, they could not switch allegiance at the national level without threatening their electoral base at the state level. A second important factor was that the BJP, right up to the 2004 general election, was widely perceived to be electorally successful – an asset as a partner in national and state-wise alliances – and this served to maintain existing coalition ties.

The greatest political shock to face the NDA was the Gujarat massacres of 2002. The failure of the BJP Government in Gujarat and the leadership in New Delhi to take decisive action against rioters can be seen to have been a key factor in the escalation of communal violence in that state. This was a clear violation of the manifesto commitment of the NDA, yet there was only muted protest from the coalition partners of the BJP. While the TDP leader, Chandrababu Naidu, called for the removal of the Gujarat Chief Minister Narendra Modi, and Mamata Banerjee boycotted a meeting of the NDA Co-ordination Committee, there was only one resignation from government over the issue (Ram Vilas Paswan (JD (U))). A censure motion in the Lok Sabha on the Government's handling of the Gujarat massacres was comfortably defeated (276 votes to 182), despite the abstention of the TDP.[19] The explanation appears to be grounded in perceptions of the electoral impact at the state level. First, in Gujarat the BJP fought against the INC on its own, and so the Gujarat massacres did not recast the nature of party competition. Second, the electoral resonance of the events was unclear, and there appeared to be no significant backlash against the BJP. Indeed, the state assembly elections that followed the massacres saw the BJP government returned to power in Gujarat, and the 2004 national elections saw little evidence that the events led to a national vote swing against the BJP (Datar 2004).

The 2004 general election showed the continuing success of parties organised on a purely regional basis. The importance of such parties, measured by their ability to win seats in the national parliament, means that neither the BJP nor the INC could hope to form a government without the co-operation of regional parties. From alliance building, to government formation, and portfolio allocation, the role of state-focussed partners continues to play a major part in the democratic government of India. This influence leads to outcomes which are contrary to some of the basic expectations of coalition theory. While a minimal winning coalition may be an optimal outcome, this is subject to satisfying the demands of alliance partners, and the high price that can be exacted by a coalition member holding a pivotal position. This can lead to the construction of larger-than-minimal coalitions to support a government in Parliament. The endurance of a coalition is largely determined by the state-level context; with partnerships based on a common-interest within competitive state-wide party systems. Coalition partners' ability, or even desire, to affect national politics, are largely dependent on the perceived impact on particular states. The ability to distribute benefits and direct national policy through control of the government in New Delhi plays a subsidiary role, evinced by the reluctance of some parties to accept ministerial posts and simply support from 'outside'. This leads to a situation where the coalition supporting the government is oversized, but the sub-set of this coalition actually taking ministerial offices (and the other direct perks of central government) is often smaller than the minimal size.

The NDA Government (from 1999 to 2004) was the first national coalition government in India to complete a full, five-year term in office. The very stability of the NDA Government, with the BJP core surrounded by numerous state-based parties, was remarkable in itself. Part of the explanation was the experience gained from earlier failed attempts at coalition management and the conciliatory leadership of Prime Minister Atal Behari Vajpayee. A more powerful reason, however, was the effect of the pragmatic electoral alliances that provided an element of common interest between the BJP and its coalition partners. The segmented nature of the electoral arena meant that some parties were situated within the coalition, while others were content to support from 'outside' (and parties such as the Trinamul Congress moved between these positions). Portfolio allocation and policy direction were determined by the balance between the broad interests of the BJP and the state-specific interests of coalition partners. This balance fluctuated according to the cycle of national and state elections. While coalition partners were able to exercise some influence over national policies, this did not extend to holding the BJP to account for its failure to prevent the Gujarat massacres of 2002; the most flagrant violation of the conciliatory manifesto which was supposed to provide a common policy platform.

The analysis of the NDA Governments shows that coalition building in a federal electoral system can confound theoretical expectations. The balance between state-specific and national interest can lead to apparently sub-optimal outcomes, an example of Tsebelis's theory of nested games. Coalitions may be oversized, and coalition partners may not take part in the direct distribution of ministerial benefits, in return for autonomy. This in turn means that national policy may be determined according to the interests of sub-sections of coalition members, rather than a more general accumulation of influence, driven by the electoral dynamics at both the national and state level.

Notes

1 Examples include de Swaan (1973), Pridham (1986), Laver and Schofield (1990), Laver and Budge (1992), Müller and Strøm (2000).

2 For a discussion of the role of the *formateur*, see Browne *et al.* (1984: 188–9). A further institutional benefit given to the party asked to form a government after a general election is influence over the nomination of two additional members of the Lok Sabha, ostensibly to represent the Anglo-Indian community under Article 331. The nomination of these members, both of whom supported the BJP-led government, helped achieve a majority in the Lok Sabha in 1998 and 1999.

3 The recommendation of the Commission are also discussed in Adeney and Singh's contributions to this volume (Chapters 5 and 7 respectively).

4 Confusingly, the Eighty-Fourth Amendment Act was the outcome of the Ninety-First Amendment Bill. Operational effect was given through the Delimitation Act 2002. Other constitutional amendments are discussed in Adeney's chapter in this volume (Chapter 5).

5 In terms of regional redistribution, the reallocation of seats is essentially a zero sum game. The states which lose out in terms of representation will be counter-balanced by those who gain. This could be disguised by increasing the total number of seats to be redistributed; a tactic that has been used in every previous delimitation (McMillan 2000: 1273).

6 This is particularly relevant in the Indian context, where constituencies tend to be very large (both terms of geographical size and number of electors), and where information from opinion polls is notoriously inaccurate and only available at state or national levels.

7 Cleavage conflict is related to the ability to maintain support from a party's voters when entering a coalition: if joining a coalition is likely to alienate a party constituency, then the costs are likely to outweigh any benefits (Dodd 1976: 59).

8 Just over 50 per cent of a membership of 545. The exact threshold is complicated by the provision of two nominated seats to represent Anglo-Indians, and the role of the Speaker. In 1998 the position in the Lok Sabha was further complicated because the results from a number of seats were delayed, because of elections postponed due to adverse weather conditions and the Election Commission forcing re-polls.

9 The Kashmir National Conference (which won 4 Lok Sabha seats), the Manipur State Congress Party (1), Sikkim Democratic Front (1) and Mizo National Front (1).

10 In their analysis of the support base of the INC in the late 1990s, Heath and Yadav (1999) show that the vote base for the INC varied across states according to the opposition it faced, marginalising its appeal as a catch all-party.

11 The Communist Party of India (CPI) has tended to take a more pragmatic approach to participation in coalition governments, which has seen it tolerate co-operation with both Congress and the Jana Sangh.

12 At the national level, such a situation occurred in 1979, when the INC supported the Government of Charan Singh; in 1989 when the Left Front and BJP supported the Government of V.P. Singh; in 1990, when the INC supported the Government of Chandra Shekhar; and from 1996, when Congress supported the Deve Gowda and I.K. Gujral Governments.

13 Bueno de Mesquita (1975: 26) argues that there is no association between the size of parties and their payoffs from participation in government.

14 When Balayogi was killed in a helicopter crash in March 2002 the TDP did not press its claims over the selection of a new Speaker, and Manohar Joshi of the Shiv Sena was elected as Speaker in May. This was seen as part of the TDP's wish to distance itself from the BJP Government in the aftermath of the Gujarat massacres.

15 The distribution of portfolios among the NDA was made somewhat easier by the fact that some parties refused to take office.

16 An attempt was made to measure the influence of various ministerial postings on the basis of budget allocations. Budget allocations were seen as a proxy for the 'wetness' of the ministerial posting: the discretionary funding available to each minister. This analysis has been left out of this chapter, but details are available from the author.

17 Information taken mainly from a review of Keesing's (1998–2003) and press cuttings.

18 Changes in the use of Article 356 are also discussed in this volume by Adeney (Chapter 5).

19 Omar Abdullah of Kashmiri National Conference Party also abstained over the issue and offered his resignation from the government, which was not accepted. He eventually resigned in December 2002, after his party's poor performance in the Jammu and Kashmir elections in October 2002.

2 The shapes of Hindu nationalism

John Zavos

Introduction

> The Congress era in Indian politics is over. The era of the BJP has begun.
>
> (Bharatiya Janata Party 2004: 1)

This statement by BJP President Venkaiah Naidu in his introduction to the party's *Vision Document 2004* demonstrates the confidence with which the BJP approached the elections to the fourteenth Lok Sabha. The document goes on to sketch out a set of long-term strategies for India's development under BJP rule. These strategies include commitments to the construction of a 'magnificent Ram temple at Ayodhya', banning religious conversions 'through fraudulent and coercive means', and working for consensus on a Uniform Civil Code (Bharatiya Janata Party 2004: see 'Highlights' and 'Our Basic Vision and Commitments'). These may all be perceived as key Hindu nationalist concerns: issues that have been foregrounded not just by the BJP, but also by other Hindu nationalist organisations, and used as focal points of mass mobilisation campaigns over several decades. If there really was to be an 'era of the BJP', then attention to these issues would surely mark its progress.

Nevertheless, this specific document was not the manifesto with which the BJP went to the polls. The party was standing at the heart of a coalition, the NDA, and it campaigned on the basis of the NDA's manifesto. The *Agenda for Development, Good Governance, Peace and Harmony* mentions neither conversions nor the Uniform Civil Code, and its reference to Ayodhya is pitched only at the level of calling for 'dialogue . . . in an atmosphere of mutual trust and goodwill', and that all should accept the judiciary's verdict on this matter (National Democratic Alliance 2004: 'Other Commitments'). High profile campaigning leading up to the general election was marked by the relative absence of unequivocal Hindu nationalist issues. The clearest indication of this was Deputy Prime Minister L.K. Advani's *Bharat Uday Yatra* (Rising India Pilgrimage). Advani is notoriously linked to the idea of the *yatra* (pilgrimage) because of his 1990 *Rath*

Yatra, a procession from Somnath to Ayodhya in a bus decorated to resemble the *rath* (chariot) of the Hindu god Ram. Until Advani was arrested as he attempted to cross into Uttar Pradesh from Bihar, the procession had advanced inexorably on Ram's kingdom of Ayodhya in order to reclaim his birthplace, leaving a string of riots in its wake. In 2004, however, Advani stated that 'this is not a rath yatra like the one I undertook last time. This is only a yatra in a bus' (*Frontline* 2004a). Advani's 2004 *yatra* still claimed to be about the regeneration of the nation, but the emphasis was on economic and governmental rather than cultural regeneration – stimulated by the stability of Prime Minister Vajpayee's 'towering personality' (Bharatiya Janata Party 2004: 1).

The different positions represented by the *Vision Document 2004* and the NDA manifesto encapsulate a level of uncertainty about the relationship between the NDA in government and the ideology of Hindu nationalism. This perception is supported by regular discussion in the media of the extent of *Hindutva* (lit. Hinduness) influence on NDA Government policy. The disputed site in Ayodhya, for example, provided plenty of occasions to raise this issue.[1] Hindu nationalism, it seems, was both there and not there. It may not be immediately evident, but it looms; our perception of the NDA and its period of office is coloured by the assumption of its presence. How far was the NDA Government a Hindu nationalist government? To what extent was the broad project of Hindu nationalism constrained by the pressures exerted by the BJP's coalition partners?

Asking such questions focuses attention on the nebulous, slippery character of the concept of Hindu nationalism. There is a lack of certainty about its position and status in contemporary politics. In this chapter, my aim is to identify the 'shapes' of Hindu nationalism, the shadows it casts in the arenas of Indian politics, in order to gain some perspective on these questions. I aim to focus on the delineation of these shapes, by mapping out key themes of Hindu nationalist thought, and examining the contexts in which this thought has emerged. The focus on shapes is appropriate, because so many Hindu nationalist ideas are concerned with the issue of 'shaping' – in particular, as I will argue, shaping Hindu society into a form that reflects the perceived glory of the Hindu 'race'.

As much of this work is to do with the development of ideas and the formation of identities, however, we need to recognise the limitations of the shape metaphor. Ideas and identities are dynamic; they are, one might say, natural shape-shifters. Using the plural is partly an attempt to accommodate this observation. It also serves to emphasise a key point I want to demonstrate in this essay: that Hindu nationalism is not so much a clearly defined movement and ideology, as a broad field of thought. As such, its contours *do* change, assuming different shapes in different contexts. It is hoped that exploring some key component themes will provide a means of identifying the constituent elements of those shapes. In the context of the volume, this may help us to work towards an assessment of the significance of Hindu nationalism in the NDA, and more specifically, to address the questions I have posed above. In the first instance, then, I want to examine some of the key contexts through which Hindu nationalism emerged. This demands a brief visit to the nineteenth century, when the issue of shaping was the subject of intense and wide-ranging dialogue in relation to a much broader, but intimately related area of thought and practice: that of Hinduism itself.

Hinduism, Hindu politics and secular politics

The nineteenth century witnessed the rapid development of modern Hinduism. Various modern-style organisations, established and run largely by middle class Hindus, were influential in this process. They contributed to the emergence of the idea of Hinduism as an objective phenomenon, comparable to other, similar phenomena (the 'world's religions'). It is widely understood that such organisations, and their ideas about Hinduism as an objective phenomenon, developed as a form of cultural resistance to colonial rule. Swami Vivekananda, for example, was the leader of the innovative Ramakrishna Math and Mission. In 1893, he spoke in Chicago at the self-styled 'World Parliament of Religions'. There he explained how India's spiritual traditions could provide salvation to the Western world, which had become manifestly alienated and debased because of the extent of capitalist development. Vivekananda spoke as a representative of Hinduism. In common with many others at this time, he implicitly invoked the idea of Hinduism as a concrete reality, even if the parameters – the shape – of that reality were by no means a settled fact. Indeed, debates over the shape of the religion during this period were themselves a powerful force in the invocation of objectified Hinduism (Zavos 2000).

Vivekananda's stance at Chicago is indicative of what Partha Chatterjee (1993: 6) sees as a conceptualisation of two 'domains' by indigenous thinkers during this period: the 'outer' domain of materialism – economy, statecraft, science and technology – which was dominated by the West; and the 'inner' domain of the spirit – the home, the family and religion – in which India maintained a superior status. This recognition of spiritual superiority, exemplified by Vivekananda, was critical to the development of nationalist consciousness in India. It provided a key stimulus to the emergence of national identity, and thus ensured that Hinduism had a major role in the fashioning of this identity.

The key political organisation of Indian nationalism, the INC, was convened in 1885, somewhat against the grain of these developments in cultural consciousness. In its first few years it was dominated by an approach which sought to capture the air of an official opposition to the colonial government. Its statements were couched in a quasi-parliamentary language and it directed its attention towards the state, despite its rather weak claim to represent the 'Indian people'. Almost immediately, this approach to nationalism was challenged by competing voices among the indigenous elite, as well as by non-elite groups who questioned the right of elites to represent 'the people'. In these dialogues, Hindu symbols and Hindu events were invoked and reinvented as part of the cultural repertoire of emerging nationalism. Very quickly, the culture of quasi-parliamentarianism associated with the early Congress became one among many voices feeding into the national movement, and as a result, the Congress movement emerged in the twentieth century as a very broad umbrella-type organisation, accommodating a variety of different views of the nation.

In such contexts, the notion that Hindu nationalism and Indian nationalism formed two distinct ideologies had little meaning. Despite the emergence of the Hindu Sabha movement in the early twentieth century in north and northwest India, the lines of opposition between Hindu nationalism and Congress nationalism remained only very vaguely drawn. The evidence suggests that there was a constant blending and borrowing of ideas. This was demonstrated graphically by the fact that many prominent figures in the INC and the Indian national movement more generally were also involved in the developing Sabha movement. For instance, Punjabis Lala Lajpat Rai and Swami Shraddhanand were important figures in both movements, as well as being prominent Arya Samajists. B.S. Moonje was involved both in the INC and the emerging Hindu nationalist movement in Nagpur.

Perhaps the most famous of these 'crossover' figures was V.D. Savarkar, the President of the Hindu Mahasabha between 1937 and 1943. In earlier years, Savarkar (1947) had written a significant Indian nationalist text about the 1857 rebellion against the British. He had also been transported for life to the penal colony of the Andaman Islands in 1910 for his part in a conspiracy to assassinate two British officials. In the classically heroic Indian nationalist context of this incarceration, Savarkar was to produce what was to become a seminal text of Hindu nationalism: *Hindutva/Who is a Hindu?* (1989). This short but rather verbose text presented the 'Hindu race' as a strong, martial people, who had been struggling for a thousand years or more with various foreign invaders from the north and west.

Hindutva/Who is a Hindu was first published in 1923. In the early 1920s, both nationalist mobilisation and communal violence were intensifying. As the profile of communalism as a political issue expanded, a strain of militant secularism became increasingly prominent within the Congress-led nationalist movement. In this view, national liberation was characterised in the classic liberal democratic sense, namely through the creation of a nation-state governed by the rule of law, in which issues of culture and religion would be ushered into the private sphere (Pandey 1990: Ch. 7). The secular tendency never eroded the different approaches to nationalism which were extant under the broad umbrella of the INC, but it was sustained as a kind of hegemonic rhetoric within the organisation. During the final years of British colonial rule in India, the predominance of this rhetoric enhanced the sense of difference between Congress nationalism and Hindu nationalism as represented by the Mahasabha and other organisations. In addition, since the rhetoric of secularism was developed in contradistinction to communalism, Congress politicians increasingly represented Hindu nationalist ideology as a form of communal ideology.

By emphasising these developments, my intention is to provide perspective on the developing structure of political alignments in the post-independence period. Hindu nationalism became situated as a communal ideology, in contrast to Congress nationalism, in a manner that marginalised the dialogue, the interaction and blending of these areas of thought about Indian politics and culture. Hindu nationalism developed into a kind of trope, which acted to define or affirm the non-communal credentials of the INC, a position which was only emphasised by the traumas of partition and the assassination of Gandhi. This process has done much to obscure the embeddedness of Hindu nationalism in developing ideas about Indian culture and social relations among political elites. Recognising the shapes of Hindu nationalism, then, means looking beyond the discourse of communalism and acknowledging the network of contexts in which key ideas emerged.

Hindu nationalism: some central ideas

As noted above, Savarkar's text *Hindutva/Who is a Hindu* was to emerge as a significant articulation of Hindu nationalist thought. Other key texts have been the writings of Deendayal Upadhyaya and the work of M.S. Golwalkar, especially his two books *Bunch of Thoughts* (1966) and *We, or Our Nationhood Defined* (1944).[2] Together, these sources provide us with insight into some component elements in Hindu nationalist thought, but one thing we should emphasise is this: they do not form a coherent body of work or the consciously progressive development of an ideological position. Perhaps this is best illustrated by the fact that although Savarkar is often described as 'the ideological father of Hindu nationalism' and *Hindutva/Who is a Hindu* as 'the classic text of Hindu nationalism' (Varshney 2002: 65), one will not generally find this book in *Sangh Parivar* bookshops in India, nor will one find reference to Savarkar on major Sangh websites.[3] This is principally because Savarkar was never a member of the RSS, and therefore cannot, in that organisation's version of history, be portrayed as too central to the development of Hindu nationalism. But it also reiterates the fractured quality of this set of ideas, its existence as a broad field of thought, interacting with other fields of thought, rather than as a clear ideological programme. In this section, I want to unpack some of the themes that might help us to identify the parameters of this field of thought. In doing so, the issue of interaction will be emphasised; although it is hoped that acknowledging this interaction will help us to identify a distinctive profile for Hindu nationalist thought.

(i) Who is a Hindu? The formulas of nationhood

This question, which forms part of the title of Savarkar's 1923 work, is at the heart of ideas of Hindu nationalism. It is a question that may be related directly to those processes of objectification we have noted above associated with the development of Hinduism. Indeed, the difficulties experienced by elites in the late nineteenth and early twentieth century in conceptualising Hinduism as a religion, and the tensions that subsequently emerged, were highly influential in the development of major lines of Hindu nationalist thought. This is because these were, in the absence of any theological coherence, debates about the parameters of Hinduism as a social phenomenon. Where one drew the boundaries of Hinduism and how its shape was articulated, formed key underlying questions in the contest over whether and how the religion needed to be 'reformed' or 'regenerated'. Two broad patterns of response emerged: one which sought to articulate the idea of Hinduism through the restructuring of society, as exemplified by some elements within the Arya Samaj; and one which sought to articulate the idea of Hinduism through the consolidation of the existing structures of society, emphasising the 'organic' unity of the component parts.

Savarkar answers his own question by emphasising and extending the latter response. *Hindutva/Who is a Hindu?* constructs a notion of Hindu nationality that is catholic, embracing a broad range of religious and cultural systems. This catholicity is characteristic of the spiritual, universalist approach to Hinduism and Hindu culture developed in the nineteenth century by figures such as Vivekananda. At the same time, however, Savarkar's notion works obsessively on the boundaries of this range, producing some formulaic models through which an individual or a group may be identified as Hindu or not. There is, for example, the widely recognised formula of *pitribhum–punyabhum* (fatherland–holy land) (Savarkar 1989: 111). Whoever can identify India as both may be considered as Hindu. In consonance with this formula, he develops the idea of *rashtra-jati-sanskriti* (nation-race-culture), as components of Hinduness (Savarkar 1989: 116). Identification with the Hindu race and nation is encompassed by the recognition of *pitribhum*; whereas identification with culture is encompassed by the recognition of *punyabhum*. On this reckoning, Savarkar's key social exclusions are of Muslims and Christians, in that they locate their holy land, their cultural identity, outside India. This formulaic approach has proven to be remarkably resilient, turning up in later Hindu nationalist works, although not always attributed to Savarkar.

Golwalkar develops a similar approach in *We, Or Our Nationhood Defined*.

He develops a formula based around what he terms the 'famous five unities' (1944: 18) of territory, race, religion, culture and language. These may be related to the Savarkian formula of *pitribhum* (territory, race) – *punyabhum* (religion, culture, language), and they follow the same pattern of emphasising a broad, catholic approach to cultural and religious identity, while identifying exclusions in a quite uncompromising manner. Golwalkar also identifies Muslims and Christians as key exclusions, although he moves on to encompass communists as anti-national or an 'internal threat' (Golwalkar 1966: 187ff.). This reflects a developing concern, in the immediate pre- and post-Independence era, with the strength of the left in Indian politics.

The quality of inclusion and exclusion formulas identifying Hinduness forms the basis for a consistent area of Hindu nationalist action: resisting conversion. The critical exclusions exemplified in the *pitribhum–punyabhum* formula mean that conversion to Islam or Christianity amounts to a process of 'de-nationalisation'. Indeed, this term was used by the RSS organiser, Kishore Kant, to describe the activities of Christian missionaries in northeastern states during the 1990s (*The Asian Age* 1998: 1 January). At the same time, there has always been recognition of the vulnerability of certain groups to the 'threat' of conversion. These are principally low caste and tribal groups, those who exist on the fuzzy margins of Hinduness – in a way that Savarkar would have regarded as anathema – and who suffer oppression precisely because of their status within Hindu society (Zavos 2001). The success of conversion campaigns among low caste or tribal groups, then, appears both as an indication of the fragility of Hindu society, and a confirmation of fears about the erosion of Hindu identity. As such, resisting conversion has always been a key concern of Hindu nationalism because it operates as a means of affirming and consolidating the idea of a broad notion of Hindu identity, on the basis of the *pitribhum–punyabhum* and other associated formulas.

(ii) Hinduness – a question of culture

In a rather paradoxical fashion, we can see that as well as rationalising exclusion, the formulaic approach is designed to encompass a broad range of traditions, including such historically resistant traditions as Buddhism and Jainism. Savarkar is able to do this because he begins with the idea that Hinduness – or *Hindutva* as he coins it – is not so much a religious as a cultural signifier, based on an identified continuity of blood in the Hindu 'race'. 'Hinduism,' he says, 'is only a derivative, a fraction, a part of *Hindutva*' (1989: 3). Through this distinction, Savarkar is able to go on to construct a grand, catholic vision of Hindu identity as diverse, yet unthreatened by that diversity. The diversity itself is perceived as characteristic of Hindu culture.

As a model of cultural development, we can relate this idea to some classic accounts of Indian syncretism and tolerance, such as Jawaharlal Nehru's *Discovery of India*. Nehru notes that 'the mind of India' has been occupied for millennia by 'some kind of a dream of unity'. Within this idea of unity, he states that 'the widest tolerance of belief and custom was practiced and every variety acknowledged and even encouraged' (1985: 62). Of course, Nehru is insistent on embracing Muslim and Christian communities within this model, but the premise of 'unity in diversity' is similar to that of Savarkar. The latter's ideas about Hindu culture, then, to a certain extent reflect a broader discourse about the Indian nation.

Interestingly, Golwalkar almost reverses Savarkar's formulation of the relationship between Hinduism and Hinduness. He claims that culture is 'but a product of our all-comprehensive Religion, a part of its body and not distinguishable from it' (1944: 22). This difference is partly explained by the use of contrasting conceptions of religion. Savarkar works with a narrow definition of religion, based on the idea of individual commitment and spiritual fulfilment. Golwalkar works with a different kind of concept altogether, a broad, all-encompassing concept, which provides a kind of framework for belief, culture and social organisation. Indeed, Golwalkar criticises the narrow conception of religion in *We or Our Nationhood Defined*. It is possible that this critique is aimed at Savarkar, the 'secular Hindu'; certainly there is a reverse echo of Savarkar's statement quoted above, when Golwalkar states that the individual spiritual fulfilment view is 'but a fractional part of Religion' (1944: 23).

Golwalkar's conception of religion is rather as a broad framework, which 'by regulating society in all its functions, makes room for all individual idiosyncrasies, and provides suitable ways and means for all sorts of mental frames to adapt, and evolve' (1944: 23). Golwalkar, then, is equally able to encompass diversity in the tradition, by broadening the idea of religion in the context of India and articulating it as 'the elastic framework of our dharma' (1966: 101). It is this very elasticity, he goes on, which operates to 'protect and maintain the integrity of our people', as various sects had emerged to counter threats to the framework; Sikhism, for example, 'came into being to contain the spread of Islam in Punjab' (1966: 103). This is highly reminiscent of Savarkar's idea of diversity as a defining feature of Hindu culture.

Ultimately, both Savarkar and Golwalkar produce approaches that attempt to resolve the threat posed by doctrinal diversity and fragmentation within Hindu identity by reference to 'framework' ideas, which endorse this diversity as archetypal. This approach, following Savarkar's articulation, has emerged in contemporary Hindu nationalism as a valorisation of Hindu culture; indeed, despite the tension noted between Savarkar and the *Sangh Parivar*, the idea of *Hindutva* has been fully adopted and is used freely in Sangh literature (although again, it is rarely attributed to Savarkar).

What, though, characterises this framework of Hindu culture or

Hindutva? Both Savarkar and Golwalkar locate the idea of Hinduness by reference to history. Even taking into account its diversity, Hinduness is rooted in Aryan civilisation and the establishment of the Vedic tradition. According to Savarkar, there was a gradual expansion of Aryan influence, leading eventually to the religious, cultural and political unification of the subcontinent under Lord Ram (1989: 11–12). These then followed periods of relative Hindu and Buddhist ascendancy, which in turn were superseded by the 'human sahara' of Muslim incursion, the beginning of a long period of struggle to maintain Hindu identity in the face of 'foreign invasion' (1989: 42–6). This interpretation of history was based on some familiar elements of nineteenth- and twentieth-century Hindu worldviews. The idea of the Vedic civilisation of the Aryans was used as a reference point by a whole host of movements and individuals involved in conceptualising Indian religion and society (e.g. Dayananda, Jotiba Phule); Ram Rajya also had a distinctive resonance as indicative of perfect governance and a harmonious society (e.g. Gandhi). And the idea of 'Muslim' rule creating a decisive break in Indian history was most familiar, and had been institutionalised in James Mill's influential early nineteenth-century *History of British India* (1817). There is nothing distinctive, then, in the use of these ideas to characterise the quality of Hinduness. They serve again to emphasise the embeddedness of the Hindu nationalist approach in developing ideas about Indian culture during the first half of the twentieth century.

This version of history is nevertheless used as the basis for the development of some further key elements of Hinduness as Indian culture. Perhaps most significant is the valorisation of the geography of India.[4] This key feature is clearly indicated by the emphasis on the land in Savarkar's *pitribhum–punyabhum* formula. He writes:

> Yes, this Bharat bhumi, this land of ours that stretches from Sindhu to Sindhu is our Punyabhumi, for it was in this land that the Founders of our faith and the seers to whom 'Veda' the Knowledge was revealed, from Vaidik seers to Dayananda, from Jina to Mahavir, from Buddha to Nagasen, from Nanak to Govind, from Banda to Basava, from Chakradhar to Chaitanya, from Ramdas to Rammohun, our Gurus and Godmen were born and bred. The very dust of its paths echoes the footfalls of our Prophets and Gurus.
>
> (Savarkar 1989: 112)

Here, Savarkar articulates archetypal diversity as indicative of Hinduness through the land itself – the dust of its paths is representative of Hindu culture. Golwalkar, who delineates Bharat as 'a land with divinity ingrained in every speck of its dust ... the holiest of the holy, the centre of our utmost devotion' (1966: 86), reiterates this kind of reverential approach.

Again, this reverence is present in a broader discourse on the Indian nation during this period. Varshney has used the example of Jawaharlal Nehru's will, in which he expresses a desire for some of his ashes to be thrown into the Ganga, because that river has been 'a symbol of India's age-long culture and civilization, ever-changing, ever-flowing, and yet ever the same Ganga' (2002: 63). Varshney makes a distinction between Nehru's view of the river, and that encompassed by Hindu nationalism, on the basis that Nehru's vision of sacred geography was 'metaphorical', rather than 'literal'. The quality of this distinction is not clear, particularly since he goes on to say that the 'emotions and attachment generated by the geography were equally intense' (2002: 63). Rather than emphasising difference, we can see here again the way in which Hindu nationalist thought has emerged within a broader complex of ideas about the emerging nation, and that the idea of polarisation between these ideas is apparently untenable.

One further aspect of Hinduness as Indian culture needs emphasising at this point. This is the focus on Ram and Sita, the heroes of the *Ramayana*, as archetypal Indians. There has been a fair amount of work in recent years on the developing ways in which these figures have been represented in art, film and other media. The emphasis of this work has been on the representation of Ram as a martial hero, defending the honour of Hinduism with the aid of a mighty bow (Kapur 1993). Sita has operated increasingly as the site of that defence, a meek and pure individual who needs protection from violation (Basu 1995). In the context of *Hindutva*, these figures are national, rather than religious. Hence, the desire in recent times to build a temple at the proclaimed 'birthplace' of Ram in Ayodhya is perceived as a national project, and resistance to this project is interpreted as anti-national, regardless of your religious persuasion.

This valorisation of Ram and Sita is indicative of a wider point on the idea of Hinduness or *Hindutva*. It denotes a set of ideas that is consciously articulated as cultural, rather than religious, and yet there is constant slippage into what we might perceive as more clearly religious territory. On the one hand, this appears to be a reflection of slippage in the original *pitribhumi–punyabhumi* formulation, which claims to include on the basis of cultural space, but clearly excludes on the basis of religious identity. On the other hand, it is also a reflection of the problematic identification of Hindu nationalism as religious nationalism, if religion is defined as a discrete category, in the manner critiqued by Golwalkar as noted above. To an extent, this *is* a set of ideas that exists in broader discursive fields than those signified by such a category.

(iii) Sangathan – ordering society

Nothing demonstrates this latter point more clearly than what has emerged as the most influential organisation propagating Hindu nationalism during the twentieth century: the RSS. As is well documented, the Sangh emerged in the mid-1920s with specific cultural objectives (Anderson and Damle 1987; Bhatt 2001; Hansen 1999; Jaffrelot 1996; Zavos 2000). It was established in Nagpur in Central Provinces, a city with a minimal Muslim minority, and its first formal public action was at the Ram Navami festival at nearby Ramtek. The Sangh volunteers, led by the founder of the organisation Dr. K.B. Hedgewar, engaged in a form of crowd control, enforcing queues, providing drinking water, and keeping an eye on commercial activity at the festival, among other tasks.

This first public action is interesting because it exemplifies two significant features of Hindu nationalist thought. First, as we have just noted, Ram was an important cultural symbol of the nascent Hindu nation. Here was an intervention in a festival dedicated to Ram. However, the Sangh was apparently not interested in the form of religious practice articulated at the *mela* (festival); rather, it pursued the objective of establishing a sense of order within this environment. Not only does this reiterate the idea of the focus on Ram as a cultural, rather than an explicitly religious symbol, it also points us towards the second significant feature: the establishment of a sense of order, discipline and organisation in Hindu social and cultural relations. This idea, expressed in Hindi as *sangathan*, has emerged as a fundamental Hindu nationalist concern.

I have written extensively elsewhere on the significance of *sangathan* to the development of the Hindu nationalist movement (Zavos 2000), and there is no need to reproduce these arguments here. What I do want to emphasise is the specific trajectory of this concern with discipline and organisation. *Sangathan* is significant because it is directed at the organisation of society. A Hindu nationalist vision of the Hindu nation is intimately bound up with the progressive realisation of a society which operates harmoniously, in an integrated fashion. Most generally, this vision has been articulated as a kind of organicist approach: society operates like a body, each component part having its own valuable function. Golwalkar comments:

> All the organs, though apparently of diverse forms, work for the welfare of the body and thus subscribe to its strength and growth. Likewise is the case with society. An evolved society, for the proper functioning of various duties, develops a multitude of diverse functional groups. Our old social order laid down a specific duty for each group and guided all the individuals and groups in their natural line of evolution just as the intellect directs the activities of the innumerable parts of the body.
>
> (1966: 100)

The ideal Hindu, then, knows his place in this organism. Fulfilling one's function in the organism, in a disciplined and orderly manner, is each individual's dharmic duty. Members of the Sangh organisation – to a certain extent the *swayamsevaks* (volunteers), but more specifically the *pracharaks* (full-time workers) – act both as a vanguard working to bring this society into being, and as examples of how to conduct oneself in accordance with dharma. In fact, the Sangh itself has been described as a model for Hindu society; the RSS ideologue M.G. Vaidya, for example, has described the Sangh as 'not an organization in society, but of society' (Zavos 2000: 196).

Such a vision, of course, entails addressing the issue of caste, and Hindu nationalism is rather ambivalent on this issue. At times, a full-fledged defence of the caste system has been articulated; at others, a 'return' to *varnashrama dharma*[5] is advocated; at others, the Sangh's vision is perceived as the eradication of caste altogether. A consistent element in this position, however, is a non-confrontational approach to established caste structures. Any transformation of caste structure is perceived as occurring through 'organic' development, rather than as requiring radical change. This approach reflects the development of Hindu nationalist thought in high caste, middle class social groups, and explains the strong antipathy to any forms of independent low caste assertion (Zavos 2001).

This refers us back, of course, to the concerns noted earlier over the shape of Hinduness in the modern world. The organisation of society emerges as a key means of articulating this shape. As an institution, the RSS has consistently focused on this objective and rationalised its actions in relation to it. Indeed, one way of understanding the *Sangh Parivar* is as a project to establish a focused presence within the various spaces of society, with the objective of demonstrating the Sangh's vision of organisation in microcosm and in relation to specific issues. Politics and the state may be regarded as one of the identified spaces.

(iv) Integral humanism – the politics of social order

The argument that politics must be seen as a component space within the Hindu nationalist conception of society is exemplified by the idea of integral humanism. This term enjoys a prominent profile in the BJP's main website (along with the notion of *Hindutva*), and it refers to a set of ideas developed in the 1950s and 1960s by Deendayal Upadhyaya.[6]

Upadhyaya was an RSS *pracharak* who had been influential in the Bharatiya Jana Sangh since it was established in 1951 as the *Sangh Parivar*'s first venture into the world of post-Independence politics. Integral humanism was fully articulated as a political programme in 1965. In a series of lectures, Upadhyaya sought to pitch this programme into what he perceived as a sea of cynicism and opportunism in politics. 'Parties and politicians have neither principles nor aims nor a standard code of conduct,' he opined. In particular, he pointed to Congress as lacking any kind of ideological coherence. 'If there can be a magic box which contains a cobra and a mongoose,' he continues, 'it is Congress' (1965: Ch. 1).

The set of ideas which he went on to develop are based around a series of key themes. First, the need to articulate specifically Indian answers to modern problems (through, for example, promoting *swadeshi* and small scale industry); second, the need for politics to be practised in consonance with the *chiti* (specific essence) of the Hindu nation; and lastly, the need to sustain the 'natural' balance between the individual and different institutions in society – institutions like the family, caste and the state – by acting in accordance with principles of *dharma*. This set of themes has been interpreted as an incorporation of Gandhian idioms into Hindu nationalist politics, in order to enhance the potential for forging alliances with other anti-Congress forces, after twenty years of total domination of the polity by that party (Hansen 1999: 84–6). Integral humanism, then, may be interpreted as a means of increasing the possibilities of power. As it so happens, new possibilities were created in the late 1960s and early 1970s, particularly in association with the Gandhian political leader, J.P. Narayan. The involvement of Hindu nationalist forces in Narayan's anti-Indira agitations undoubtedly gave the Jana Sangh the credibility to take a share in power in the post-Emergency Janata Party coalition government (Graham 1990). It is quite possible, then, to view this key element of Hindu nationalist ideology in terms of electoral strategy, a resolve to bid for power in the late 1960s. A similar interpretation of the VHP strategy around the issue of the Babri Masjid in the 1980s is also well established (Jaffrelot 1996). In these interpretations, Hindu nationalism as ideology is framed to support the primary interest of an organisation or set of organisations in state power.

The trajectories of Hindu nationalist thought discussed so far in this chapter, however, must lead us to consider a different kind of interpretation in relation to integral humanism. In particular, Upadhyaya's ideas appear to follow the logic of the emphasis on the organisation of society as a principal objective. This may be seen in the key role he gave to the concept of *dharma* (duty) in his lectures. *Dharma*, that is, in the same sense noted in relation to the Hindu nationalist vision of society: a harmonious, integrated system in which each individual and group has a specific function or duty. Although Upadhyaya presents *dharma* as part of an integrated regulation of human activity based on *purushartha* (the four universal objectives of humanity), in his discussion he demonstrates this integration by referring each objective (and in particular the 'worldly', political objectives of *artha* (gain) and *kama* (pleasure) to *dharma*. 'Dharma,' he says, 'defines a set of rules to regulate the social activity, Artha and Kama, so as to progress in an integral and harmonious way, and attain not only Kama and Artha but also Moksha eventually (Upadhyaya 1965, Ch. 2). Without reference to *dharma*, then, other objectives may not be reached.

The invocation of *dharma* indicates a further articulation of the idea of order or organisation of society as central to a Hindu nationalist world-view. Upadhyaya interprets *dharma* as a kind of dynamic network of inter-related regulations by which life should be led. It is these regulations that govern social relations. Upadhyaya seeks authority from the *Mahabharata* to argue that in the *kritayuga* (the first of the four eras of the world), 'there was no state or king. Society was sustained and protected mutually by practicing dharma' (1965: Ch. 3). In subsequent *yugas* (epochs), he explains, 'disorganisation came into existence', and as a result, the state was introduced as an additional form of regulation, but the state was only ever legitimate if it operated in accordance with dharma. The primacy of society, then, is clear here, and the state exists as an institution – 'an important one, but not above all other' (1965: Ch. 3) – which is framed and governed by this idea.

This approach locates integral humanism within the context of developing Hindu nationalist ideas focused primarily on the transformation of society, rather than viewing it as an instrumentalist appropriation of Gandhian idioms designed to increase the possibility of power. There is certainly evidence of the appropriation of Gandhian idioms, if not ideas, in Upadhyaya's lectures, but what this demonstrates primarily is interaction in ideas about the development of society. I have argued elsewhere that Gandhian idioms, ideas, and strategies were quite significant in the articulation of Hindu nationalism in the 1920s (Zavos 2000: 189–91). This significance was not because of instrumentalist appropriation, or indeed because Gandhi was a surrogate Hindu nationalist. Rather, Gandhian ideas and Hindu nationalist ideas developed in the same discursive spaces, drawing on a similar range of ideas about and experiences of history, culture and political mobilisation.

Whether in the 1920s or the 1950s, the dialogue between Gandhian and Hindu nationalist ideas has to be viewed as a straightforward element of the development of ideological forms. These are, after all, perspectives on the world which exist primarily in what Stuart Hall has called the 'mental frameworks' of people, both individually and in groups (1996: 26). These individuals and groups exist in time and space, and they formulate their 'mental frameworks' in accordance with the 'languages, the concepts, categories, imagery of thought and systems of representation' which are available to them (1996: 26). In this context, the blending of ideological forms, the borrowing of idioms and symbols, the adaptation of existing ideas has to be perceived as the way in which meaning is constructed. The structure of Indian politics, with its sharp division between the secular and the communal, does not help us to recognise this point. In the final section of this chapter, I want to demonstrate how the shapes of Hindu nationalism can be perceived in a variety of areas of Indian social and political life, which do not necessarily conform to this bi-polar structure.

Recognising the shapes of Hindu nationalism

A key conclusion to be drawn from this analysis is that Hindu nationalist ideas about identity, culture and politics draw on and to some extent reflect the construction of ideas about the Indian nation and its cultural heritage in the late nineteenth and twentieth centuries. Nevertheless, I have suggested that the use of formulas and explicit religious symbols to draw the boundaries of national identity may be construed as distinctive. Two lines of thought – the obsessive concern with conversion and the aggressive assertion of ownership over sites projected as sacred – are indicative of this distinctiveness.

Yet even here, there is a degree of embeddedness in broader fields of thought. Perhaps the clearest post-independence example of this point is the restoration of the Somnath temple in 1947/8. This was carried out under the auspices of an INC government, with the Home Minister Sardar Patel noting that 'the restoration of the idols would be a point of honour and sentiment with the Hindu public' (Jaffrelot 1996: 84). INC involvement in this project is often perceived as indicative of the presence of 'Hindu traditionalists' in the party, a group who are distinguished from Hindu nationalists through the comparative weakness of their ideological commitment, or through their primary concern for the promotion of culture rather than opposition to the other (both ideas are expressed in Jaffrelot 1996: 83–4). This distinction is, I feel, rather over-wrought. The ideas underpinning the approach of Patel and others in the INC during this period are clearly informed by the same kind of concern for Hinduness overrun by Muslim 'invaders' as those noted earlier as indicative of Hindu nationalism. Again, we get an indication of the fuzzy boundaries of this field of thought, rather than its clear distinctiveness from Congress nationalism.

Conversion issues also indicate a broader reach for ideas associated with Hindu nationalism than the formal organisations of the *Sangh Parivar*. The conversion of some *Dalits* to Islam in Meenakshipuram in 1981 is a good example of this, in that the concerns expressed about this event were far broader than those generated by the Sangh. Jaffrelot notes that 'leading articles in newspapers not known for their support of Hindu nationalism suggested that the converts had been paid sums of money', and that the whole process had been sponsored by rich Arab nations inspired by pan-Islamism (1996: 341). This view was also taken by certain sections of the INC Government, and the *Indian Express* published a poll revealing that as many as 78 per cent of north Indian urban Hindus wanted the government to ban conversions in the wake of Meenakshipuram (Jaffrelot 1996: 341). Such figures, of course, need to be taken with a pinch of salt, but these responses do indicate again a degree of embeddedness of some key ideas associated with Hindu nationalism in Indian political life. The shapes of Hindu nationalism, in this sense, are not necessarily constrained by the limits of the *Sangh Parivar* and other overtly Hindu nationalist organisations.

A further conclusion concerns the focus on society rather than the state, through the realisation of correct *dharma*. Formal politics and the control of the state is significant, but it needs to be placed within the context of this broader focus, which conceptualises society as a range of segmented areas and 'functional groups', as Golwalkar would have it. This point is graphically demonstrated by the network of organisations that constitute the *Sangh Parivar*. These organisations focus on a variety of issues, from tribal welfare to education to labour relations, and this is an expanding network across areas of social and cultural life.

The RSS – the 'parent organisation' – maintains a loose, rather informal sense of control over the Sangh network. The current *sarsanghchalak* (leader) of the RSS, K.S. Sudarshan, explained the relationship in a recent interview. 'For the overall development of society', full time RSS workers are encouraged to enter 'different fields according to their abilities'. Their general objective is common: 'to try to find solutions to problems in those assigned areas, under the *Hindutva* ideology'. Although the organisations are independent, Sudarshan continues, the RSS maintains a guiding relationship with its workers, who remain *swayamsevaks* (RSS cadre) (*Outlook* 2003: 30 June). It is well known, for example, that the Prime Minister and his deputy during the NDA's tenure, A.B. Vajpayee and L.K. Advani, have remained as *swayamsevaks*. Other key figures in the BJP, for example, Gopinath Munde and Murli Manohar Joshi, have also followed this path. Key leaders in the VHP, such as the international secretary, Ashok Singhal, are also *swayamsevaks*, as are other key Sangh figures such as the leader of the Swadeshi Jagran Manch (SJM, an affiliate of the RSS set up in 1992 to oppose economic liberalisation), Dattopant Thengadi.

Joshi and Singhal demonstrate the route taken by ambitious *swayamsevaks*. Joshi joined the RSS, at the age of 10, in 1944. While pursuing academic studies, which culminated in a PhD in Spectroscopy from Allahabad University, he became increasingly involved in the Sangh's student organisation, the ABVP, achieving the status of General Secretary of this organisation in the early 1950s. In 1957, he joined the Bharatiya Jana Sangh and enjoyed increasing prominence in the Uttar Pradesh hierarchy of this organisation, before becoming General Secretary of the BJP in the 1980s, President in the early 1990s, and a key cabinet minister in Vajpayee's administration, first as Home Minister, then taking charge of three ministries: Human Resources Development (including education), Science and Technology and Ocean Development. It is in the HRD ministry where he has really made his mark, instigating policy initiatives in the education sector, which demonstrate the Sangh's desire to shape national consciousness.[7]

Singhal also hails from Uttar Pradesh, having been born in Allahabad in 1927. He also pursued a technical education, achieving a BSc from

Benaras Hindu University in Metallurgical Engineering. He joined the RSS as a *swayamsevak*, before becoming a *pracharak* (full-time worker), and eventually being assigned to the VHP in 1980. At this dynamic period of the organisation's history, Singhal rose quickly to become its general secretary in 1986. Singhal later indicated the role the RSS had to play in the development of different areas of social life by calling them 'ascetics in the real sense'. He identified 'service' as 'the key word of our culture, and Sangh's swayamsevaks are symbols of service. Today in all spheres of activity such workers are needed' (cited in Katju 2003: 68).

The complexity of the Sangh network has increased over time, as new institutional layers are created. For example, the VHP established the Bajrang Dal, initially as a sort of youth wing. Over time, the Bajrang Dal has developed into a kind of confrontational front for the VHP, providing foot soldiers in key campaigns such as that over the Ram temple in Ayodhya. The Bajrang Dal also operates as a continuous activist presence in local situations, providing its own version of 'socio-religious policing' to guard the honour of local Hindu girls, protect local cattle and local temples, and so on (Katju 2003: 52). Likewise, the SJM is another organisation which has gone on to develop more focused organisations, such as the Centre for Bharatiya Marketing and Development and the *Swadeshi Vichar Kendra*.[8]

Given these developing, dynamic networks, it is not surprising that the Sangh has developed a diversity of approaches to the idea of 'finding solutions to problems' using '*Hindutva* ideology' (see Sudarshan's comments in *Outlook* 2003). Nothing has brought this diversity into focus more than the period of NDA rule. The BJP's perceived inability to find the kind of solutions demanded by different Sangh organisations has induced sharp criticism. Ashok Singhal, for example, commented in 2003 that 'Atal and Advani have backstabbed the VHP' because of the government's reticence over temple construction in Ayodhya (*Free Press Journal* 2003). Also in 2003, national convenor of the SJM, Muralidhar Rao, described the Vajpayee government's economic policies as 'dubious, deviant, diluted', particularly in relation to disinvestment and the World Trade Organisation (*Telegraph* (*Calcutta*) 2003). As a result of this divergence, the BJP was not able to rely fully on the grassroots cadre of other Sangh organisations during the 2004 general election campaign. At the BJP's National Executive meeting held in July 2004 to review election performance, L.K. Advani stated that there had been 'a sense of alienation in our Parivar and a weakening of the emotional bond with our core constituency' (*Frontline* 2004c). As if to reinforce this point organisations such as the SJM and the VHP have shed few tears at the fall of the NDA Government. Muralidhar Rao has gone so far as to welcome the Common Minimum Programme of the incoming INC-led United Progressive Alliance, commenting that the NDA had 'lost touch with the masses' (*The Tribune* 2004e). It appears from this evidence, then, that the constraints of coalition government have caused a fracturing – and therefore weakening – of Hindu nationalism as a political force.

The arguments presented here, however, suggest that any assessment of the influence of Hindu nationalism in political terms needs to recognise that this is a set of ideas which is located in a much broader space than that represented by the BJP. Because they overlap and blend with other key discourses on Indian society, culture and identity, these are ideas which are manifested in a wide range of political actions and articulations. In addition, the focus identified here on social relations and social development demands a broader understanding of what constitutes politics. For example, in tribal areas of states such as Madhya Pradesh and Orissa, the Sangh affiliate Vanvasi Kalyan Parishad has been increasingly active, reshaping tribal religious practices within a Hindu framework (*Frontline* 2004b). In the arena of education, the Sangh now has a network of schools, many run by the Vidya Bharati Akhil Bharatiya Shiksha Sansthan. The Vidya Bharati system supervises over 18,000 schools across India, with 1.8 million students and 80,000 teachers focusing on Sanskrit, moral and spiritual education, yoga and physical development.[9] The political impact of Hindu nationalism really needs to be measured in terms of its continuing activism in such arenas, where politics is manifested not in terms of formal state institutions, but as a contest for power in a network of localised institutions and practices (Zavos *et al.* 2004: 3).

An approach which focuses on the political impact of organisations such as Vidya Bharati can also help us to locate Hindu nationalism in the context of government. It is no coincidence that one of the most significant areas of policy development during the NDA's tenure has been in the area of education. From the National Council for Educational Research and Training (NCERT) to the Indian Council for Historical Research, Hindu nationalist approaches have been vigorously promoted; further reshaping ideas about Indian history and society in a wide range of schools, colleges and universities.[10] In order to recognise Hindu nationalism as a feature of the NDA Government, then, we need to look particularly at those policy areas, such as education, which impact on the structure and development of social relations.

Hindu nationalism continues to be an influential force in the development of worldviews in India, through the interaction and overlap of ideas as highlighted in this chapter, and the vigorous, diversifying development of Sangh activities through its affiliate organisations. In the final analysis, the shapes of Hindu nationalism cannot really be contained in the arena of formal politics. Recognising the impact of Hindu nationalism means looking beyond this arena, beyond the state and the immediate problems posed by coalition politics, to the ways in which its key ideas resonate in the broad spaces of Indian social and cultural life.

Notes

1 See, for example, *Frontline* (1999b); *The Hindu* (2002a).
2 In more recent years, the ideas extant in these texts have been developed by ideologues such as Sita Ram Goel, Ram Swarup, H.V. Seshadri and P. Parameswaran, in a succession of cheaply produced pamphlets and larger works distributed through the network of the *Sangh Parivar*.
3 This is largely the case, even though during 2003 and 2004 there have been successive disputes between the BJP and its opponents over Savarkar's status as a national figure and a freedom fighter.
4 See also Jaffrelot (2004).
5 Trans. Order of society in accordance with the duties of the four classes and the four stages of life.
6 See www.bjp.org/philo.htm.
7 See the contribution by Marie Lall (Chapter 8) in this volume.
8 See www.swadeshi.org/aboutus.
9 See www.vidyabharati.org.
10 See the contribution by Marie Lall (Chapter 8) in this volume.

3 In part, a myth

The BJP's organisational strength

James Manor

Introduction

In 1999, this writer visited the offices of three political parties in Patna. Bihar's State Assembly was in session, so he expected the parties' head-quarters to be more active than usual.

He first went to the INC office. It was open, but not a single person was present during the hour that he waited there. Then he went to the office of the state's ruling party, the RJD. Here one man was present, but sound asleep on a mat on the floor.

He then moved on to the office of the BJP. There more than a dozen people were busily conferring, writing and talking on the telephone. When they were asked about the party's activities in the state, they provided an extremely cogent, detailed explanation of their clearly defined roles, and the organisational structure within the state headquarters. Then this writer asked about how the organisation extended out into various districts and beyond, to rural areas where most voters live. The answers became rather tentative and vague. He was told – thrice – that 'as you know, we are a cadre-based party'. But little more of substance was provided. This seemed odd at the time. But the vibrant scene at the BJP office offered such a stark contrast to the other two offices that he saw little reason to question a widely held belief. This is the notion that in Bihar and most other Indian states, the BJP has a stronger organisation than its rivals – a penetrative structure, consisting of full-time activists or cadres,[1] which is capable of penetrating effectively below the district level into sub-district and local arenas.[2]

Its allegedly strong organisation is sometimes seen as a factor that can help the party to compensate for other, quite serious problems that it faces.[3] Three of these are especially important. The first is the failure of the Hindu nationalist agenda to attract broad popular support – across India generally, and in most individual states. The second is its poor performance in office at the state level, which has meant that only one of its incumbent Chief Ministers has ever won re-election on the strength of his government's record on governance and development – Bhairon

Singh Shekhawat in Rajasthan in 1994.[4] (Narendra Modi won re-election in Gujarat in 2002, but for other, unsavoury reasons.) The third is the BJP's status as a relatively minor force across much of eastern and southern India.

But is its organisation actually all that strong? After his visits to the party offices in Patna, this writer was surprised to discover that in Bihar, the BJP organisation is actually rather weak, especially when one looks beyond the capital and certain other urban pockets. Later, he was even more surprised to discover that in Madhya Pradesh – where the BJP looms larger than in Bihar, as one of the two main parties – its organisation again had few cadres and failed to penetrate into rural areas effectively.[5] Finally, he had long known that the BJP has a very frail, poorly led organisation in Karnataka.[6]

This triggered enquiries about the strength of the BJP organisation in other important states, the results of which are presented in this chapter. They indicate that in a great many states, the BJP is weaker, less well led, and penetrates less effectively into rural areas where elections are won and lost than is normally supposed. We can say about most states what Ghanshyam Shah said about the BJP in Gujarat: that it has '*posed* . . . with considerable success, as a cadre-based party', but that there was 'hollowness' to this claim (emphasis added, 1998: 259, 262). In many states, it has a solid organisation in some urban enclaves – but only *some* – and in a few eccentric rural pockets.[7] Indeed – most astonishingly of all – in many (and probably most) states, its organisation is weaker than that of at least one other party, even where other parties also have insubstantial organisations. This chapter sets out evidence on these issues, and then considers some of the implications of this – for the BJP, for other parties, and for democracy and communal accommodation in India.

It should be stressed that this study is exploratory and does not purport to be definitive. It is intended as an invitation to others to examine these matters in greater depth. Such studies are badly needed because the BJP's organisation has received remarkably little attention in recent years. Analysts have concentrated instead on the party's strategies, its discourse, the images that it projects, its social base, its share of the votes in various elections, its outreach to groups that have not traditionally supported it, the tension between pragmatism and purity, among other issues. All of these things are important, and several of them bear directly on its organisation. However, so far we have heard surprisingly little about the BJP organisation *per se*.[8]

The type of organisational weakness analysed here

This chapter concentrates on one particular aspect of the BJP's organisation. It questions the widespread notion that the party has a cadre-based structure that is capable of penetrating into sub-district and local arenas across rural India. In doing so, it does not argue that the party's organisation is weak *in general*. In certain other – but in electoral terms, less important – ways, the BJP organisation tends to be strong in many (though not all) parts of India. The idea that its organisation is strong is in part a myth, but *only* in part. Let us consider some of its genuine strengths.

The BJP's internal processes are more institutionalised and democratic than are those of most other parties in India, although the degree of institutionalisation is sometimes overstated. Its organisation is also comparatively well disciplined – although we need to be clear about the kind of discipline we are discussing.

Certain kinds of indiscipline and, indeed, infighting within the BJP, have at times loomed large in recent years. In Madhya Pradesh, for example, conflicts developed over the award of tickets for the state election of 1993. Two years later, internal party elections could not be held there – a first – because 'tensions were so acute'. In 1997, party elections were delayed in places owing to 'intense infighting' which, in Bhopal District, led to violent clashes (Jaffrelot 1998a: 279, 284, 288). Then, as the 1998 Lok Sabha election approached, violence over nominations within the BJP's state headquarters office reportedly led to over 50 people being hospitalised.[9] That is serious indiscipline, even by the sorry standards of the INC.

In some other respects, though, discipline within the BJP has remained impressive. Its organisation is more capable than those of most other parties of maintaining control over what may be politely termed 'fundraising'. It manages this in a more centralised and disciplined manner, in order to provide more resources for the party and less to individuals. For instance, one well-informed source in Madhya Pradesh explained that in the INC, fundraising and profiteering are decentralised. INC leaders at the state level 'loot, but share the loot' with party colleagues at lower levels. 'In the BJP, that is not allowed. Certain key figures in a state government, at high levels but not at the top, are in charge of it. The party retains most of the money'.[10]

The BJP is also remarkably effective at persuading its state-level units to accede to instructions from their national leaders. As will be discussed below, this particular strength is also one source of the BJP's weakness as a penetrative force.

Finally, the BJP's organisation is also harder to break than are other parties.[11] The 'breaking' of party organisations – that is, the process by which a party's members are induced to defect to other parties – has been a significant theme in recent years in several states, especially, but not only in Bihar and Uttar Pradesh. The BJP has suffered from this at least once – in Chhattisgarh after Ajit Jogi became Chief Minister in 2003 – but that was an unusual instance.[12] The difficulty in breaking the BJP organisation was apparent in late 2003, particularly in Uttar Pradesh, when Chief Minister

Mulayam Singh Yadav managed to break other parties to secure his majority in the state assembly, but not the BJP. He may have held back partly in order to develop a more accommodative relationship with the BJP, but he also appears to have viewed the BJP organisation as more difficult to break.

As Jaffrelot has shown, there are two main reasons that the BJP is difficult to break. First, people who have left the party tend strongly *not* to flourish outside it. Second and more importantly, it deploys people with RSS backgrounds as *sangathan mantris* (organising secretaries). They form a core element within the organisation, and maintain more coherence than is found in most other parties – although that coherence has diminished in recent years (Jaffrelot 1998a: 269–72). Jaffrelot reports that, at one time, these people began to develop 'a dense network of local committees' in Madhya Pradesh, 'by utilizing the existing RSS network' (1998a: 269).

It should be stressed, however, that this writer's research in Madhya Pradesh in early 2003 indicated that by then, the BJP *per se* did not possess such an organisational presence at the local level across most of that state.[13] Two things may explain this. First, the 'dense network' may not have extended as far as party leaders would have wished, and over time, it may have decayed – partly as a result of groupism within the BJP. Second, many RSS activists in Madhya Pradesh had cooled in their enthusiasm for the BJP, because they were dismayed by said groupism and by the national leaders' de-emphasis of the Hindu nationalist agenda since the mid-1990s. It is plausible to assume that similar things have happened in a number of other states.

So, to reiterate, this discussion deals with just one type of organisational weakness. This is the BJP's failure in most parts of India to develop cadre-based structures that are able to penetrate effectively into sub-district and local arenas in rural areas – *where election outcomes in almost all Indian states are decided*. This weakness leaves the party with a limited capacity to convey messages from the national and state levels to important interests, and to deliver goods and services to them. It also makes it difficult for the party to convey information upward about the concerns, preferences and problems of interest groups. So it damages not only the electoral prospects of the BJP, but the party's capacity to govern effectively and responsively when it takes power at the state (or for that matter, the national) level.

Before we turn to a state-by-state discussion of the BJP's organisation, it is necessary to comment briefly on one specific issue – the degree to which it is justified to speak of the BJP and the RSS as distinct entities. We sometimes hear it said – in the Indian press and in some academic analyses – either that these two bodies are one and the same, or that the RSS controls the BJP. There is no doubt that there is some overlap between the two organisations – in two senses. First, many people in the BJP organisation are currently members of (and even office-holders within) the RSS, or have had close ties to the RSS in the past. Second, the BJP often seeks proactively to insert RSS operatives at key points in its organisation or even – as we shall see in connection with state assembly elections in December 2003 – to draw RSS cadres *en masse* into its activities. Therefore, it is a mistake to claim that these two organisations are either identical and interchangeable, or that the RSS controls the BJP. It has exercised considerable influence over the BJP at certain times, and in certain places. But its influence varies greatly from time to time and place to place, and that influence almost always falls well short of outright 'control'. This is apparent from the research of many leading authorities on Hindu nationalism, several of whom are cited below, and from this writer's studies of politics in several Indian states over the last decade.[14]

The BJP's organisational weakness – state by state

Let us begin with the regions in which the BJP is weakest: the south and the east. In two southern states – Tamil Nadu and Kerala – the BJP's organisation is decidedly frail. In Tamil Nadu, party-building has progressed less far than in the other three southern states. It has only a tenuous reach beyond a limited number of urban pockets. In Kerala, the RSS is solidly established in certain urban centres and some sub-regions, but the BJP *per se* has far less strength. As its new leading mobiliser in Kerala recently said, 'The BJP (has) had a negligible presence in the state's polarised polity.'[15] In both of these states, the BJP has (not surprisingly) been unable to win a significant share of the popular vote.

In the other two southern states, the party has at times attracted substantial numbers of votes – nine per cent in Andhra Pradesh at the state election in 1999 and 28.8 per cent in the 1991 parliamentary election in Karnataka – although nothing approaching that on most other occasions.

In Andhra Pradesh, the BJP's electoral alliance with the TDP at the 1999 state election did not yield benefits that could facilitate organisation building. The ruling party starved it of advantages. After a membership drive in 2001–02, the BJP managed to develop networks of activists in most cities and in a small minority of rural arenas. But the TDP refused to permit it to contest elections from those areas in 1999, and a similar pattern prevailed in 2004. The state-level unit of the BJP initially declared itself in favour of statehood for the Telengana sub-region, in order to enhance its popularity and organisation-building efforts there. But the party's national leaders then compelled it to abandon that posture[16] – in part because it was inconvenient to the TDP. This undermined the standing of the BJP in Telengana, and damaged morale within the state unit more widely. It thus remains a rather marginal force in Andhra Pradesh, albeit one whose vote share may exceed the difference between those of the TDP and its main rival, the INC (as it did at the 1999 state assembly election).

Until the 2004 state assembly election in Karnataka, the BJP played a marginal role there.[17] At times, it *appeared* to be reasonably strong. It was the official opposition for a brief period after the 1994 state election, and again after the 1999 state election. Despite this, other opposition parties – the INC between 1994 and 1999 and the Janata Dal from 1999 to 2004 – were far more plausible alternatives to the ruling parties than was the BJP.

Thus, at the 1999 state assembly election, the INC – which had been badly mauled in terms of seats at the previous state election, but which had an organisation of far greater substance, reach and penetrative power than the BJP – swept back to power on the basis of popular disenchantment with the Janata Dal. The BJP's national leaders forced the state-level unit of the party into an illogical, last minute alliance with the Janata Dal. That contributed to the scale of the INC victory. However, no serious analyst should believe that if the BJP had been free to oppose the Janata Dal in 1999, it would have had a chance at capturing power. Its organisation was, and is, too weak – concentrated in urban areas and eccentric rural pockets – most notably Coorg (Kodagu) and the two coastal districts. It has also been incompetently led at the state level for over two decades, which has undermined organisation building.

The BJP ceased to be a marginal force at the Karnataka state assembly election of 2004. It gained the largest number of seats in a hung assembly, although it still came second to the INC in total votes received. It was then denied the chance to govern by the formation of a coalition between the Congress and the Janata Dal (Secular) (JD (S)). On close examination, this improved performance turns out to owe little to the organisational strength of the BJP. Indeed, it still lacks penetrative capacity in nearly all rural areas of the state. Its gains at that election are mainly explained by its success in winning support from Lingayats in *part* of northern Karnataka – in the so-called 'Bombay' Karnataka – something that it accomplished despite this organisational weakness. It should also be noted that the BJP failed to win many seats in the *other* northern sub-region, Hyderabad Karnataka, because the JD (S) captured most of the anti-Congress vote there *despite* a rather frail organisation.

The decision of the other two parties in Karnataka – both of which have more penetrative organisations than the BJP – to form a coalition government in May 2004, following the state assembly election, will probably qualify as an historic miscalculation that will enable the BJP to take power at the next state assembly election. By combining, they leave the BJP as the only alternative available to disgruntled voters if they govern poorly. The early evidence of infighting within the governing coalition strongly suggests that they will indeed govern badly. The INC and the JD (S) would have been better advised to permit the BJP to form a minority government, and then to have thwarted most of their initiatives by using their majority in the state assembly. They could then have won a subsequent state assembly election by arguing that the BJP had provided wretched government, but short-term calculations blinded the leaders of those two parties to this opportunity. The main point to stress in this discussion, however, is that both the BJP's rise in Karnataka and the likelihood that it will form the next government there do not imply that its organisation is capable of penetrating into rural arenas. It is weaker in that connection than either of the other two parties in the state.[18]

Let us now turn to the eastern states. In Bihar, the picture is somewhat brighter for the BJP. Over the last 15 years, it has made some headway in developing its organisation, so that it is no longer dominated – as it was in the 1980s – by urban trading castes. During the 1990s, the party attracted activists from a wider array of upper caste groups. This enabled it to capture much of the old upper caste base of the INC, and to penetrate into rural areas across much of the state. Activists' relative inexperience still limits its impact, but the RSS (which is especially strong in tribal areas), and the informal higher caste networks of BJP operatives, compensate somewhat for this deficiency.[19]

When we turn to Orissa, we encounter the kind of dismal situation for the BJP that it faces across most of the south. In that state, the BJP formed an alliance at the last state election with the BJD, and they have governed the state in a coalition led by that party since then. But the BJP's efforts since 1999 to strengthen its badly under-developed organisation have been damaged by its association with a ramshackle ally led by a capricious Chief Minister, Naveen Patnaik. So the BJP organisation in Orissa remains quite insubstantial.

One study of the 1998 Lok Sabha elections in West Bengal initially provides rather surprising news – namely, that 'the BJP has improved its once insignificant organisational base to the extent that it has a party structure in place *throughout all localities* of the state' (emphasis added, Gillan 1998: 2391). But a careful reading of what follows indicates that, however extensive this organisation was, it lacked efficacy. It amounted to 'an organisational foothold' which enabled the party to gain only 'a limited following in a number of districts, particularly in the border areas of the state'. Although the BJP won one seat at the 1998 Lok Sabha election in the state – its first, in the constituency of Dum Dum – it could not be said to have 'built up to the victory . . . by means of consistent organisational and electoral growth'. Instead, Gillan argues that 'the BJP vote share (in that constituency) has fluctuated over several elections'. Gillan adds that the party's organisation also exercised a rather tenuous hold over its activists, given 'the frequent instances over the last ten years of party workers moving between' the BJP and the INC (1998: 2392, 2395). So in West Bengal once again, the party's organisation appears to lack the capacity to penetrate effectively below the district level.

Let us now turn to northern, central and western India, where the BJP has long had greater organisational strength and electoral success. As state elections approached in Rajasthan and Madhya Pradesh in late 2003, the

BJP's organisation was seen by many analysts to be so incapable of penetrating below the district level that it could only win if it drew RSS cadres into the campaign. It was not just independent observers who took this view. The national leaders of the BJP agreed, and decided to sideline – one analyst used the word 'demolish'[20] – the party's traditional leaders at the state level, and thus much of its organisation. Relative outsiders were projected as the pre-eminent figures in the campaigns, namely Vasundhara Raje Scindia in Rajasthan and Uma Bharti in Madhya Pradesh. Senior party operatives from New Delhi – Pramod Mahajan in Rajasthan and Arun Jaitley in Madhya Pradesh – were inserted as the campaign coordinators. A senior RSS leader in the latter state told a *Hindustan Times* interviewer that the party's organisation 'was in a messy state', so that from mid-2002, 'the RSS took over the reins of the election'[21] – as it did in Rajasthan (and apparently in Chhattisgarh).

Large numbers of RSS activists from other states (Maharashtra and Gujarat) were also brought in. The RSS was persuaded to play the dominant role in these states by offers of immense influence during the campaigns and (apparently) after victory was achieved. These states witnessed RSS campaigns, rather than BJP campaigns, and they succeeded in ousting incumbent INC governments.[22] When we see the BJP's national leaders and RSS activists within these states acknowledging – implicitly, sometimes even explicitly – that their party organisation lacked penetrative capacity, we can be reasonably sure that the assessment presented here is accurate.

The case of Rajasthan deserves a little more comment. How do we explain the failure of the BJP to develop a penetrative organisation there? The party there was long dominated by one man – Bhairon Singh Shekhawat – twice Chief Minister of the state, and currently India's Vice President. Both in government and in opposition, he succeeded in maintaining his pre-eminence within the BJP by pursuing two main strategies; neither of which lent itself to the construction of a penetrative party organisation.

Let us first consider relations between the BJP under Shekhawat and other parties. He constantly cultivated cordial personal ties to leading figures (and even to individual legislators) in those parties. This minimised resistance to his initiatives, and it helped him to maintain his image as a moderate. To lend credence to this image, he needed to play down communal issues. That impelled him to remain somewhat aloof from the efforts of RSS activists to promote Hindu extremism at the grassroots, especially among tribals – efforts which bore political fruit, especially at the 2003 state assembly election, after Shekhawat had left state politics. He also restrained himself and BJP activists from organisation building in rural areas – partly because a strong, penetrative organisation would threaten his personal pre-eminence, and partly because it would alarm politicians in other parties with whom he had developed congenial ties that served him well.

If we look at the internal affairs of the BJP in Rajasthan, we find that Shekhawat projected his influence through highly *personalised* networks. He selected individual members of the party who were close to him and helped them to develop political bases within various sub-regions of the state. Some of these people developed networks that enabled them to make their influence penetrate downward in rural areas, but these tended to be personal structures with the BJP label attached to them, rather than the other way round. Within Rajasthan, Shekhawat preferred to stand back from the BJP as an institution. He was, thus, not entirely displeased when at the 1994 state assembly election, his party fell just short of a majority in the assembly. This required him to offer cabinet posts and other enticements to a few independents and others in order to govern – and it meant that the survival of his government hinged on him, and on his long-standing ties to non-BJP leaders. All of this contributed to his disinclination to construct a penetrative organisation that might take on a life of its own.[23]

The available evidence on Uttar Pradesh is quite limited, and we badly need further research on this crucial state. It is clear that in some parts of the state, the BJP possesses some penetrative capacity. For example, in the area around Agra, it has greater strength than in the neighbouring districts of Madhya Pradesh.[24] The same appears to be true in some, but not most other parts of Uttar Pradesh. But the dependence of the BJP upon the influence of certain caste leaders – not least Kalyan Singh – indicates that the party's organisational strength in rural parts falls well short of what it requires.

In Punjab, the BJP organisation is reliably seen to be less strong than in several other northern states – for example, Madhya Pradesh where it is distinctly weak. The party in Punjab is largely dependent on RSS cadres during election campaigns. It is strong mainly in urban areas, but it also has modest strength in the Majha region (Gurdaspur and Amritsar Districts) and in the Doaba regions between the Sutlej and Beas rivers. It has only a few pockets of strength in the state's largest region, Malwa. Its electoral prospects depend on whether or not it has an alliance with the Akali Dal.[25]

In Haryana, the BJP organisation is in a shambles. It has never been a cadre-based party with a wide network. It was captured right from the beginning by what is called pejoratively 'the GT Road party' (that is, by Punjabi refugees who settled close to the Grand Trunk Road that passes through Haryana). As a result, the party never developed a strong organisational presence among the local Haryanvis and was confined to Punjabi pockets, mainly in urban areas. Whatever strength it has is on loan from the RSS.[26]

In Gujarat, the behind-the-scenes influence of Narendra Modi, while Keshubhai Patel was Chief Minister after 1995, caused a deeply damaging split in the BJP organisation into RSS and non-RSS factions (Shah 1998:

262). Modi's subsequent takeover of the BJP government in the state, and his autocratic approach to governing, have deepened the split still further.

In quite recent times in rural Maharashtra, the BJP has missed significant opportunities to acquire the penetrative capacity that it has always lacked in most parts of the state. When it governed during the late 1990s, it was mainly its coalition partner, the Shiv Sena, that made inroads into the influential sugar cooperatives in western Maharashtra which had long been a INC stronghold. This was done, in part, by changing the boundaries of zones within which cooperatives can deliver their produce to sugar mills. That required very visible action by the state government, so the process was plainly known to BJP leaders there. But they did far less than the Shiv Sena to follow up with efforts to insert their own loyalists into the cooperatives. This episode strongly suggests that for the BJP, the creation of an organisation capable of penetrating rural areas was a low priority. The party may have been somewhat complacent in this connection because it believed that the RSS possessed that capability, in *some* parts of the state. But it was a serious – and revealing – omission.[27]

It is also worth briefly considering the BJP's organisational problems in *comparative* context. In how many significant states do other parties have stronger, more penetrative organisations than the BJP does? The answer is 'in an extremely large number'.

This is, not surprisingly, true in the four states where other parties have *quite* strong or *very* strong organisations. In West Bengal, the CPM's organisation is very strong. In Kerala, the CPM is less strong than in West Bengal, but is still quite strong.[28] In Andhra Pradesh, the TDP under Chandrababu Naidu after 1995 developed a solid, penetrative organisation that is undoubtedly quite strong.[29] Likewise, in Tamil Nadu, the DMK has an organisation that is still, surprisingly (after many years in the wilderness) quite strong. The BJP organisation in these states is vastly weaker than those of these four parties.

But when we look further afield, to states without strong parties, it is remarkable how often the BJP comes off second best, compared to its rivals. Indeed, in several states, it is weaker than not one but *two* other parties. In Karnataka, it is clearly less strong (at present and at all times in the past) than the INC. And at most times over the last 20 years, it has been less strong than the Janata Party or Janata Dal. It is also certainly weaker than two other parties in Kerala, Andhra Pradesh, Orissa, Haryana and Punjab. Moreover, it is arguably weaker than two other parties in West Bengal and Tamil Nadu.

This long list reflects dismally on the condition of the BJP's organisation. To say that it has less penetrative capacity than the wretched BJD in Orissa – and that it may have less than the chaotic AIADMK in Tamil Nadu or the severely faction-ridden INC state units in West Bengal and Andhra Pradesh[30] – is to offer a severe indictment.

The BJP's position, in comparative terms, is more encouraging in

Bihar. One party has a stronger organisation, but it is the Communist Party of India-Marxist Leninist (CPI-ML) which plays little part in electoral politics. The BJP there has a superior organisation to that of the INC which, according to Shaibal Gupta, 'is in very bad shape', and to the ruling RJD of Laloo Prasad Yadav. The RJD, argues Gupta, 'is really without any organisation', but it compensates with its strong, informal networks among disadvantaged castes and Muslims.[31]

If we consider states that have something close to two-party systems, in which the BJP is one of the two parties, the picture that emerges is only somewhat brighter for the party. In Madhya Pradesh over the last ten years, the INC has had a rather weak organisation, but it has consistently had more substance and reach than the BJP. The same is true across most of Rajasthan. If the BJP organisation is on level terms with that of the INC in Chhattisgarh, this is not saying much since the latter has been greatly damaged by former Chief Minister Ajit Jogi's extravagant and breathtakingly unwise over-centralisation of power while in office in the period before the 2003 state election.

In Gujarat, Ghanshyam Shah's comments (noted above) on the hollowness of the BJP's claim to have a cadre-based organisation inspire the suspicion that the INC is more penetrative there. The BJP used communal polarisation at the last state election as a means of compensating for its organisational weakness and its poor performance while in power over the preceding years.

This leaves only a small number of states where the BJP's organisation is (or at times has been) stronger than its rivals. In Delhi, for example, the BJP – unusually – has a reasonably strong organisation. However, we would expect that this would take place in a predominantly urban arena and it is compatible with the argument set out so far.

Implications: organisational weakness and Hindu extremism

What are the wider implications of the BJP's organisational weakness? We shall consider the connection with coalition politics presently, but let us first examine its implications for a further upsurge in Hindu nationalist extremism.

Organisational inadequacy creates serious problems for the BJP at election time. Most obviously, it means that the party lacks a reliable instrument for reaching most voters. But the difficulties do not end there. It also implies that, to do well in election campaigns, the BJP must rely on RSS cadres in many states. That raises several further dilemmas.

First, the RSS is more concerned than is the BJP with the pursuit of the Hindu nationalist agenda. This can prove a major inconvenience to the BJP when – as is common at the time of writing, across much of India – the party's leaders believe that stressing that agenda will not win them broad popular support. So while they may need RSS cadres to man (and that is the accurate word) their election campaigns, by doing so they come under pressure to emphasise issues that may alienate or bore many voters.

One particular type of voter, who seldom gets enough attention, is worth a brief comment here. Many people in India who have at times considered voting for the BJP are attracted because the party appears to represent orderliness, discipline, responsibility and maturity.[32] Such people sometimes compare the manner in which those who attend BJP election rallies are guided in an orderly manner into different sections of the space for the meetings, thus avoiding the over-crowding and chaos that often attend the rallies of other parties. Such people are likely to be put off by the extremism in which activists from the RSS and other elements of the *Sangh Parivar* sometimes engage. They are repelled by what Harish Khare (2003) calls the 'continued weakness for wanting to operate outside the legal system', and by activists who are 'ill at ease with the constitutional constraints and obligations'. There is also clear evidence that communal violence alienates the business community which has provided the BJP (and for that matter, the RSS) with much of its funding (Jaffrelot 1996: 478).

Another part of the problem is the tendency of the RSS to be a diffident partner for the BJP. This has happened at different times and in different places for different reasons. In some parts of India – and, to a degree, in India as a whole – between 1980 and 1989, when Indira Gandhi and then Rajiv Gandhi were clearly in the ascendancy, many RSS cadres turned to the INC as the party that was most likely to achieve some of its cherished goals. They did so in part because they found the BJP's political prospects depressing, but also because they were dismayed at the party's dilution of Hindu nationalist ideology, its 'efforts to attract Muslims', its strategy of alliance-building with other parties, and its aim to form a coalition government (Jaffrelot 1996: 327). In that period, Paul Brass witnessed RSS cadres canvassing for INC candidates in Uttar Pradesh – as a result of a decision by the RSS leader in the state.[33] Andersen and Damle (1987: 231–2, 234), Graham (1987: 15), Katju (2003: 63) and Jaffrelot (1996: 374, 377) offer evidence from other states to reinforce this point.

That problem was eased when the BJP's fortunes revived after 1989, but some hesitations in the RSS remain. And they are reinforced by a second difficulty – the distaste that many RSS members feel towards politics and the ambiguities that attend it. This has diminished somewhat in recent years, but it remains a reality. Graham (1990: 48) as well as Andersen and Damle (1987: 125, 157, 208, 227) stressed this, even *before* the BJP began admitting large numbers of prominent people whose commitment to Hindu nationalism was open to doubt. That distaste has grown with the inclusion of such people, and it intensified further after 1998, as BJP leaders shelved most elements of the hardline agenda in order to keep the NDA together so that they could govern at the national level.

The presence of RSS cadres in BJP campaigns has also made it more difficult for the party to develop links to independent, small time political 'fixers' at and below the district level in various states who can serve as a significant resource at election time.[34] And when the party has succeeded in forging such links, that in turn has put off some RSS cadres.

When BJP election campaigns stress developmental issues – as they did successfully – although their definition of 'development' was exceedingly narrow,[35] in unseating INC state governments in Madhya Pradesh, Rajasthan, and Chhattisgarh in 2003, this also causes dismay among many RSS cadres who are more preoccupied with Hindu nationalist issues. Roads, electricity supplies and service delivery are seen as legitimate issues to some in the RSS, but they leave many cold.

All of these things have inspired diffidence within the RSS towards BJP appeals for help in and between election campaigns. The BJP managed to overcome this in the 2003 state assembly election campaigns in Rajasthan, Madhya Pradesh and possibly Chhattisgarh, by offering the RSS immense influence both during the campaigns and once governments were formed in those states. By contrast, activists from the VHP and the Bajrang Dal largely sat out those campaigns, which suited the BJP (Manor 2004). This approach – of using the offer of a dominant role to the RSS in order to draw it into the action – may be a sign of things to come, which is a worry for many secularist Indians. It may also be a device to achieve what Jaffrelot calls the 'restoration' of *sanghathanism* (dominance) by those (often RSS members) who seek a firmly controlled BJP organisation (1998a: 283–4). But the possibility of RSS diffidence still remains a worry for the BJP (Jaffrelot 1996: 326–30), not least because the party's organisation lacks penetrative capacity.

We need to look beyond the RSS, and to consider another aspect of the link between organisational weakness and extremism. In some countries, organisational weakness has contributed to political extremism. This is – in complex ways – central to the story of Sri Lanka since the mid-1950s. Politicians there who head parties with frail organisations have repeatedly used bigotry to compensate for their parties' organisational incapacity to mobilise voters (Manor 1994: 770–84).

We have seen examples of this in India, but it has (so far) been the exception rather than the rule. The INC made some use of this in anti-Sikh newspaper advertisements and comments by its leader in the 1984 general election campaign. But the most startling and systematic example was the BJP's recent, successful re-election campaign at the state level in Gujarat.

As an election loomed there, Chief Minister Narendra Modi could see that he was likely to lose. This was largely explained by the poor record of the BJP government in the state during its years in power – although that record owed something to the weak BJP organisation which was ineffective at developing understandings with interest groups that might vote for the party. Modi recognised that the BJP's organisation lacked the strength to compensate for that poor performance with efficient election campaigning. So if he was to be re-elected, he needed something else to sway voters. Communal polarisation – to which Modi had long been devoted in any case – provided the answer. Ghastly riots ensued, and he was swept back to power in their aftermath.[36]

That episode firmly established such tactics as an option in the minds of BJP leaders. But the distaste that this approach inspires among some of those leaders, and more crucially, doubts about whether it would work in other parts of India[37] have so far kept this from becoming the party's preferred option. Its state assembly election campaigns in late 2003 focused more on development issues than on communal provocation – in part because incumbent INC governments in the various states were seen to be vulnerable on development, at least as the BJP defined it. This was true, even in Madhya Pradesh, where the BJP campaign was led by Uma Bharthi who has often played the firebrand in the past. Her restraint owed something to the small number of Muslims in that state (less than 5 per cent of the population) and to the failure of Hindu extremists to evoke much popular response.

One incident in mid-2003 vividly illustrated this latter point. A fire-breathing VHP leader, Acharya Dharmendra, entered Madhya Pradesh and made an incendiary communalist speech in a district town. He was promptly arrested on orders from the INC Chief Minister, Digvijay Singh. Dharmendra refused to pay his bail, in the expectation that large numbers of angry Hindus would gather to demand his release. After several days passed without any significant protests, he meekly handed over his bail, and left the state.

There is, however, no guarantee that the Modi option will never be seized upon by other BJP leaders. Some prominent national leaders of the party already have taken that view. This approach appears, on present evidence, unlikely to work. But that will not necessarily prevent it from being adopted. It may need to be tried and to fail before the option is shelved or ruled out.

Even if the party stops short of the Modi option, yet gives the RSS the kind of post-election dominance that it was apparently promised in Rajasthan and Madhya Pradesh, something similar may result. We must ask how long RSS activists will be content with BJP governments in such states emphasising development. The answer appears to be 'not for long'. Pressure from the RSS appears likely to compel such governments to stress Hindu nationalist themes. But given the lack of appeal – so far – of such themes in states other than Gujarat, any emphasis given to them is likely to undermine the interests and the popularity of the BJP.

Implications: organisational weakness and coalition politics

How does the organisational weakness of the BJP connect to a core concern of this book, namely the relationship between coalition politics and Hindu nationalism? There are three things to say here.

First and rather obviously, organisational weakness helps to make it necessary for the BJP to seek coalitions at the national level, since that weakness is one of the things that prevents the party from winning anything approaching a majority in the Lok Sabha. It is, however, not the *main* reason for its failure to do so. The main explanation for that lies in two patent facts: that Hindu nationalism does not inspire sufficient popular support, and that regional parties have consistently attracted substantial numbers of votes since 1989.[38] So if the BJP suddenly acquired a penetrative capacity, it would not be enough to win majorities in Parliament. But organisational weakness still contributes significantly to its inability to do so.

Second, if we turn things around and look at the connection from the other end, it is also possible to say that the pursuit of majority coalitions in the Lok Sabha contributes to the BJP's organisational weakness at the state level – in at least *some* important states. Consider two examples.

In Andhra Pradesh, the BJP's national leaders have insisted – in 1999, and again in early 2004 as a state election loomed – that the state-level unit of the party make an electoral alliance with the TDP, and that it accept unfavourable deals on seat allotments. The reason was that the national-level BJP saw the TDP as crucial to its goal of constructing a majority within the Lok Sabha. In 2004, this caused serious demoralisation within the state unit of the BJP. Between the 1999 and 2004 general elections, the Andhra Pradesh Chief Minister and his TDP dealt harshly with his BJP electoral allies – as if they were adversaries – in the same manner in which he treated the opposition INC. The BJP in the state had to submit to such affronts, on orders from national-level leaders. In 2004, they were confronted with the prospect of similar treatment for a further five years. The deep dismay that this caused has contributed to the organisation's continuing weakness in that state.

In Karnataka, during the state assembly election of 1999, we witnessed a more breathtaking imposition from on high. Between 1994 and 1999, the BJP had been the official opposition in Karnataka. During this period it had aggressively criticised and undermined the ruling Janata Dal at every opportunity. It had even carefully cultivated support among important interests that were hostile to the Janata Dal. Nevertheless, at the eleventh hour, the Karnataka BJP was forced to align itself with one element of the despised Janata Dal – because national BJP leaders believed that it would yield dividends in the Lok Sabha election in Bihar. This provoked deep anger within the state unit of the BJP, further eroding its already frail organisation. Consequently it sent the party down to an embarrassing defeat in Karnataka at the hands of the INC. BJP activists, relating that chain of events to this writer, broke down in tears.

Finally, one recent trend identified above may undermine the BJP's efforts to construct and sustain heterogeneous coalitions at the national level (and in states like Uttar Pradesh, where it is also necessary). What will happen if (to compensate for the BJP's organisational incapacities) the RSS is given greater influence in governing states, like Rajasthan and Madhya Pradesh? It seems only a matter of time before BJP governments in those states stress the Hindu nationalist agenda more energetically than in the past – and more energetically than at the national level. That would make coalitions at the national level (and in places like Uttar Pradesh) more diffi-cult to construct and sustain, because it would alienate the vast majority of coalition partners who are averse to Hindu nationalism. The point here is that the organisational weakness discussed here may, indirectly, contribute to the BJP's difficulties in gaining control at the national level.

The BJP's central leaders and the problem of organisational weakness

One last question is worth considering here. How aware are the BJP's national leaders of the kind of organisational weakness discussed here – their party's lack of penetrative capacity? We have clear evidence that *at times*, they have recognised this and taken action to remedy the problem. This was apparent during the state assembly election campaigns in Rajasthan, Madhya Pradesh and possibly Chhattisgarh in late 2003. They systematically marginalised the old-line leadership of the party in these states, parachuted in alternative leaders and organisers, and took pains to draw RSS cadres into the fray.

But that is not the whole story. At other times, their actions have done further damage to already weak organisations at the state level – to promote good relations with regional parties in the interests of building coalitions that can yield majorities in the Lok Sabha. We have seen that this has happened in Karnataka and Andhra Pradesh, and it may have occurred in Orissa, Bihar and elsewhere. The compulsions of alliance-building have taken precedence over the strengthening of the BJP's organisation. Similarly, national-level politics have taken precedence over the BJP's interests at the state level.

That is arguably a rational decision by the BJP's senior leaders, and does not imply a failure to recognise organisational weakness at the state level. It does not call their competence into question. But something else does. In some states, they have persisted for exceedingly long periods with state-level leaders who are unimaginative and sorely lacking in political skills. This has, for example, long been true in Karnataka – which is the party's most promising region in the whole of the east and the south. In that state, the BJP's national leaders have given control of the party unit to a man who is inept, autocratic and either unwilling or unable to engage in organisation building. Cases like that – and there are others – raise questions about whether the party's national leadership has at times allowed itself to be deceived by the myth that the BJP has a cadre-based organisation capable of penetrating into sub-district arenas.

This chapter has argued that the BJP's organisation is weaker than many people believe in at least one important respect. In most Indian states, it lacks a cadre-based structure – or any structure – that can penetrate below the district level and project its influence within most sub-district and local arenas.

The party's organisation is reasonably strong in several other respects, although these strengths do not entirely compensate for this particular weakness. For example, the BJP is able to ensure that state-level units comply with instructions from the national level. This helps the party to develop coalitions at the national level, but it undermines the credibility and organisational strength of the BJP in some important states. Moreover, the BJP organisation is harder to break than are other parties. That is useful to the party, but it does not do much to make it more capable of winning elections or of governing effectively once elected.

Organisational discipline enables the BJP to raise funds in a more efficient and centralised manner – funds for the party rather than for privateers – than can other parties. This again is helpful to the BJP, but money does not suffice to win most elections. If it did, then more incumbent state governments – which almost always have more money than their challengers – would have been re-elected in recent years.

The BJP can call upon an auxiliary force, the RSS – the like of which is available to no other party – to help win elections at the state level when incumbent parties other than the BJP are vulnerable. This occurred in December 2003 in Madhya Pradesh, Rajasthan and Chhattisgarh. Nevertheless, there are limitations to the advantage that this provides to the BJP. The RSS cannot help to unseat incumbent governments that are not vulnerable – as we saw in Delhi on that same occasion. In many states (especially, but not only in the east and the south) the RSS lacks the strength to ensure election victories.

We also need to ask whether the RSS can help the BJP, once it is elected in such states, to govern more effectively and responsively. Will it help the BJP to gain re-election in such places? The answers are unclear, but there are good reasons to doubt the utility of the RSS on both fronts. It is worth recalling the sole occasion on which a BJP government at the state level was re-elected thanks to its record on governance and development – Rajasthan in 1993. The RSS played little role there. The explanation had much more to do with an adroit Chief Minister and with the imaginative programmes that he and his team had created. And he deliberately kept well aloof of the RSS. There is no evidence that the RSS can assist in generating and implementing such programmes.

So even though the BJP's organisation is weak only *in part*, the part in question is vitally important both in winning elections and in governing effectively, imaginatively and responsively once it takes power at the state level – and perhaps also at the national level. A continuing dependence on the RSS after election victories (which we may now be seeing in Madhya Pradesh, Rajasthan and possibly Chhattisgarh) is not a satisfactory way to overcome this weakness. It creates as many problems as it solves.

The BJP aspires to be 'the natural party of government' in India, but at present it falls far short of that goal. It has no hope of winning a parliamentary majority on its own in the foreseeable future – indeed, it has very little hope of gaining anything close to a majority. When we ask why, two answers usually loom large. Other parties, not least small regional parties, have greater appeal to voters and Hindu nationalism does not inspire sufficient popular enthusiasm. The evidence provided here suggests one further explanation. The BJP's lack of a strong, penetrative organisation impedes its capacity to reach the electorate and to govern effectively when – despite this disability – it gains power.

Notes

1 Christophe Jaffrelot (1998a) has explicitly described the BJP as 'a cadre-based party'. This chapter argues that such claims tend strongly to be over-stated. Jaffrelot also states, convincingly, that divisions within the BJP should be seen as 'groupism' rather than 'factionalism' – because the latter word implies struggles '*between individuals to whom local activists pay allegiance*' (the emphasis is Jaffrelot's). He contrasts the BJP's cadre-based character with that of other '"aggregative parties"' which cash in on the influence of local politicians and notables', although he rightly notes that the BJP has become somewhat more aggregative in recent years (1998a: 275–6)

2 Upon reading these comments in draft, Paul Wallace stated that he had had a very similar experience in Hyderabad several years ago – long before the BJP had begun to develop its organisation in Andhra Pradesh.

3 See, for example, Zerinini-Brotel (1998: 77). This idea is usually not stated as plainly as it is in that paper. It tends to be presumed and implied – partly because, as we shall see, the party's organisation is seldom explicitly analysed.

4 Note that this election victory occurred after a spell of President's Rule in the wake of the destruction of the Babri Masjid. But in this writer's view, it seems fair to describe this as the 're-election' of a BJP government which had – just previously – held power in Rajasthan.

5 This comment is based on visits to the state in 2002 and (twice) in 2003.

6 I have discussed this in various places, for example Manor (1998: 163–201).

7 In Karnataka, for example, the party has a strong organisation in Coorg, and in the two coastal districts where the composition of society differs radically from the rest of that state.

8 For example, most of the contributors to the most wide-ranging recent assessment of the BJP in several states (who include this writer) – Hansen's and Jaffrelot's volume tends to deal with the party's organisation by implication or barely at all (1998a).

9 Interview with reporters at the *Hindustan Times*, Bhopal, 6 December 2003.

10 Interview with Dr Sunilam, MLA, a member of the Samajwadi Party and a famously incorruptible figure, Bhopal, 16 December 2003. This may not have been true in Maharashtra when the BJP held power in an alliance with the Shiv Sena. So much money was diverted that the state's previously impressive reputation to fiscal responsibility was destroyed. Extremely well-informed sources in that state and in the west insist that the responsibility for that lies mainly with the BJP – and not the Shiv Sena which grew frustrated at its inability to match the BJP in 'fund-raising'.

11 The BJP has done some breaking of other parties in recent years. In Uttar Pradesh in 1997, for example, it broke both the BSP and INC and, thereby, took power in the state (Hansen *et al.* 1998: 314).

12 This incident is not to be confused with Jogi's failed attempt to induce such defections *after* the 2003 state election.

13 There is evidence to suggest that the BJP organisation in Madhya Pradesh was beset by serious problems far earlier. One report from 1990, for example, stated that, 'The average run of BJP workers, with few exceptions, have tended to behave like Government employees, casual and indifferent in their demeanour' (*The Hindu* 1990).

14 Those states are Haryana, Uttar Pradesh, Bihar, Orissa, Rajasthan, Madhya Pradesh, Chhattisgarh, Andhra Pradesh, Tamil Nadu, Karnataka and Kerala.

15 This was Krishna Kumar, former Congress minister in the central government, who defected to the BJP and was assigned the task of building the party in Kerala (quoted in *The Hindu* 2003h).

16 These comments are based on information from Benjamin Powis who was doing doctoral research on local politics in the state.

17 Far greater detail is provided in Manor (1998: 163–201).

18 These comments are based on interviews with activists from all three parties, and with analysts, in Bangalore, 7–14 May 2004. I am (not for the first time) especially grateful to E. Raghavan and Imran Qureshi for their insights. It is worth noting that a recent effort by the *Sangh Parivar* to foment communal polarisation through an agitation over a place of worship in Chikmagalur District failed to gain the BJP any advantage at the 2004 election. This is no surprise, given the state's record of Hindu–Muslim accommodation.

19 I am grateful to Shaibal Gupta for these points.

20 Interview with Amitabh Singh, Bhopal, 8 December 2003.

21 Interview with *kshetra pracharak* Narmohan, *Hindustan Times*, 6 December 2003. The words quoted are those of the reporter, summarising Narmohan's views.

22 On Madhya Pradesh, see Manor (2004). A close reading of press reports from Rajasthan and Chhattisgarh indicates that similar things happened in both states.

23 I am grateful to Rob Jenkins and Sanjeev Srivastava for evidence on Rajasthan.

24 I am again grateful to Rob Jenkins for this observation. It was corroborated in an interview with Digvijay Singh, former Congress Chief Minister of Madhya Pradesh, New Delhi, 15 May 2004.

25 I am grateful to Harish Puri for this information. He was drawing upon RSS and BJP contacts.

26 I am grateful to Yogendra Yadav for these comments.

27 I am grateful to Rob Jenkins for this evidence from Maharashtra.

28 This comment is based on T.J. Nossiter's comparisons of the CPI-M in these two states, and on discussions with numerous specialists in the politics of the two states.

29 Benjamin Powis has collected especially telling evidence on this in his doctoral research at the Institute of Development Studies, University of Sussex. I am also grateful to K. Srinivasulu for insights in this vein.

30 For a recent example of divisions within the Andhra Pradesh Congress (a very old story), see *The Hindu* (2004b).
31 This again is based on comments by Shaibal Gupta.
32 This writer has met a great many such people over the years, but see also Table 8.2 in Shah (1998: 260). Respondents in a 1991 survey in Gujarat cited, as one of their two most important reasons for preferring the BJP, their perception that it was a 'Good party/*disciplined* party/listens to us' (emphasis added). The other main reason was the wish to 'give them a chance'. These things were far more important than the quality of BJP candidates and the party's pro-Hindu stance.
33 Communication from Paul Brass, 14 October 2003.
34 For a more detailed discussion of 'fixers', see Manor (2000).
35 See, for example, Manor (2004).
36 See the contributions in this volume by Alistair McMillan (Chapter 1), John Zavos (Chapter 2), Subrata Mitra (Chapter 4), Nitya Rao (Chapter 6) and Meghnad Desai (Chapter 13) for perspectives on the 2002 Gujarat riots.
37 Attempts at communal polarisation were not successful at the subsequent state election in Himachal Pradesh.
38 I am grateful to Yogendra Yadav for stressing this point

Part II
Domestic governance

4 The NDA and the politics of 'minorities' in India

Subrata K. Mitra

Introduction

The success of the NDA in forming a government in 1999 was seen by many as the harbinger of a systematic onslaught on the status and dignity of India's minorities. The anxieties were caused mainly by the fact that the BJP, as the largest member of the coalition, secured for itself the Ministries of Home, Law, Human Resources and Scheduled Tribes and Castes. These Ministries have significant implications for India's minorities. Although it moderated its positions on key policy issues in order to appeal to a wider section of the electorate, the BJP had campaigned from a platform of 'Hindu' nationalism, a slogan that gave primacy to an exclusive and homogenising model of the nation over one committed to the accommodation of religious and cultural diversity. However, despite some highly publicised attacks on churches and missionaries as well as the Hindu–Muslim riots of 2002 in Gujarat – in which the role of the BJP Government in Gujarat and the NDA in Delhi has been vigorously criticised in the media and by human rights groups (Jaffrelot 2003) – the end of the term record of the NDA Government, relative to the initial scepticism, appears to have been positive with regard to its minority policy. An analysis of media reports and party documents confirm that the NDA stood by the assurances it gave to the minorities in its National Agenda of Governance, although there were attempts at change that were resisted by the BJP's coalition partners in the NDA. In terms of official policy, the political consensus on safeguarding the growth of a plural society that has evolved in India since independence has held during the watch of the NDA. National statistics on riots show a downward trend.[1] Have poachers then become gamekeepers?[2]

The chapter poses this question with regard to the 'minorities' policy of the NDA. Though these policies and executive action were articulated in the name of the ruling NDA coalition, in terms of their origin, these were mostly initiatives of the BJP. The chapter analyses them through the position the NDA took on issues affecting minorities as well as on the larger vision of the nation and the state within which these specific policies were conceptualised.[3] I explain here why, contrary to expectation, the BJP/NDA did not upset the status quo with regard to citizenship rights and dignity of minorities, while trying, howsoever feebly, to question the very concept of minority in Indian politics. The consequence of this double effort – to accommodate minority interests while trying to query the concept of minority itself – gives a Janus-faced character to the NDA's minority policy. I explain this in terms of the spatial distribution of preferences in the Indian electorate, the countervailing forces of Indian politics, the internal dynamic of the NDA coalition, the relative power of the exclusivist organisational core of the BJP compared to its parliamentary wing, and the political acumen and negotiating skills of the NDA leadership.

'Minorities' in Indian politics: the genealogy of an essentially contested concept

Judging from its contradictory empirical meanings, contentious genealogy and the history of conflict on and around it, the term 'minority' is an 'essentially contested concept' in Indian politics.[4] Undeterred by any such theoretical misgivings, the Constitution of India and the vested interests that have grown around it, see minority as an unambiguous, directly measurable and legal construct, intended to promote the welfare of vulnerable sections of society. 'Minority', in this formulation, is the vulnerable 'Other' of Indian politics, locked in mortal combat against the powerful, indigenous 'Majority'. Defenders of, what I would call, an unproblematic and essential view of minorities were apprehensive about the long-term implications of the logic of parliamentary democracy in India based on the simple plurality electoral law, for they saw the potential for the collective strength of an organic Hindu majority crushing non-Hindu minorities.[5]

A brief genealogy of the issue of minority in Indian politics will set the concept in the context of its historical evolution. More ideological tool than philosophical category, controversy over the concept of minorities was a regular feature of Indian politics under colonial rule. The British, both solicitous and strategic, set themselves up as defenders of the minority. Following the transfer of power, the fear of persecution of 'minority' communities by the 'majority' became one of Nehru's main concerns. More recently, with the meteoric rise of the BJP to power in the 1990s following the destruction of the Babri Mosque in 1992, the fate of India's non-Hindu communities has become a cause for world-wide anxiety. In a charged political atmosphere polarised around the issue of the ascendance of Hindu 'fundamentalism', a theoretical analysis of the interaction of the minority as an inherited concept and the logic of post-independence politics has not been possible. This chapter responds to this lacuna by problematising the concept of minority in Indian politics through a focus on the politics of minorities of the NDA.

Elections and the politics of minority discourse in India

There are no specific provisions in the Indian Constitution dealing with majorities. Minorities are considered as cohesive natural groups; but majorities are understood as political coalitions who do not deserve any extra protection, for the sum of their individual rights is considered to be sufficient for the articulation of their political demands. Group rights are conferred on sections of society whom the makers of the Constitution considered vulnerable. Benefits and protections are conferred on groups in order to preserve their identity as groups. The fixed definition of minorities as a reliable guide for action is contested by the meanings attributed to it in its political usage. In his essay, 'Who are India's Minorities?' Weiner (1986: 101) points out the empirical ambiguity that underpins the concept.[6] In his analysis, the ambiguity regarding who is a minority transmits itself to the majority as well (1986: 117). On the basis of a large number of empirical anomalies, he concludes:

> Clearly India contains such a medley of religious, caste and linguistic groups that the sense of belonging to a minority depends upon where one lives, how much power and status one has, and one's sense of community threat. . . . In the Indian context, it is a way of calling attention to a situation of self-defined deprivation.
>
> (1986: 101–2)

If the lawmakers of India were aware of the empirical uncertainty underlying the concept of minority, there is little indication of it in the definition of minorities and minority rights in the Indian Constitution.[7] Possibly to promote its enthusiastic commitment to nation-building and social engineering and to forestall further uncertainty in its meanings, the Indian legislation gave a fixed meaning to the concept of minority, defining it as 'Muslims, Christians, Sikhs, Buddhists and Zoroastrians (Parsis)'.[8] Moreover, Article 29 of the Constitution contains a number of provisions for the protection of interests of minorities. Thus, Article 29(1) confers the right to the conservation of distinct language, script or culture to any section of the citizens of India. Article 29 also requires the State not to deny admission into any educational institution maintained by the State or receiving aid out of State funds to anybody on grounds only of religion, race, caste, language or any of them. In addition, Article 30 affirms the right of minorities to establish and administer educational institutions. Finally, Article 29(2) prohibits the State from discriminating against any educational institution in the allocation of grants 'on the ground that it is under the management of a minority, whether based on religion or language'.

Weiner's inference is significant for our purpose: 'minority and majority status is a matter of self-ascription as well as objective definition. What is a majority from one perspective is a minority from another' (1986: 101).

The quickening of the pace and reach of India's competitive electoral arena has also given voice to the inner contradiction of minority as a concept to different political constituencies. One direct outcome of this process is the emergence of a Hindu 'majority' as a political idea (Mitra and Fischer 2002), claiming to speak in the name of India's Hindus, who represent 83 per cent of the population. The reaction to this is the apprehension, both academic and political, of a tide of creeping 'Hindu fascism', barely concealed under the cloak of majoritarian democracy.[9]

To counter this allegation of majority communalism, which they see as an electoral liability, the BJP/NDA developed a range of social and economic policies of engaging the minorities which amounted to a 'non-essentialising strategy'. The BJP, a political party, keen like all organisations of the genre, on achieving power and sustaining its hold on it,[10] had actively sought to dispel its 'anti-minority' image even before the formation of the NDA. The demolition of the Babri Mosque provoked tactical voting on the part of the minorities, damaging the BJP in the 1993 Assembly elections (Ghosh 2003: 234). The poor electoral showing of the BJP provided the context for a major strategic re-think with regard to minorities. The party conclave of the BJP in Sariska in 1994 was perhaps the main turning point towards an explicit formation of a policy of accommodation towards the minorities (*The Economic Times* 1994). Another report quoted Advani as warning 'Muslims to be aware of both Congress and their leaders and repose faith in the BJP'. When a journalist sought to know exactly which measures the BJP was contemplating for the welfare of Muslims to win their confidence, Advani said that 'the BJP will protect their lives and they will enjoy equal justice' (*The Indian Express* 1993). Another report from the same period – tragically anachronistic in view of the violent events in Gujarat in 2002 – has Keshubhai Patel, the then Gujarat Chief Minister, saying that 'Muslims have nothing to fear under the rule of the BJP Government in Gujarat and can look forward to getting a much better deal than what they got during Congress (I) rule'. Following Sariska, the BJP maintained that Muslims were as patriotic as Hindus, but had been 'misled and misused by the Congress (I)' (*The Statesman* 1995).

This effort to wean minorities in general, but Muslims in particular, away from the INC was reinvigorated once the BJP came to power in 1998. In my analysis, the strategy has consisted of the demonstration of the shared interests of non-Hindu communities with those of Hindus, and engaging with social groups on the basis of concrete demands for material welfare, security and citizenship rather than exclusivist slogans of identity politics. It may, however, be argued that all parties, in the face of intense competition for political support, say things that they do not follow up on afterwards. Therefore, one can reasonably ask, was the call to non-essentialise the minority identity merely rhetorical or was the party able to back it up with actual performance once in government? The question can be answered by first looking at the material that the party has itself put forth, and then through an evaluation of its issue positions in the media and by academic analysts.

The approach of the 1998 general election generated new tactical thinking within the BJP. For instance, one of them concerned circulating the Koran in Sanskrit. Rather than harping on the essential differences between Hindus and Muslims, the strategy was to concentrate on specific needs that are common to both. Anandan in *The Indian Express* reports that:

> High on the agenda . . . is a follow-up of the resolutions with regard to the minorities at the Goa convention of the party early this month. In that convention following BJP president L.K. Advani's call to 'remove misconceptions (about the BJP) in the minds of the minorities', the party resolved to revive the earlier Congress slogan of Hindu-Muslim *bhai-bhai*, invoking the brotherhood of Hindus and Muslims. The more well-known of the resolutions were the three Ts – *taaleem* (education), *tanzeem* (organisation) and *tijarat* (employment) for Muslims.
>
> (Anandan 1995)

The appropriation of the Congress slogan of brotherhood of Hindus and Muslims was further reinforced with a 'guarantee to every Muslim' by Advani of 'security, justice, equality and full freedom of faith and worship'. Going all out to woo the community in the last lap of the party's campaign, he said 'no BJP government will tolerate any dilution of this guarantee' (*The Telegraph* 1996). This had a follow up in a 'long interview to a private television channel' by Vajpayee who said that 'all Muslims should be able to live with self-respect and honour'. According to Vajpayee, '[f]or this, Muslims should give all support to my government', adding that he could 'not understand why the community was keeping away from the mainstream' (*Mid-Day* 1996). Further appropriations of INC policy regarding non-Hindu groups included efforts by Advani who, according to one press report, 'praised Jawaharlal Nehru for his secular policies and promised to create a riot-free, violence-free and discrimination-free India when the BJP comes to power at the Centre' (*The Times of India* 1997).

Despite these efforts, or perhaps because of them, the BJP's policy of engaging minorities was received with considerable scepticism. To wit, Aslam Sher Khan, a former Union Minister, was one of the most prominent Muslims to have joined the BJP. However, it is reported that 'he quit the party within one year after realising that the BJP had no love for Muslims and *Dalits* and wanted to use them as a ladder to achieve power' (*The Asian Age* 2000). Nevertheless, the upper echelon of the BJP and its Muslim spokespersons were undeterred by such internal bickering. Support for the policy of accommodating Muslims came, primarily from Prime Minister Vajpayee, who claimed that

> his bus initiative to Lahore had greatly blunted the 'false image' of the BJP of being an anti-Muslim party (and that) the BJP finds a 'radical change' in the attitude of Muslim voters and is confident of getting 'a

major share of their votes' . . . as the party has given them a feeling of national pride unlike the so-called secular parties which always portrayed them in a poor light.

(*The Hindustan Times* 1999)

In addition, the Union Minister for Textiles, Syed Shahnawaz Hussain (a Muslim member of the NDA cabinet) refuted reports that 'the Centre had reduced the Haj subsidy this year and said the subsidy would continue'. He noted that '[t]he Vajpayee Government had increased the Haj subsidy by 22 times from what it was during the Congress rule', due to the increase in airfares (*The Hindu* 2003c).[11] The NDA Government also highlighted its appointment of two individuals from minority communities (Tarlochan Singh and Dr M.S. Usmani) to the two leading positions in the National Minority Commission. The NDA showed considerable skill and planning behind these key appointments to such a politically sensitive body.

Integral humanism: BJP's counter formulation to Nehruvian secularism

The official policy of the BJP on minorities was formulated in their 1998 election manifesto. Its social agenda, a key component of its manifesto, was derived from 'Integral Humanism' a concept that it promoted as superior to the fuzziness of secularism. The 1998 manifesto claimed that:

> Our ideology rules out contradictions between society and its very components, as also between society and the individual . . . The BJP's concept of social justice, therefore, does not seek to create rifts and schisms between various sections of society, but aims at removing social and economic disparities . . . An ideal society is not one that is compartmentalised in segments, but is an integral whole, harmonious and conflict-free.
>
> (Bharatiya Janata Party 1998)

These notions were spelt out in terms of a number of subsidiary ideas, such as equal rights for all in *satta* (power), *sampatti* (prosperity), and *samman* (dignity). Moreover, the BJP committed itself to:

> a casteless socio-economic order that will effectively provide access to equal opportunity for all citizens, irrespective of their caste, creed, religion and gender (and) if necessary, through legislation, to dismantle practices, customs, beliefs, usages and institutions, which in any manner hurt the dignity of an individual.
>
> (Bharatiya Janata Party 1998)

These detailed provisions for promoting the welfare of SCs, STs and OBCs was in the name of the promotion of social harmony, and 'positive secularism'. The manifesto described it as 'Justice for All, Appeasement of None'.

The party was keenly aware of the need to appeal to minorities for support and offered to provide credit, training and recognition to artisans and craftsmen from minority communities and to 'amend Article 30 of the Constitution suitably to remove any scope of discrimination against any religious community in matters of education' (Bharatiya Janata Party 1998). The 1998 manifesto also vowed to:

> set up special courts to try cases of communal violence and, if necessary, amend existing laws to provide for exemplary punishment to those inciting or taking part in communal or sectarian violence.
>
> (1998)

The manifesto gave detailed attention to specific facets that have been of special concern to the Muslim community, particularly dealing with the operation of *wakf* (religious property trusts). The BJP committed itself to:

> create a riot-free India; protect wakf properties from being usurped by unscrupulous individuals and help wakf boards to develop these properties for the welfare of poor Muslim families; ban job advertisements which require applicants to declare their religion.
>
> (1998)

While the BJP was keen to attract support from non-Hindu communities, it was careful to distinguish its policy from what it has criticised as pseudo-secularism and vote-bank politics. To make the point, it reaffirmed what it rather euphemistically described as 'Our Commitment to Kashmiri Pandits', which puts the onus of Kashmir's ills on 'separatist and sectarian militancy in Jammu and Kashmir'. The plan of action that the manifesto offered, namely a phased return of the refugees, including Pandits and Kashmiri Muslims, to the Kashmir Valley and a home rehabilitation scheme, is yet another indication of the non-essentialising strategy, capable of offering a concrete plan without necessarily referring to identity politics.

In the 1998 manifesto, the BJP restated its engagement with minorities in terms of dual commitments to 'genuine secularism' and specific welfare measures for the SCs, STs and OBCs. The former, can be seen as an authoritative expression of the party's ideological position. The manifesto asserted that:

> We are committed to establishing a civilised, humane and just civil order; that which does not discriminate on grounds of caste, religion, class, colour, race or sex. We will truly and genuinely uphold and practise the concept of secularism consistent with the Indian tradition of '*Sarva panth samadara*' (equal respect for all faiths) and on the basis of equality of all.

> We are committed to the economic, social and educational development
> of the minorities and will take effective steps in this regard.
>
> (1998)

Having served in power for 13 months, the NDA Government claimed
to have achieved the listed results to the previous commitments. Under
the subheading of 'Our Achievements in 13 Months', the NDA's 1999
Manifesto listed an extensive list of its efforts on behalf of minorities. They
included, among others, the following summary of achievements:

- An increase in allocations to the National SC and ST Finance and
  Development Corporation for the purpose of providing loans at con-
  cessional rates.
- The issuance of a multiyear, Rs 208 million grant for SC/ST students
  in the northeast during each year of the 9th Five Year Plan.
- The revamping of the National SC and ST Finance and Development
  Corporation, National Backward Classes Finance and Development Corporation, and the National Minorities Development and Finance Corpo-
  ration (NMFDC).
- The setting up of a shop in Delhi to provide marketing support for
  items produced by Tribal Communities and handicapped persons.
- The reactivation of the National Handicapped Finance and Development Corporation.
- The issuance of grants to 95 educational institutions managed by
  minorities.
- A 50 per cent increase, during the 1998–99 financial year, in allocations to improve the financial position of *Wakfs* and *Wakf* Boards.
- A 250 per cent increase, during the 1998–99 financial year, in dis-
  bursements to the NMFDC for the purpose of economic development
  of thousands of families belonging to minority communities.
- The expenditure of Rs 22 million for the purpose of providing pre-
  examination coaching to 6,030 candidates belonging to minority
  communities (National Democratic Alliance 1999).

The above record of achievements with regard to minorities, gives a
detailed account of the claims made on behalf of its non-essentialisation
strategy. A careful perusal of these claims helps identify the social groups
that have been targeted by the BJP/NDA under the rubric of its reformu-
lated minority policy.

Claims, counter-claims, performance

Ironically, the NDA's minority policy appears to have displeased just about
every political formation in India, including those on the Left who see it as
'anti-secular', to the extremists of the Hindu religious right, who found BJP's

commitment to *Hindutva* lukewarm and opportunistic. It is important to step outside partisan views and analyse the specific policies in terms of the issue positions of the NDA and those of the parties opposed to it. This is where the insights provided by Wright (2001: 3–7) are extremely helpful.[12] On the basis of an analysis of the Indian media, he gives a detailed account of 12 issues where the BJP/NDA was faced with a choice between an accommodation of minorities or their exclusion from national politics. We shall analyse Wright's observations in terms of three groups of issues respectively: issues with implications for models of nation-building, those relevant to state-formation and finally, issues that have a direct implication for social justice.

With regard to the first category, a long-standing demand of Hindu nationalism has been to create a nation that would draw its legitimacy from a set of sacred symbols, of which the cow is a core element. Accordingly, efforts to ban cow slaughter have been at the forefront of the policies of Hindu nationalist parties and movements. As such, the passage of an anti-cow-slaughter bill – in the form of an amendment to the Prevention of Anti-Social Activities law in Gujarat in the year 2000 – was seen as an avowal of the enactment of Hindu nationalism through legislation. The legislative coup did not go unnoticed. Wright observes that one of the two Muslim MLAs protested against the bill, saying that it was meant to harass the minority community during *Bakr Id* (the feast of sacrifice, an important Muslim holiday). However, Wright wryly comments that the bill was passed with the unanimous support of both the BJP and the INC, and that, as in Sri Lanka, the minority has no chance when the two major parties agree.[13]

On a second sensitive issue, with regard to school prayers, the BJP-led coalition in Uttar Pradesh sought to make the singing of *Vande Mataram* (India's national song) and *Saraswati Vandana* (a Hindu hymn) compulsory for government schools. The songs were considered by the Muslim *ulema* (clerics) to be idolatrous, and a *fatwa* (edict) was issued for Muslim parents to withdraw their children from the schools if the state government persisted in its efforts. Then a crucial component of the state's coalition, the Lok Tantrik Congress, expressed reservations about forcing students to recite a hymn linked to Hindu nationalism. In turn, NDA Government's Home Minister, L.K. Advani, took a position against compulsion too.

Another contentious issue was a programme, which, according to the left, was intended to rewrite textbooks in a manner so as to glorify Hindu heroes over Muslim rulers.[14] Wright (2001: 4) reports,

> At the centre, this took the form of the government packing the governing Board of the Indian Council of Historical Research and withdrawing some already written textbooks from publication. However, strident criticism at the state education ministers' conference compelled Human Resource Development Minister, Mr Murli Mahohar Joshi, to back down.
>
> (Baweja 1998; *The Times of India* 1998c)

In this case it was an NDA Government ally, M. Karunanidhi, the DMK Chief Minister of Tamil Nadu, who objected to the inclusion of material from the Vedas and Upanishads in school curricula, 'which to this party smelled of Northern imposition on the South' (Wright 2001: 4).

A cohesive nation ensconced within a strong state has been one of the main objectives of Hindu nationalism. The BJP/NDA efforts to check the growth of *madrassas* (Muslim schools) and to clamp down on unauthorised immigration from Bangladesh have been justified by the government in terms of this objective. Thus, the legislation in Uttar Pradesh requiring permission from the local administration for the erection of religious structures was intended to check the 'ominous growth of madrasas and masjids in the Nepal border region' (Wright 2001: 4). The Indian police and military feared these were being used by Pakistan's Inter-Services Intelligence (ISI), as safe houses for Kashmiri militants determined to wreak havoc and promote communal disunity (*The Times of India* 1999). However, Muslim organisations suspected that the ulterior motive of the BJP state governments was to inhibit or even reduce Muslim organisations. Meetings and demonstrations were staged against the Bill (*Dawn* 2000b). Nevertheless, it passed both houses of the legislature only to be delayed by the Governor who refused to sign it and referred it to India's President Narayanan, who was nominated to this high office by the previous INC regime.

True to style, Prime Minister Vajpayee played it safe by sending the Bill mentioned above, once it was passed by the Uttar Pradesh legislature to a multiparty committee for review, even though previous INC governments had passed similar laws in Rajasthan and Madhya Pradesh. A senior BJP leader was quoted as saying, indiscreetly, that '[t]he BJP cannot afford the ire of Muslims and other minorities in UP' after dropping Chief Minister Kalyan Singh, an OBC, for a high caste politician' (*The Times of India* 2000a).

A related proposal was the Criminal Law Amendment or 'Prevention of Terrorism Bill' to replace the lapsed TADA (Terrorist and Disruptive Activities Prevention Act), a controversial law under which many Muslims had been held without trial. This, of course, attracted the criticism of civil rights groups, both domestic and international, as well as Muslim organisations that rightly feared discriminatory and arbitrary arrests of minority members (*EPW* 2000c: 1066–71; *Dawn* 2000a; *The Times of India* 2000b). Coalition partners, whose members have long suffered police harassment when they were in opposition, also weighed in against the bill. Finally, the BJP/Shiv Sena coalition in Maharashtra attempted to make a big issue about deporting illegal immigrants, chiefly Muslim Bangladeshis and Pakistani 'overstayers'. Subsequently this also became an issue in New Delhi during slum clearance. Bengali infiltrators had long been a source of conflict in Assam, especially in those areas where it borders with Bangladesh.

The NDA saw illegal immigration as a threat to the reversal of the religious and linguistic ratio in States bordering on Pakistan and Bangladesh. An attempt by the Gujarat police to order a census of 'criminal and communal elements' to stem the tide, evoked sharp reactions from human rights and minority organisations in the state, and eventually had to be withdrawn before the High Court could rule on its constitutionality. An incongruous alliance of civil rights activists with employers, rather than legislative opposition, may have sunk the project, just as it did in the US.

Finally, the attempts of the NDA Government to promote women's empowerment through the legislation to reserve one third of the seats in the Parliament for women was thwarted through a coalition of left secular parties and the Congress who saw this as an insidious attempt by Hindu nationalists to increase their numbers because, if the Bill were to pass, the likely beneficiary would be upper caste Hindu women (*The Times of India* 1998b; Ausaf Saied Vasfi 1998; Wright 1997: 852–8).[15]

Similarly, the NCRWC was depicted as an attempt to induct the spirit of *Hindutva* into the constitution and resisted from within the coalition by the Samata Party, Trinamul Congress, DMK and TDP.

Thus, according to Wright, notwithstanding its ideological stance, in practice, the BJP has had to 'modify and soften or even defer some of its main platform planks' strategically, in order to mobilise support and sustain the coalition government. Success has come at a price, for it has lost some of the 'most dedicated and effective cadres of the *Sangh Parivar*'. Wright concludes: 'Democracy and coalition politics do tend to deradicalise extremist parties, but at the cost of effectiveness of governance' (2001: 7). Commenting on the NDA policies on the whole, Wright says that these policies have been far more status quo oriented than the impression one might get. 'The requirements of coalition building have indeed compelled the BJP to retreat on most of its historic as well as some new issues to the exasperation of its non-party organisations, the *Sangh Parivar* (RSS, VHP and Bajrang Dal)'. Accommodation of minorities within a redefined political space with a demonstrably Hindu bias rather than the dissolution of their distinctive identities appears to have become official BJP policy. 'Hinduvadis still claim that all they are trying to do in this regard is to end "minority appeasement" and make good Indians out of the Muslim minority, not to expel or exterminate them. If this goal is in fact true, then the charge of the left and secularists that the Hinduvadis are "fascist" is misdirected' (Wright 2001: 3).

The Janus face of NDA's minority policy: a necessary ambivalence?

Any general inferences one might have drawn from the possible hiatus between the professed policies of the NDA and their actual implementation pales into insignificance in view of the Gujarat riots of 2002; the one incident whose memory has since become for many people the one and exclusive criterion to evaluate the minority policy of the NDA. True, the riots took place in Gujarat and not in central territory. Thus, constitutionally, the primary responsibility for law and order lay with the state government of Gujarat. The fact of the matter is that the BJP was the ruling party in Gujarat; and that the BJP-led central government could have been more effective in its efforts to maintain order in Gujarat. During the event, speculation has been rife with regard to the complicity of Chief Minister Narendra Modi and its condoning by the central government's Home Ministry. By reopening the *Best Bakery* case (in many ways a test case to establish the possibility of official involvement with the communal violence against Muslims) and moving it out of Gujarat, the Supreme Court itself has cast its vote in the camp of those who see in the Gujarat riots a complete negation of all the claims made by the BJP/NDA to prove their credentials with regard to equal right to citizenship and dignity by India's non-Hindu minorities.[16] Instead of a policy and practice of non-essentialisation of the 'Other', in the opinion of many observers, what one finds, instead, is essentialisation and polarisation.[17]

To what might one attribute the behaviour of the NDA Government – error of judgement, masterly inaction or deep conspiracy – during the crucial aftermath to the outbreak of the Gujarat riots? The lack of firm and purposeful reaction on the part of the NDA Government – reminiscent in many ways of the initial inaction of the Rajiv Gandhi Government in 1984 in the face of the anti-Sikh riots in Delhi following the assassination of Indira Gandhi by her Sikh bodyguards – probably supports all three of these explanations and thus challenges the claim of the BJP being minority-friendly. Be that as it may, the acrimonious debate on the allocation of blame is far from over. One clear implication, relevant for this chapter, to arise from this epochal event is the tremendous scepticism and cynicism that it has given rise to in respect of the efforts of the BJP/NDA to appear minority-friendly.

The perceived and actual contrast between the BJP's claims and its performance gives its minority policy a Janus-faced ambivalence. To explain the underlying contradictions of policy and performance as sheer opportunism is simplistic, for what else should one expect from political actors in any event? The external perception of the NDA's minority policy as convoluted and contradictory and the genuine dilemma that this policy in general, and Gujarat Chief Minister Narendra Modi in particular, have generated within the decision-making circles of the BJP calls for deeper analysis. The BJP's strategic location within the political context of contemporary India and the distribution of preferences over issues seen as crucial by the minorities, and the shifting landscape of coalitions and social bases of political formations, are more promising lines of inquiry. The answers to the perceived gap between policy and practice are to be found in the logic of vote maximisation, coalition formation and maintenance, and the larger frame of India's institutional arrangement and the countervailing forces that underpin them. I shall deal with these points briefly.

A core hypothesis emerging from spatial models of voting behaviour and party strategies (Downs 1957; Riker and Ordeshook 1973) suggests that all political parties must, simultaneously, seek to get the maximum share of the vote and make necessary ideological compromises. At the same time, though, they must try not to go too far off their ideological moorings, so as not to lose their distinctiveness and the support of core followers. This double bind sometimes makes them take fuzzy positions. With regard to the position on Muslims and Christians, two minority groups that function as an indicator of BJP's social policy, the data presented in Tables 4.1 and 4.2 show how those who claim to have voted for the BJP in the previous parliamentary election are disposed.

Table 4.1 gives the impression of the growth of more harmony than disharmony between Hindus and Muslims during the NDA's watch, a fact which is supported by a higher percentage of those claiming to have voted for the BJP as compared to the electorate as a whole. Table 4.2, on the other hand, tells another story. In this case, though there is a slightly higher percentage for those who believe injustice has been done to Christians among the electorate as a whole, in the case of the BJP, the percentages are exactly in the opposition direction, with about 28 per cent disagreeing that injustice has been done to Christians as compared to 18 per cent of BJP voters who acknowledge that injustice has been done to Christians.

From Table 4.1 and Table 4.2 we can conclude that, although the BJP/NDA have seen it as appropriate to stay within the main thrust of Indian opinion with regard to good communal relations between Hindus and Muslims, attitudes differ within the party with regard to the posture to take to attitudes towards Christians who have rapidly displaced Muslims as 'pampered minorities' in the eyes of the BJP.

Minorities themselves, to go by public opinion figures, have emerged as assertive and conscious of their rights, questioning the image of helpless vulnerability that one so often comes across in the national and inter-

Table 4.1 Response to statement: 'There is greater brotherhood among Hindus and Muslims' (figures represent percentages)

Party respondent voted for	Disagree	No opinion	Agree
Congress or its allies	24.9	40.9	34.2
BJP or its allies	22.5	34.1	43.4
LF	33.1	34.5	32.4
BSP	20.0	49.8	30.2
Others	23.0	40.7	36.3
Total	24.5	37.8	37.7

Source: CSDS (1999).

national media. Our findings (Mitra and Singh 1999: 141) from a survey of the national electorate in 1996 reinforce this picture. Asked, 'do you think your vote has effect on how things are run in this country, or do you think your vote makes no difference?', 60.3 per cent of Muslims and 66.4 per cent of Christians answered in the affirmative; compared to 58 per cent for Hindus and 58.6 per cent for the population as a whole. Similarly, the findings from a question regarding institutional legitimacy indicated a higher level of support for the institutions of parliamentary democracy for Muslims and Christians than Hindus, and the electorate as a whole. Asked, 'Suppose there were no parties or assemblies and elections were not held, do you think that the government in this country could be run better?' Muslims and Christians answered in the negative, with 72.1 per cent and 73.4 per cent, respectively; whereas the corresponding figures for Hindus was 68.2 per cent, and the population as a whole, 68.8 per cent (Mitra and Singh 1999: 144).

The attitudinal evidence of empowerment of minority groups is reinforced by a different form of evidence we get from Weiner (1986). This consists of a meticulous analysis of India's electoral demography in terms of bastions of minority strength. Weiner showed how national 'minorities' are actually majorities in a number of Indian States, such as Jammu and Kashmir (Muslim), Meghalaya (Christian, Tribal), Nagaland (Christian, Tribal), Punjab (Sikh), Arunachal Pradesh (Tribal), Mizoram (Christian), in a number of districts (where the majority character has important implications for district level democracy) and urban communities (where majority strength directly translates into municipal politics). Thus, independently of special institutions to protect minority interests, the sheer logic of majoritarian democracy itself propels minority interests into the political arena.

A complementary picture to these images of efficacy and legitimacy is to be found in a national consensus about the responsibility of the government to ensure the protection and welfare of minority communities (see Table 4.3). Once again, it should be noted here that the majority of those claiming to have voted did so in the affirmative to the question: 'It is the responsibility of the government to protect the interests of the minority

Table 4.2 Response to statement: 'Injustice has been done to Christians' (figures represent percentages)

Party respondent voted for	Disagree	Don't know/no opinion	Agree
Congress or its allies	13.9	58.5	27.6
BJP or its allies	27.7	54.5	17.8
LF	13.3	51.6	35.1
BSP	5.9	82.7	11.4
Others	17.1	59.9	23.0
Total	19.3	57.1	23.5

Source: CSDS (1999).

communities. Do you agree?'. Though, their percentage is lower than the Congress and the Left parties.

A point that needs to be made here is that while national minorities are regional and local majorities in several contexts, they are not the same minorities, and following Weiner's (1986) figures, the cross-cutting nature of the various different criteria of the minority status makes for social heterogeneity and, therefore, political fragility. The support for minority rights thus continues as a powerful sentiment but not necessarily as concrete policies.

As we have found in our analysis of the discourse on India's personal laws (Mitra and Fischer 2002), a combination of Muslim assertiveness and the countervailing forces of India's institutional design has forced the pace of legal uniformity to slow down.[18] The Constitution of India has not taken a categorical position on this issue because of its dual theory of rights. On the one hand, it supports the notion of methodological individualism, which gives the political majority the right to define the laws of the country through the mechanism of the plurality system and parliamentary democracy. On the other hand, the commitment of the state to minority rights protects their core beliefs from legislative and administrative interference.

The personal law system is a test case for this duality. A large number of violent conflicts and judicial controversies have taken place on this issue. The constitutional solution to the contradiction inherent in the personal law system has taken the form of Article 44 of the Constitution. It provides a non-binding directive to the state to take steps in the direction of a unitary system of personal laws for all the citizens of India regardless of their religion. A majority-driven system can be legal, according to the narrow letter of the law, but still unjust because it does not embody the will of the people it constrains. Evidence from survey research shows considerable support in the electorate as a whole (including those who claim to have voted for the BJP in the 1996 parliamentary election) for a plural, rather than a unitary, personal law system.

Table 4.3 Response to statement: 'Government is responsible for the protection of the interests of minority communities' (figures represent percentages)

Party respondent voted for	Disagree	Don't know/no opinion	Agree
Congress	7.4	27.5	65.1
BJP or its allies	10.8	32.2	57.0
NF	8.6	28.9	62.6
LF	5.7	19.8	74.5
BSP	13.4	35.4	51.2
Independents	3.5	23.9	72.6
Others	4.4	27.8	67.8
Total	8.2	29.3	62.5

Source: CSDS (1996).

Whereas the BJP in the past had placed a Uniform Civil Code high on its electoral agenda, it has not pursued this any further once in power. The BJP's solicitude for the sentiments of non-Hindu communities is reinforced by the imperative of coalition politics. The coalition partners of the BJP – particularly those like the TDP, Trinamul Congress and the Samata Party – locked in competition against the INC in their regional arenas are sensitive to the Muslim and Christian vote in their respective states and have tended to act as watchdogs for minority interests within the coalition. The BJP itself is acutely aware of the need for compromise, for this was the very issue on which the first coalition government of the Janata Party (1977–79) had polarised and the Jana Sangh members were isolated. This led, eventually, to the collapse of the coalition government in 1979, and the return of the INC to power under the leadership of Indira Gandhi. The NDA leaders appear to have remembered the bitter lessons of coalition management from this first venture.

The influence of the distribution of preferences in the electorate, party competition and coalition manoeuvres in terms of moderating the minority policy of the NDA, is reinforced by the ubiquitous presence of India's nongovernmental organisations (NGOs). As agents of protest and interest articulation, they have increasingly emerged as defenders of minority rights. Human rights activists, NGOs and other civil society organisations have emerged during the rule of the NDA as an important part of the political system. They have created political pressure on those involved in the decision-making process. Their advocacy of minority rights, particularly in riot affected areas, has become a prominent and influential factor in the political process.

Finally, the institutional arrangement of the state has once again shown its resilience, for watchdog bodies like the press, and the judiciary did not decline under NDA rule. There are several institutions that are responsible for the amelioration of the fear of persecution and unfairness that members of vulnerable social groups experience on an everyday basis. The National Commission of Minorities, whose financial and political independence are guaranteed by the constitution itself, is further designed to recruit its top officials from among the members of the minority community itself. Several of its functions have important implications for the effectiveness and judicial neutrality. It undertakes investigations of the conditions of minorities at its own initiative, and suggests appropriate measures in respect of any minority to be undertaken by the central government or the state governments. The Minorities Commission is no paper tiger. For instance, the Commission, while performing any of its functions, can exercise all the powers of a civil court trying a lawsuit. This new landscape of power and countervailing forces which give much greater visibility to violence against socially marginal groups, is a radical departure from the situation after India's Independence where the lot of minorities was much more beholden to the intents and activities of the government of the day.

Conclusion

Weiner (1986) whose meticulous study gives an insight into the inner contradictions of minorities seen as cohesive social groups, had forecast two
likely scenarios for their future on the basis of a statistical analysis of
minority policy during the first four decades after independence. He
wrote that:

> A pessimistic scenario is one in which majority–minority conflict
> increases, state governments do not demonstrably increase their
> capacity to deal with these conflicts, the centre by its actions provokes
> opposition to central authority, and the growth of violent conflict
> leads to greater coercion and the use of the armed forces. An opti-
> mistic scenario is one in which leaders at both the national and state
> levels demonstrate their skill at accommodating the demands for sub-
> stantial administrative decentralization and prove skilful at reassuring
> minorities without threatening the cultural identity and interests of
> majorities. *We can make no predictions about which scenario is most likely.*
>
> (1986: 130, emphasis added by the author)

Have we, in the light of our analysis of the NDA's minority policy, come
any closer to making short-term predictions in terms of the parameters
laid down by Weiner? Once again, testifying to the essentially contested
character of the issue, there is likely to be room for disagreement. For
those who see the 2002 Gujarat riots as the only significant fact of the
NDA's minority policy, the first of the two possibilities outlined by Weiner
would seem more likely. My understanding of events points in the direction of the second of the two scenarios. For its part, the NDA with all its
difficulties of balancing partisan interests within its broad rubric of the
National Agenda of Governance managed to project a coherent, non-
threatening image of *Hindutva* as concept and practice.[19] The Government's subsidy of the *Haj* (pilgrimage to Mecca) continued as before,
where one set of supplicants has replaced another at the patronage
network of culture-management. In retrospect, if one were to consider
only the minutiae of legislation and administration, *plus ça change* rather
than a radical change in the institutional arrangement, and political practice would probably be the more appropriate description of the minority
policy of the NDA. Why many of the statistical details mentioned in this
chapter have not made their way into the international media, where the
spectre of rising Hindu 'fundamentalism' remains the main focus, is
beyond the remit of this chapter.

On the basis of a chronology of minority-related issues, this chapter has
analysed minority politics during the stewardship of the NDA and, in the
light of the evidence thus uncovered, has attempted to link the anomalies
of the minority discourse to the essentially contested character of the

concept of minorities in India. I have argued in this chapter that the minority policy of the NDA – a combination of accommodation and questioning – has been marked more by continuity of the pre-NDA consensus than a radical discontinuity. However, there have been attempts at change that have been undermined by the BJP's coalition partners and ultimately withdrawn by the BJP. Engaging the 'Other' by focusing on specific interests rather than staying aloof on the lines of essentialised identities has been the main thrust of the NDA Government's minority policy.

Many of the assumptions that underpin NDA's minority policy may appear half-hearted and unconvincing to those who take an essentialist position on minorities. They would expect a more robust defence of India's public sphere from what they see as a steady, incremental and insidious induction of Hindu symbols into the core values of the state. Why does the judiciary then not defend the pristine purity of India's public sphere? The controversy generated by the '*Hindutva* judgment' of the Supreme Court, particularly, the judgment by Justice Verma[20] has, at least for now, been put to rest thanks to the position taken by the Supreme Court on the *Best Bakery* case where the court has stood by its proclaimed intention to defend minority rights. But, while by taking an unambiguous position on minority rights in the *Best Bakery* the Supreme Court might have given a temporary reprieve from controversy, the deeper, long-term cause of uncertainty is still there. The very fact that the judgment by Justice Verma was seen by specialists as 'open to interpretation' (Jacobsohn 2003), is an important fact that we need to examine carefully.[21]

The moot point in this debate is how one can reconcile respect for the sentiments of Hindus with the sense of vulnerability and anxiety of non-Hindus in the public sphere of India. Jacobsohn argues that the judgment of Justice Verma did not *see* the contradictions between what he considers the ontology of the Hindu middle classes and the epistemological rigour of positive law.

Analysis of the political shades of grey that underpin the discourse on, and around minorities, in India contain much that is useful. Properly harvested, these empirical details can point one towards new political structures and institutional arrangements conducive to the growth of a sense of common citizenship in India. That political and academic analysts sometimes miss these finer points can only be attributed to the polarisation of political debate in India on the issue of secularism, another essentially contested concept, which has focused attention on the spectacular incidents of the political theatre (Ayodhya 1992 and Gujarat 2002), and kept attention away from the small prints on progress with regard to the empowerment of socially marginal groups.

The VHP and some members of the BJP have expressed their anxiety, concern and preferences for a culturally cohesive nationalism, just as the articulate and alert secular lobby has come to the strident defence of a social vision that ignores all distinctions based on primordial identities, except when it becomes a source of political vulnerability. But these abstract, ideological shots are usually fired by the articulate, elite adversaries over the heads of the people in everyday life who are actually locked in conflict over such concrete details as places of worship, right of passage for religious processions or petty discrimination on the grounds of belief. In view of the fragility of many of India's institutions and the historical void that underpins them,[22] the need for a general, dynamic and comparative analysis of public policy, rooted in the political reality and conscious of the historical legacy, has never been greater.

Acknowledgements

The author is thankful to Katharine Adeney, Alexander Fischer, Kenneth McPherson, Marie-Therese O'Toole, Malte Pehl and Lawrence Sáez for their comments on an earlier draft of this chapter.

Notes

1 The level of riots per million of population, having reached their highest point in the mid-1980s, have steadily declined since. This trend has remained unaffected during the period of NDA rule (see Mitra 2003a: 673). However, there are two methodological problems that should be taken into account here. First, there is no exclusive link between riots and minority politics as riots may also be caused by food shortages, water, reservation policies, caste and land related conflicts. Second, the riot statistics as reported in Crime in India (Home Ministry) recorded riots as the units of analysis and does not take into account the duration or number of deaths involved. I am grateful to Alexander Fischer for pointing this out to me. See Wilkinson (2000) for a discussion of the problems of measurement.

2 Opinions vary sharply with regard to the BJP's change of stance on religious minorities. A succinct summary of the media reports is available in Wright (2001). Speculation on this is widespread in the Indian media. Thus, 'The BJP hasn't changed the System. The System has changed BJP' (Mukhopadhya 2004: 10).

3 See Weiner (1986) for an excellent introduction into the problematic character of this concept.

4 'Minority' as a term of political discourse displays all the attributes of an essentially contested concept such as internal complexity, variability in meaning, the capacity of the concept to adapt itself to varying circumstances, while there is a common consent on the original exemplar, and most important of all, the absence of a direct way of verifying the concept empirically (see Cox *et al.* 1985: 30).

5 'Hinduism' is as much of a contested category as 'minorities'. The claims for homogeneity made by the ardent advocates of *Hindutva* are not sustained by ritual or practice. See von Stietencron (1989) and Sontheimer (1989).

6 He cites a quotation from Wright (1983: 412) on this point: 'It is taken for granted that the Hindus are a majority ... but to say so is totally wrong. The vast masses of people that are called Hindus are a vast congeries of sub-caste minorities ... whereas the Muslims form the actual majority.'

7 Basu points out a certain ambiguity in the use of the concept as it shifts

between religious, linguistic or cultural minorities. These are non-overlapping categories, in the sense that one may be a minority according to one of them, but might, at the same time, belong to the 'majority' in terms of the others (2000: 388).

8 The definition comes from the Central National Minority Commissions Act, 1992, a core legal text in this area. This legal definition is contested by Weiner (1986), who takes a broader view of minorities, among whom he includes the SCs and STs.

9 One of the leading voices articulating this argument is that of Paul Brass (2003: 301). See Hansen (1999, 2001), Mahmood (1996) and Jaffrelot (2003) for a broad formulation of the scenario where the Hindu majority is projected as a potential danger for the non-Hindu minority. See Varshney (2002) and Mitra (2003a) for an empirical demonstration of how and why this prognosis does not work.

10 This is a point developed by Meghnad Desai (Chapter 13 of this volume).

11 I do not have any means of independently verifying the statistics. The significant fact here is the implication of this claim which, to my knowledge, has not been contradicted, for the BJP discourse on minorities.

12 I am grateful to Professor Theodore Wright for having brought this article to my attention.

13 Vigorous opposition by the allies of the BJP within the NDA coalition stymied the efforts of the Union Agriculture minister to introduce the 'Prevention of Cruelty to Cows Bill, 2003'. The message of the BJP's allies, whose opposition to the bill was more vigorous than that of the Congress was 'Do not take our support for granted' (Rajalakshmi 2003).

14 For more information on this effort, see Lall's contribution to this volume (Chapter 8).

15 See the contribution by Nitya Rao (Chapter 6) in this volume for an alternative perspective.

16 Zahira Habibulla (2004).

17 See Jaffrelot (2003: 8) for a gripping and graphic account of the brutal attacks on Muslims which supports this line of thinking.

18 The Indian debate on the personal law system revolves around the model of a unitary legal system, applicable to all citizens of the country regardless of their religion. The advocates of this position draw on the European tradition of positive law, theories of the modern state and social legislation for the empowerment of women. Its opponents deny the secular state the right to interfere with personal law in the name of their sacred origin in religious tenets. India's non-Hindu, but most of all, conservative Muslim opinion, are closely identified with this position.

19 Statements like 'For the BJP, *Hindutva* is its soul, *Hindutva* is its ideology. But we do not blend *Hindutva* with politics' by Mukhtar Abbas Naqvi, BJP spokesperson, bear out this impression (*India Today* 2003: 7).

20 'Any speech wherein expression *"Hindutva"* or "Hinduism" are used, irrespective of their meaning, cannot by itself fall within the ambit of seb-sec. (3) of Section 123 (Representation of the People Act (1951)/Section 123 (3A) Corrupt Practices.)' AIR 1996.

21 See Shankar (2003: 54) for a critique of Jacobsohn's analysis of the verdict in the *Hindutva* case.

22 See Nandy (1983) for a psycho-historical analysis of colonial rule and its implication for the hiatus between the post-colonial state and Indian society. Saberwal (1986: 4) refers to institutional fragility as 'social blanks'. Sharma (Sharma 2003) examines the scope for commensurability of the paradigms represented by India's liberal institutions and *Hindutva*.

5 Hindu nationalists and federal structures in an era of regionalism

Katharine Adeney

Introduction

Constitution design is controversial, especially designing structures to accommodate 'ethnic' identities. Constitutional recognition (or non-recognition) of 'ethnic' identities is a very public form of recognition, and debates concerning this issue are always controversial (Adeney 2002: 8–9). Amending a constitution to recognise new identities or to change their public recognition is even more fraught. This is because recognition is linked to access over power and resources. Once amendments are accepted, they become entrenched in their own right.

This is why it was so contentious when the BJP manifesto of 1998 and the NDA manifesto of 1999 proposed to create a Constitutional Commission. The INC and the two main Communist Parties opposed it, fearing that the BJP would use it to change basic features of the constitution (Sachar 2000). However, this concern was overstated – Article 368 of the constitution requires that such a '[b]ill is passed in each House by a majority of the total membership of that House and by a majority of not less than two-thirds of the members of that House present and voting'. In addition, many amendments, most of which concern the relations of power between the Union and the states, require ratification by not less than half of the states by resolutions in their legislatures. Given the diversity of the popular bases of the political parties within the NDA, agreement on any controversial changes would have been highly unlikely. But this was not the only reason that the opposition was concerned. As Christophe Jaffrelot (1996) has discussed, the discourse of the State is as important as laws and constitutions. According to Bogdanor (1988: 5), '[a] working constitution in a democracy implies reference to certain norms and standards which lie beyond and outside the document itself'. The concern was that the purpose of constituting the Commission was to introduce contentious issues into national debate.

Hindu nationalism and federal forms of government

At the outset it is important to note that 'federal forms of government' can encompass many different constitutional forms. There is no *necessary* relationship between the level of centralisation within a constitution and whether that country is a federation or not. Federations are defined by the division of sovereignty to, at least, two territorially defined levels of government. They are not defined by the extent of powers that are allocated constitutionally to the lower territorial tier of government; although federal forms of government *are* usually more decentralised than their unitary counterparts. Similarly, there is no necessary relationship between a federal system of government and the protection of minority rights (Adeney 2002: 11–12). If a federation is organised around units defined by ethnicity then that ethnic group has some protection within that unit from the centre. But even if the federation is organised on 'ethnic' criteria, a territorially concentrated group can be outvoted at the centre by a coalition of other 'ethnic' groups or a dominant 'ethnic' group. Potentially even less secure are minorities within states (e.g. Urdu speakers in Uttar Pradesh or Muslims within Gujarat). The Indian federation does possess mechanisms to protect these minority communities, although they have not always been effective.

Hindu nationalism has historically had a mixed attitude to federal forms of government. This makes it difficult to determine whether the BJP was constrained by its coalition partners. One of the big unanswered questions when the BJP-led coalition came to power in 1998 – and again in 1999 – was whether the BJP would remain true to its Hindu nationalist agenda. In assessing the BJP's operation of the federal provisions it is important to recognise that centre–state relations cannot only be understood through constitutional provisions. The day-to-day operation of these provisions is vitally important. In addition, constitutional structures constrain as well as enable governments and the individuals that comprise them, but the extent to which agency is possible is hugely significant (Adeney and Wyatt 2004: 4–6).

Zavos defines Hindu nationalism as an 'ideology seeking to imagine or construct a community on the basis of a common culture' (2000: 5). But this says nothing about *specific* forms of governmental structures. Jaffrelot also makes the point that the RSS 'did not regard State power as the most important object of conquest – they preferred to work at the grassroots level with a long-term perspective' (2000: 353). Indeed, Hindu nationalism, in Chetan Bhatt's words

> retained an ambiguous relationship to the Hindu State or Hindu Government ... the latter represented territorially bounded sovereignty political and administrative structures based on permanent Hindu majority rule.
>
> (2001: 42)

Hindu nationalist thought favours a strong centre; being committed to the unity of the Hindu nation; but is simultaneously committed to the decentralisation of authority to panchayats. It has sought to create a strong state and does not see decentralisation at the *local* level as incompatible with this. This is because, as Hansen argues, the BJP's commitment to

> subdividing the Indian States into smaller units and regions . . . is . . . informed by a desire to limit the considerable power of the States, the regional sentiments, and vernacular public arenas (and) . . . strengthen . . . the Union government.
>
> (1999: 221)

Hindu nationalist thought views federal forms of government, especially those that design the provincial units around 'ethnic criteria', as destabilising strong and effective government, and potentially undermining the territorial unity of the country. It is for this reason that they advocated the creation of 100 *janapadas* (administrative divisions grouping together several districts). These divisions were deliberately intended to divide 'linguistic zones and ensure . . . that they did not become mini-nations' (Jaffrelot 1996: 130). They were also intended to build a strong state. Indeed, the Jana Sangh organised its internal organisation along these lines (in contrast to the INC which had organised its internal organisation along linguistic boundaries).[1] Hindu nationalists were therefore committed to 'national' federalism rather than 'multinational' federalism (O'Leary 2003: 6). Federalism can be convened on administrative rather than cultural lines. An administrative, rather than an ethnic rationale, must be used as the primary explanation behind the creation of the three new states in 2000,[2] as well as a perception of the perceived electoral advantages for the BJP.

It is therefore hard to draw any definitive links between Hindu nationalism and particular forms of federal design. Hindu nationalism has differed over time and between Hindu nationalists. The only way forward is to point to particular attitudes at moments in time. Despite the general commitment to a national rather than multinational federation, the Hindu Mahasabha did *not* oppose the linguistic reorganisation of states in the 1950s. To wit, the All Indian Hindu Mahasabha asserted that it endorsed 'the demand for the formation of States on a linguistic basis and the rectification of boundaries of the existing States wherever necessary' (Hindu Mahasabha 1954). Was this an early example of the compromises Hindu nationalists were prepared to make in order to secure wider support? Yet this view was qualified in the same statement.

> The Mahasabha has always believed that Hindustan is one homogeneous country and regards States as administrative units, though

the Mahasabha stands for decentralisation in certain spheres of national development, it cannot regard different States as different nationalities.

(Hindu Mahasabha 1954)

In addition, the Hindu Mahasabha argued that the State Reorganisation Commission's (SRC) recommendations needed to be modified in relation to religious communities. For instance it claimed that '[t]he Sikhs should gladly share with other Punjabi speaking people in the development of their future destiny as one indivisible linguistic unit and as an essential limb of the Indian nation! (quoted in *The Hindu* 1955a).

The Jana Sangh adopted a similar view in regard to language and religion.

The Bharatiya Jan Sangh stands for a unitary form of Government with decentralisation of powers to the lowest levels. Till that is achieved we are in accord with the principles formulated by the Commission for the Reorganisation of States.

(quoted in *The Hindu* 1955b)

This was partially because opposing linguistic reorganisation would have been unpopular, and as Jaffrelot notes, the Jana Sangh did not hesitate to exploit linguistic feelings (1996: 130). The limits on the recognition of linguistic and religious differences was not converted into an 'absolute faith' (Graham 1990: 99). Despite this, in common with the Mahasabha, it retained concerns about the process. Graham opined that:

In the debates about [linguistic reorganisation] the Jana Sangh proposed the absorption of small units into larger territories within a federal framework but it also reaffirmed its faith in a unitary system under which India would have had a single cabinet and a single legislature, based on a system of about one hundred regional assemblies.[3]

(1990: 99)

An area where the Jana Sangh were less willing to compromise, partially because of religion, was in the Punjab after independence. The Jana Sangh opposed the division of the Punjab, a stance that cost it many votes (Jaffrelot 1996: 131). It did so partially for strategic reasons – Punjab being a border state with Pakistan. But it also opposed the division because it viewed the Sikhs as a sect of Hinduism. However, it conceded that people in the Punjab should have the choice between using Punjabi or Hindi and between the two scripts – Devanagari and Gurumukhi.[4]

Hindu nationalist parties have therefore reached compromises with, what they have regarded as, 'anti-national' forces in the past. In its 1967 manifesto, the Jana Sangh conceded 'that the public service entry examinations could be taken in the regional languages' (Jaffrelot 1996: 226).

This makes it less surprising that they have recently entered into, and encouraged, a coalition with political parties that are regionally based, either espousing a regional agenda, or a caste agenda that is regionally defined. As Varshney and Sridharan analyse, the BJP cannot come to power at the Centre using its 'natural' constituency. To come to power at the centre required entering alliances with regionally based parties to expand the size of a future coalition (2001: 216). This pragmatic policy ensured that it was able to form governments in 1998 and 1999. It *is* significant that it was willing to compromise on its agenda in order to do this; dropping controversial pronouncements from its manifesto.

There were no *major* strains to centre–state relations during the NDA's tenure in office (although to some extent this depends on what is defined as a 'major strain'). However, tensions undeniably existed. Was there relative harmony because the BJP was constrained by its coalition partners? Partially. This pragmatic policy ensured it was able to remain in power for

Table 5.1 Topics in the 1999 NDA manifesto relating to constitutional and legal reforms

---

a) Appointing a Commission to review the Constitution of India;
b) Commitment to the devolution of more financial and administrative powers and functions to the states including the Sarkaria provisions relating to Panchayats;
c) Commitment to a Backward Area Commission to identify least developed areas and recommend comprehensive measures for their development;
d) Committee to study the feasibility of all 19 languages in Schedule Eight of the constitution as official languages[a];
e) Examine problems of border states;
f) Take measures for ensuring a fixed term (five years) for all elected bodies including legislatures and replace no confidence motions with German system of Constructive vote of no-confidence;
g) Introduce necessary electoral reforms to deal with defections and the criminalisation of politics;
h) Introduce a revitalised northeastern Council, ensure territorial integrity of the states of the northeast;
i) Set up a National Judicial Commission to recommend judicial appointments in High Courts and the Supreme Court and draw up a code of ethics for the judiciary;
j) Provide eligibility criteria that only naturally born Indian citizens hold the high offices of state-legislative, executive and judicial;
k) Establish a National Register of citizens and a multi-purpose identity card for all citizens;
l) Undertake all necessary legislative and administrative measures to ensure the right of franchise of the Armed Forces through proxy voting and or any other method.

Source: Summarised from National Democratic Alliance (1999).

Note
a In 1999 there were only 18 languages in the Eighth Schedule. The 19th language mentioned is the official language of English – not counted as a 'national' language.

its full term in office, something few observers would have been willing to bet on.[5] Yet, as demonstrated, Hindu nationalists' attitudes to federal design and centre–state relations have been adaptive and accommodative in the past. The lack of a unified 'federalism' or a unified 'Hindu nationalism' goes a long way to explaining the pragmatism, even if this says nothing about a commitment to the rights of religious minorities.

The manifesto commitments of the NDA were extensive in the area of constitutional and legal reforms, as can be seen in Table 5.1. Many, although not all, of the above commitments were put into effect – and were uncontroversial, or designed to *prevent* a change to the status quo. Under the NDA, 15 Constitution Amendments Acts were enacted, one of which still requires ratification by half of the states before coming into effect. These amendments can be seen in Table 5.2. Not all were directly related to centre–state relations, some were unconnected and others were tangentially related such as the amendment to prevent the redistribution of seats between the states of the Union, albeit vitally important for centre–state harmony.[6] Many amendments concerning reservations and qualifications for SCs and STs restored the status quo after Supreme Court judgements challenged elements of reservation policy.

Table 5.2 Constitutional amendments under the NDA

Amendment	Bill number	Purpose	Date passed
Seventy-Ninth	Eighty-Fourth	To extend the time period for the reservation of seats for SCs and STs for another ten years.	21 Jan. 2000
Eightieth	Eighty-Ninth	Related to Tenth Finance Commission. Changing share and types of taxes states can receive.	9 Jun. 2000
Eighty-First	Ninetieth	Changed constitution in response to Supreme Court judgement that reserved quota of jobs for SC/ST could not be 'carried over' so that the reservation would exceed 50 per cent in any one year.	9 Jun. 2000
Eighty-Second	Eighty-Eighth	Supreme Court said it was not permissible to relax qualifying level for SC/ST. Constitution changed to make it permissible.	8 Sept. 2000
Eighty-Third	Eighty-Sixth	Amend Seventy-Third Amendment Act that made it mandatory to allocate SC seats in Panchayats. Arunachal Pradesh, with no SC population was exempted from this provision.	8 Sept. 2000
Eighty-Fourth	Ninety-First	Postpone re-adjustment of state's seats in the Lok Sabha until 2026. Refix SC/ST seats according to 1991 census.	21 Feb. 2002
Eighty-Fifth	Ninety-Second	Amend Article 16 of the constitution to allow for seniority to play a role in SC/ST appointments.	4 Jan. 2002

Table 5.2 Continued

Amendment	Bill number	Purpose	Date passed
Eighty-Sixth	Ninety-Third	'The state shall provide free and compulsory education to all children 6–14 years old and shall endeavour to provide early childhood care and education for all children until six years old and a parent or guardian to provide opportunities for education to his child or, as the case may be, ward between the age of six and 14 years.'	12 Dec. 2002
Eighty-Seventh	Ninety-Sixth	Refix SC/ST seats according to 2001 census.	May 2003
Eighty-Eighth	Ninety-Fifth	Allow centre to levy service tax and allow the states the centre to collect and appropriate this tax.	May 2003
Eighty-Ninth	Ninety-Fourth	There shall be separate National Commissions for SCs and STs.	Aug. 2003
Ninetieth	Ninety-Ninth	To keep intact the representation of the ST and non STs in Assam.	Aug. 2003
Ninety-First	Ninety-Seventh	Insert into Article 75 of Constitution • Total number of ministers, including the PM or the CM, 'should not exceed 15 per cent of the total number of members' of the House of the People or the Legislative Assembly of a state. • If disqualified from being member of the Legislative Assembly under Paragraph Two of the Tenth Schedule (defection), also disqualified from being able minister until the term expires or they are re-elected. • Also disqualified from holding a remuncrative political post until term expires or re-elected. • Paragraph Three of the Tenth Schedule to be omitted (that disqualification on ground of defection shall not apply in case of split).	Dec. 2003
Ninety-Second	One Hundredth	Provides for inclusion of Bodo, Dogri, Maithili and Santhali languages in the Eighth Schedule.	24 Dec. 2003

Source: GoI (2000a–e, 2002a–c, 2003a–f).

Many of the above amendments are not relevant to centre–state relations and as such are not discussed in this essay. In this chapter I focus on the issue of state finances and changes in relation to the border states. In addition, there are important issues relating to centre–state relations that were not covered in the manifesto commitments, such as the use of Article 356.

Finances

As Rob Jenkins reminds us, 'Fiscal federalism is, in many ways, the heart of the Center–State relationship, in India as in most other federal systems' (2003a: 618). The Indian federation has historically been centrist in its financial provisions. In recent years, economic decentralisation has occurred as a result of economic liberalisation. However, these changes have meant that the states have generally experienced a decline in the level of fiscal transfers from the Centre. This is important because the states have controlled few sources of revenue, and the ones they did were not lucrative, and subject to immense variation. In addition, while economic liberalisation provided the states and the parties that controlled them with the ability to attract investment directly; this investment has not been spread evenly. At the same time, fiscal constraints have limited public investment creating greater interest in private investment.

These changes are the result of global pressures and structural changes rather than being confined to the period of the NDA Government. Despite this, the decisions of the governing coalition in this area *had* the potential to influence fiscal federal relations and reveal much about the linkages between coalition politics and Hindu nationalism. The BJP now favours allocating 'a fairer share of central revenues' (quotation taken from 1996 BJP Manifesto quoted in Varshney and Sridharan 2001: 216), a necessary concession to expand its vote share. It has also embraced the economic liberalisation of the economy which has enabled the states to seek their own investment opportunities. This is in contrast to the *Swadeshi* ideals of the RSS – again demonstrating the pragmatism and compromises of the BJP.

One of the significant changes made under the NDA was the Eightieth Constitutional Amendment of 2000 (GoI 2000b). This amendment changed the tax raising powers of both Union and states, so that the states would receive up to 29 per cent of the *net* proceeds of all Union taxes and duties. This Act required '*all* Central taxes and duties (except surcharges and certain sales taxes) to be shared between Centre and States' (Chandrasekhar and Ghosh 2000, emphasis added by the authors). Before this amendment only selective taxes were shareable and vertical transfers had declined. This was a welcome change in the distribution of finances between the centre and the states. Yet these changes came with qualifications. First, the transfers were downscaled from the recommendations of the Tenth Finance Commission, which had recommended 29 per cent of the gross proceeds of the taxes be shared (*EPW* 2000a). Second, these changes were well under way in the Ministry of Finance *before* the NDA came to power.[7] Finally, at the same time as Yashwant Sinha claimed this amendment proved that the NDA was operating in the spirit of 'cooperative federalism', he changed unilaterally the Terms of Reference (TOR) of the Eleventh Finance Commission to recommend that the grants to the states be conditional on their reduction of their fiscal deficit.[8] The TOR not only encroached on states' autonomy by making a former entitlement conditional, but it was introduced without consultation to the Inter-State Council (ISC). This was unwise from the point of view of amicable centre–state relations, given that a meeting of the ISC was scheduled for only three weeks later. The bypassing of the ISC gave the impression of the centre unilaterally implementing financial reforms. Many of the states vociferously objected to the underhand way in which this was done at the meeting of the ISC on 20 May 2003 (*EPW* 2000b).

The report of the Eleventh Finance Commission was submitted to the President in June 2000. It came under sustained attack by the states, including members of the NDA. The TDP, a vital supporting member of the NDA met with all the members of the Commission.[9] The Eleventh Finance Commission had changed the weightages relating to population size, reducing them from 20 to 10 per cent. The Commission accorded a weightage of 7.5 per cent to fiscal discipline. These two changes have adversely affected Andhra Pradesh as has the reduction in the weightages of efficiency parameters, such as a state's efforts in collecting taxes (reduced from 10 to 5 per cent) (Muralidharan 2000). Despite this, Naidu wielded his influence as a supporting member of the NDA to influence favourably the centre's economic decisions affecting his state (Echeverri-Gent 2002: 48).

All these trends are important because public investment has declined at the same time as other pressures have increased on states. Large differences have developed between the different states of the federation, not only in terms of per capita income but also with respect to economic, demographic and developmental growth levels. Although these challenges were not exclusively the result of NDA policies, the inter-state differences in growth, development and population growth are vitally important issues for centre–state relations.

One final and recent change in relation to federal finance that deserves scrutiny is the Constitution (Ninety-Fifth Amendment) Bill 2003.[10] This permitted Service Tax to be levied by the Union (which previously had done so by default through entry 97 on the Union List) but to be collected and appropriated by both the Union and the states. The Statement of Object and Reasons appended to the Bill states that:

> [t]he States have taken a unanimous decision to replace their existing sales tax system with the system of Value Added Tax (VAT) from the 1st April, 2003.[11] In this context, with a view to widening their tax base, the States have suggested that they should be enable [sic] to collect and appropriate tax on services.

> (GoI 2003f)

The statement added that as the 'service sector accounted for 48.5 per cent of the country's [GDP in 2000–01] ... the proposed amendment would help in significant augmentation of revenues of the States' (GoI 2003f). Although it has not yet been ratified by the requisite number of states, only the AIADMK voted against the bill in the Rajya Sabha (on the grounds that 'the right to levy service tax should be with the States') (Parsai 2003). This could have a significant impact on state revenue in the future as '(t)he services sector has almost been outside the tax net during the previous decade' (*EPW Research Foundation* 2004: 1843) Therefore, in relation to federal finance, the states have secured more resources, even if the centre has at times acted without consultation. Whether this lack of consultation can be attributed to the individual in charge of the Finance Ministry at the time, or was related to the ideology of Hindu nationalism is difficult to say. But the change does mitigate the economic centrism of the centre, with the BJP acting pragmatically in this regard, as it has done so in relation to economic liberalisation more generally. However, this change will not address the disparities between the states, which remain the biggest threat to long-term and stable centre–state relations and state–state cooperation. But these disparities are not within the purview of any central government to solve easily, especially in an era of coalition politics.

Border states

The 1999 National Agenda for Governance included a promise to sort out the northeast of India. The northeastern states pose many challenges to the central government. Elsewhere, Manor (1996, 2001) has argued that the diversity of India has facilitated democracy and the stability of the country, but stresses that the extreme diversity in the North East is problematic for ethnic conflict regulation and the stability of the Indian state and democracy. It is hard to disagree. The SRC deliberately avoided re-organising the states in this area because of the extreme diversity (SRC 1955). Religion, tribe, language and dialect internally divide the states of this region.

The border states have suffered a very high number of deaths. Definitive data are impossible to acquire, and figures vary widely, but the numbers of deaths are much higher in these states, even when compared to other infamous incidents of violence such as the communal riots after the demolition of the Babri Mosque or the carnage in Gujarat in 2002 (Adeney 2003: 224). This disparity is even greater when the differences in population sizes are taken into account.

Therefore, accommodating these regions is an important challenge for the Indian federation. As said, the conflict is a political one. By many standards the northeastern states are not backward. Mizoram has the highest literacy rate in India while Nagaland, Tripura and Manipur are all above the national average. Their per capita incomes are, by Indian stand-

ards, very high (Das Gupta 1998: 187–8). The smaller states in the northeast 'have a considerably higher per capita plan outlay allocation than the
national average for all States' (Das Gupta 1998: 211). In terms of budget
transfers, 'those that have done best are the delicate border States'
(Jeffrey 1994: 188). This is not to deny that these states feel isolated from
India, and feel that they have not been integrated into the Union.

Harish Khare argues that the BJP 'has made a fetish of having introduced
creativity in the Indian federal structure'. He elaborates that they have

> carried forward the dialogue process with the insurgents in Nagaland,
> worked out an agreement with the Bodos and established a Bodo Ter-
> ritorial Council, and agreed to sit across the table from the All Party
> Hurriyat Conference in Kashmir.
>
> (2004)

The BJP continued with the reorganisation of the political structures of
the northeast of the country – although it did not *initiate* this process.
Despite the fact that it was continuing rather than initiating this process, it
is significant that the BJP has constitutionally recognised 'ethnic' identities that 'undermine' the unity of the 'Hindu nation'. Hindu nationalists
had recognised these identities previously (e.g. the Jana Sangh conceding
the legitimacy of regional languages being used for public service examinations), but this time it was actively pursuing it.

That recognising identities can be divisive is illustrated by the zero-sum
nature of many of the claims by groups of the northeast. One example of
this is that extending the ceasefire agreement with the Nagas to areas
outside Nagaland has concerned Manipuris. Advani stated that the NDA
was committed to the integrity of the states of the northeast. However,

> [i]t has been a longstanding demand of the NSCN to merge all Naga-
> dominated areas in the Northeast with Nagaland. This is why the chief
> ministers of the other States [were] wary of the extension of the cease-
> fire to their territories.
>
> (Singh, O. 2001b)

Unsurprisingly, the CPI-ML Manifesto for the 2004 Lok Sabha elections
argued that the BJP seeks to split the movements in the northeast in the
interests of creating,

> disharmony and even [to] engineer inter-tribal clashes so that the[y]
> can fish in the troubled waters of the North-East and advance its sec-
> tarian agenda. The ceasefire accord with the Nagas created unprece-
> dented unrest in Manipur, and the accord with the Bodos ... has left
> the Assam hills simmering.
>
> (2004)

The BJP's perceived partisan support for the Naga cause had electoral consequences. For instance, the party suffered in the 2002 state assembly elections in Manipur because of its perceived support for a Greater Naga-land. The issue has continued to affect the BJP and in October 2003 Vaj-payee had to reiterate publicly his rejection of a Greater Nagaland in the absence of a consensus being reached between the affected communities (*The Hindu* 2003f).[12]

In Assam, the issues were just as complex. In 2003, a tripartite Memo-randum of Understanding was signed between the Bodo Liberation Tigers, the Assam Government and the Centre. It 'envisage(d) the cre-ation of Bodoland as an autonomous self-governing unit within Assam' (Mody 2003). A Bodoland Territorial Council (BTC) of 46 members was created, replacing the existing, but ineffectual, Bodoland Autonomous Council. In the new BTC 40 seats were elected – among these, 30 were reserved for tribals, five for non-tribals and five for other groups – and six nominated by the Governor 'from communities not otherwise represen-ted' (Mody 2003). This agreement required the amendment of the Sixth Schedule of the Constitution, which was passed in August 2003, creating a Bodoland Territorial Council Area District (BTCAD).

Later that month, the parliament passed the Constitution (Ninety-Ninth Amendment) Bill, 2003 (GoI 2003c).[13] This Act provided for pro-tection of the rights of *non-tribals* by keeping intact the existing representation of the Scheduled Tribes and Non-Scheduled Tribes in the Assam Legislative Assembly from the BTCAD.

In all these cases, as with the creation of the three new states in 2000, electoral processes and longer-term games were at work. The BJP has worked hard to gain support of the *Adivasis* (tribals) who are a high pro-portion of the population of the northeastern states. Their support in the state assembly elections of November 2003 was crucial, especially in the new state of Chhattisgarh. Their votes were also important in other states, such as Gujarat (Yadav 2004). Although the electoral gamble has not worked in the BJP's favour in all cases – witness the INC's victory in the Uttaranchal state assembly elections in 2002, and the failure of the BJP to win more than one seat in Jharkhand in the 2004 general election – the electoral dimension was an important factor for the BJP.[14] In addition, the creation of the three new states is indicative of the perceived security of the Hindi heartland. The fact that worries about the fragmentation of India based on the absence of 'a large, powerful and well-organised State in the Gangetic Valley', as expressed at the time of the SRC (1955: 246) are no longer paramount indicates that a sea change has taken place in the considerations of the Indian elite (especially among Hindu national-ists) for whom such concerns have even greater resonance given that this used to be their 'natural' constituency.[15]

In addition to federal reform, developments in Kashmir have been encouraging. The BJP long opposed Article 370 giving the state special status, but it was under the NDA that fair state assembly elections were held in Kashmir in October 2002. They were not classified as *free* and fair by international observers because of the violence perpetuated by groups opposing the elections (BBC 2002). Notwithstanding this, these fair elections were a major development, the significance of which should not be downplayed. Although it can be argued that the Election Commission of India secured the fairness of these particular elections, this has not always happened in the past. There is no necessary incompatibility between opposing the special status of Kashmir – guaranteed in Article 370 of the constitution – and allowing free and fair elections. Indeed, one could argue that opposing the special status of Kashmir requires at the very least, a commitment to free and fair elections in the state. But it remains significant that these elections resulted in the National Conference, a BJP supporter, being voted out of office.

As argued before, the existence of disharmony between groups is not necessarily a sign of divide and rule, often only related to the size of the political cake that is being divided. However, although there is nothing inherent within a federation that requires minority protection; in most federations protection for minority communities within the states exist. India is no exception. Although Brass (1982) points out that minority rights depend on the cooperation of the state governments and Wilkinson (2000) has stressed this point more recently, especially in relation to law and order, all states *are* constitutionally required to provide adequate primary education facilities for children of minority-language groups, or if numerous enough, to permit them to set up their own educational institutions (this provision also applies to religious groups). While linguistic minorities have been discriminated against, the President of India is empowered to appoint a special officer for linguistic minorities; there is therefore a complaints procedure whereby they can seek redress from the centre. Second, at the state level, the constitution prohibits discrimination in the allocation of public funds to religious minority schools.[16]

Therefore when discussing centre–state relations, the treatment of minorities is relevant. On the latter, the BJP falters. One of the aims of the BJP in courting tribal and *Adivasi* communities has been to perpetuate religious tensions, as seen in Gujarat. As Kumar and McMillan point out, in the 2004 general election,

> [t]he Congress leads among the Adivasis ... but only by nine points. This is one section that the BJP has consciously and successfully wooed in the recent years. While the NDA has lost votes all over the country and across all social segments, it has actually improved its votes among the Adivasis by five percentage points.
>
> (2004)

This is not to dismiss all the incentives the BJP has undertaken. Late in 2003, a further constitutional amendment was introduced, recognising four new languages in the Eighth Schedule of the Indian constitution, with a promise to recognise many more. The languages of Bodo, Dogri, Maithili and Santhali were recognised. One press report commented that:

> Mr. Advani said the Constitution Amendment to include Bodo was brought in as part of the memorandum of settlement between Bodos, Assam Government and the Centre. Santhali language was included to keep the balance as it is a widely spoken language by another tribal group in the area.
>
> (*The Hindu* 2003b)

India Business World, moreover, argued that the BJP 'decided to include Dogri language to win back the confidence of the people of Jammu region ... where it faced [a] rout in the last assembly elections' (2003). The initiative was welcomed by the Kashmiri Chief Minister, as well as the Jammu political parties who claimed credit for the initiative (*The Tribune* 2003b). The BJP ultimately failed to reap electoral rewards in the 2004 general election, the BJP losing the seats it had won in 1999 in Udhampur and Jammu.[17] This is a significant shift in the BJP's position towards the 'unity' of Hindus.

The recognition of regional languages as official languages in the constitution has been an important element of the Indian state's accommodation of its diversity over time. As argued previously, although the BJP has historically had a commitment to a unitary Hindu nation – it recognised and accepted the power of linguistic identities in the 1950s and 1960s. All these newly-recognised languages are sub-state languages and were demanded by local BJP units for electoral reasons.[18] However, the manifesto of the NDA appeared to suggest the opposite policy. The recognition demonstrated a renewed pragmatism and redefinition in what is required for the security of the 'Hindu nation'.

Article 356

Of course, just as interesting and significant as what has been amended, are the things that were *not* amended. The BJP introduced no proposal to amend the constitution to implement the constitutional changes recommended by the NCRWC in regard to Article 356.[19]

The emergency powers outlined in Article 356 have been used 115 times since independence (Adeney 2003: 257–9). This was an issue over which the NCRWC commissioned a separate report. The discussion about Article 356 was an important one for members of the NDA and prominent within recent constitutional debates and discussions on federalism in India. The Supreme Court's Bommai judgment (Bommai 1994), following the dismissal of the BJP state governments after the Ayodhya demolition, drastically altered the rules of the game by requiring that Article 356 should not be imposed before the state government has a chance to prove its majority on the floor of the house and adequate warnings have been issued by the centre.

In both 1997 and 1998, (then) President Narayanan refused to impose President's Rule. He argued that using the criteria laid down in the Bommai judgement, the state government must a) be warned and given the chance to change its policies, and b) given the chance to prove its majority in the state assembly. When the NDA was in power, Article 356 was only used four times. In February–March 1999 it was imposed on Bihar for 26 days because of the decline of law and order in that state before the Rajya Sabha refused to ratify it. It was imposed in Manipur in 2001 for 276 days, being lifted in March 2002. This followed the collapse of a coalition, and continued in light of violent agitations within the state. It was imposed in Uttar Pradesh in March 2002, following the results of an inconclusive state assembly election, and was lifted 68 days later in May 2002. Finally, it was imposed for 17 days in October 2002 in Kashmir while the People's Democratic Party (PDP) and the INC negotiated the terms of the coalition formation.

The NCRWC rejected the abolition of the article. 'Article 356 should not be deleted. But it must be used sparingly and only as a remedy of the last resort and after exhausting action under other articles like 256, 257 and 355' (Recommendation 166).[20] The one constitutional change they recommended was that 'the State Legislative Assembly should not be dissolved either by the Governor or the President before ... Parliament ... has had an opportunity to consider it' (Recommendation 173). They also recommended that 'The Governor should not be allowed to dismiss the Ministry, so long as it enjoys the confidence of the House' (Recommendation 168). None of these proposed constitutional changes were implemented.

Regardless of the lack of constitutional changes, following Narayanan's precedent it will be difficult to impose President's Rule in the future. Even if a future governing coalition gained a majority in both houses it would be hard to impose Article 356 given the opposition of many of the state-based political parties, of which all future governments are likely to be comprised.

Any discussion of Article 356 in the context of centre–state relations is of course, made all the more poignant by the fact that the BJP refused to use the Article to dismiss the Modi administration in Gujarat. Modi's BJP administration was widely condemned for, at best, failing to prevent the violence of February/March 2002 and, at worse, aiding and abetting it (Human Rights Watch 2002). During the violence, in which up to 2,000 people, mainly Muslims died (Ali Engineer 2003), several opposition political parties called for the imposition of Article 356 – a much better case is harder to think of in recent times – but the NDA did not. The reticence of political parties, such as the TDP, to condemn the BJP was seen as a sign of their political weakness, but must also be seen as an example of their unwillingness to sanction the dismissal of a state government by a mechanism through which they had suffered in the past. The BJP was, therefore, using trends in centre–state relations to its advantage, as arguably it had been doing in wooing *Adivasis*. This is an example of a federal mechanism which could have protected a minority community deliberately *not* being used.

All the above is indicative of the fact that in recent years a wider consensus has evolved on the use of Article 356. At the eighth meeting of the ISC, held in August 2003 in Srinagar, 'Advani, said it was decided that Article 356 should be used as a measure of "last resort" and not as an initial preference' (Misra and Fazili 2003) and '[i]t was decided that the Union Government could consider incorporating suitably the essential features of the Bommai judgement in the Constitution' (Prime Minister's Office 2003).

This is a change that has been wrought by politics as much as by ideological commitment. As Venkatesan argues, the BJP's experience of coalition politics has meant

> that its earlier obsession with the principle of a 'strong Centre *vis-a-vis* the States', in conformity with its nationalistic and patriotic platform, would yield little political ground.
>
> (2003)

The INC in its turn, despite its use of the power in the past 'has realised the need for constitutional safeguards against the misuse of the Article, as the party is in power in many States and face[d] the risk of politically motivated action by the Centre' (Venkatesan 2003). Interestingly, unlike in the second ISC when four Chief Ministers called for the abolition of the article (Sáez 2002), only Punjab and Tamil Nadu called for its abolition in 2003. Despite the consensus to retain the power, the ISC argued for a constitutional change along the lines of Bommai. However, no constitutional bill was introduced under the NDA.

Conclusion

Many of the changes identified above were significant for centre–state relations, especially the consensus over the changes to be made to Article 356 and the political reorganisation and accommodation of groups in the Northeast. However, to a large extent, they built on policies of the previous administration. The NDA, and BJP as the majority party within it, were reacting to the changes of economic liberalisation, the *Bommai* judgement and the proliferation of political parties with a regional and secular focus without doing anything to bring these changes about. In addition, while the behaviour of the BJP within the coalition was ostensibly pragmatic, the old adage remains; it is impossible to say whether it would remain pragmatic outside the constraints of a coalition. The events in Gujarat, though, are not an encouraging example and the recently passed anti-defection law made it difficult for smaller coalition partners to defy the BJP. As one commentator has suggested:

> What few had foreseen was the way in which such smaller parties would slowly be marginalised within the NDA by the BJP ... Nowhere was this as clearly illustrated as in the Gujarat carnage of 2002, when the sound and fury of the pluralist allies fell far short of a complete break. It has been equally clear in the way key portfolios like telecommunications ... moved out of the orbit of smaller allies and firmly into the BJP's own sphere of influence.
>
> (Rangarajan 2004)

In addition, there were several issues over which the BJP was less willing to compromise, even with its own coalition partners. The BJP may have been generally pragmatic in relation to centre–state relations, partially because its own ideology in relation to federalism is ambiguous, and partially because it was pursuing a longer-term endgame. But in relation to issues such as education, the situation has been rather different (Ansari 2001).[21] The BJP ignored the concerns of its coalition partners, notably in Jammu and Kashmir and Meghalaya as shown here, and over the changes to the curriculum (Ansari 2001) and the Government Advisory Board bypassed the states in the consultative process over this issue.[22]

Moreover, other issues, although not specifically discussed in this chapter, such as the dispute over the application of the Prevention of Terrorism Act (POTA), will have growing import in centre–state relations. Many 'saw the gamut of discursive practices surrounding the act as attempts by the ... (BJP) to find a substitute for Ayodhya' (Kumar Singh 2004). POTA was used in controversial circumstances by Jayalalitha, Chief Minister of Tamil Nadu, to imprison the general secretary of the MDMK, Vaiko.[23] The Government initially refused to condemn the 'misapplication' of the Act. On the one hand, this could be seen as positive development regarding the autonomy of the states vis-à-vis the centre – the centre refusing to intervene even though a non-member of the NDA imposed the Act on a coalition partner. However, the *initial* refusal to address the concerns of the MDMK and DMK (the centre subsequently condemned the misapplication of the Act) has to be seen in the context of the politics of the NDA and those internal to Tamil Nadu. In the last year of its administration, the BJP moved much closer to Jayalalitha, thus the refusal to deal with the demands of the DMK was seen by some commentators as a move to force the DMK out of the alliance to let the AIADMK come back in (Tripathi 2003).[24]

Coalition partners expressed concern that the interests of the smaller parties were 'being pushed aside by the dominant players ... the BJP chose its alliance partner to its advantage even though it hurt the political interest of another [party] in the coalition' (Suryamurthy 2003). As Kumar Singh (2004) points out, irrespective of the decisions taken and the manner in which the law was implemented, there has been a centralisation of security matters in the hands of the centre. This fits in with the centralising agenda of Hindu nationalism. In addition, the perception has been that POTA has been deployed disproportionately against Muslims. One example was '[t]he Gujarat government, for instance, had charged 131 persons, all Muslims, accused of being involved in the Godhra arson case under POTA' (*EPW* 2003).

On the 16 December 2003, the Supreme Court ruled that there was a distinction to be made between subjects that fell under 'public order', a state subject and 'situations of terrorism'. As discussed by Kumar Singh (2004), the Supreme Court ruled that parliament had legislative competence in the latter on the grounds that terrorism was an issue that could not be confined to one state only. Following this, in March 2004, the Supreme Court ruled that despite the new Uttar Pradesh state government under Mulayam Singh wanting to withdraw proceedings against 'Raghuraj Pratap Singh alias Raja Bhaiyya, independent MLA and [former] minister in the BJP-BSP coalition government in the State' they could not do so (Kumar Singh 2004). The court ruled that the proceedings for withdrawal could only be initiated by the centre, even though law and order is a state subject.

To conclude, it is notable that parties, such as the AIADMK, took it upon themselves to out-BJP the BJP as seen in the anti-conversion bill that banned religious conversions by 'allurements or force' introduced in Tamil Nadu in October 2002[25] and the refusal of Jayalalitha to condemn the violence against Muslims in Gujarat.[26] Others have perceived themselves as being too weak to challenge the BJP (the TDP in the wake of the Gujarat violence). However, there is little chance that a major reform of the federation would have been successful, or even advocated by the BJP, precisely because of the ambiguity in Hindu nationalist thought in this regard. In the current political climate, centralisation is not an option; any expansion of the BJP seeking to become the majority party in states such as Tamil Nadu would require recognition of regional identity and autonomy. Yet, the long-term endgame of Hindu nationalism may mean that their aims could be achieved by less drastic institutional changes. It is in this spirit that the personnel changes made to the National Human Rights Commission (NHRC) and Social Science Research Council (SSRC) by the NDA may have longer-term implications for the Indian polity, and religious minorities specifically.

Acknowledgements

The author would especially like to thank Christophe Jaffrelot, Therese O'Toole, Lawrence Sáez and Andrew Wyatt for their comments on earlier drafts of this chapter, in addition to the participants at ICS in February 2004 and at NETSAPPE in Paris in June 2004.

Notes

1 I am indebted to Christophe Jaffrelot for bringing this important point to my attention.
2 Although the creation of Jharkhand had a tribal basis, the boundaries of Jharkhand do not correspond to the historic 'Jharkhand'. The creation of the three new states has been eloquently discussed by Emma Mawdsley (2002).
3 These regional assemblies are the *Janapadas* discussed earlier.
4 However, the BJS did not endorse the Sachar formula, which divided the state into a Punjabi speaking and a Hindi speaking part. Both parts had to learn the other language but only from the last class of primary education.
5 An almost exception was Wyatt, who argued that the '1999 result has given the alliance a working majority and it may come close to completing a full term in office' (2001: 389).
6 As discussed by Alistair McMillan's contribution to this volume (Chapter 1).
7 I would like to thank John Echeverri-Gent for alerting me to this fact, and he discusses the issue in Echeverri-Gent (2002: 40).
8 This move had been proposed by the Ministry of Finance in 1999.
9 I am indebted to Aseema Sinha for bringing this to my attention.
10 Which will become the Constitution (Eighty-Eighth Amendment) Act.
11 Although most states have 'drafted and modified the VAT Act . . . the country is not yet close to its implementation' (*Rediff.com* 2004).
12 In the 2004 elections the INC held the seat for Nagaland – the BJP did not stand in the constituency.
13 Which became the Ninetieth Amendment to the Constitution.
14 The BJP won ten out of the 11 seats in Chhattisgarh in 2004 and three out of five in Uttaranchal.
15 The BJP won only ten seats in the 2004 general election. This compares unfavourably to the 1999 result when they won 29 seats (although this was out of 85 seats), and even more unfavourably to previous elections (57 seats in 1998, 52 in 1996 and 51 in 1991). See the contribution by Christophe Jaffrelot in this volume (Chapter 12).
16 The extent to which this has been applied in a neutral fashion under the BJP government is discussed in Marie Lall's contribution to this volume (Chapter 8).
17 Although this was a trend seen elsewhere, as is discussed in more detail by Christophe Jaffrelot (Chapter 12).
18 I would like to thank David Stuligross for this observation.
19 A recommendation of the Commission, although not a proposed constitutional amendment.
20 But they argued that a new *convention* should be encouraged that the Centre should use Article 355 and issue directive to states to ensure compliance with the law before Article 356 is used.
21 The issue of education is discussed by Marie Lall in Chapter 8 in this volume.
22 I am indebted to E. Sridharan for bringing this to my attention.
23 Vaiko had given a speech supporting the LTTE, a proscribed terrorist organisation under POTA. He made the speech in July 2002 and remained imprisoned for 19 months until February 2004, See Subramanian (2004).
24 This strategy proved to be fatal for the BJP and the AIADMK in the 2004 General Election.
25 Similar laws already existed in Madhya Pradesh, Arunachal Pradesh and Orissa (Sathiya Moorthy 2002). Jayalalitha withdrew this Act after the failure of the AIADMK to win any seats in the 2004 election.
26 This action has been discussed in more detail by Wyatt (2004).

6 Social justice and empowerment of the weaker sections and gender rights

Nitya Rao

Introduction

The concept of social justice has been on the agenda of the Indian Government since independence, starting with Nehru's vision of liberating 'the minds and bodies of ordinary Indians by purposeful acts of economic and social transformation' (Corbridge and Harriss 2000: 20). Conceptually, this idea as it developed in India, seems to fit with the work of John Rawls (1971), who writing on the question of justice in a constitutional democracy, highlighted that individual differences cannot be negated, but should be used for maximising social advantage. The principle of justice as fairness should be used for constructing a common citizenship rather than the notion of natural liberty.

While the concept of justice then forms the foundation of the Constitution of India, the notion of empowerment is a much more recent one, at least in the way it is used in the global development discourse, and its specific focus on women. The women's movement, however, does not just see empowerment as a means to reverse subordination, but also as a positive development of internal strength, the right to determine life choices and influence processes of social change, often collectively.[1]

Interestingly, while the term 'gender' seems to have replaced the word women in the political language of today, there is nothing that follows the title in the manifesto or commitments to explicate this issue. Scholars, such as Vina Mazumdar,[2] would argue that while discussing the rights and aspirations of women, it is better to use the term 'women' directly rather than mystify the discourse by using 'gender'. Further, in a plural society such as India, women cannot be separated from their caste, community or class identity; hence, efforts to pursue gender equality have to be contextualised within particular settings.[3]

This chapter starts with a brief overview of social justice as a priority concern of the Indian government post-independence and the shaping of this agenda through the past five decades. As part of this discussion, I explore three major issues, namely, reservations for the socially and culturally marginalised groups, enhancing the status of women and women's empowerment and the issue of regional injustices leading to the demand for and creation of four new states. The core of this agenda appears to be a concern for equitable development based on a redistribution of opportunities and resources.

The motivations and push factors for these different strands of the social justice agenda have however varied both in time and intensity, in response to the differing political ideologies of the parties in power as well as pressures created from below – by the political mobilisation of caste, linguistic and regional groupings, leading to differential rates of progress. The issue of reservations received a fillip in the late 1980s with the adoption of the report of the Mandal Commission by the National Front coalition government in 1989–90. Women's empowerment and gender justice however had come into sharp focus earlier with the research and advocacy of the women's movement during the International Women's Decade (1975–85) and the setting up of a series of official committees and commissions thereafter. The regional autonomy demand mainly emerged from local, indigenous movements, some of them existing from before independence.

Fortunately or unfortunately, these agendas have moved forward when their relationship with vote-banks and political support for the government in power have been clearly established. Among the three issues, women's rights and gender justice was not seen as directly translating into votes, hence never received the same political commitment compared to the policy of caste-based reservations. With the state assembly elections in December 2003 in the north Indian states of Rajasthan, Madhya Pradesh and Delhi, revealing women solidly voting for women leaders, the situation might change in the future.

The second part of the chapter examines the commitments made in the NDA manifesto to the social justice agenda and assesses the achievements of the government. How far do outcomes or non-outcomes reflect the double contradiction faced by the BJP-led NDA Government: first, the compulsions of coalition politics that made the government retain caste-based reservations to which the BJP was opposed, and second (and perhaps more importantly), the tensions between the moderate face of the party and the more radical and intolerant movement face of the RSS and other members of the *Sangh Parivar* (Basu 2001)? Balancing these two contradictions has often led to a double-speak on social justice issues, the ultimate agenda then remaining at a standstill.

The focus of the analysis is the national level, but where appropriate, state-level examples from NDA run or NDA partner-run states are used. This choice is made because the NDA's Charter of Commitments includes a mix of national-level and state-level subjects. For instance, while one strand of the women's empowerment agenda refers to bringing in legislation for the reservation of women in Parliament and the state assemblies – a national-level debate – a second refers to free education, essentially a state subject.[4]

Historical roots of the social justice agenda

The reservation policy

The Fundamental Rights and Directive Principles of the Constitution of India enshrine in them the basic tenets of equality, freedom, justice, liberty and fraternity for and among all citizens of the country, irrespective of caste, class, sex and religion. Caste consciousness or division is not a new phenomenon in India but was brought into the public political sphere by the colonial government, which started recording caste identity in census operations from 1881. After India's Independence, Nehru and other leaders of the INC wanted the caste system to disappear. Yet given the historical disadvantage of certain groups in Indian society and the need to provide a level playing field, after heated discussions in the Constituent Assembly, a policy of 'reservations' in government employment, political representation and educational institutions was finally accepted (Gupta 1997a). Articles 341 and 342 of the Constitution empowered the President of India to establish lists of SCs and STs, who were eligible for reservations. These lists were restricted to a single state, and once issued, could be changed only by an Act of Parliament. Yet, as experience has shown, it has not been difficult to expand membership.

In addition, Article 340 gave the power to designate a third category eligible for reservations, namely, the Other Backward Castes (OBCs). A detailed list of 2,339 groups – constituting the OBCs – was, in fact, created in 1955. However, the government of that time found an exclusive reliance on caste-based categories unacceptable, as caste is a social attribute that cannot be acquired, changed or shared with the larger group. If it becomes the key deciding factor, not only would it create opposition over time, but also strengthen exclusive groups rather than building a common fraternity. Therefore this proposal was shelved. While reservations were thus introduced, a compromise was devised, clarifying that they were time-bound, with the clear aim of reversing starting inequalities and disadvantages within a decade through the universalisation of basic services and a planned economy. Successive governments however have found it hard to withdraw the principle of reservations, as gaps in educational achievement and public employment have not disappeared.[5]

In 1978, following the decision of the state government of Bihar to provide reservations to the OBCs, the central government appointed the Mandal Commission to investigate the relationship between the OBCs and government at all levels. Its report, issued in 1980, recommended that 27 per cent of central government civil service jobs be reserved for the OBCs, in addition to the existing 23 per cent for the SCs and STs. However, the report was ignored until 1989–90, when the National Front government, led by V.P. Singh, decided to implement its recommendations. At the same time, with the intention of abolishing untouchability by making it a cognisable offence, the Scheduled Castes and Scheduled Tribes (Prevention of Atrocities) Act was passed in 1989, amending the earlier Untouchability Offences Act of 1955. The National Commission for Scheduled Castes and Scheduled Tribes was also set up in 1990 through the Constitution (Sixty-Fifth Amendment) Act (GoI 1990).

The adoption of the Mandal Commission Report somewhat changed the original philosophy of reservations by clearly identifying the potential of cultural identity as a key strategy for enhancing political influence and thereby seeking subsidies and favours for the entire caste/group.[6] Given the competition for scarce resources, it became necessary to be able to establish a clearly identifiable group and exclude non-members. Post-1989, caste-based mobilisation has become very important in legislative politics. This is visible in the expansion of seats of the regional and factional parties, representing particular caste groups in India's national Parliament from approximately 21 per cent in 1952 to 33 per cent in 1998 (Osborne 2001: 677).[7]

During this period, however, one finds a mixed trend in the economic sphere. Caste-based occupational specialisation appears to be dissolving in the 'new' sectors of the economy (based on merit and education), spurred by economic liberalisation policies, while caste clustering still prevails in the more traditional occupations. Therefore, SCs continue to constitute a majority of agricultural labour in the rural areas, but also sweepers in government employment – both seen as low status jobs and inappropriate for higher castes.[8]

While one does find considerable variance in wealth and income even within castes, the SCs and STs still constitute the majority of the poor (who are also predominantly rural and employed in agriculture), and their numbers have been increasing. The proportion of STs among the poor has increased from 14.8 to 17.5 per cent, SCs has stayed constant at 27.5 per cent and other castes has decreased between 1993–94 and 1999–2000 (Dev 2003: 8). While official recommendations to use income and wealth as criteria for reservations exist, these have never been implemented. The NDA Government initiated a move to amend Article 15 of the Constitution to include economic marginalisation in addition to social, cultural and educational backwardness towards the end of its term, but this proposal did not come up for discussion in the Lok Sabha.

Clearly, the lack of an economic criterion and growing dependence on caste reveals the importance of electoral rather than broader social justice objectives in the reservation policy. The relentless expansion in the proportion of Indians covered by reservations, by encouraging alliances along caste and ethnic lines, appears to have strengthened social divisions and sharpened resource conflicts between groups (Rudolph 2004). While rollbacks in reservations have not been possible, the actual measures in favour of the SCs and STs have been quite modest (Galanter 1997).

This is to a large extent the result of the BJP ideology of an organic society, based on principles of social harmony and social assimilation and an attempt to diffuse caste contradictions rather than addressing them head-on. As the BJP manifesto, while accepting reservations, asserted, 'the path to progress ... lies not through social division brought by casteist politics but through social harmony' (quoted in Jaffrelot 1998b: 33). Reservation appears to be one area where the BJP itself lacks faith, but had to compromise its ideology and principles due to the compulsion of coalition politics.

Women's empowerment and gender rights

Ambedkar raised the issue of gender justice soon after independence in tandem with the formulation of the Indian Constitution. He drafted the Hindu Code Bill, which enshrined certain basic tenets on which there could be no compromise – the right to divorce for the woman, outlawing of polygamy, granting of inheritance rights, recognition of inter-caste marriages – to name a few. The Bill was violently opposed in the lower house of Parliament, the Lok Sabha, as it presented a challenge to the existing patriarchal social framework. Over the next few years, legislation on many of these aspects was separately formulated and passed. India now has fairly comprehensive legislation in a range of fields to give teeth to the constitutional provisions of equality as enshrined in Articles 14, 15, 16 and 39 (GoI 2003g: 28–9).

The narrative of gender rights is one of official commissions and working groups leading to a barrage of legislation as well as projects. Women's continuing disadvantage was publicly highlighted in 1974 with the publication of the Report of the Committee on the Status of Women in India (CSWI). This brought to light the fact that while life expectancy in general had improved, there was a distinct differential between sexes, reflected in the steady decline of sex ratios since 1921. The progress of literacy among women was dismal, with a rate of 18.4 per cent for females against 39.5 per cent for males. The most glaring discrepancy perhaps was the declining participation of women in the labour force from 34.4 per cent in 1911 to 17.35 per cent in 1971 (Indian Council of Social Science Research 1975). The vast gaps across development sectors led to women's empowerment being in the forefront of national policy during the International Women's Decade 1975–85, finding a prominent place for the first time in the country's Sixth Five Year Plan (1980–85). Considerable legal reform and new legislation to protect women was passed during this period, such as the 1984 amendment to the Dowry Prohibition Act, 1961, that made women's subjection to cruelty a cognisable offence. Later, based on the provisions of the Seventy-Third and Seventy-Fourth Constitutional Amendments (passed in 1992), one-third of seats in local government were reserved for women, across caste categories.

Following on efforts by successive governments in India, the NDA Government declared 2001 as the Women's Empowerment Year and brought out a National Policy on Women's Empowerment. Yet this appears as a wish list of programmes, rather than identifying priority areas for women's empowerment. While employment had been identified as a critical sector of gender disparity by all the earlier reports and studies, emphasis on this has slipped considerably, the focus shifting to self-help, assisted by some credit. This is perhaps related to the declining role of the state in the economy and its inability as well as unwillingness to influence the policies of the private sector. But more so, it appears linked to a particular construction of women's role and identity in society – while women are encouraged to seek employment, this is presented within a paradigm of self-sacrifice and caring for the family (Basu 1999). The dominant position of men within the family is acknowledged; hence, women's work is positioned as secondary and in the nature of 'helping out'.

A second priority area for women – health – has also more or less disappeared from the agenda, except for reproductive and child health (RCH). This appears connected to the population control agenda, while also reinforcing women's role as mothers, rather than enhancing women's control over their bodies and sexuality.[9] A third area of disparity is education. The recent introduction of the National Programme for Girls Education has the stated objective of bringing 100 per cent of girls into the education system, but as Benei has noted, schooling is a very important tool for reproducing particular understandings of the 'nation' and of 'culture' (2001: 195). The Department of Education under the NDA Government was firmly under the control of the RSS, represented by Murli Manohar Joshi, which made consistent efforts to revise text-books in order to emphasise Hindu nationalist constructions of education and national identity as well as impose a stringent moral code in the guise of 'value education'.[10] Adult literacy meanwhile has entirely fallen off the agenda, not least because of its links to radical, democratic forces in the country, despite its recognised contribution to women's empowerment in the early 1990s.

Formation of new states

The demand for regional autonomy to facilitate better utilisation of local resources and speed up the process of development with local control has emerged at regular intervals in different parts of the country. Soon after independence the government was forced to reorganise state boundaries based on cultural and linguistic criteria. There was a second wave of state reorganisation in the 1960s and 1970s, often based on 'nativist' and 'sons of the soil' demands for economic opportunities and preferences (Gupta 1997b: 230; Weiner 1978). Several regions which had been refused statehood in the past, such as Jharkhand, however, kept up the pressure for statehood mainly on economic grounds.[11]

While the demand for the formation of separate states is thus long-standing in several cases, the late 1980s saw an acceleration of these movements. The language of social justice now came to be used to justify this demand in regions or in respect to groups that appeared to be neglected by the respective state governments due to geographical, cultural, educational or other reasons. The movements for Jharkhand, Uttaranchal and Chhattisgarh have been prominent in this regard. In Jharkhand, for instance, while mineral and industrial development did take place in the 1960s and 1970s, a majority of those who benefited were immigrants into the region – 10 per cent of immigrants appropriated 50 per cent of the industrial jobs (Sengupta 1982: 18).

Through the States Reorganisation Act, 2000, the Parliament led by the NDA Government effected the formation of four new states – Jharkhand, Chhattisgarh, Uttaranchal and Delhi. Yet questions persist in relation to the parameters used for granting separate statehood to some regions and not to others. For instance, the demand for Vidarbha in Maharashtra, Telengana in Andhra Pradesh and Kamtapur in West Bengal have also been in existence for a while now. While governance and socio-economic development are the stated objectives of new state formation, clearly there are issues of power and political mileage involved in this process (Sharma, S. 2003). Once again one can find contradictions between ideologies of the BJP and its coalition partners: the ideology of social assimilation and a unitary state opposed by one of political decentralisation and the assertion of group identities. The cases of Chhattisgarh and Jharkhand might appear as compromises with regional groups. However, it is significant that both being tribal-majority areas, it could also be seen as an effort to bring them under the larger political project of *Hindutva*, as I discuss in the next section.

Much of this larger social justice agenda thus has its roots in earlier decades, and is not new to the NDA Government. It has been adopted by the NDA partly due to its diverse constituency and the difficulties of rolling back such an agenda, but also as an attempt to extend the *Hindutva* project. This is clearly visible in its lack of attention to SCs on the one hand (a demand of coalition partners), but additional attention to tribal areas and the effort to manage tribal mobilisation within the Hindu fold. While presenting itself as a champion of women's rights, in line with RSS ideology, women's public 'extra-domestic identity' is situated within a framework of 'authoritarian community commands'; in service of the nation rather than with a view to securing gender justice (Sarkar 1995: 189). The next section lists the specific action points promised by the NDA Government in its Charter of Commitments and attempts to assess both their scope in relation to the larger goals as well as achievements.

The NDA and social justice

SCs, STs, backward classes and minorities

The most controversial aspect of the social justice agenda has been the policy of caste-based reservation and the socio-economic development of SCs, STs, OBCs and minorities. When the BJP-led NDA came to power, there was a fear of rollback in this agenda, given the BJP's support base among middle-class and upper-caste traders and business groups. However, the NDA's manifesto commitments (1999) included the following provisions:

- the interests of SCs/STs and OBCs will be adequately safeguarded by appropriate legal, executive and societal efforts and by large scale education and empowerment;
- provide legal protection to existing percentages of reservations in government employment and educational institutions at the centre and state levels;
- continue offering assistance to SCs, STs and OBCs to ensure their speedy socio-economic development;
- remove the last vestiges of untouchability from our society;
- present a National Charter for Social Justice (*Samajik Nyay*) based on the principle of social harmony.

The pulls of coalition politics made the government retain its commitment to reservations, yet it is significant to note the addition of the last point – a reflection of the *Sangh Parivar*'s societal ideology as articulated by the prominent RSS ideologue, Deendayal Upadhyaya. While continuing with the policy of reservations in educational institutions and public employment, the government set up a separate Ministry of Tribal Affairs in 1999 to provide focused attention to the social and economic development of the STs. For the same reason, the Commission for SCs and STs was bifurcated, with a new Commission of Scheduled Areas and Scheduled Tribes being constituted and the National Scheduled Tribe Finance and Development Corporation (NSTFDC) was separated from the National Scheduled Caste Scheduled Tribe Corporation.

The main direct strategy for tribal development since 1954 has been through the Tribal Sub-Plans (TSPs). Apart from its contribution to the TSPs, the new Ministry has a series of small and ad hoc schemes such as scholarships, hostels, book banks, exchange visits, vocational training centres, grants-in-aid to NGOs, village grain banks and contribution to the NSTFDC. Given that its total expenditure in the year 2002–03 was around Rs 10,000 million, out of which Rs 8,000 million was allocated to TSPs and under article 275(1) (GoI 2003h) it is not clear to what extent the various schemes of the Ministry can actually contribute towards the socio-economic development of the tribal people of the country. Ultimately, one needs to recognise that administrative costs have been considerably enhanced by the creation of new institutions.[12]

With the creation of a separate Ministry of Tribal Affairs, the Ministry of Social Justice and Empowerment is now charged with the welfare and protection of the SCs, OBCs, minorities and disabled persons. It is also meant to work towards the mainstreaming of such groups in society by ensuring the effective implementation of laws passed for the protection of their interests. Of the total Tenth Five-Year Plan outlay of Rs 85,300 million (for the period between 2002–07), approximately two-thirds (namely Rs 57,860 million) is allocated to Scheduled Caste Development (GoI 2003i). Even though the SCs constitute a larger proportion of the population, the allocations on an annual basis are as small as those for tribes.[13] Once again, expenditure heads include scholarships, hostels, book banks, assistance to NGOs and contributions to the NSCFDC.

Even a cursory glance reveals that Tribal Affairs, even though separated from the Social Justice Ministry, carries an almost identical agenda. The purpose of creating additional institutions thus appears to be political – to sidestep lower-caste parties on the one hand, while weakening the assertiveness of the marginalised – threatening Hindu nationalism, by splitting the SCs and the STs on the other.

The SCs are relatively well organised under the fold of parties such as the BSP. While negotiating alliances with the BSP and other lower-caste parties, the above steps seem to have paved the way for the BJP to make inroads into the tribal vote-bank. The history of tribal areas in the central Indian region in the last decade has been one of growing Hinduisation. This has often led to severe conflicts with Christian missionaries, engaged in education and health interventions in these remote areas, especially around the issue of conversions (Hardiman 2000).[14] Apart from the physical manifestation of these conflicts in terms of attacks on Christian missionaries, the Hindu organisations have also concentrated on expanding their own constructive work programme in these areas. It is no coincidence that all the tribal-dominated regions in central India at present have BJP (Rajasthan, Gujarat, Madhya Pradesh and Chhattisgarh) or BJP-led coalition (Jharkhand) governments. During the NDA's second term, Orissa and Andhra Pradesh had state governments that were members of the NDA. The strategy of separating tribals from the scheduled castes and consciously investing resources to Hinduise them, seems to have paid off in electoral gains.[15]

How did this happen, given the figures presented earlier on increasing poverty levels among the STs during the last decade? As Hansen and Jaffrelot (1998b) discuss, while the BJP essentially carries within it an upper caste, Hindu view of society, in order to gain and retain power, it had to find ways of dealing with low-caste mobilisation. It did this through the philosophy of integral humanism, articulated by RSS ideologues, such as

Madhav Sadashiv Golwalkar and Deendayal Upadhyaya. While drawing on Gandhian principles of *swadeshi* (Indianisation), *sarvodaya* (welfare) and *gram swaraj* (village governance), these were selectively appropriated to establish discipline and give primacy to cultural-national values based on the subservience of the individual to society. This has been characterised by Richard Fox as an ' "ideological hijacking" to appropriate the legitimacy of the Gandhian idiom in Indian politics' (quoted in Hansen 1998: 295).

The BJP's model of rural development, as articulated by the DRI, consists of four pillars: self-reliance, education, health and good behaviour. Kakuta, in her analysis of the DRI's Chitrakoot Project, finds that the focus of the rural development project was more on behaviour (to keep in check 'bodily needs and animal-like behaviour' (2002: 81–2)) than on poverty and disparity. It was concerned with a process of cultural assimilation by giving Hindu names to tribal children, constructing temples to Hanuman or Shiva, and creating a Hinduised school environment. Within this Brahmanical view, poverty of the SCs and STs is attributed to their laziness, lack of education and alcohol consumption; all individual attributes rather than structural factors. Given the basic organic conception of society that legitimises social hierarchies (based on caste, ethnicity or gender), it is then no surprise that poverty reduction or the redistribution of assets has not been a state priority, rather the emphasis has been on social assimilation and behaviour change. This is expected to lead to social harmony and in turn enhance national strength. Social inequalities and conflicts are under-played in this discourse.

It is also important to highlight briefly the NDA's policy towards religious minorities, particularly Muslims and Christians. The pressure of coalition politics and the need to negotiate alliances to stay in power meant that the BJP had to tone down its core commitments in terms of disbanding the Minorities Commission that was set up in 1992, abrogating Article 370 of the Constitution that gives special privileges and status to Jammu and Kashmir, or enforcing a Uniform Civil Code based essentially on Hindu laws. However, the largely assimilationist agenda did seek to eradicate legal and political recognition to cultural and religious differences, in the process confirming the inferiority of marginal groups and minorities and questioning the fundamental principles of pluralism (Hansen *et al.* 1998). While religious minorities have never been included in the regime of caste-based reservations, even though a large majority of them (especially Christians) were SCs who converted in order to escape social ostracism and as a step to upward mobility, they have increasingly been projected as 'anti-national' within the *Hindutva* discourse. Basu (1995) notes that the BJP has to foster Hindu–Muslim violence to gain Hindu votes and does so by portraying the Muslim community as a threat, but given the economic and political realities, it is hard to project Muslims as dominant. They, in fact, seem to be over-represented among the poor, with lower access to public employment, education and health services.[16] As Jeffery and Jeffery (1999) find in their study of four villages in rural Bijnor, this is in no small measure due to the systematic discrimination by local state processes, controlled by upper-caste Hindus.

In terms of overt action, while the NDA Government at the centre has not engaged in communal violence directly, the pogrom against Muslims by the BJP government in Gujarat in February–March 2002, led by Chief Minister Narendra Modi, and condoned by the centre, is a reflection of their ideology and attitude vis-à-vis minorities. It however also reflects a conflict over economic resources.[17] As Harriss-White (2003) notes, one of the aims of the *Hindutva* project is to defend the space for Hindu accumulation, while at the same time imposing a more uniform ethical discipline in markets, based on Hindu norms. Projecting Muslims as exploitative and ruthless businessmen permits the generation of a discourse that is willing to allow them to live on conditions of subservience to the Hindu majority, especially its commercial interests.

Economic policy is one area that reflects the basic contradictions between the BJP and its alliance partners, as well as between the BJP and the *Sangh Parivar*. Although policies of liberalisation, capitalist growth and the dismantling of the 'license raj', that favour the BJP's middle class vote-bank, have been supported, there is at the same time a pull towards *swadeshi* and protection of the small-scale sector. While this has emerged from some of the alliance partners representing the poor and low castes – such as the Samata Party – it has more strongly been demanded by the RSS, seeking to maintain cultural harmony, with consumerism propagated by foreign companies typically seen to erode the cultural ethos (Hansen 1998). The compromise appears to have been to allow processes of liberalisation to take their course, but to manage inequalities and tensions by an emphasis on strong societal discipline and national pride within a *Hindutva* framework. As Corbridge and Harriss note, 'people are not empowered by land or wages alone ... the victims of discrimination can also be empowered by a heightened view of their worth or honour' (2000: 216).

Clearly, the issue of the socio-economic development of SCs, STs and minorities is not a straightforward one. One finds mixed signals in this regard emerging from NDA-led state governments. Activists see the policies of liberalisation and privatisation as a clear sell-out to global forces, with small sops being given to the poor, to create a notional sense of well-being. This disjuncture, however, is visible in the growing conflicts over basic resources, especially in tribal-dominated regions of the country.

Empowerment of women under the NDA

Women, as repositories of religious beliefs and keepers of the purity and integrity of the community, have over the last decade been at the centre of the *Hindutva* project, both in its mass mobilisation against Muslims as well as in reproducing and maintaining a puritanical Hindu ideology in society. The NDA's Charter of Commitments, though limited in scope, appears to favour women's rights. They include provisions to:

- legislate for reservation of 33 per cent of seats in Parliament and State Assemblies for women;
- institute plans to provide free education for girls up to college level, including professional courses;
- set up a Development Bank for women entrepreneurs in the small-scale and tiny sectors.

By their own assessment, after the first 13 months in government, there was no progress on the agenda for women's empowerment (NDA 1999: 22). The fate of the Women's Reservation Bill (WRB), introduced first in 1996 as the Constitution (Eighty-First Amendment) Bill, in 1998 as the Constitution (Eighty-Fourth Amendment) Bill, and then again in 1999 as the Constitution (Eighty-Fifth Amendment) Bill, remains as uncertain as ever. Despite several attempts it has not been passed by Parliament.[18] While the original feminist argument in favour of the bill was in terms of creating equality of opportunity, the main opposition arose from the politics of caste identity that argues against women as a unified and homogenous collectivity. Uma Bharti, briefly the BJP Chief Minister of Madhya Pradesh in 2004, for instance, while supporting reservations for women, asserts that a backward caste or *Dalit* woman is doubly oppressed, and so should have a place within the quota. The issue of 'quotas within a quota' reflects the reality that gender identities cannot be separated from caste, religious and even class identities (Menon 2000).[19] Such a shift in perspective is now visible in both the debate around the WRB and the Uniform Civil Code. The feminist movement distanced itself from the Uniform Civil Code once it realised that the BJP and *Sangh Parivar* were using this platform to curb minority rights. While appearing to serve women's interests, they were demonising Muslim men and Muslim personal law (pointing to practices of polygamy and the triple *talaq*) as backward and discriminatory towards women (Hasan 1999). The women's movement is now seeking to support initiatives for reform within different communities.

While all the parties seem to outwardly at least support the call for women's reservation (with the exception of the Samajwadi Party), feminist critics feel that, in fact, none of the parties are really prepared to displace men from politics (as this would indeed be one of the practical implications of such a move unless of course the total number of seats in Parliament is increased).[20] Otherwise, even without legislation, they could have increased the number of women candidates supported for elections. State assembly elections in December 2003 revealed that less than 10 per cent of the total contestants were women, with the BJP fielding a total of 56 and the Congress 65 women candidates in the states of Madhya Pradesh, Rajasthan, Chhattisgarh and Delhi (Sharma, V. 2003).[21] In the 2004 general election, it was worse, with women constituting 6 per cent of total candidates (354 out of 5435) (Election Commission of India ND). Therefore, while discursively supporting reservation for women, there has been no shift in the nature of electoral politics to provide women more space in decision making within parties.

Public activism within the *Sangh Parivar* clearly supports conservative views of women by eulogising women's domestic roles and the sanctity of motherhood. As Desphpande (2001) illustrates, using the case of the Shiv Sena's Mahila Aghadi in Mumbai, the emphasis is on women's duties as mothers and wives. They are allowed to take jobs, but this must be with the consent of the family and preferably as teachers or social workers linked to the organisation, which is projected as an extension of the family. While they are required to support male activities for electoral and political purposes, they do not have any formal positions within the Sena organisation, with patriarchal, family-oriented values constantly being reinforced. Women, however, are provided physical training ostensibly for self-protection against the Muslims, who are thoroughly demonised. While addressing women's practical needs as well as issues of violence does lead to a degree of personal empowerment (Sarkar 1995), such case studies suggest that the real purpose of women's mobilisation is to use them as a tool in propagating the *Hindutva* ideology; creating a sense of threat to Hindu women from the 'other' and then legitimising the use of violence to combat this threat (Basu 1999), rather than gender justice.

The NDA's second theme regarding women's empowerment, namely, free education for girls, is not a new one. In fact, free education is assured to all children up to the age of 14 by the Indian Constitution. Consequently, a majority of states in the country already have such a provision, including special benefits for girls from SC/ST and OBC communities. Given the goal of Education for Women's Equality in the National Policy on Education, 1986 (NEP 1986), successive governments have attempted to promote girls' and women's education.[22] India is also a signatory to international commitments such as 'Education for All' in Jomtien, 1990 and the 'Dakar Framework for Action', 2000.

Alongside an effort to streamline different educational initiatives under the umbrella of the *Sarva Shiksha Abhiyan* (Education for All Campaign), a few special schemes have been launched to give a push to girls' education. For example, the National Programme for Education of Girls at Elementary Level (NPEGEL), seeks to ensure full coverage of girls through a coordinated and holistic strategy of residential and non-residential bridge schools for 9–14-year-old girls, upgrading of primary schools to the middle level, early childhood care centres and the appointment of gender coordinators at the cluster-level to ensure gender-sensitive education provision.

Such schemes can definitely support girls' education, but the basic problem of supply remains. As several studies have shown (PROBE 1999; Ramachandran and Sahjee 2002), a major barrier to girls' education appears to be the non-functioning of schools, rather than poverty or the unwillingness of parents to educate girls. In Dumka district of Jharkhand, for instance, 1,200 posts of schoolteachers at the primary and middle level have been vacant for over five years. In January 2004, the NDA Government appointed 276 new teachers, but this still leaves a considerable backlog, with clear implications both for the functioning of schools and for the quality of education. Five-hundred-and-fifty para-teachers, on a meagre honorarium of Rs 1,000 per month and with ten days of training have also been appointed. While not a solution for encouraging good equality universal education, this is a strategy being adopted across the country, especially in north India, as it gives flexibility in recruitment, with preference often being given to RSS volunteers in BJP or NDA-led states. Apart from economically benefiting the support base, this strategy has the added advantage of informally Hinduising the education system, by positioning teachers who would be willing to Hinduise the school environment by introducing rituals such as the morning prayer, physical training, singing of patriotic songs and so on.

Another trend, visible in states such as Andhra Pradesh, governed by an ally of the NDA during its tenure in office, is towards privatisation of primary education. Private schools are mushrooming not only in urban centres, but also in the rural hinterland. Those with any resources prefer to send their children to private schools, as at least there is some visible sign of learning taking place in these schools. Girls tend to lose out to boys in this competition for scarce resources, due to the persistent social expectation of men as 'providers'. Girls continue to attend government schools with poor facilities and lack of teachers and receive a poorer quality of education. The policy of the NDA to achieve 100 per cent coverage through the appointment of para-teachers, while failing to recruit and appoint trained teachers, signals towards communalisation of education on the one hand and enhanced disparities in learning achievements between girls and boys as well as the better off and the marginalised on the other.

While the focus has been on primary and secondary education, free higher and professional education to girls remains an unattended agenda item. This is revealed by the Tenth Five Year Plan's (2002–07) commitments to empower women that include an 'endeavour to put into action the governmental commitment of providing free education for girls up to the college level, including professional courses' (Planning Commission 2002: 4). While the enrolment of girls in higher education has increased and is likely to increase further in the future, the labour markets subsequently discriminate against women. As Harriss-White (2003) illustrates in her case study of a small town in Tamil Nadu, the labour markets are strongly gendered with decision-making, technical and managerial functions the domain of men. She, however, hints that the rapid expansion of computer and information technologies, with a large number of women, could contribute to changing gender relations in the labour market. This discrimination and segmentation in the labour markets has been aggravated by the *Hindutva* ideology that allows women to work, but only take such jobs that enable them to meet family demands and responsibilities.[23]

In terms of the commitment to setting up a development bank for women entrepreneurs in the small-scale and tiny sector; this has yet to happen. The *Rashtriya Mahila Kosh* (RMK, National Credit Fund for Women) continues to function, but given its limited resources, its coverage too remains limited.[24] However, the NDA Government tried to increase access to credit for women through the establishment of new micro-credit mechanisms as well as linkages with the National Bank for Agriculture and Rural Development (NABARD) and other nationalised banks. The Self Help Group (SHG) linkage programme has grown from support to 500 SHGs in 1992 to 500,000 in 2002, covering over 40 million poor people, 90 per cent of them being women.[25] Nevertheless, problems of uneven regional coverage (with the majority of groups being in Andhra Pradesh) and loans that are smaller than the credit requirements remain.

The NDA Government also introduced three special programmes for the empowerment of women.[26] The common strategy of all these programmes is the formation of women's SHGs and helping these establish credit and bank linkages. While several small income generation projects have been set up through these SHGs, there is enough evidence globally on the limitations of small women's projects (Buvinic 1986; Mehra 1997), especially when faced with competition from mass-produced, cheap products from multi-national corporations. Further, while micro-finance interventions and income generation projects may contribute to some stability in livelihoods, they are unlikely to help these women either come out of the poverty trap or indeed transform gender relations significantly. In sum, the NDA's policy of forming women's SHGs as a vehicle of empowerment, while in the right direction, tended to become a mechanical exercise for generating small savings and perhaps accessing credit. Social norms and gender inequities are rarely challenged or indeed changed.

New states

> Commitment to give full statehood to Delhi and also create Uttaranchal, Vananchal and Chhattisgarh as new states.

The NDA Government was clearly successful in pushing forward its agenda in terms of formation of the new states promised in the manifesto through the States Reorganisation Act, 2000. The fact that the plateau region of southern Bihar was named Jharkhand, and not Vananchal, appears as a key compromise made by the BJP due to pressure from local groups and regional allies. However, how far these new states have in fact contributed to meeting the aspirations of the local people, to promoting socio-economic development of the region or indeed addressing the key concerns raised by the people's movements that had been struggling for the creation of these states, is not yet clear.

The simple logic of social justice in the formation of these new states is one of better utilisation of resources for the benefit of the local people through decentralised control. The arguments of 'regional neglect' and 'internal colonialism', as used by the Jharkhand and Chhattisgarh movements, were thus wiped out.[27] These two states particularly, on account of the concentration of tribal populations, were seen to have certain specific cultural, social, and economic needs. Several moves have been made to acknowledge cultural identity. These include the appointment of a tribal leader as Chief Minister, the recent inclusion of Santhali – the language of the largest tribal group in Jharkhand – in the Eighth Schedule of the Constitution,[28] and special self-employment schemes for tribal youth.

One, however, finds much less priority to tribal groups in the formulation of economic policies. The strategy adopted for economic growth in both Jharkhand and Chhattisgarh is one of industrial and mineral development largely through encouragement to the private sector. Not only can reservations not be imposed therein, but capital for investment, lying mainly with big industrialists and the multinational corporations on the one hand and socially advantaged local groups, mostly Hindus, on the other, needs to be encouraged. Thus, there is a priority focus on infrastructure development as well as attempts to liberalise the protective land legislation (such as the Chota Nagpur and Santal Pargana Tenancy Acts in Jharkhand[29]) in a unilateral manner.

Mining leases are being rapidly granted in both states, without consultation with the tribal people. It is true that mines and industries generate short-term benefits through wage employment, but for the STs and SCs, without appropriate technical qualifications, these are at the lowest level, and on unhealthy terms and conditions. Microlevel fieldwork in the state of Jharkhand (Rao 2003a) revealed that while wage employment has been generated, much of the land, earlier used for cultivation or grazing, is now lying waste. Further, the sudden availability of cash, without sources of investment, has led to growing consumption of liquor and social disruption in the region. The Ministry of Tribal Affairs corroborates Rao's findings when it states, 'It has been a myth that industrialisation would lead to a corresponding improvement in these sectors among the tribal' (Ministry of Tribal Affairs ND).[30]

While the social justice agenda has progressed within a macrolevel framework, there is a need to devolve further the control over resources and decisions in order to meet the stated goals. The economic growth and industrialisation driven development agenda based on hi-tech capital investment of the Jharkhand or Chhattisgarh governments is not easily compatible with democratic decentralisation and control over resources by local communities. Jharkhand is perhaps now the only state in the country that has not conducted *panchayat* elections, but has been manoeuvring to postpone them indefinitely.

Perhaps the growing opposition to and organisation against some of these measures needs to be considered a positive development, with the tribals realising that even with a tribal CM, they still need to protect their everyday livelihood interests. The governments in both Jharkhand and Chhattisgarh have been trying to counter this opposition either through the use of force and threats (violence being an accepted strategy of the *Sangh Parivar* for 'ensuring good behaviour'), or by providing some small sops in return. Jharkhand has seen a large number of cases being filed against tribals opposing some of these state actions, including arrests of tribal leaders and their undue harassment. On the other hand, there are publicised measures such as the digging of a tank in every village, or the provision of buses for cooperatives of tribal youth, or then the provision of communication through wireless technology in each *panchayat*. Therefore, 'development' is in fact taking place, but on the terms and in the vision of the NDA government running the state (Rao 2003b; Kakuta 2002).

Conclusion

What this review suggests is that the NDA Government has in fact carried forward the social justice agenda in some respects. A major achievement has been the creation of new states and the special emphasis on tribal development. Field-level evidence from tribal-dominated areas of the new states, as well as other parts of the central Indian region under the rule of NDA-partner Governments, however, point towards the fact that economic development policies seem to have benefited urban, private capital rather than the poor, who are faced with rising prices and excluded from the 'new' regime of accumulation. Class differentiation among tribals, as between entrepreneurs and peasants, appears to be increasing, but as mentioned earlier, inequality does not really seem a concern of the BJP given its ideology of social harmony and society as a unified, organic entity. Institutions of redress too have been withering away for the poor and replaced by local control by the mafia or others constituting the 'shadow state' (Corbridge and Harriss 2000). In the BJP-led and NDA-run states, one has often found the *Sangh Parivar* engaging in forms of social and moral policing, punishing those whom they perceive as disrupting social harmony.

Some compromises have been made with parties representing the SCs, such as the BSP, but in material terms, the condition of the SCs has not improved significantly over this period. For the minorities, life has become more insecure, their property has been threatened, and the message that social assimilation is the best strategy for survival been strongly given. If they fail to adopt a subservient stance in relation to the majority, then the use of violent attacks is almost viewed as legitimate.[31]

The NDA's achievements in the field of women's empowerment and gender rights too were limited. While none of the NDA's manifesto commitments were achieved, positive steps include the adoption of the National Policy on Empowerment of Women in March 2001 (GoI 2001a), enhancing government accountability towards providing equal opportunities to women by tracking budget expenditures as well as promotion of women's SHGs linked increasingly to government financial institutions. How far these measures will go in terms of ensuring gender equity remains uncertain, especially in a context where women's literacy, participation in political decision making at the higher levels and enhancing equality in work opportunities, no longer seem to be priorities. Women are seen as supporters of men, rather than individuals in their own right and this has contributed to the rather half-hearted attempts to include women more centrally in party structures and political decision making. It is worth noting that the BJP's caste-based allies have tended to agree largely with this view, as they typically see women as dividing the movement for group rights.

To conclude, I would like to return to the issue of vote-banks and their ability to change institutional practice. The BJP has attempted to maintain its upper-caste, middle-class vote-bank by facilitating economic liberalisation and capitalist growth. Even where it has fielded low-caste or tribal candidates, they are not seen as representing their respective caste or ethnic group in ideological terms, hence have often not won the elections. The BJP has, therefore, sought to deal with lower-caste mobilisation by building alliances with caste-based and regional parties that represent such groups. At the same time, it has used the language of 'social harmony' to reduce mistrust of these groups towards itself. As far as tribal groups are concerned, however, it has tried to extend its own vote-bank, by providing economic concessions, creating separate state institutions for tribal development, alongside ideological indoctrination (using populist religious parlance or 'Ram-Hanuman idiom') through an extensive network of educational institutions.

What the 2004 elections appear to have shown is that the rural poor are not taken in by rhetoric. They expect concrete changes in their life conditions – education, health and employment opportunities being key. Neglect of the poor, lower castes and women by the NDA Government has cost them their power.

Notes

1 Rowlands (1998) expresses these different forms of power in terms of power over, power within, power to and power with, respectively. See also Batliwala (1993) and Kabeer (1999) on this point.

2 Personal communication December 2003.
3 This view was articulated by the third world women's network, DAWN, during the Third International Women's Conference at Nairobi in 1985. See Sen and Grown (1987) and Mohanty (1991).
4 As per Article 45 of the Constitution.
5 Despite reservations for the past five decades, the literacy rates of SCs and STs continues to be below the national average of 52.21 per cent (37.8 per cent for SCs and 29.6 per cent for STs in 1991). The prescribed quotas in groups A and B of the central government services are also rarely filled, with SCs averaging 10–12 per cent and STs 3 per cent (Louis 2003). The same holds true for even the more advanced states. Karnataka, for instance, has a literacy rate of 38 per cent for SCs and 36 per cent among STs against a state average of 56 per cent in 1991 (Manasa 2000). Figures for SCs and STs for 2001 are not yet available.
6 See Chatterjee (1999) for SCs, Gupta (1997a) for OBCs and Baviskar (1997) on the use of tribal identities as a political resource. Organisations of these groups have focused on political power and cultural identity, with a relative neglect of economic issues (CWDS 2003).
7 The Bahujan Samaj Party, for instance, is clearly identified as a dalit party.
8 Louis (2003: 2476) finds that 40 per cent of sweepers are SCs, much over the prescribed quota.
9 The document 'National Population Policy: Perspectives from the Women's Movement' presents a critique of the population policy. The document however also collates the correspondence and dialogue with different policy makers and political leaders on this issue (CWDS 1997).
10 This conservatism and intolerance of any form of deviation is further reflected through the attack on films such as Deepa Mehta's 'Fire' and 'Earth', art exhibitions of painter M.F. Hussain or the attack on shops selling Valentine's Day cards by activists of the ABVP and Bajrang Dal.
11 The movement for regional autonomy in Jharkhand existed even before India gained independence in 1947. Yet when the states were formed on linguistic criteria, none of the tribal languages of the region were seen to be sufficiently widespread to warrant separate state status, hence the demand was refused.
12 Given a tribal population of 8 per cent, almost 80 million, the per capita expenditure works out to Rs 125 per year. With deductions for overheads, the actual resources available to the tribals would be even lower.
13 The number of SCs is estimated to be around 160 million or 16 per cent of the total population.
14 A case in point is Gujarat, where the BJP government sought to legislate against conversions in the mid-1990s.
15 Adeney's chapter makes a similar argument and the results of the 2004 election confirm the BJP's success. See Chapter 5 in this volume.
16 The tenth plan allocation for minorities is only Rs 2,900 million, even though they constitute over 12 per cent of the population. The annual expenditure for 2001–02 and 2002–03 has been dismal at around Rs 50 million (GoI 2003i).
17 See Hardiman's (2002) discussion of the Godhra violence from a historical perspective.
18 The Common Minimum Programme of the UPA government has also committed itself to legislating for women's reservation in Parliament and the State Assemblies.
19 See Sonalkar (1999) and Raman (2001) on this point.
20 See Sharma, K. (1998: 17) for a discussion of this point.
21 In the 2003 elections, the three states of Madhya Pradesh, Rajasthan and Delhi have women Chief Ministers. Yet in these states the number of female contestants were only 9, 7.6 and 9.5 per cent respectively. The number of women

elected (19, 12 and seven) constitute 8, 6 and 10 per cent of these state assemblies (Election Commission of India ND).

22 Key initiatives in this regard were the introduction of the Integrated Child Development Services (ICDS) for early childhood education and care and the Mahila Samakhya Programme for Women's Education in the mid-1980s.

23 'Caring' work such as teaching and social work are encouraged.

24 Since its inception in 1993, the RMK has built alliances with 1,066 NGOs in the country and disbursed Rs 890 million under its various schemes including Revolving Funds, crop credit and off-farm activities, small consumption loans, micro-credit for skill upgradation, etc. (GoI 2003i).

25 This is perhaps the largest microfinance programme in the world operating through 444 banks (44 commercial banks, 191 RRBs and 209 cooperative banks) in all districts of the country. The cumulative loan in March 2003 was Rs 10,263 million and refinance was Rs 7,965 million. See the NABARD website for further information www.nabard.org/roles/mcid/highlights.htm.

26 These include Swayamsidha in 650 blocks of the country, Swashakti in nine states (Bihar, Haryana, Gujarat, Karnataka, Madhya Pradesh, Uttar Pradesh, Jharkhand, Chhatisgarh and Uttaranchal covering 323 blocks) and the UNFPA funded Integrated Women's Empowerment and Development Project in Haryana. The total outlay for the five-year period (2002–07) for the Swashakti and Swayamsidha Projects is only Rs 750 million and Rs 2,000 million respectively. When divided by the number of women needy of the support, the investment appears negligible.

27 See, for instance, Ghosh and Sengupta (1982), Munda (1988) and Corbridge (2000) in the case of Jharkhand. For a discussion of Uttarakhand, see Menon (1998).

28 Discussed in more detail in Adeney's contribution to this volume (Chapter 5). Bodo, Dogri and Maithili were also recognised.

29 It is on account of such protective legislation that the tribals in these regions have retained the status of cultivators and not been reduced to agricultural labourers. For India as a whole, Louis (2003) points out that 54.5 per cent of STs are classified as cultivators as against only 25.4 per cent of SCs.

30 The sectors here refer to education, health and infrastructure development.

31 While Muslims have been the main targets, Christians have not been left out either in states such as Jharkhand, with even disadvantaged Christian villagers being targets of attack.

7 Managing the anti-corruption rhetoric
The National Democratic Alliance, transparency and corruption

Gurharpal Singh

Introduction

The late W.H. Morris-Jones once noted that 'corruption – the fact itself, but even more important, the talk of it – occupies a great place in Indian politics' (1971: 62). This observation was intended to draw attention to the folklore about corruption and its underlying assumptions about political authority and power. Since the 1970s, however, political corruption has moved from folklore to occupying a centre stage in Indian politics with few national or regional administrations which can claim an unblemished record. 'Corruption in public life', as a recent editorial in an English daily lamented, 'is one of the most daunting issues facing the country. Things have come to such a pass that all politicians evoke public ridicule' (*The Tribune* 2003e).

In undertaking an evaluation of the performance of the last NDA Government in this highly contested area we are faced with a number of obvious difficulties. How, for instance, are we to assess its record? In what ways is it possible to distinguish the constraints on the leading party, the BJP, from the overall functioning of the government? And what if anything does the record of the NDA inform us about the broader understanding of political corruption in India?

This chapter addresses some of these concerns by outlining the background to the good governance and transparency agenda which emerged in the 1990s. It then highlights the legislative and other reforms undertaken by the NDA during its period in office. These reforms are then compared with the actual record of governance, especially given the high profile corruption scandals that took place during these years. Finally, attention is drawn to the limitations of anti-corruption drives in today's India by focusing on a case-study where an NDA regional partner, the Shiromani Akali Dal (SAD) in Punjab, was subjected to an anti-corruption campaign after 2002.

Political corruption, transparency and the good governance agenda

Although concern with political corruption has been a regular feature of Indian politics, the year 1991 marked a distinct turning point in policy interest in the subject. The process of economic liberalisation begun that year did not only arise from the 'Washington Consensus', the neo-liberal agenda for 'good governance', but it also spawned a myriad of NGOs, local groups and political activists keen to lock into the broader process by mobilising support for domestic political reform. Economic liberalisation, it soon became apparent, would be incomplete without the wholesale reform of political institutions crafted during the colonial period. Whereas these institutions worked reasonably well during the heyday of INC hegemony, with increasing political decay, deinstitutionalisation and the rise of national opposition parties, the rights of citizens could no longer be forsaken for the imperatives of command politics. Indeed, in the 1990s, the demands for political reform were strengthened by fragmentation of the national political universe and increasing regionalisation. It was against the background of weak national governments in the mid-1990s that political corruption emerged as a national public policy concern (Singh 1997b). Whereas national governments proved ineffective in developing systematic policies to tackle corruption in public life, the Supreme Court – often at the prodding of reform activists – made some pioneering judgements, sometimes in response to well-publicised financial scams (Das 2001: 163). These judicial initiatives also coincided with national and international surveys which reflected poorly on India (see Vittal 2001). In the mid-1990s, voter confidence in the political system plummeted so badly that one opinion poll even indicated a majority preference for a national leader 'who [was] corrupt but efficient to one who [was] honest but inefficient' (Singh 1997b: 222). By the late 1990s, therefore, there was a significant policy agenda centred on the need to control political corruption, empower transparency in governance and implement good governance as an agenda cross national and regional government (Singh 2004). How this agenda was articulated, legislated upon and managed, will probably remain one of the enduring legacies of the NDA.

The NDA and reforms

The NDA came to power as a coalition with a difference, untainted with any association with the institutionalised 'licence permit raj' of INC regimes. The BJP, its major constituent, was viewed by many as a cadre party that had consistently opposed corrupt governance and projected an image of a clean, disciplined organisation. Certainly it was part of the BJP's rhetorical appeal to upper castes and the middle classes who were often unexposed to the experience of government by the party in the states (Tully 2000). But the NDA's commitment to good governance in the 1999 election manifestos was couched in general terms, namely of the need to provide 'honest, transparent, and efficient government capable of accomplishing all-round development'. In order to achieve these goals, the manifesto promised:

> time-bound programmes of needed administrative reforms including those for the Police and Civil Services ... [and] electoral reforms on the basis of the recommendations of the Goswami Committee, the Inderjit Gupta Committee and the Law Commission Report so as to deal with the malaise of defections, corruption and criminalisation of politics, and to prevent electoral malpractices.
>
> (National Democratic Alliance 1999)

Specifically, corruption was to be tackled by enacting 'the Lok Pal Bill with adequate powers to deal with corruption charges against anyone, including the Prime Minister'. In the administration of justice, the NDA coalition promised not to 'allow discrimination between the rich and the poor, the empowered and the powerless, [and to] restore the majesty of law and the objectivity of the state' (National Democratic Alliance 1999).

What have been the actual achievements in light of these manifesto commitments? Broadly-speaking these can be categorised into three: reviews undertaken to identify areas needing action, legislative changes enacted in response to judicial (Supreme Court) rulings and legislation introduced specifically with the aim of curtailing abuse of public office.

Reviews: National Commission on the Working of the Constitution (2000–02)

Perhaps the most sustained focus on corruption and transparency during the NDA's tenure was provided by the Report of the NCRWC (2002). Despite the controversy surrounding the objectives of the Commission, the report – drawing as it did extensively on the backlog of inquires and judgements from the early 1990s onwards – provided sober reflections on the subject with its implications for the working of the Constitution and the political system. In its overall judgement the Commission did not mince its words:

> There is pervasive impurity [in] the political climate and [in] political activity. Criminalisation of politics, political corruption and the politician-criminal nexus have reached unprecedented levels needing strong systematic changes.
>
> (NCRWC 2002: 51)

This emphasis on the subject was evident in the stress on the need to reform the administration, judiciary, the electoral system and the funding of political parties. The nature of these observations is too extensive to summarise here, suffice to say the general tenor of the analyses can be gauged from the recommendations made (NCRWC 2002).[1] Among them it included:

- a comprehensive law regulating political parties, including the requirement for transparency in funding and declaration by candidates for election of assets and pending criminal cases;
- amendments to the Representation of People's Act (1951) to prohibit candidates with criminal records from contesting;
- limits to the size of Council of Ministers to 10 per cent of the total strength of the lower house;
- removal of parliamentary immunity for corrupt politicians;
- re-examination of constitutional guarantees for civil servants from the immunity from prosecution (article 311) and 'oath of transparency';
- a Freedom of Information Act;
- Public Interest Disclosure Act (Whistle-Blower) Act;
- amendments to the Prevention of Corruption Act (1988);
- Central Vigilance Commission Bill; and
- Lok Pal (Ombudsman) Bill.

These long-standing reforms were seen as essential to restrict the scope for discretion and unaccountable behaviour by public officials and politicians, while increasing the penalties for transgression. That the report subsequently became embroiled in political controversy is another matter. What is important for us to acknowledge, however, is that many of the recommendations of the NCRWC became the signposts around which the NDA's initiatives were formulated.

Responses to judicial (Supreme Court) rulings

Several of the proposals made by the NCRWC emerged in response to impending decisions of the Supreme Court. Of particular note were the recommendations to pass the Civil Vigilance Commission Bill, the Lok Pal Bill and the Presidential Ordinance (2002) relating to the disclosure of election candidates' financial and criminal background. Yet the way in which these initiatives were implemented suggested that the NDA's commitment to reform, transparency and anti-corruption was influenced as much by its desire to manage the process as the need to establish transparent and un-corrupt outcomes.

The campaign to prevent election candidates with criminal backgrounds from standing for public office was initiated by the Election Commission in January 1998, when candidates were directed to file affidavits on their criminal past. In May 2002, reform groups issued a writ petition to secure for voters the right to information related to the criminal record of candidates. Although the NDA Government successfully appealed against the decision, it subsequently lost in the Supreme Court, which upheld the fundamental right of voters to know the background of the candidates. When in June 2002 the Election Commission issued a notification mandating the disclosure of criminal record of candidates in elections, the NDA Government overturned the verdict with a Presidential Ordinance, a move which had the backing of all the major political parties and was later legislated upon with amendment to the Representation of People's Act (1951).[2] This remarkable *volte face* was not left unchallenged. In March 2003, in a bold judgment, the Supreme Court struck down the Amendment and restored its order of May 2002 (*Deccan Herald* 2003). The judgment's implications were wide-ranging and included the need for election candidates to declare assets, liabilities, and dues to financial institutions in respect of candidates themselves and also members of their families. How these provisions will be put into practice remains to be seen.[3]

A similar chain of events followed the NDA's piloting the Central Vigilance Commission (CVC) Act (2003) and the Lok Pal Bill (2003). The background to the CVC legislation can be traced to the Supreme Court ruling in the Hawala Case (1997), which recommended that the Central Bureau of Investigation's (CBI) independence and ability to investigate cases against VIPs be strengthened by its administrative supervision by the CVC (which should be given statutory status), the ending of the Single Directive (which limited the CBI's scope for inquiries against senior civil servants), and the establishment of new guidelines for the appointment of the CVC and the Director of the CBI. But converting this judgment into legislation was an exceptionally drawn out affair. Initially two ordinances were passed and two Bills had to be introduced on separate occasions. In its final form, the new Act more or less neutralised the key tenets of the judgment. Following recommendations by the Joint Parliamentary Committee, chaired by Sharad Parwar, the Single Directive was reinstated. Moreover, the Act limits the CVC's superintendence of the CBI to offences alleged to have been committed under the Prevention of Corruption Act (1988) only – leaving a loophole for the government to influence cases that are being investigated by the CBI under other laws. The definition of a 'public servant' under the Act is restricted to 'civil servants', thus excluding politicians whose cases would be supervised by the Union Government (Joshi, G. 2003). This legislation was so badly drafted, with obvious loopholes and deliberate contravention of the Hawala Judgment, that its enactment immediately invited a judicial challenge from reform-minded activists. As of the time of the writing of this chapter, the matter is currently pending before the Supreme Court. In its defence, the previous NDA Government (1998–99) argued that it had introduced the Bill without the Single Directive clause, but that the Joint Parliamentary Committee in its report to Parliament suggested the re-introduction on the grounds that 'no protection was available to the person at the decision-making level' (*The Times of India* 2004c).

The Lok Pal (Ombudsman) Bill (2003), a key manifesto promise, suffered a worse fate. The institutional needs for an ombudsman were recognised in the early 1960s, but progress was painfully slow as the bureaucrats initially directed the proposal against politicians rather than civil servants. Supreme Court judgments in several cases have repeatedly called for the establishment of an ombudsman to deal with the caseload that is unnecessarily referred to the courts (*The Tribune* 2002e). Partly in response to these pressures, the NDA Government first introduced the Bill in 1998, then 2001 and yet again, in 2003. The Bills were drafted to include the Prime Minister's Office under its purview, a recommendation opposed by the NCRWC. The Bills' progress has followed a well-trodden path. In the need to reach a consensus, they were referred to a Joint Select Committee of the Parliament, which responded so slowly that legislation lapsed due to the lack of parliamentary action on the Bill. Unsurprisingly, the latest version of the Bill (introduced in 2003) became victim of the early dissolution of Parliament in January 2004. Filibusters and engineered delays were the preferred tactics of politicians to regulate themselves. As Rajeev Dhavan has wryly noted, post-colonial India 'has evolved virtually no independent mechanism to investigate corruption. Neither politicians nor bureaucrats want to investigate their own corruption. They make sure no real investigation happen' (*The Hindu* 2003g).

The Freedom of Information Act (2002) is another initiative that arose from court rulings. Several judgments – including the right to information about election candidates – had given broad interpretation to article 19(1) of India's Constitution, which guarantees the right to free expression and speech, including the right to know. Efforts by Ram Jethmalani, then the NDA Minister for Urban Development, to open up his Department were opposed by the Cabinet Secretary with a court writ blocking the move – a procedure itself challenged by reform activists. In order to deal with the matter the Government took repeated adjournments and finally submitted the Bill (2000). These delays led to an exceptionally unusual ruling from the Supreme Court in 2002 which 'directed that if the legislation was not passed before the next date of hearing (in January 2003) the court would consider the matter on merits and pass the order'. It also added a powerful caveat that 'even if the legislation were passed, the court would examine whether the legislation was in conformity with the right to information as declared by the court' (Bhushan 2002).

Despite this ruling preliminary assessments of the Act suggest it is exceptionally weak when evaluated against four criteria: its scope, the exemptions, the independence of institutions that would adjudicate disputes and sanctions against refusal to disclose or wrongful disclosures (Bhushan 2002). In its present form, the Act is noticeably weaker than existing state acts on freedom of information. In view of these serious shortcomings, it is to be expected that the legislation when it comes into force – it is yet to be effected – will be seriously contested in the courts.

Other legislation

In addition to these initiatives, there have been two other pieces of legislation that require discussion. The first piece of legislation, the Election and Other Related Laws (Amendment) Act 2003, marked a partial implementation of the promise to reform the funding of political parties as recommended by the Gupta Committee. This legislation does not impose the kind of regulation of political parties recommended by the NCRWC, but it is nevertheless a notable measure of reform with three major provisions. First, it provides open contributions to political parties and affords full tax exemption to individuals and corporate bodies for all contributions to registered parties – companies had been banned from making donations between 1969 and 1985. Second, it ends a loophole introduced in 1974 into the Representation of People's Act (1951), whereby expenditure by political parties was exempt from election expenditure ceiling. Finally, it introduces provision for indirect public funding of recognised political parties by granting them a share of broadcasting time on private and public electronic media and allowing the supply of election materials (Narayan 2003).

Commenting on the debate on the legislation, the Union Law Minister Arun Jaitley said, 'This legislation was meant to infuse accountability in the entire process of corporate donations to political parties' (*The Hindu* 2003e). Whether these intentions are realised remains to be seen since much party election expenditure continues to be generated from illegal sources. The onus is clearly on the monitoring processes to make the legislation effective.

The second piece of critical legislation, namely the Constitution (Ninety-Seventh Amendment) Bill 2003, was passed by Parliament (GoI 2003d). The Bill approved key changes to the anti-defection laws and limited the size of the Council of Ministers to 15 per cent of the strength of the lower house of national and state parliaments. This legislation had been recommended by several government commissions and review committees – including the NCRWC[4] – and received bipartisan support in Parliament. But while the provision relating to the size of ministries was given six months to take effect, the defection provision became effective immediately, prohibiting defectors from holding any office until they were re-elected. Critics suggested the measure was intended to control rebellious party backbenchers; in reality, it was a response both to political pressure and outstanding Supreme Court judgments in cases of defection in Goa and Manipur (*The Tribune* 2003f).

If measured against the NDA's manifesto commitments, as well as the recommendations of NCRWC, the reforms passed by the NDA Government mark a substantial advance in an area seriously neglected by all previous administrations. With the exception of the Lok Pal Bill, the NDA administration has a justifiable claim to have held firm to a large measure of its promises. Nonetheless, it is important to remember that no administration, whatever its ideological complexion, could for long have avoided the momentum for reforms that gathered pace against the backdrop of economic liberalisation, the decline of one-party dominance, and the increasing assertiveness of the Supreme Court which had passed judgments strengthening the individual's rights to transparency, information and 'good governance'. The imperative nature of some of these judgments compelled the NDA Government to legislate, very often against its will. At the same time, it would be churlish not to acknowledge that this process was hastened by work of reform activists, as well as some pro-reform ministers within the administration who responded favourably to the case for change.

A more critical assessment, on the other hand, would highlight the delays, the restrictive nature of the changes and the areas that have been left untouched. Police and civil service reforms, two of the key manifesto commitments, have avoided serious consideration. No landmark measures have been taken against public service transfers, the single most lucrative source of income generation for regional and national politicians alike.[5] Judicial reforms necessary to make the new legislation effective still awaits needy consideration, though the newly established National Judicial Commission should help to check the increasing tide of corruption in the legal system. This corruption was recently exemplified by a Magistrates' writ against the President secured by a journalist in Gujarat with a bribe of Rs 40,000 (*The Tribune* 2004b). Arguably without judicial reforms, many of the enabling features of the legislation are unlikely to make much impact and may well remain confined to a small constituency of middle-class reformers or single-issue local organisations.

Corruption and transparency: the NDA and governance

Legislation and reforms give only a partial insight into the record of the NDA which must also be assessed with reference to the actual experience of the coalition's governance. The years 1999–2004 witnessed some spectacular scams which provide important clues to dissonance between professed manifesto claims and the daily administration of government. In this section, we assess some of the major corruption scandals which occurred during the Thirteenth Lok Sabha (1999–2004), and the innovations introduced to manage the fallout arising from them.

Tehelka.com and 'Coffingate'

Throughout 2001, the NDA reeled under a flood of allegations which began with the *Tehelka.com* scandal in March. The Internet news portal –

in a sting operation – secretly filmed defence officials and BJP party chairman, Bangaru Lakshman, accepting a bribe of Rs 100,000 from a supposed representative of a defence supply company. In the immediate furore that followed the revelations, George Fernandes, the Defence Minister, resigned.

The NDA Government's initial response was to procrastinate and victimise its opponents. The Venkataswamy Commission, set up to investigate the episode, was scheduled to report within four months, had failed to do so almost 18 months later. *Tehelka.com*'s financial backers, meanwhile, were subjected to harassment, regular raids by income tax authorities, and attempts were made to tie them to a financial conspiracy to rig prices on the stock exchange (Singh 2003: 156). Meanwhile, George Fernandes, who had vowed not to re-join the government until he was cleared by the inquiry, re-entered the Cabinet through political pressure on the Prime Minister.

No sooner was Fernandes re-admitted to the NDA cabinet than his political career plunged into further turmoil in December 2001 when the so-called 'Coffingate' scandal broke in Parliament. The fraud involved officials in the Ministry of Defence authorising payments of US$2,500 per coffin destined for Indian casualties of the Kargil War (1999), the actual price was US$172 per casket. Opposition parties, which had earlier accused the NDA Government of avoiding discussion of the Central Vigilance Commissioner's investigation into defence deals since 1989, now launched a sustained disruption of Parliamentary business, and for almost 20 months refused to recognise Fernandes' reinstatement (Singh 2003: 156).

The NDA Government remained unyielding against this political pressure, but suffered another setback when, in November 2002, Justice Venkataswamy moved to a new post as Chair of the review panel of Customs and Excise. He was replaced by a retired Supreme Court judge, Justice S.N. Phukan, who had been appointed by the NDA Government – unlike his predecessor who had been nominated by the Supreme Court (*Rediff.com* 2003).

The proceedings of the Phukan Commission[6] have been highly contentious. The Phukan Commission's decision to send the tapes of the original sting – accepted as authentic by the Venkataswamy Commission – for forensic examination in the United Kingdom aroused immense suspicion. Although the Commission's interim report, which dealt with defence deals between 1981 and 2000, acknowledged the involvement of middlemen and recommended action against certain officials for their alleged role in 'deals', it was received with hostility by the NDA's parliamentary opposition, largely because Justice Phukan did not give 'a clean chit to Mr George Fernandes'. In the Commission's defence, Justice Phukan suggested that only the findings and recommendations of the report should be made public, because the rest was not for public consumption due to considerations of 'national security' (*The Tribune*, 2004d).

Unit Trust of India and securities scam

In 2001, two financial scandals occurred which had wide-ranging implications. In the first scandal, overseas companies with nominal capital holdings, often amounting to only a few dollars, colluded with local stockbrokers and foreign institutional investors to rig share prices of equities. This scheme resulted in profits worth Rs 35 billion (US$729 million) which were repatriated illegally (*India Today* 2002a). This scandal was followed in July with the price collapse of Unit Trust of India's (UTI) US-64 fund. The UTI scandal also took the lid off a 'promoter–politician–financier' network: UTI had invested funds in 285 companies that did not exist, gave unusually generous guarantees to leading industrial houses and wantonly ignored the advice of its own analysts (*Frontline* 2001). The UTI's director was found to have engaged in private deals, which also included buying shares in Cyberspace, a software company with alleged links to the Prime Minister's Office (*India Today* 2002b; 2002c; 2002d).

Widespread public anger at the US-64 fund collapse – which affected several million small time investors as well as allegations of the Prime Minister's son-in-law's lobbying for investment in Cyberspace – prompted the UTI chairman to offer his resignation. Given the gravity of the charges against him, the issue was referred to a Joint Parliamentary Committee investigating the securities scam. However, the reports of this Committee, far from proving hostile to the NDA, absolved Finance Minister Jaswant Sinha of any wrong doing and instead placed blame on bureaucrats and the chairman of UTI. Detailed criticism of the report from insiders, on the other hand, indicates that it was a 'corporate eyewash'. Leading industrial houses and official financial institutions, which had been allegedly implicated in the scandals, were cleared of murky dealings at the behest of a cross-party lobby of MPs on the committee who were active in representing business interests. 'Nothing in the report,' concluded one assessment, 'guaranteed that the new set-up will be only more accountable or foolproof. . . . It is only when the guilty are made to account for their lapses that future scams can be avoided' (*Newsinsight.net* 2002).

Petrol pumps and public sector units

A major scandal arising out of routine administrative discretion occurred in August 2002, with the allocation of licences for petrol pump and liquid gas agencies by Ram Naik, the Minister for Petroleum and Natural Gas. Presumably, following conventional practice of previous INC administrations, the Minister approved the allocation which included a large number of BJP applicants. 'Pumpgate', as the scandal came to be known, led to four days of sustained disruption in Parliament by the NDA's opposition. In turn, the parliamentary activity sparked great public outcry which, according to Inder Malhotra, exposed the BJP (NDA) as 'corrupt as everyone else in India's political system' (*Financial Times* 2002).

Vajpayee responded to this orchestrated opposition by issuing an order cancelling all the allocations of licences for petrol and gas agencies since January 2000. This dramatic act, however, was challenged by the allottees before the Supreme Court which reversed the order in all but 413 cases and ruled that the Government's action had been motivated by a desire to save face and 'enable it to escape the scrutiny of allotments' (*The Hindu* 2002c). The court established a committee to investigate 'tainted' allocations as well as the procedure of allocations.

An equally partisan exercise of executive power was found in the efforts of six Union ministers (two from the BJP and four from NDA allies) to squeeze funds out of the heads of Public Sector Units (PSU) by threatening to launch vigilance raids. For instance, one PSU chief complained that he was asked to provide 20 million rupees for party funds by a Minister. He alleged that when he refused to pay the bribe, he was denied his extension. Others who refused to comply were threatened with transfers, CBI raids and, ironically, complaints to the CVC. It is also alleged that one PSU chief was forced to release Rs 5 million to an unregistered NGO run by his Minister's daughter.

When the issue was brought to the notice of the Prime Minister by the Central Vigilance Commissioner, considerable efforts were expended. First, in attempting to deflect the matter and then, reluctantly, acknowledging that the meetings between the CVC and the Prime Minister and the Cabinet Secretary had taken place, although the NDA Government claimed that no culpable ministers had been identified (*The Tribune* 2003d; *Newsnight.net* 2003). Ironically, the one minister who did eventually resign – as a result of an unrelated episode – was Dalip Singh Judeo, the Union Minister for the Environment and Forests. He was caught on video tape accepting a bribe in a mining deal quoting a Bollywood couplet *'pasia khuda to nahin, par khuda se kam bhi nahin'* (Money is not everything, but still you need money) (*The Times of India* 2004a). After several days of procrastination, counter allegations that the videos were unauthentic and calls by the NDA's parliamentary opposition for an investigation by a Joint Parliamentary Committee, the Prime Minister was pressured into conceding in the Lok Sabha that the CBI would conduct a full enquiry. In response to suggestions that the CBI was the PM's poodle, he asserted, tongue-in-cheek, that: 'The CBI has full functional autonomy and, under the recently enacted Central Vigilance Commission Act, the superintendence of the CBI in relation to offences under the Prevention of Corruption Act has been vested by the government in the CVC' (*The Tribune* 2003c).

Taj Corridor, Telgi, Jogi, Dubey

Vajpayee's pained assurance failed to dispel the view among non-NDA parties that the CBI was an instrument of government control. These impressions were certainly reinforced by the speed, and then the delay, with which the former Uttar Pradesh Chief Minister, Mayawati Kumari and Uttar Pradesh officials were indicted in the Rs 1,750 million Taj Corridor scandal *(Frontline* 2003a). It was also reinforced by the not so subtle pressure by the Minister for Home Affairs, L.K. Advani, to ensure the *Telgi* (paper stamp) scandal being investigated by the Maharashatra government was supervised by the CBI, much to the chagrin of the state's INC administration (*Newsinsight.net* 2003). Moreover, the speed with which the Central Government announced a CBI probe into the efforts of the former Chhattisgarh Chief Minister, Ajit Jogi, who was caught on tape trying to bribe a potential BJP splinter group after the state elections, also raised concerns (*Frontline* 2003b). Most incriminating of all, for a Prime Minister who has tirelessly projected an image of a caring national patriarch, was the death of an Indian Administrative Service (IAS) whistleblower, Satyendra Dubey, following his complaint to the Prime Minister's Office of 'looting' in Bihar of a $12-billion scheme to build 12,000 kilometres of roads across India. Dubey's death was all the more shocking, for it is alleged to have occurred after a leak of his complaint from the PMO's office (BBC 2003a).

From the way the NDA managed the scandals noted above, a common pattern is discernible. When scandals broke there was a general tendency to respond with denials or – if confronted with irrefutable evidence, as in the cases of *Tehelka.com* and Judeo – to allege that it was a well-planned conspiracy of entrapment by political opponents. This approach was then followed by systematic blame displacement in which the authenticity of the evidence was questioned. Where inquires become inevitable, efforts were made to expand their remit to include previous administrations – Coffingate, *Tehelka.com*, UTI and the securities scam – so as to mitigate the outcomes either by implicating previous administrations or by structuring the need for consensual outcomes.

The NDA, like all other previous administrations, was unrelenting in its victimisation of opponents. According to Jethmalani, a former minister, the administration 'behaved worse than Indira Gandhi during the Emergency ... [and its] conduct was totally undemocratic' (*The Times of India* 2004b). Despite the protestations of the Prime Minister, the administration made capricious use of the CBI to embarrass political opponents to the point where non-NDA state governments frequently refused to countenance probes by the central agency (*The Tribune* 2004c). Finally, the NDA Government relied heavily on the charismatic and personal appeal of Vajpayee to deflect serious probes. His personal integrity – and that of a few other ministers – enabled the coalition to insulate itself from Bofors-like scandals which could have disabled the core central leadership. It was perhaps because of this insulation that the NDA was able to sustain broad appeal even when its record of governance was no less distinguished than its predecessors.

NDA corruption, transparency, and the states: a case-study of Punjab

The gap between the NDA's rhetoric and its policies on fighting corruption and promoting transparency was even wider at the state level. Whereas the scandals at the national level highlighted the pervasiveness of a political culture of corruption, developments at the state level seemed to underline the assumption that reforms intended to limit the abuse of public office would have negligible deterrent effect and, if anything new regulations might actually increase the potential for rent-seeking. The contradictions in seeking to reform a deeply corrupt political system were graphically illustrated in the state of Punjab, where the SAD, a NDA partner and regional ally of the BJP since 1997, was subjected to an anti-corruption campaign by an INC administration from March 2002. In an all too predictable turn of events, the latter itself became ensnared in allegations of wrong-doings, thereby exposing the limits of anti-corruption drives.

The SAD and the BJP in Punjab formed a strategic alliance just prior to the landslide victory in the 1997 state assembly elections (Singh, G. 1998). The formation of the SAD administration in Punjab was followed by the success of the NDA in the 1998 Lok Sabha elections, but this quickly turned to a rout in 1999. Despite this reversal the Alliance held, reinforced by the 'normalisation' process in Punjab after nearly two decades of terrorism and endemic violence in which over 30,000 had died (Singh 2000). By 1996, the costs of counter-insurgency operations by central and state governments had almost bankrupted the state government, and when the SAD–BJP coalition returned to office on a manifesto commitment of rural populism that included free electricity for rural users, the fiscal deficit soon increased to unmanageable proportions.

Against this financial background the SAD–BJP administration in Punjab quickly adopted the 'Haryana model': that is, everything for which an unofficial charge could be levied was levied. Government employee transfers, promotions, and contracts were placed on tariffs collected by an array of middle-men.[7] Ministers were more or less allowed to 'privatise' corrupt practices in their chosen portfolios. Most brazen of all, the Punjab Public Service Commission Chairman, Ravi Sidhu, who had earlier been appointed by the erstwhile INC administration, converted his position to one of auctioning public appointments in connivance with the administration. Sidhu is alleged to have operated under extensive patronage, accommodating the offspring of high officialdom, leading judges and of course, those willing to pay the going tariffs.[8] Prakash Singh Badal, the Chief

Minister, his son and his wife, it is alleged, in addition to superintending the process amassed assets worth Rs 43 billion ($961 million), which included several hundred million dollars' of property overseas, was a sum, according to one estimate, that was 'ten times the state's outlay on education ... well over half of its planned expenditure... and 8 percent of India's entire projected defence expenditure for 2003–4' (*Frontline* 2003c). 'Corruption', under the Badals, the leading state daily surmised, 'had become a way of politico-administrative life' (*The Tribune* 2002a).

Captain Amrinder Singh's INC administration which came to power in March 2002 had a single issue programme: to expose SAD–BJP graft. Soon after taking over it took the lid off simmering scams: Sidhu was arrested in a glare of publicity, SAD ex-ministers were charged, and Singh promised that Badal and his family would be brought to book. However, these efforts ran into all too predicable road blocks. The Sidhu case opened an elaborate web of complex dealing in which senior officialdom, including High Court Judges, had secured government posts for their children and relatives, an expose which the High Court first sought to control and then had to concede under pressure from Public Interest Litigation (*The Tribune* 2002b).

While the Punjab INC Government sought to cancel some of the appointments made during Sidhu's tenure in office, irregularities were reported in the cancellation process itself. Singh's efforts to find a High Court Judge to undertake a judicial probe of Badal's administration – in contravention of Punjab's Lok Pal Act (1996) – backfired when it was discovered, to great embarrassment, that the nominated judge faced serious allegations himself. Apparently, he had pressured an additional judge – a relative of the Chief Minister of Haryana – to secure a waiver on his son's loan of Rs 20 million from the Haryana Financial Corporation (*The Tribune* 2002c). Simultaneously a bitter dispute erupted between the Vigilance Bureau (staffed by the police), which was conducting the process of investigations, and the IAS cadre which sought to protect IAS immunity from prosecution by limiting the power of the former (*The Tribune* 2002d). These administrative difficulties were further compounded by political division within the INC as the Chief Minister used the campaign to discipline his own rank-and-file and outmanoeuvre his main opponent within the party who was framed for embezzling funds from the Chief Minister's Relief Fund in the previous administration (*The Tribune* 2004a).

In 2003, the anti-corruption campaign became increasingly bogged down in procedural, judicial and political challenges. It took over 20-months to frame charges against the Badals, which were eventually timed to stymie internal opposition to Singh's Chief Ministership and enhance the INC's prospects in the December 2003 state assembly elections. The anti-corruption campaign, apart from its partisan nature, also revealed the deep extent of administrative and political decay within the Punjab political system in which a highly politicised bureaucracy, itself seriously implicated in systemic corruption, was able to frustrate a campaigning government.

In the absence of civil groups with an abiding interest in controlling corruption or promoting transparency, the anti-corruption campaign stood exposed as the new governing formula bereft of any ideology or meaningful policy commitments. In a role reversal befitting a Bollywood epic, Singh, the champion of 'good governance', the maharaja who had come down from his palace in Patiala to clean up Punjab politics, found himself at the centre of allegations that his son took a $100,000 kickback in a telecommunications venture floated by the state (*The Tribune* 2003g). Rejecting a probe by the CBI – which Singh alleged was controlled by the NDA – he ordered a judicial probe into the allegations. Naturally, as these events unfolded, the NDA administration continued to give steadfast support to the Badals and the SAD, and periodically threatened Singh's government with New Delhi inspired leaks.[9] Paradoxically, George Fernandes, his own denouement notwithstanding, declared at a major public rally in defence of the Badals that 'any attack on [the] SAD ... is an attack on the NDA government' (*The Tribune* 2003e).

Conclusion

Any serious evaluation of the NDA's record on transparency and anti-corruption has to balance the achievements with practice and the ability of the reforms to deliver on the ground, especially at the state level. A charitable reading of the last five years' of central governance would argue that the NDA administration has put in place a comprehensive architecture of reforms which will, in due course, substantially reduce the incentives for corrupt behaviour by public officials and politicians through, among other things, increasing transparency in all spheres of public life. As democratisation cascades beyond a tiny minority of vocal reform activists, the reforms will, it is often argued, surely bite even in states, like Punjab, which are traditionally ranked low in what might be called India's unofficial index of the political culture of development. These reforms, it should be recognised, have been undertaken by a loose coalition, which has fulfilled most of its manifesto commitments.

A less sanguine assessment, in contrast, would argue that there was no qualitative or behavioural departure in the NDA Government's efforts to manage the reform process, characterised as it was by the presence of an ominous hand guiding the reforms and institutions to partisan advantage. Uniquely there was virtually no ideological distance between the BJP and its coalition partners in dealing with the subject. The fortunes of both were intertwined in efforts to successfully manage the fallout from political scandals, frustrate opponents and ensure partisan advantage from the new reforms. Indeed, the lack of a serious commitment to establish independent institutions with effective regulatory functions was self-evident, signified by the emergence of a new style in *how* to manage political corruption scandals. This style, moreover, exudes an assured professional self-confidence in being able to adapt the anti-corruption rhetoric to the exigencies of Indian political life in a manner which clearly signals the arrival of political spin-doctoring and the death of the familiar Congressite Orwellian double-speak.

Like most governments in South Asia today, the NDA administration used the anti-corruption agenda to control opponents, disarm internal dissent, and in the face of external and internal pressures for greater regulation, where possible, indulge in familiar patrimonial Machiavellianism. Because of these actions, the reforms may well remain on paper or, inadvertently, bring into the public sphere the underlying ambiguities about the meaning of corruption in Indian public life. General angst about corruption sits uncomfortably alongside popular support for the Jayalalithas, Yadavs and Badals, on the one hand, and widespread corrupt practices by the 'victimised' middle-classes, on the other (Singh 1997b: 221–2).[10] India, forever the exceptional case, may well prove that procedural transparency can happily co-exist with record levels of corruption. As with understanding India's democracy, understanding corruption in Indian public life calls for a greater intellectual imagination and effort than has been expended hitherto (Singh 2002).

Acknowledgements

The author is grateful to the Nuffield Foundation for a Social Science Small Grant that enabled him to undertake interviews in India during April–May 2003.

Notes

1 These are only some of the main recommendations. For a comprehensive review, see the full text of the report. Also see the discussion of the NCRWC by Katharine Adeney in Chapter 5 of this volume.
2 The inserted amendment was as follows: 'Notwithstanding anything contained in any judgement, decree or order of any court or any directive, order or any other instruction issued by the Election Commission, no candidate shall be liable to disclose or furnish any such information in respect of his election, which is not required to be disclosed or furnished under this Act, or rules made thereunder.' This is also discussed by Alistair McMillan's contribution to this volume (Chapter 1).
3 Before the elections it was unclear whether the returning officer has the power to bar candidates with criminal records and outstanding dues from contesting. For details of the affidavits that the candidates are required to complete, see the Election Commission website at www.eci.gov.in/forms/NewForms_fs.htm.
4 The NCRWC recommended that the size be limited to 10 per cent of the strength of the lower house in national and state legislatures.
5 For a more detailed discussion of the role of transfers in corruption, see Wade (1985).

6 The Phukan Commission of Inquiry was established to investigate the *Tehelka.com* scandal. For details about the Phukan Commission, see Swami (2004).

7 Interview with a journalist, Chandigarh, 15 April 2003.

8 The Sidhu scandal is still in the process of being brought before the courts. For a detailed coverage, see *The Tribune* from mid-March to August 2002.

9 Parkash Singh Badal acknowledged he had complained to the Prime Minister about his treatment by Chief Minister Amrinder Singh and that the Directorate of Revenue Intelligence was probing the allegations against Raninder Singh, son of the Chief Minister (*The Tribune* 2004c).

10 Corrupt acts by India's middle-classes are rarely written about, largely misunderstood and often justified as necessary evils in a corrupt polity and society. But given the Indian middle classes' wholesale disinclination to pay taxes, especially income tax, it is probably necessary to be circumspect about the nature of anti-corruption rhetoric and movements in India, see *Financial Times* (2002).

8 Indian education policy under the NDA government

Marie Lall

Introduction

The NDA Government has been seen widely as not implementing its nationalist agenda during its time in power, focusing instead on the development of high tech industry and economic issues relating to the growing middle class. However, on the education front, policy and practice pointed in a very different direction. During the five years of its full term of office (1999–2004), the NDA Government made sure that they quietly and unobtrusively replaced key people in the education department and changed curriculum and textbooks. The leading party in the NDA, the BJP, recognised that education policy was an effective means to promote and spread its nationalist ideology.

During its rule, the BJP and the *Sangh Parivar* hoped that by educating the next generation within their chosen ideology they would make *Hindutva* thought the norm. *Hindutva*, the essence of being Hindu and leading a Hindu way of life, is based on the premise that India is a Hindu nation. It emphasises the two-nation solution by which all Muslims and all Hindus should have a country to call their own. Any non-Hindus in India would have to accept either the majority's domination or leave. This intolerant view means that all non-Hindu communities in India, but especially the Muslim community, are seen as separate, second-class citizens.

Visible signs of the spread of intolerance in education only started to emerge towards the latter part of the full term of the NDA Government when books, critical of certain aspects of Hinduism or Indian history, started to be removed from school bookshelves. Likewise, academics with dissenting views, both foreign as well as Indian, found themselves threatened by members of right wing radical groups. Although this phenomenon did foster a limited debate in the Indian English language press, it failed to make an impact as a national issue. However, the BJP attempting to socialise a whole new generation of 'new Indians' has to be seen as one of the most radical policy changes in Indian political and social history.

This chapter presents a brief overview of the main changes in education policy under the NDA Government and it will study their effects on the future of Indian education. It briefly describes the development of education since India's independence and the main issues that have formed policy. It will then discuss the role of politics and national identity formation in education, before analysing the BJP's election manifesto. The rest of the chapter will focus on what may be termed as the 'saffronisation' measures taken by the NDA Government and the effects that these have had on India's education infrastructure.

The main issues of education in India

Since Independence in 1947, India has developed a system of education for both boys and girls, which reaches down to the village level. In the 40 to 50 years of slow expansion that followed, India's education infrastructure has developed some of the best higher education institutions in the world (such as the Indian Institutes of Technology (IITs) and Indian Institutes of Management) and yet some of the worst basic education provision prevails in the rural and tribal areas.

The empowerment and re-distributive effects of education have been at the core of India's aim to provide basic education for all. The main issues concerning education have until recently centred around literacy and access to schooling rather than the content of the curriculum. Literacy has always been the central issue in India's education debate as it is viewed as the catalyst for social and economic change (Drèze and Sen 2003: 3). This is evident by the contrasts between the record of different states, whereby Kerala with India's highest literacy rate has done economically much better than many of the northern Hindi belt states where the literacy rate is far lower.

According to the Seventh Schedule of the Indian Constitution, the responsibility for education is shared between the central and the state governments. The central government focuses on setting policy, stimulating innovation and planning frameworks. The responsibility of individual state governments lies in running the education system, which in turn exacerbates the disparity in the quality of education provision as each state has differing resources to allocate to education. It is the inadequacy of resources which has recently become the most pressing and central issue. The other is the question of quality versus quantity. When resources are scarce, what are the state's priorities? Again here, the southern, and in large part richer states, do better than the poorer, northern states.[1]

The Kothari Commission[2] (1964–66) made recommendations for India's modern education policy. Only in the early 1960s was there a feeling that a separate Commission was needed to modernise the Indian educational system. There had been some prior steps to plan education; among others there had been a committee on integration that focused on national integration through education. In light of India being a developing country, its main priorities were listed as increasing productivity, developing social and national unity, consolidating democracy, modernising the country and to develop social, moral and spiritual values. In order to achieve these aims, according to Article 45 of the Indian Constitution, the main pillar of Indian education policy was to be free and compulsory education for all children up to the age of 14.

In 1986, Rajiv Gandhi's INC Government wanted to reform the system in a way that would not only raise the level of quality and quantity of education, but would also safeguard the basic Indian values of secularism, socialism and equality, which had been promoted since Independence. To this end, the government was to seek resource support from the private sector to complement government funds (NEP 1986: Paragraph 11.1; Shukla 1988: 31). The government also declared that it would accept larger responsibility to enforce 'the national and integrative character of education, to maintain quality and standards' (NEP 1986: Paragraph 3.13; Shukla 1988: 6). This means that the central government retains significant influence over policy and programmes. The 1986 policy may be remembered for promoting privatisation, but it was clear in its emphasis on secularism and promoting science as goals of education.

When it was re-discussed at length in 1992, the 1986 National Education Policy was judged to be a sound way forward for India's education system. The new emphasis was to expand secondary education and continue the focus on education for minorities and women. However, in no way did the revisions alter the secular nature of the Kothari Commission or their re-emphasis in the 1986 reforms.

The politics of education

Politics and education policy in India can never be separated. In any country, the government will try to shape the future by putting its mark on the school curriculum in order to influence the thinking of future generations. This is the case as much in countries with a democratic tradition as well as dictatorships and countries with a fundamentalist leadership.

At Independence, India was a secular state. The concept of secularism, though, was only enshrined in the Constitution at a much later date, in part because the broad consensus among the Indian elite that took over in 1947 did not feel the need to emphasise what was seen as the obvious cornerstone of the Indian Republic. While Pakistan had been created as a Muslim country, India had from the start clearly been a multi-religious country with a secular government. Article 30 of the Constitution of India clearly states that there will be no discrimination against any educational institution on the ground that it is under the management of a minority. Moreover, under the provisions of Article 28 (1) religious instruction is barred in state funded schools, and Article 29 (2) provides any person, irrespective of identity, has to be admitted to any institution receiving state funds and give equal and due respect for all religions. It is true to state that this understanding was very much one of elite thinking, and religion continued to play a major role in the daily life of Indian society. Religion slowly crept back into politics under the rule of Indira Gandhi (1966–77, 1980–84) and has remained there ever since, being used by politicians to muster support from vote banks. However, since officially there was still a separation between religion and state affairs it did not enter the broad field of education.

Throughout the 1970s until the mid 1990s, the main concerns of Indian education policy was, as described above, the issue of the shortage of teachers in rural areas, the level of literacy among the wider population and equity in education for women, the SCs and STs. As a result of the inegalitarian distribution of education resources across much of the rural and tribal areas, first Christian missionaries – and later the RSS – set up school networks in remote areas, supplementing, and sometimes replacing state education. This was the first level at which religion and education started to mix.

Since the mid-1990s, the issue of voluntary and forced conversions have become major issues in tribal areas, as Christian missionaries have been depicted as using their schools and medical surgeries to increase their flock. With BJP backing, the RSS network started to expand its influence, using the same means (schools and medical services) to try to reconnect the tribal population to 'Mother India' and to *Hindutva*.

The BJP first managed to form a government in 1998 and again in 1999. It is one of the many fronts of the RSS, a 'cultural' organisation set up in 1925 by Dr. K.B. Hegdewar. Its aim was to promote India as a Hindu nation where minority religious groups would be subordinate to Hindus. M.S. Golwalkar, who became chief of the RSS in 1940, laid down the RSS ideology in *We or Our Nationhood Defined*. He wrote:

> [I]n Hindusthan, the land of the Hindus, lives and should live the Hindu nation. . . . The foreign races in Hindusthan must either adopt the Hindu culture and language, must learn to respect and hold in reverence Hindu religion, must entertain no idea but those of the glorification of the Hindu race and culture, i.e. of the Hindu nation and must lose their separate existence to merge in the Hindu race, or may stay in the country, wholly subordinated to the Hindu Nation, claiming nothing, deserving no privileges, far less any preferential treatment – not even citizen's rights.
>
> (1939: 62)

In 1998, the BJP had a nationalist agenda that included the introduction of a Uniform Civil Code under Hindu law and the construction of the Ram temple at Ayodhya.[3] However, one has to remember that in order to stay in power, the BJP had forged an alliance with 14 other parties, many of which were regional and secular in nature. It was the impact of coalition politics upon the NDA Government which in effect stopped the BJP from implementing the more radical parts of its nationalist programme. The BJP strategy has been to implement change slowly and mostly on less visible ground.

Education and national identity

The essence of the educational process itself, according to Pai and Adler, is fundamentally similar in all societies. They argued that, '[e]very culture attempts to perpetuate itself through deliberate transmission of what is considered the most worthwhile knowledge, beliefs, skills, behaviours, and attitudes. This deliberate transmission of culture is called education' (2001: 40).

Education is seen as one of the central tools in modern society to shape national identity. National identity formation partially relates to the construction of a state identity over time (Adeney 2003: 161–2). Governments have the ability to control and impose curricula in schools and with it define the identity discourse of the day. This can be done in overt ways or sometimes in less obvious forms. For instance, Sleeter (forthcoming) argues that '[s]tate-mandated curriculum can be understood as one form of an overlapping web of state-produced discourse that puts some order on the messiness of real life from an elite point of view'.

Being a product of the elite in power, it is also a flexible construction that changes over time and according to the ideals and ideology of the current government (Adeney and Lall forthcoming). For any Indian government, the question of national identity has always been a problematic one because of the many differences on the basis of caste and religion, which have traditionally divided Indian society. At Independence, India's diaspora was seen as very much part of the nation. However, at Independence, a statist definition promoted by Nehru, excluded the diaspora in India's nation building efforts (Lall 2001: 88). Instead, the thrust was to make sure that equality for all groups within India became a corner stone of the new country.

According to the Anthropological Survey of India, more than 4,000 distinct communities inhabit India. Their identity and cultural profile is shaped by their environment, language, occupational status and religion.[4] Nehru believed that India, being such a diverse country, could only be united on the basis of shared history and universal education.[5] Education, just as matters of the state, had to be kept strictly separate from religion. Religious education in schools entirely state funded is to this day forbidden.[6] Shared history emphasised mainly the independence struggle and getting rid of the British colonial power. Nehru saw in this a great bonding process between the diverse communities. However, shared history also went back to pre-colonial times and emphasised the integration of the Mughal invaders. The Muslim community was – despite the controversial nature of India's Partition – never to be depicted as a separate, non-Indian group. This was in effect a mutually reinforcing strategy: education for all (the structural element) and an inclusive curriculum 'for all' (the content element).

The Hindu nationalist agenda, however, has always been very different from that espoused by Nehru and the mainstream of the INC. Using Golwalkar's aforementioned definition as the basis for what Hindu nationalists would like young Indians to learn at school, involves a radical re-articulation of Indian identity. It shifts secular Nehruvian ideology to religion, from plurality to unity, from equality to hierarchy, from co-existence to oppression. Any identity works by preferring and privileging certain aspects over their opposition. The Hindu nationalist discourse emphasises the following tenets: We are Hindus, because we are not Muslims (or Other), and we do not want to be Muslims (or Other), because they are morally, socially and politically inferior.

From the perspective of Nandini Sundar (forthcoming) '[w]hen it comes to debating the nation's past or understanding contemporary society, the RSS/BJP agenda may seem not very different from that of conservatives elsewhere'. She wearily adds that,

> what makes the RSS agenda more dangerous is that it is not just a question of giving excessive weight to certain people or certain periods in history over others, of leaving out women and minorities, or its preference for so-called 'facts' over ways of thinking, but its readiness to distort accepted truths with the express desire of creating hatred for minorities.
>
> (Sundar forthcoming)

As will be discussed later in this chapter, the NDA Government did try to rewrite the curriculum and change the content of textbooks in BJP-led states. If nationalist policies were to be implemented nationwide, India's multicultural heritage would be destroyed from below by teaching children to see India as solely a product of Hinduism. In this setting, Taneja (2003) argues that '[a] whole generation would grow up with their collective memory of a shared heritage destroyed and with ideas and information that have no basis in reality'.

The NDA's education policy – polarisation of society along communal lines

The NDA election manifesto for the 1999 general election included a separate section on education entitled 'Education for all'. Its preamble stated:

> It is sad that fifty years after independence, the cherished goal of universal primary education enshrined in the Constitution, which was to

have been implemented by 1960, yet remains to be achieved. In recent years, State support for education has been wholly inadequate. Quality education is fast becoming the preserve of the social and economic elite of the country. We hold that education is both a human right and a means to bring about transformation to a dynamic, humane, thinking society.

(NDA 1999)

According to the above, the main aims are in harmony with those of the previous governments and the education reforms implemented under Rajiv Gandhi (1984–89). The main excerpts of the actions and goals listed in the manifesto (reproduced in summary form below) do not place emphasis on any communal line or fundamentalist approach. In fact, they seem wholly reasonable steps in light of India's main education problems. The principal NDA goals were to expand the education infrastructure, increase literacy and discourage foreign influences.

- Increase state spending on education progressively to 6 per cent and more of our Gross National Product within five years.
- Achieve near complete functional literacy in five years, particularly by mobilising societal participation and full literacy by the year 2010.
- Accord priority to free primary education and enrol the help of locally-funded non-government organisations in this area; also integrate early childhood care and pre-primary education with primary education.
- Offer incentives in the form of free text books, mid-day meals and nutrition programmes and stipends to check dropout rate so that at least 80 per cent of children, both boys and girls, who enrol, complete primary school education.
- Set up a special monitoring authority to scrutinise the quality of education and remove gender disparity.
- Ensure autonomy to universities and to colleges under them. Rid them of corruption and other baneful influences. Encourage them to mobilise resources for research and higher education and provide academic freedom to our scholars, especially in the social sciences.
- Restore to teachers self-esteem and make teaching a respectable profession.
- Create centres of educational excellence in our academic system that can set an example and build self-confidence.
- Launch a scheme for low interest bank loans for meritorious students who want to go in for higher education.
- Thwart attempts by dubious, so-called foreign universities, colleges and institutes to open branches in India and prevent the outflow of foreign exchange on studies abroad unless the course is relevant to our needs and requirements.

- Provide specialised opportunities for highly talented students at school level.
- Ensure that traditional knowledge and skills are preserved and disseminated.
- Seek the help of industrial establishments for rapid proliferation of technical education.
- Encourage the enrichment, preservation, and development of all Indian languages, including Sanskrit and Urdu.
- Encourage greater participation of social and charitable institutions in expanding the network of educational institutions and in improving their standards.

On the basis of this manifesto, there seems to be no reason to expect that the Hindu nationalist agenda would be pushed through schools or other educational institutions. The only exceptions seem to be the last two points, which could have pointed to a hidden agenda, whereby the 'Hinduisation' or 'saffronisation' of Indian education could be promoted through the use of language or religiously inclined organisations.

In practice, the increased use of the RSS to provide schools and furnish other types of less formal education provision in tribal areas all over India, especially in Madhya Pradesh and the northeast, have been a part of this drive to include pro nationalist organisations in educating the less nationalistic inclined areas in India. The inclusion of Urdu next to Sanskrit is an interesting contrast, as it could have been expected that the BJP would have promised to concentrate its efforts on languages linked to the Hindu community.[7]

When the NDA came to power in 1999, the BJP decided to retain control of the two most senior positions in the human resource development portfolios, which included education policy. Two BJP hardliners, Murli Manohar Joshi and Uma Bharti, both of whom had played a significant part in the Ayodhya Ram temple agitation during the 1990s that had been organised by the RSS, took on these offices. Much of what the NDA manifesto called for was not implemented. Instead, the focus of the NDA's education policy became the 'Hinduisation' or 'saffronisation' of curricular content. In fact, Murli Manohar Joshi oversaw the expansion of the network of RSS schools and the appointment of RSS people or sympathisers to top national education bodies such as the NCERT[8] and the University Grants Commission (UGC).[9]

The new approach in the NDA's education policy should not be a surprise. As early as the State Ministers' Conference, held in October 1998, the new agenda had been publicised. According to Taneja (2003), '[i]n fact it is quite clear what the agenda paper at the Conference meant by the abrogation of Articles 29 and 30 of the Constitution'. Taneja added that 'Uma Bharti, the Union Minister of State in the Ministry of Human Resources did not take long to pronounce that the Kashmir problem finds its roots in the teaching pattern in the Madrasas and that there is a need to closely monitor them' (2003).

Policy in practice

In the state schools things started to change. The NCERT issued the National Curriculum Framework in 2001 for school education. This document was heavily based on the RSS ideological agenda and on the premise of a slogan used by Murli Manohar Joshi to justify the new framework: 'Indianise, nationalise and spiritualise'.[10] The discursive implications of this slogan are enormous: India is not really Indian; it needs to be 'Indianised'. It is not a proper nation, because it contains too many un-Indian elements, so it needs to be nationalised. And this, of course, is achieved by finding and invoking its true (Hindu) spirit. In this view, all foreign elements have to be purged from the curriculum. These include the British legacy as well as aspects of Indian culture, which are seen as having been introduced by the Mughal invaders. This links straight back to Golwalkar's text of 1939, which emphasises *Hindutva* as the only true basis of Indian identity.

The new policy involved a massive revision of school textbooks. The revisions were contested by a petition to the Supreme Court brought by three activists who argued that the NCERT had not followed the correct procedures of consultation with the states and that it sought to introduce religious teaching, which is forbidden by Article 28 (1) in the Constitution of India. This appeal, however, was rejected by the Supreme Court.[11]

The revised history and social science textbooks, which were subsequently released, seemed to want to re-write history, justifying an anti-minority outlook. According to Chandra (2002) '[p]rofessional historians soon detected a number of flaws, such as the statement that killing cows was forbidden in the Vedic period, or the failure to mention Gandhi's assassin (from the RSS)'.

The BJP argued that if history was one sided it had to be corrected. Objectionable material, which was deleted from the textbooks, included material written by four prominent Indian historians: R.S. Sharma, Romila Thapar, Bipin Chandra and Harbans Mukhia. None of them were asked about the changes made to their textbooks. Officially, 16 pages in three history textbooks used in secondary education history classes were removed. This included a paragraph detailing that there was no archaeological evidence of settlements in and around Ayodhya around 2000 BC.[12]

In an interview, Murli Manohar Joshi explained that changes were made to textbooks after complaints were received from Jains, Sikhs, Jats and other communities who felt aggrieved by how certain things were depicted in the old textbooks. In the interview, Joshi argued that:

> We examined them and the NCERT made a decision to delete them. . . . Certain authors of history have tried to distort history. They

have given it a purely leftist colour. They say that India had no history
of its own because they are guided by Marx. They teach the history of
a nation that was mainly defeated and conquered by foreign powers.
It's a travesty of facts and an attempt to kill the morale of a nation.

(Sharma 2002: 215)

Aside from accusing India's historians of an underhand communist
agenda, Joshi also denied any RSS involvement and any *Hindutva* agenda
in the corrections made to the history books. He said that:

Nobody from the RSS has ever talked to me on this issue (. . .) They
(the protesting historians) think that I will foist a Hindu agenda. No, I
will teach correct history. I will teach Marxism but I will also teach the
failures of Marxism. Why should they object to it? I have only an
Indian agenda.

(Sharma 2002: 216)

Joshi's main contention has been that in all the science books all the
discoveries have been ascribed to the western world. He disagreed with
this orientation. Instead, he posed the question: 'Was the invention of
computers possible without the invention of the Indian binary system,
zero and one?' (Sharma 2002: 208).

During the NDA's tenure, much of the Hindu nationalist agenda was
pushed through the teaching of 'moral' education and general knowledge
that focused on the 'pride of being Hindu'. Indian culture was presented
as Hindu culture, ignoring the pluralistic roots and the contributions of
the Muslim and other minorities. Non-Hindu communities were characterised as foreign, in part owing their religious allegiance to a country
outside India. This was a total reversal of the Nehruvian roots of Indian
education as it had been taught for over 50 years. With it came the reversal of the definition of Indian national identity as being inclusive of all the
different communities in India. The Human Resource Development
Minister responded to the widespread criticism from the historical profession by calling it 'intellectual terrorism unleashed by the left . . . more dangerous than cross border terrorism' (*The Indian Express* 2001).

The debate, which was labelled by the press as the 'saffronisation' of
education, became a national issue in the summer of 2001 when even the
coalition partners of the NDA let it be known that if the Human Resource
Development Ministry insisted on the new agenda, states not ruled by the
BJP would refuse the textbooks and the changes made to the syllabus. The
criticism of the new education policy was based on two main arguments.
First, that they were directed by the communal agenda of the *Sangh
Parivar* and were contrary to the principles enshrined in the constitution.
Second, that the subject of education was the individual states' respons-
ibility and changes could not be imposed unilaterally from the central

government, thus no curriculum could become national policy without the mandatory endorsement by the states. Through these debates, the BJP remained isolated in parliament, not supported by its own coalition partners.

The dispute is exemplified by the relationship between the central government and the state government in Delhi. The state government there has taken the unusual step of creating its own textbooks. Delhi's INC Chief Minister Sheila Dikshit said she had no problems with the old textbooks and would have happily reprinted them. However, the NCERT refused permission and insisted that the new textbooks, with the historical revisions, be used. Thereafter, the Delhi state government fought back by creating its own books (Joshi, P. 2003).

It is evident that in the name of curriculum reform there had been an attempt to rewrite textbooks along communal lines on a scale that would have submerged all secular interpretations in school level teaching. In Uttar Pradesh, for example the RSS undertook the task of rewriting, along communal lines, the history of every district in the state.[13] The Indianisation of history would do away with any contributions from minority groups.

Based on a reading of curricular changes, Taneja (2003) shows some examples from the revised history textbooks. They include some of the following items:

- The Aryans are shown as the original inhabitants of India and the builders of Indian civilisation. In contrast, the coming of Muslims is depicted as an intrusion that shattered the imagined homogeneity of the Indian community.
- The ancient period of history, especially the Mauryan and the Gupta period, is painted as 'Golden' because the rulers during this time are seen to be Hindus, and the medieval centuries are seen as the advent of darkness, a threat to culture, and an attack on Indian civilisation.
- The Moghul emperors, especially Aurangzeb, are painted as cruel tyrants without reference to the medieval context in which these rulers acted.
- When studying the Nationalist Movement, Muslims are portrayed as the enemies of the nation and are held responsible for India's Partition, while Hindu communal forces are depicted as the greatest patriots and nationalists.

Aside from what was happening in state schools during the NDA's tenure, the RSS started to expand its influence through the education and health sectors. They feel they can emulate the work of Christian missionaries in reaching members of SCs and STs, who are not part of the BJP's natural vote bank. In providing help and support, the RSS hoped to instil *Hindutva* in all segments of society.[14]

The first Saraswatu Shishu Mandir was established in 1952 by some RSS members whose aim was to contribute to 'nation building' through education. There are now more than 50 state and regional committees affiliated to Vidya Bharati, the largest voluntary association in the country.[15] These coordinate around 13,000 institutions with 74,000 teachers and 1.7 million students.[16] The expansion of the network of RSS schools was a major pillar in this strategy, essentially going against the traditional separation of education and religion. Funds for this expansion have been collected through various means, including charities operating in the West. In fact, according to a recent report published by *Awaaz*, a London based secular network, almost a quarter of Sewa International earthquake funds raised from the British public to help Gujarat have been used to build RSS schools (Awaaz 2004).

The centre of teaching in RSS-sponsored schools revolves around the concept of *Sanskrit Gyan* (knowledge of culture). *Sanskrit Gyan* texts are taught in Vidya Bharati schools and *Shishu Mandirs* (temples for children). The RSS, however, also sponsored an agenda paper on education. The central government tried to present this agenda – which suggested that *Sanskrit Gyan* and similar texts could be made compulsory for all schools – before the Conference of the State Education Ministers in October 1998.

RSS schools teach a distinctive perspective of history. In these schools, students are taught such 'facts' as that Homer adapted Valmiki's *Ramayana* into an epic called the *Iliad;* that the Egyptian faith is based upon Indian traditions according to Plato and Pythagoras; that the cow is the mother of all; that Jesus Christ roamed the Himalayas and drew his ideas from Hinduism. The interesting thing here is that *Hindutva* emphasises the universalisation of Hinduism as the source of all human wisdom, at the same time as setting Hindus apart from non-Hindus.

But most importantly, these RSS schools are being legalised and could have, under legislation proposed during the NDA's tenure, received state funding. According to Taneja,

> Through a directive that makes all schools running for 10 years automatically entitled to affiliation and recognition, the BJP govt. has ensured large transfers of state funds to RSS schools in the states of BJP govt., especially if it can be easily shown that govt. schools are not functioning well.
>
> (2003)

Undermining higher education, other educational institutions and committees

Although the BJP manifesto is very clear that it supported the independence of higher education institutions, in practice the NDA Government increased control and centralisation. According to Mehta '[e]very major institution of higher education, from the Indian Institutes of Management to the IITs, from universities to professional bodies such as the council of architects, from private institutions to foreign players are now subject to a single-point agenda that defines higher education policy: control and centralisation' (2004).

During the NDA's period of governance, vice chancellors of various universities were appointed with the sole criteria of sympathising with the new policies. Nalini Taneja cites the example of Delhi University. She writes that:

> In Delhi University, while the BJP was holding the State Government, all democratic norms were flouted and the functioning and role of the statutory bodies such as the Academic Council completely undermined. Governing Bodies of Delhi Administration and other colleges were filled with known sympathisers of no academic achievements or interest in education with a view to ensuring appointment of affiliated persons as Principals for the colleges. Appointments to teaching posts were similarly ensured through this process.
>
> (2003)

Similar problems have been observed in Himachal Pradesh where all three state universities are being run by RSS cadre. Formal academic qualifications do not seem to be only criteria for admission any longer. In addition, problems were reported at the Aligarh Muslim University, where the student union's president had been dismissed illegally by the Vice Chancellor.

Under the NDA, the UGC had its authority and autonomy undermined with regard to teachers' salaries, promotions and working conditions. The UGC is being used to commercialise education and to cut state funding. Personnel at the National Institute of Planning and NCERT have also been changed. The three historians (Romila Thapar, Bipin Chandra and Satish Chandra) whose texts were scrapped from the national textbooks were dropped from the NCERT board.

To date, there have not been any studies conducted on how change of senior personnel at the universities has affected the curriculum. However, it seems inevitable that the political outlook of the heads of the higher education institutions would taint the teaching and research of those institutions.

Aside from rewriting textbooks and replacing senior personnel at universities, the government has also placed pro *Hindutva* personnel in the right places within national education institutions.[17] For instance, several historians appointed to the Indian Council of Historical Research (ICHR) are known to have supported the VHP campaign on Ayodhya. The Indian Council of Social Science Research has been staffed with RSS supporters. In Simla, the Indian Institute of Advanced Studies has a new pro RSS chairman. In the National Museum, galleries were renamed and the choice of items displayed reflected the *Sangh Parivar*'s view of Indian history. Similarly, the Indian Institute of Mass Communication has a new chairman on the executive council who is known to have RSS affiliations. The advisor to the director of the All India Council for Technical Education has RSS links as well.

During the years of NDA rule, budgetary allocations in science and technology were shifted to focus on military and nuclear research to the detriment of research in the fields of health, agriculture and general science education. More significantly, there has been a change in discourse among certain academics on the ground. One of the senior professors interviewed by this author at IIT in Delhi said:

> For 50 years – since independence there has been a policy to enhance the history of minorities disproportionately. All this government is doing is putting the history of the Hindus into the right perspective (...) If you go to JNU (Jawaharlal Nehru University) you can still find those who toe the old socialist line that the old interpretation of history is right and the new take on it is wrong.[18]

It would have been inconceivable to hear such a statement anywhere in the academic community even a few years ago. The greatest success of the BJP education policy seems not to have been the introduction of new textbooks with a revised history and science curricula, nor even the emergence of RSS activists at the helm of national education institutions; it is the fact that the logic of their discriminatory discourse has permeated the intelligentsia. While it is easy to conceive that a less well-educated rural population would accept as true the 'Hinduised' interpretation of India's past, it is difficult to understand how such discourse has been accepted and swallowed whole by the educated middle classes. This is especially the case for the generation who grew up with Nehru's secular ideals of constructing an inclusive Indian national identity. The greatest danger is the erosion of the concept of this inclusive, statist identity, which allows for the different communities to live with each other.

At JNU, there were changes as well. Professors and students explained that *pujas* (Hindu prayers) had started in the student halls of residence. As a reaction, Muslim students had been doing *namaz* (Muslim prayers) in the refectories. Consequently, the university gave a neutral space outside of the halls, but on campus, for all religious activities to take place. Again, it should be emphasised that even until the late 1990s it would not have been possible to conceive that religion would play any kind of public role in JNU's student and university life. Nevertheless, one of the professors interviewed by this author tried to make reassuring comments. 'India is such a large country that changes like this cannot happen over night. There are plenty of people who oppose these changes'.[19]

It might well be that there are many people who oppose such changes, and individual state governments have defied the BJP, refusing to adopt the new textbooks. However, the speed at which the discourse among the urban middle class has been changing is breathtaking and should cause concern.

Conclusion

The effects of the new policies have gone much further than schools, universities and education institutions. While the changes in these institutions have been largely conducted quietly, and public debate has been limited, there has been a new development on the book-publishing front. Very active *Sangh Parivar* members have taken it upon themselves to intimidate authors and publishers when they have found books critical of Hinduism or *Hindutva*.

Books that allegedly show Hinduism or the Hindu Right in a poor light have been attacked. For instance, a civil injunction was laid against historian D.N. Jha's book on beef-eating in ancient India. Likewise, two commissioned volumes on the freedom struggle, which included documents showing that the RSS and Hindu Mahasabha collaborated with the British, were withdrawn from publication by the ICHR.

In January 2004, Oxford University Press withdrew a book in India written by James Laine, an academic from the University of Minnesota. The withdrawal of the book, titled *Shivaji – the Hindu King in Islamic India*, took place after violent protests by extreme right groups who were upset by anecdotes about Shivaji's personal life, especially those concerning his paternity[20] (*THES* 2004). The research centre in Pune, BORI, where the book was researched was also vandalised. The Laine controversy has caused consternation within the academic community. However, Sharad Pawar, a former INC member, and now leader of the Nationalist Congress Party observed that '[r]esearch scholars should not tarnish the image of inspiring personalities' (*THES* 2004).

While this controversy seems to point to a 'book burning' type strategy, things are not quite that simple. On the political front there seems to be a two-pronged approach. On the one hand, the NDA Government was instigating slow changes behind the scenes, which included curriculum and personnel changes as described above. On the other hand, there were sometimes violent protests by activists of various *Sangh Parivar* affiliated organisations, almost as if to see how far they could go. The violence appears to have been condoned by the NDA Government, largely because it did not take any action against the protesters despite the damage they caused.

What is interesting to note is that, even in the run up to the 2004 general election, these education issues did not make waves in the press. The discourse of the average middle classes had changed. For those who live in rural areas, the critical issues were roads, water, electricity and jobs, and to a lesser degree, access to education. The possible reason for this is that religion and its role in society has always been a complicated subject in India. Although India is a secular state, religion has been used in politics when it suited a particular politician. However, in principle, religion was a matter of the private sphere and totally separate with regard to education. Nevertheless, the coming to power of the BJP-led NDA alliance has shown that in India secularism is to date still a contested concept.

For the 2004 general election, the NDA's manifesto changed slightly in its emphasis on education; moving towards a more 'communal' and nationalistic stand. Compared to the 1999 NDA manifesto, three points stood out in the 2004 version:

- The focus on Indian culture, heritage and ethical values in syllabi will be strengthened. Character-building and all-round development of the student's personality will be emphasised. Sports, physical training and social service will be mainstreamed into the educational system.
- The growing de-emphasis of Bharatiya languages in school and college education will be checked. Teaching in the mother tongue will be encouraged.
- Efforts will be intensified for the propagation of Sanskrit.

In essence, this shows that the BJP was more confident than ever that it could push its nationalist agenda through the education portal. While issues pertaining to the Ram temple at Ayodhya and the Uniform Civil Code might still be seen as divisive within society, there was little or no resistance to changes on the education front. Although the NDA did not win re-election, the BJP and its allies did not lose the 2004 general election because of their nationalist agenda. The 2004 general election was not about endorsing or rejecting *Hindutva* and fundamentalism, but principally about jobs, roads, water and electricity. Despite a good monsoon, high economic growth at around 7.5 per cent, and the peace talks with Pakistan, an INC-led Government has been formed. The electorate rejected policies, which in effect widened the economic gap between rich and poor.

The INC and its allies will have a heavy burden improving rural economic problems. In the field of education, they will have to reverse the policy and personnel changes that were implemented by the NDA. The fact that the BJP, as the leading party in a minority governing coalition, utilised education to re-educate the Indian population by stealth is enough reason to pay close attention to this policy arena in the future. The new INC-led coalition will have to review the new textbooks and the new curriculum, and rid it of its chauvinistic, nationalistic content. The silence on this issue needs to be lifted and the debate on what has been happening to the education system needs to be made public. If they fail to do so, secularism will continue to be eroded throughout the educational system. Their task will be made more difficult by the fact that a large section of the educated middle class and the intelligentsia had jumped on the ideological bandwagon of Hindu nationalism and had accepted the tenets of its discourse. It is important to remember that the original fears that the BJP would impose *Hindutva* in India have subsided. This means that if the Congress Party does not get it right, they could be voted out in five years time, and we could see a revival of Hindu nationalism again.

Acknowledgements

The author is grateful to Andreas Behnke and David Gillborn for their comments and ideas which allowed her to develop this chapter.

Notes

1 For a detailed analysis on the dilemmas of resource allocation and planning, see Raghavan (2003).
2 See Sharma (2002) for a detailed analysis of the Kothari Commission.
3 In 1992, 'Hindu' *kar sevaks* under the leadership of the BJP and other members of the *Sangh Parivar*, demolished the Babri Masjid, a fifteenth century mosque in Ayodhya. Despite the lack of historical evidence, they claimed the mosque had been built over an earlier temple commemorating the birthplace of the Hindu god Ram.
4 This survey also shows that Hindus and Muslims share more than 95 per cent of characteristics of various kinds that are common and that it is shared lives that have given shape to the diverse cultural expressions. Among other things the studies also show that nobody today can be characterised as an original inhabitant or a foreigner, see details in Taneja (2003).
5 More on the construction of Indian national identity, see Adeney and Lall (forthcoming).
6 See specifically Article 28 (1) of the Constitution of India which provides that no religious instruction shall be provided in any educational institution wholly maintained out of state funds.
7 However, in the 2004 election manifesto Urdu was dropped.
8 The NCERT, though an autonomous body, draws up the national curriculum framework and publishes textbooks which are used as models by most state governments.
9 The detailed list of posts which was offered to RSS members and sympathisers is discussed at a later stage in this chapter.
10 This attempt to 'Indianise' at the university level includes introducing courses like Vedic rituals and Vedic Astrology.
11 Judgment by Justice M.B. Shah, D.M. Dharmadhikari and H.K. Sema in Writ Petition (Civil) No. 98 of 2002, Ms. Aruna Roy and others vs. Union of India and others.
12 'Archaeological evidence should be considered far more important than long family trees given in the Puranas. The Puranic tradition could be used to date Rama of Ayodhya around 2000BC but extensive excavations in Ayodhya do not show any settlements around that date' (Sharma 2002: 198).
13 The RSS has a separate Institute known as the *Bharatiya Itihas Sankalan Samiti*, with 400 branches all over the country, for coordinating and giving direction to this effort. One of the key 'achievements' of this Samiti is the 'cleansing' of Christian influence on historical chronology (Taneja 2003)

14 See the contribution in this volume by Nitya Rao (Chapter 6).
15 For a more detailed description of the RSS sponsored *Vidya Bharati* network, see Sharma (2002).
16 *Vidya Bharati* institutions function under a variety of names such as: *Shishu Vatika, Shishu Mandir, Vidya Mandir, Sarasvati Vidyalaya,* etc.
17 See Taneja (2003) for more details on personnel changes.
18 Anonymous interview conducted at IIT Delhi on 11 January 2004.
19 Anonymous interview conducted at JNU on 16 January 2004.
20 Shivaji is admired for his stand against the Mughal Empire and is considered a national hero.

Part III
External factors

9   The NDA and the politics of economic reform

Rob Jenkins

Introduction

The NDA Government continued the process of economic reform initiated by the INC Government in 1991, and sustained by the United Front Government during 1996–98. Faced with the need to deepen second-generation reforms, the NDA encountered a more complex set of challenges than its predecessors. The political implications of a broadened agenda – combined with shifts in the nature of party competition, federal relations and political mobilisation, not to mention the economy itself – have made managing the politics of economic reform particularly daunting during the NDA era.

In common with the other contributions to this volume, this chapter assesses the role of coalition politics, ideological constraints and external forces in shaping the NDA's performance in power. The chapter argues that the content, pace and sequencing of economic reform was to a considerable extent influenced by all three factors, though not necessarily in ways that might have been predicted at the time the NDA came into office. In the area of economic reform, the NDA faced the challenge of preventing the three constraints from merging together in ways that would make the task of liberalising the Indian economy even more daunting than it already was. Aspects of *Hindutva*, for instance, were constantly in danger of becoming wedded – through such RSS-linked front organisations as the SJM – to a form of economic nationalism that cast *external forces* (such as the World Bank, the International Monetary Fund (IMF) and multinational capital generally) as the nefarious drivers of the government's liberalisation programme. To the extent that the BJP's junior coalition partners were susceptible to the economic nationalism aspect of this logic, the three forces were often perilously close to solidifying into a formidable composite constraint. This was prevented both by skilful politics on the part of the coalition's managers, and also by certain structural factors. For instance, while the idea of economic nationalism was appealing to certain NDA elements (for crass political reasons as much as any ideological commitment to economic autarky), the *Hindutva* thrust given

to these ideas by the likes of the SJM was anathema to them, indeed dis-
crediting the otherwise sacrosanct idea of *swadeshi* in certain quarters.[1]

The relative influence of each of these three factors on the process by
which the NDA pursued economic liberalisation varied across time, across
policy domains and across reform tasks. Perhaps the most notable trend
has been the continuity in the tactics used to manage the politics of
reform. The NDA Government continued with the tendency towards
Machiavellian politics displayed by its predecessors, including continued
reliance on India's federal institutional structure to negotiate awkward
political dilemmas.

Whether the momentum of reform slowed under the NDA, or whether
(as the World Bank argued in 2003) 'the pace of reforms has slowed since
the mid-1990s' (2003: i), depends very much on one's view of what constitutes 'reform', whether the earlier stages of reform are considered politically less demanding than later stages, and how much allowance is made
for the broader economic environment within which reform takes place.

Indeed there are inherent analytical obstacles that confront any analyst
seeking to characterise the NDA Government's performance on economic
reform. The first is the difficulty of determining the appropriate standard
against which to assess performance. Should we adopt process standards –
indicating policy measures introduced – or outcome standards, indicating
what the policies yielded? If we adopt process standards, as this chapter
mainly does, should these be conceived of dichotomously – either a reform
was or was not effected – or 'continuously', on the basis of gradual progress
towards a policy shift? The case of labour policy illustrates this point. While
legislative amendments to the much-criticised Industrial Disputes Act (IDA)
of 1947 were not affected – to say nothing of its outright abolition, as some
might like – steps in this direction were taken, such as clearance by the
cabinet of certain IDA amendments.

Were we to adopt outcome measures, even more problems would arise.
Certain policy changes take years to have an effect. But should initial indi-
cations of impact count? And if shorter-term indicators are used, is there
not the potential problem that some of these impacts may rely upon perceptions influenced by *other*, non-economic aspects of policy? For instance,
how much foreign direct investment (FDI) India receives may be affected
as much by investor perceptions of communal stability and regional security as by India's relaxation of investment rules. Even a focus on the political implications of reform, which usually manifest themselves more
quickly than do the economic effects, does not overcome the familiar difficulty of gauging their net *impacts*. This has two aspects: across and within
constituencies. The overall balance across constituencies is difficult to
assess because, while reform may have worked to the advantage of some
social groups, it may well have hurt other interests. The ability of the
'winners' to substitute for the loss of support from the 'losers' is uncertain
at best. Making assessments within constituencies presents problems as

well. When a group is affected by more than one type of 'reform', there are few universally reliable, and comparatively applicable, measures for determining whether, in the case of an individual household or medium-sized firm (to say nothing of a diversified conglomerate), the losses from one species of reform – such as changes to the tax code – are fully offset by other aspects of liberalisation, such as increased foreign competition resulting from reduced tariff and non-tariff barriers to international trade.

In addition to the difficulty of deciding upon the most relevant agenda items for political analysis there is a second obstacle to assessing the NDA's performance. This is the problem of determining the validity of basic economic indicators associated with second-generation reforms. Huang and Khanna (2003), for instance, argue that we must challenge our most basic assumptions about what phenomena require explaining. For instance, China's lead over India in terms of FDI inflows, they argue, is quite possibly grossly overstated. This is because Chinese tax laws create incentives for economic actors to conceal earnings and to bring them back into circulation in the form of foreign investments, namely the phenomenon known as 'round-tripping'. While China's figures have been overstated – Huang and Khanna claim that estimates could be up to *twice* as high as actual inflows – India's numbers have been understated. It is possible, they argue, that India's foreign investment levels are double what the official statistics indicate. If they are right, then the two countries' respective foreign investment performances, in terms of inflows as a percentage of gross domestic product (GDP), are pretty close to converging, with investment into China equalling 2 per cent of total domestic output compared to a figure of 1.7 per cent for India.

Regardless of whether a process or outcome standard is considered most appropriate, what constitutes an acceptable threshold for successful reform remains unclear. Should the NDA be judged against its manifesto commitments? Or would the known preferences of key decision makers within the BJP be a more appropriate standard? Or given that manifestos are, in practice, aspirational statements rather than realistic commitments, should the NDA's reform performance be judged against *ex ante* expectations (voiced by journalists, economists and others) about how far its reform programme was likely to go? Or should its performance be assessed against the standard set by international development institutions: the reform milestones in bilateral and multilateral aid programmes? How about comparing the NDA against its predecessors in the post-1991 era, the Narasimha Rao government or the United Front? But the tasks, and the times, were different then.

In the end, there is no obvious method for arriving at a completely satisfactory standard. Judgements must be made on a case-by-case basis. Either way, advancing the process of economic reform into a new generation will present the new government with a huge range of political problems, not least the sheer enormity of this ever-expanding agenda, which includes the deepening of existing structural reforms as well as the need to address issues of equity, to place public finance on a more sustainable footing, to stand up for India's interests in multilateral trade negotiations, to upgrade the country's decaying infrastructure, and to combat the corruption that drains both public resources and entrepreneurial energy. Moreover, each of these issues and the tradeoffs involved in prioritising among them involves acute political dilemmas.

Before proceeding further, one final caveat is in order. The NDA Government's ability to advance the reform agenda would have been severely handicapped had not other enabling factors been present. For instance, one macro-level condition that permitted the generally liberal course of reform to persist was the positive performance of the Indian economy. Inadequate progress on certain indicators, such as the consolidated (central plus states) fiscal deficit as a proportion of GDP, has been eclipsed in public discussions by the high annual GDP growth figures (particularly in a world marked by meagre economic growth in most countries during the period under investigation). Likewise, headline-grabbing statements such as the size of India's foreign-exchange reserves (which stand in such great contrast to the 1991 situation), or the fact that during at least one quarter during 2003–04 India balanced its current account for the first time in a quarter-century, have also become salient in economic debates. All of this has taken place in a low-inflation context; this was critical, as India's polity is notoriously averse to even mild inflation (at least by the standards of other developing countries).

Conceptualising the second generation

There is no universally accepted definition of what constitutes a second-generation reform agenda. Second-generation reforms are often conceived of as delving deeper into sectoral specificities. Thomas Friedman, in his evocative style, calls this the shift from 'wholesale' to 'retail' reform (2004).[2] Others would contest such a generalisation, claiming that some basic reforms – such as rules for fiscal prudence – were usually not enacted in the first wave of reform. This is certainly true of India, and indeed of most other countries with the capacity to resist the more extreme austerity programs that characterised World Bank and IMF structural adjustment recipes of the 1980s and early 1990s.

The reason why there is no unanimity on what constitutes second-generation reform is not simply that each analyst has his or her own policy preoccupations; just as important is the widespread questioning of the standard economic prescription of privatisation, deregulation, trade liberalisation, unrestricted transnational capital flows and so forth. Doubts about the wisdom of this reform package have existed ever since the rise to prominence of neoliberal economists within the international financial institutions during the mid-to-late 1970s.[3] These began to boil over in a more concerted (and intellectually coherent) *counter*-counter-revolution during the latter part of the 1990s – first in the wake of the East Asian economic crisis, and then in the anti-globalisation protests in Seattle, Prague, Genoa, Gothenburg and elsewhere. By the turn of the millennium, orthodoxy had become heterodoxy. What John Williamson had once called 'The Washington Consensus' had fractured.

In a recent book, *After the Washington Consensus*, Kuczynski and Williamson (2003) delineated the contours of what they were promoting as a new post-consensus reform agenda. They make three main points relevant to understanding reform's second generation, and therefore to the NDA's performance during its term in office. First, any practical approach to constructing a second-generation reform agenda must include the unfinished business from the first generation. Second, second-generation reform must be centred on institution building, without which markets will not function and the reformist momentum will not be sustained. Finally, issues of equity must be addressed, for reasons of political sustainability if nothing else, and these must inform part of the way in which reform is sold to sceptical publics.

World Bank President James Wolfensohn is in almost complete agreement with Williamson. Wolfensohn (1999) sees the 'first and second generations [as] *not* being sequential'. Indeed, he maintains 'that the first and second generation actually coalesce in terms of timing' (1999). Wolfensohn also argues that

> [t]he second generation issues focus around the questions of the structure of the right institutions, of the improvement of the administrative, legal, and regulatory functions of the state, addressing the incentives and actions that are required to have private sector development and to develop the institutional capacity for reforms.
>
> (1999)

Finally, Wolfensohn wants equity and fairness not only to be part of the agenda, but also to be seen to be part of it, so that they are central to the political discourse and not just the economic strategy. As he put it, 'Second generation reforms must also address the very important question of how you build consensus in a society' (1999). The idea that second-generation reforms must address a broader social constituency and also require attention to filling in the detail of earlier broad-brush reforms is consistent with the view taken by officials in other developing countries. Guillermo Ortiz, who heads the Mexican central bank, admitted in early 2004 that the early phases of economic liberalisation in Mexico were confined largely to the domain of elite politics, but saw the 'urgency' of spreading discussions of reform into mass politics.[4] Ortiz argued that it was necessary for 'Mexico to finish the structural reforms at the micro level', and that '[w]e did the first stages of structural reform from the top down' (cited in Friedman 2004). That was the relatively straightforward part. 'The next stage is much more difficult,' he maintained, because the government will 'have to create the wider consensus to push the reforms in a democratic context' (ibid). This has clear echoes of Wolfensohn's view.

This chapter thus begins from the premise that first- and second-generation reforms are not, primarily, headings under which it is possible to list specific economic sectors (agriculture, finance), techniques of economic governance (privatisation, fiscal adjustment), or actor-related processes (labour, civil service reform). Rather, each of these familiar agenda items, as well as others not listed, is an ongoing process, consisting of more than one stage of reform. Therefore, in assessing the NDA's management of the politics of second-generation reform, this chapter does not treat any individual reform as inherently either a first- or second-generation issue. Instead, the relevant criterion is whether the NDA Government successfully advanced individual reform issues in ways likely to make them politically sustainable over the long term.

Political tactics for managing the politics of economic reform

The influence of political calculations on not just the broad parameters of economic reform, but specific measures as well, dates to the very beginning of India's economic reforms of the 1990s. In his first budget speech in 1991, which justified and gave some concrete shape to the newly launched policy of economic liberalisation, former Finance Minister Manmohan Singh (currently Prime Minister) announced a range of subsidy cuts. In the face of mass demonstrations, those relating to agricultural inputs (particularly on fertilisers) were 'rolled back', allegedly on orders from Prime Minister Narasimha Rao. By the time that the NDA Government took power, such humiliating policy 'rollbacks' had become a regular feature of the budget speech drama. Having been initiated into this curious rite following his first budget speech in 1998, Yashwant Sinha – Finance Minister during most of the NDA Government – reportedly made it his practice to draft a 'rollback announcement' even before presenting his budget to parliament. This is a stark reminder of the pervasiveness of politics in the reform process, and an indication of how responses to such pressures get institutionalised, binding future reformers.

In a study which focussed on the period from 1991–98, I argued that the reorientation of India's development strategy could be seen as a process of 'reform by stealth', an approach made possible by a combination of three factors: the political-management skills of India's politicians, the fluid institutional environment within which they operated and the political incentives thrown up by the initial policy measures they employed to address the 1991 economic crisis (Jenkins 1999).

These factors have been just as relevant during the subsequent period of BJP-led coalitions, from 1998–2004. The NDA adopted similar means to its predecessors in power. Echoing a characterisation often applied to Narasimha Rao, one of Prime Minister Vajpayee's long-time political colleagues called him 'a master of ambiguity', who 'sends different – sometimes wholly incompatible – messages to different communities'.[5] It is thus perhaps not surprising that the process of pursuing reform quietly – avoiding conflicts until propitious moments, dividing opponents, and using illiberal methods to achieve liberal ends – persisted under the NDA. Some of the means employed have remained the same since the days of Narasimha Rao; others have recently emerged.

Arun Shourie, Minister for Disinvestment, Communications and Information Technology in the NDA Government, showed his implicit appreciation of Narasimha Rao's philosophy of the politics of reform: in a world in which change is always taking place, there are advantages to harnessing the forces already in motion. When asked by an interviewer to elaborate on his characterisation of the central political dilemma facing a reformer – the need to effect 'a complete U-turn without [it] seeming to be a U-turn' – Narasimha Rao stated that accomplishing this feat becomes less difficult to comprehend '[i]f you understand that where you are standing is itself in motion'. According to the former Prime Minister, once you realise that 'you are not static' then '[t]he turning becomes easier' (Gupta 2004). Grasping for himself this dynamic of perpetual motion, Shourie described his belief that second-generation reforms are 'propelled by the opportunities that have opened up' as a result of earlier reforms (2004). His view was that, eventually, a process of self-propulsion emerges: 'one reform creates pressure that other reforms be put through. Import–export licensing is abolished. Trade increases. Traders and manufacturers demand that ports be improved so that turnaround time comes down to Singapore levels, that the DGFT (Directorate General of Foreign Trade) accepts electronic filing of forms' (Shourie 2004). Ultimately the reformer's job becomes one of guiding rather than pushing.

In the area of telecommunications reform, one of Shourie's ministerial responsibilities, the NDA demonstrated its understanding of how to use strategic delay to its political advantage in advancing the process of liberalisation. Instead of pushing ahead aggressively on certain extremely controversial reform measures, the NDA Government let events already 'in motion' overtake the status quo. Ministry officials responded to technological convergence and price distortions that had arisen in the domestic market – themselves the result of how licenses for cellular and other services were issued – by claiming helplessness in the face of forces beyond their control. Reliance Industries Limited, India's largest private-sector firm, was reportedly permitted, as a result of its alleged inside access to high-ranking politicians in the governing coalition, to poach on markets that were not within the terms of its original license. Eventually, this made a mockery of the existing system, in effect forcing reform to take place by dint of necessity rather than through a planned effort that would have required the expenditure of the NDA Government's scarce political capital. Reflecting on this process, none other than the Disinvestment Minister himself remarked that 'by exceeding the limits which restrictions sought to impose upon them', companies such as Reliance had 'helped create the case for scrapping . . . regulations' (*The Economist* 2003b). Even critics of the NDA's performance on economic reform had to agree. Referring specifically (though indirectly) to this very case, one critic regarded this as part of a larger pattern, in which

> [r]eforms in India . . . are driven by either crises or vested interests. The 1991 reforms were driven by a foreign exchange crisis; others such as the telecom reforms of 1999 (when firms migrated from high fixed license fee commitments to a lower revenue-sharing license fee regime) were driven by the needs of the private sector telecom players – indeed, even the latest move towards a unified license is being driven by the needs of one part of the industry.
>
> (*Business Standard* 2003)

The BJP, when in opposition, nuanced its anti-reformism by claiming that it opposed external sector liberalisation until internal reforms were firmly in place. It also claimed that its approach to the external sector would be guided by pragmatism, and close attention to India's national interest, rather than a dogmatic acceptance of free trade. This was symbolised by the famous statement about wanting to import 'computer chips' not 'potato chips'. The BJP's 1996 manifesto, prior to first taking office, was also careful not to dismiss globalisation entirely, instead referring to the need to adopt a 'calibrated' approach to global economic integration. These fine distinctions were, of course, an attempt to have it both ways, something to which most parties aspire. But as the BJP-led NDA adapted to the realities of power, it found this balance difficult to sustain, and before long the government was adopting means similar to those used by its predecessors.

Fiscal policy

India's composite budget deficit (which includes the combined deficits of the central and state governments, but does not include a number of off-budget liabilities) increased dramatically between 1997–98, the last year before the BJP came to power, and 2002–03. In 1997–98 it stood at roughly 7 per cent of GDP; by 2002–03 it was in excess of 10 per cent, and rising. Both higher expenditure, particularly in non-development areas (mainly government salaries and non-merit subsidies of various sorts), and lower revenue were to blame. There are limits to how quickly a government can reverse the course of trends inherited from its predecessors, particularly on government salaries; but the NDA never even appeared to try. On the contrary, it placed excessive faith in the ability of privatisation proceeds to plug its widening deficit.

One of the areas of expenditure that contributed massively to the fiscal imbalance was the power sector. Financial losses in this sector hit 1.4 per cent of GDP in 2001–02. Food and fertiliser subsidies amounted to a further 1.4 per cent of GDP in 2002–03. Adding in petroleum subsidies (0.3 per cent of GDP) brings these three items to almost a third of the total combined fiscal deficit.

Public expenditure is an area in which the NDA's performance was clearly constrained by both coalition politics and external forces. The Government of India's commitments to its international development partners – mainly international financial institutions, but also bilateral aid donors and regional development banks – should have resulted in an improvement in the country's fiscal situation. These commitments were embedded both within ostensibly binding conditionalities attached to lending instruments, and within the non-binding targets agreed as part of grant programmes. Another set of external actors, namely foreign investors, could also have been expected to act as a source of downward pressure on the budget deficit. Concerned with the impact of growing deficits on exchange rates, interest rates, consumer spending and other key indicators, both portfolio managers and multinational firms contemplating FDI should have helped to discipline the NDA Government's profligacy. An argument can of course be made that without these external pressures, India's fiscal condition would have been even worse, but this kind of counterfactual optimism is not very convincing.

The constraints imposed by coalition governance evidently exerted a much stronger influence than did the external forces. Needing to satisfy such a large range of coalition partners made the Finance Minister's job more difficult than it otherwise would have been. Though only a few of these partners were, on their own, a serious threat to governmental stability, almost all of the partners – especially those lacking control of key spending ministries in their own right – extracted expensive concessions from the coalition managers.

In the current phase of India's electoral politics, in which regional parties are significant contributors to the forging of parliamentary majorities, the category of 'coalition constraints' overlaps very substantially with what might be termed regional pressures. This, by implication, highlights the important role played by those non-BJP coalition partners that also ruled state governments. The large bloc of MPs from the TDP, which ruled Andhra Pradesh, was a crucial component of the NDA coalition's parliamentary majority. The TDP leader, and then-chief minister of Andhra Pradesh, N. Chandrababu Naidu, exerted pressure on the NDA that made it difficult, if not impossible, for the Government of India to exercise fiscal restraint. For instance, Naidu was among the main ring-leaders of a movement among Chief Ministers to oppose the Eleventh Finance Commission's recommendation that decisions on the allocation of financial transfers from the central to the state governments be linked, in part, to the performance of state governments in reining in public spending. This led to a much-publicised political storm that not only undermined the proposals themselves, but also reinforced the message that the central government could be effectively challenged when it sought to take action to restore order to the public finances. This had sub-stantial knock-on effects, as other coalition partners sought to extract fiscal concessions for constituencies located within their states. These con-cessions took the form of both changed tax rules that assisted certain sec-toral interests and spending commitments that were intended to buy political support for regional parties, who could then claim that central government largesse would not have been forthcoming had not the regional party been part of, or actively supported, the NDA.

Perhaps the most blatant example of regional lobbying was Railways Minister Mamata Banerjee's insistence that the central government approve the proposals contained within her self-proclaimed 'Bengal package'. The willingness of the NDA leadership ultimately to comply with many, though not all, of these demands for regional patronage was only partly explained by Banerjee's support for the NDA. Another contributing factor was the BJP's lack of a significant electoral presence in West Bengal. Strengthening Ms. Banerjee's hand in the provincial politics of West Bengal would have encountered far more opposition from BJP leaders, as well as from other members of the NDA who viewed such concessions through zero-sum spectacles, had the BJP been a serious contender for power in West Bengal. Such complaints could be heard from BJP politi-cians in Andhra Pradesh: the BJP-led government in Delhi was providing additional resources and policy autonomy to a state government ruled by the TDP, a party that BJP leaders in Andhra Pradesh saw as their main political rival for the one prize that mattered to them – control of the state government.

Naidu and Chief Minister Prakash Singh Badal of Punjab, also ruled by an NDA coalition partner, the SAD, were key figures in resisting proposals to reduce the quantity of foodgrains and other commodities procured by the Food Corporation of India. This caused difficulties not just for the government's fiscal position, but for the prospect of agriculture reform more generally.

The pressures from coalition politics – in its federal guise – also thwarted a number of other reforms related to public expenditure. Tax reforms, for instance, were important not only to the country's overall fiscal health, but also to removing obstacles the practical realisation of other second-generation reforms. A good example is the VAT. On 1 June 2003 India was to become the proud owner of a 'national value-added tax'

(*The Economist* 2003a). But Finance Minister Jaswant Singh backed out just before the deadline. This had happened earlier as well. It was not just traders who were aggrieved but also state governments, many of whom feared a loss of revenue, despite commitments made by officials in the central government. If India is to achieve the level of manufacturing competitiveness its boosters foresee, then reform of the system of state-level sales tax (assigned to states by the Indian Constitution) is necessary in order to create a common market. But political pressures keep intervening. As the NDA Government was voted out of office in May 2004, it saddled its successor with the financial implications of its spending commitments, particularly the estimated Rs 40 billion per year needed to fulfil the inflation-indexing commitment made to central government employees. This will eventually affect state governments as well.

To its credit, the NDA did, to the surprise of many, pass the Fiscal Responsibility and Budget Management Act (FRBMA). The FRBMA established 2008 as the target year by which India's fiscal deficit would be eliminated. On the other hand, because of the optimism of its projections – which included an expectation for growth and tax revenues to continue on an upward curve for the foreseeable future – few observers considered it likely that this target would be met. The newly-elected United Progressive Alliance (UPA) Government, which assumed office under Prime Minister Manmohan Singh in late May 2004, almost immediately shifted the deadline back to 2009.

Trade policy

Trade policy in many ways encapsulates the problems that confront any attempt to provide a clear assessment of the NDA Government's performance on economic reform. On the one hand, it could be claimed that the NDA performed exceedingly well on this front. It reduced India's average applied tariff rate from more than 35 per cent in 1997–98 to approximately 29 per cent in 2002–03. Even with a general election looming, the NDA Government announced in February 2004 a reduction – from 25 to 20 per cent – in the peak duty for non-agricultural product imports, as well as the elimination of the Special Additional Duty. Moreover, the NDA undertook a major step in the overhaul of India's trading regime by phasing out quantitative restrictions on more than 1,400 product categories.

On the other hand, there are grounds for scepticism about such achievements, and not just in terms of whether as much was accomplished as originally promised. This is because policy changes that might, on one reckoning, be counted as government actions may well have been determined by India's multilateral commitments. By far the most important are the multilateral agreements administered by the WTO. These include both sector-specific agreements, such as the Agreement on Agriculture, and those dealing with broader issues that cut across a range of sectors, such as the Agreement on Subsidies and Countervailing Measures.

Governments often have a political incentive to claim that their hands are tied, their room for policy manoeuvre constrained by international treaty obligations. To complicate matters further, frequently the nature of India's commitments is disputable, making the element of volition involved hard to determine. One example is the case of edible oil imports. Soon after quantitative restrictions on imports of this and other product categories were phased out during 1999–2001, India experienced a surge of imports that drove down prices. While this was theoretically good news for consumers – assuming that markets were responsive enough to prevent traders from cornering all the savings – producer groups were less pleased. On the face of it, the import tariff level that the NDA Government had set for various edible oils, as a replacement for the quantitative restrictions (which limited the actual amounts that could be imported), was well below the bounded rates it had committed to at the WTO. Still, despite the pressure exerted by both edible oil producers and the oilseed farmers that supplied them, the NDA Government did not increase the tariff. Why it did not is one of the disputed issues referred to above, which make the assessment of trade policy so difficult.

In this case, because India's bounded rates clearly allowed tariff increases, any excuse for non-action by the government that invoked WTO obligations would not be tenable. As a result, other explanations began to circulate, most notably the belief that the NDA Government's failure to react to the import surge was part of a half-secret bilateral deal with United States trade officials. This deal allegedly emerged from negotiations on how to respond to the ruling by the appellate panel of the WTO's Dispute Settlement Body, which had ruled that India's continued use of quantitative restrictions on a range of products was a violation of its obligations under Article XI of the 'GATT 94', one of the agreements administered by the WTO (WTO 1999). Rather than retaliate against India with increased tariffs of its own, as WTO rules generally allow winning parties to a dispute to do, the US struck a deal. How true this was in the case of edible oils is less important than the perception that arose among participants in the public debate. This is an interesting example because the political incentive created was the opposite of the one cited earlier. The NDA Government did not want to claim that its hands were tied by an international agreement: the notion that Indian farmers could not be protected because of a deal with the US administration was not considered politically advantageous, to say the least.

Another explanation for why the NDA Government failed to raise tariff levels during this crisis stressed the Finance Ministry's sensitivity to pressure from the international financial institutions and market sentiment generally. The argument made by critics was that while, under the old system, changes in the level of imports permitted under quantitative restrictions could be imposed by the Ministry of Commerce acting alone, under the newly tariffised system a tariff increase required Finance Ministry approval, and given the close association between Finance Ministry officials (the main point of contact for Bank and Fund representatives) and the multilaterals, there was built-in resistance to taking action. Again, this kind of explanation can be contested; but by entering the political rumour mill it contributed to the perception that external forces were, indirectly, shaping the manner in which India's trade policy was being implemented, an aspect of 'policy making' that must be considered when arriving at an overall assessment of government performance in this area.

Assessing the NDA's performance on trade policy reform is also made difficult because of the uncertain boundaries of this policy domain. As a result of the Uruguay Round of trade negotiations, a range of new policy areas became part of an expanded multilateral trade agenda, the logic being that policies once considered purely domestic had implications for patterns of international trade. Thus, issues such as the level of subsidies provided to agricultural producers became subjected to international disciplines. In addition to its own policy decisions, therefore, the NDA Government's performance on trade policy must also be judged on its participation in international negotiations.

There is no doubt that the NDA Government made its presence felt in world trade talks, and indeed in the routine operation of the WTO itself. Even discounting the claims made by the Ministry of Commerce – that India was instrumental in scuppering the Seattle ministerial meeting in 1999 – there is fairly unambiguous evidence that India's delegation to the Doha ministerial meeting in 2001 played a very important role. For instance, the Indian delegation helped secure a side agreement stating that public health emergencies needed to take a more prominent position in the implementation of the Trade-Related Aspects of Intellectual Property Rights Agreement (or TRIPs). India, as we have seen, was also a significant protagonist in several cases argued before various WTO Dispute Settlement Panels. India used this mechanism to press its claim that Indian textile producers suffered as a result of health and safety regulations in rich-country markets that unfairly discriminated against Indian products.

Perhaps India's most high-profile achievement under the NDA Government in the international trade arena was its role in helping to establish the so-called G-20, a loose group of about 20 developing countries whose mission was to act as a coordinated bloc on issues of mutual concern, particularly on agricultural subsidies and provisions for Special and Differential Treatment for poor countries. India, Brazil, South Africa, Nigeria and other large developing countries were able to forge this grouping in the run up to the Cancun ministerial meeting in late 2003, which was to assess progress on key issues introduced in the trade negotiating round begun at Doha in 2001. Publications of the Ministry of Commerce and Industry – the departmental reorganisation that created this joint ministry was itself the work of the NDA Government – routinely celebrated India's role in making the G-20 a workable entity, stressing that the government not only invested substantial diplomatic capital, but also used great ingenuity in tapping the intellectual resources of India's economics profession, both in India and among its diaspora (GoI 2004a: 20).

Labour policy

Labour reform – along with agricultural liberalisation – is often seen as among the most significant pieces of unfinished business from India's first generation of reforms. A complete overhaul of India's industrial-relations regime – including the conditions under which workers can be hired and fired, the rules governing union recognition, and the mechanisms for resolving employment disputes – is considered long overdue by the World Bank and other observers. India's restrictive labour regulations are widely regarded as unsuitable for its increasingly globalised economy.

Like its predecessors, the NDA continued to 'reform by stealth', facilitating backdoor policy changes rather than effecting them through overt decision making. This involved, among other things, relying on state-level leaders in India's federal system to negotiate awkward political dilemmas. Though the NDA avoided directly reforming the relevant labour legislation, during its time in power labour reform was nudged onto the terrain of mass politics through, for instance, the attempts by state governments (in Uttar Pradesh, Tamil Nadu, Rajasthan and Kerala) to take on state public employee unions in highly public confrontations. While this shift represented an important step in the direction of a second-generation reform agenda, on another key indicator – the building (or resuscitation) of institutions – there has been little progress. Indeed, a case can be made that the institutions necessary to manage the transition to a new labour-relations regime have been actively undermined, not least as a result of the Machiavellian politics mentioned earlier. The Indian Labour Conference, for instance, a tripartite body that could serve as a focal point for forging a workable compromise on many key labour issues, was marginalised.

Like its predecessors, the NDA Government was eager to promote Voluntary Retirement Schemes (VRS) to help firms to shed excess labour. While VRSs are not a substitute for the official 'exit policy' sought for so long by India's private sector, they contribute to solving the surplus-labour problems of many firms. The element of stealth derived not just from the fact that VRSs perform some of the functions that governments are too politically timid to effect by means of policy; other, more flagrant, sins of omission are involved. VRSs are often far from voluntary. Sometimes muscle power is used to intimidate workers, as governments (at the state and central level) turn a blind eye. In other cases, firms have been able to rely on the threat of keeping an employment dispute tied up in tribunals for so long that workers will never receive any payment if they refuse to sign up, voluntarily, for early retirement (Jenkins 1999).

Underhanded tactics could be found at the level of policy as well. In 2002, for instance, when declaring its intention to promote a series of Export Processing Zones (EPZs) and Special Economic Zones (SEZs) that would help India live up to its alleged 'trading superpower' potential, the government proposed to classify such zones as 'public utilities'. This would require employees of firms in these zones to provide 45 days' notice before going on strike, a substantial increase on the existing 30-day provision.

State governments have been far more active on the labour front than the central government. Whereas the central government mainly made announcements, the Madhya Pradesh state government actually watered down labour laws for firms in the Indore Export Processing Zone (EPZ) (*The Economic Times* 2003). Some state governments were reform trail-blazers in certain policy areas, which helped others – including the central government – on the path of reform. In 2002, for instance, during cabinet debates on proposed amendments to India's Industrial Disputes Act (IDA) there was explicit discussion of precursor state-level legislation in Maharashtra. Maharashtra's legislation increased the number of employees a firm could have and still be exempt from the provisions of the relevant 'exit' regulations, which require approval by the state government to retrench workers or close down an enterprise. Discussion of the Maharashtra act was said to have played a role in selling to the cabinet proposals pushed by the Government of India's Finance Ministry. Insiders vouch for the fact that 'the example of Maharashtra's Industrial Act was cited by the pro-amendment ministers led by finance minister Yashwant Sinha' (*The Times of India* 2002). The Maharashtra government had, through example, provided a powerful argument to otherwise cautious coalition managers in New Delhi. Ultimately, the cabinet approved changes to the IDA, but these never reached the statute books.

Privatisation

In the budget for 2003–04, the NDA Government stated that it expected to realise Rs 132 billion in revenues from privatisation, a large sum in both absolute and relative terms. Had the target been met, it would have been equivalent to one half of 1 per cent of India's GDP. That this represented an extremely optimistic estimate was not an unfair assessment given that privatisation had yielded only Rs 30 billion in 2002–03.

Apart from ideological reasons, and the self-interested motivations of politicians who have long used public-sector enterprises as a source of patronage, an additional reason why privatisation aroused such strong resentment was the perception among both the political class and the public that the means by which privatisation (or disinvestment, to use the NDA's preferred euphemism) was being effected had in fact involved corruption. Critics frequently pointed to the privatisation of BALCO as an example of government callousness and legally dubious manoeuvring.[6] Of course, a case could be made that the alleged corruption that was involved in privatising this or any other company was a small one-off price to pay in exchange for ridding the NDA exchequer of the ongoing financial responsibility for these enterprises. Some critics would even go further, claiming that privatisation had improved the productivity in at least some firms. Nevertheless a potent political force was created by the equation in the public mind – and, crucially, among certain NDA coalition partners – of privatisation with corruption, favouritism to foreign firms, and an abandonment of India's ideological commitment to a strong state sector. This in effect combined the three political constraints on government performance with which this chapter's analysis has been concerned.

Interestingly, despite all the concern about public perceptions of privatisation, it was not public opinion, but rather the judiciary, that most seriously damaged the NDA Government's privatisation plans. Having decided to proceed with the partial disinvestment from two high-profile state-owned enterprises in the petroleum sector – over the objections of several ministers – the NDA Government ultimately could not take action. It was not the representative aspect of democracy that was able to halt the government. When the NDA Government sought to bypass parliament, the Supreme Court stepped in. It was a liberal institution of restraint,[7] with the capacity both to adjudicate between contending branches of government and to reinterpret constitutional provisions in light of changing times, which halted the NDA Government's most significant disinvestment. This highlighted the limits to the reform-by-stealth approach to managing the politics of economic reform.

Deregulation and re-regulation

The second generation of economic reform is, as noted earlier, centrally concerned with institution building. Among the most important institutions are those responsible for managing competition and creating an environment conducive to increased private investment, both domestic and foreign. More nuanced approaches to economic liberalisation than those that predominated in the 1980s have grasped the need to accompany vigorous deregulation with a judicious measure of *re*-regulation. The NDA Government's performance in this area has, again, been mixed.

One of the least impressive cases has been in creating the institutional framework for regulating the generation, transmission and distribution of electricity. This is a crucial infrastructure sector. Nevertheless, the intensive efforts undertaken to set the conditions for new investment and managed competition – in many cases with the assistance of bilateral and multilateral development agencies – failed. Even states like Orissa that were once touted as potential success stories have little to show for all the effort. The creation of the Central Electricity Regulatory Commission (CERC) failed spectacularly to establish effective rules of the game, though there are high hopes among some observers – including those otherwise unsympathetic to the NDA – that the Electricity Act 2003, once fully in force, will have a salutary effect.

The telecommunications sector, by contrast, has witnessed a fairly healthy process of institutional development. To be sure, the Telecom Regulatory Authority of India (TRAI), the creation of which preceded the NDA, has lost important battles with Department of Telecommunications, with political decision makers (and the courts in some cases) siding against it – for instance, on questions relating to license fees and the process for setting tariffs. Slowly but steadily, however, the NDA oversaw the development of a telecommunications regulator with more organisational substance than was once believed possible.

Asking why India's telecom regulator managed to evolve into a substantial institution, while its counterpart in the power sector did not, Mukherji (2004) points to India's federal structure as an important institutional variable. Responsibility for the power sector is shared between the centre and the states, whereas telecommunications is a subject for the centre alone. As a result, India's telecom regulator could act – after a long period of maturation – as a more authoritative referee in disputes between government and private providers. Mired in provincial politics, state-level electricity regulators made decisions that rendered the CERC much less influential than it should have been.

Lal (2003) comes to a slightly different conclusion, stressing interest-group politics rather than institutional variables. He explicitly concedes some of the points made by Mukherji. (It should be noted, however, that Mukherji's explanatory framework stressed other factors as well, particularly the extent to which reform in the telecommunications sector was 'homegrown', whereas in the case of the power sector the World Bank and external consultants hired by aid agencies played a much greater role). Lal recognises that it 'has been argued that such "successful" reform is more likely in federally administered sectors like telecom, as they do not impinge directly on powerful voting interests like farmers' (2003). He stresses, however, that there is no clear correlation between central reforms being 'easy' and state reforms being 'difficult'. A more robust formulation, according to Lal, 'is that where the gulf between compensation and pain (in content, perception and time) for politically and financially powerful interest groups is narrow, reform proceeds in stealthy incremental doses. Where it is very wide (or appears to be so), as in power and income tax, it apparently grinds to a halt' (2003).

Echeverri-Gent's research on regulatory reform in the financial sector – particularly as it pertains to equity markets – suggests a similarly mixed picture. On the one hand, there was far less foreign institutional investment than either the NDA Government or many foreign analysts had anticipated. On the other hand, a number of reform measures that had long been promised by previous governments were finally implemented. India moved to a system of 'rolling settlement' periods for equity trading following Finance Minister Yashwant Sinha's announcement in 1999 that India would adopt global best practice. While it took two years – and a major financial scandal – before that pledge was fulfilled in July 2001, at least action was ultimately taken. As a result, according to Echeverri-Gent (2004), '[t]he deeply flawed account period settlement system that contributed to periodic breakdowns was replaced by a "T + 2" rolling settlement that is one of the most efficient systems in the world'. Something similar happened with derivatives trading. After repeated policy battles, in which reform advocates sought to abolish the 'carry forward' system that was used to finance speculative trading, and prompted many market crises, it was under the NDA that reform was successfully implemented, creating what Echeverri-Gent called 'a thriving derivatives market'. Again, it is difficult to determine whether the NDA was bolder than its predecessors, willing finally to take on the forces of resistance, or whether it was reaping the benefits of initial actions taken by earlier reformers (Echeverri-Gent 2004).

This raises the more general question: Which is politically more difficult: starting reform, which in some cases can be done with a stroke of the pen, or carrying through on the details, which is often what causes the real economic pain, and thus provokes the most serious political reactions? Narasimha Rao himself, not surprisingly, claimed that it was the initiation phase that was hardest. He compared the reforms introduced during his government with the further elaboration of the reform agenda during the subsequent governments, stating that liberalisation in 1991 'came from 0. Maybe negative. So taking something from 50 to 100 is making it double. But if you take it from 0 to 1, how many times is it? . . . Infinite' (Gupta 2004). He thus minimised the contribution of later governments by characterising their actions as making merely incremental changes, building on the foundations set by others (Gupta 2004). Nevertheless, precisely because many of the difficult decisions had been deferred by earlier governments, the NDA found itself with fewer reform options. A fair assessment would have to assign the NDA Government at least some of the credit for keeping the reform process on track.

Elections and reform: the closing stages of the NDA Government

By late 2003, with a general election less than six months away, and a round of important state elections in progress, NDA ministers started becoming more cautious, claiming that reform measures considered politically sensitive were significantly down the priority list. Union Commerce Minister Arun Jaitley, speaking at the India Economic Summit

2003, initially stated how positive labour reform would be for job creation, and then reassured any trade unionists that might be listening that nothing serious would be done in the short term. It was something for the next parliament. Asked when he thought action might be taken, Jaitley said 'I think in two to three years, work on labour reforms would pick up momentum' (*Hindu Business Line* 2003).

Near the end of 2003, the BJP wrested power from three out of four INC-controlled states in north India. It was a huge reversal: the BJP took 171 out of 230 state assembly seats in Madhya Pradesh, 120 out of 200 in Rajasthan and 50 out of 90 in predominantly tribal Chhattisgarh. Many in the BJP felt that the time was ripe for a further push on reform. 'We believe these polls dramatically improve the mandate to deepen economic reforms in India', a senior BJP official said soon after the verdict was announced. 'We want to bring it home to people that economic liberalisation is not some distant thing that happens in Delhi', and that it 'directly raises the standard of living of ordinary Indians, in the countryside as well as in the cities' (*Financial Times* 2004b). Jaitley, shedding his reticence of just a week earlier, asserted that the state elections results were 'a very strong vote for further economic reform' (*Financial Times* 2003).

By claiming so loudly that its victory in the 2003 state assembly elections was due to the success of economic reforms, the BJP could hardly be surprised when its defeat at the 2004 general election just months later was blamed on the political reaction to reforms as well. It is doubtful whether either interpretation was correct. For instance, nothing in the election survey data produced by the Delhi-based Centre for the Study of Developing Societies (CSDS) indicated that the NDA lost power because of a revolt against economic reform by India's voters. Neither, for that matter, were any of the three central factors discussed in this paper – ideological constraints, coalition pressures or external forces – responsible for the NDA Government's demise in 2004. The UPA Government, under Prime Minister Manmohan Singh, the key architect of the first generation of reform, will face many of the same political difficulties that its predecessor did in managing the transition to a second generation of reform built around new institutions and a greater focus on equity.

Acknowledgements

For helpful comments and criticisms, the author would like to thank Pranab Bardhan, Kunal Sen, Barbara Harriss-White and other participants at the two seminars where various portions of this paper were discussed – in February 2004 at the Institute of Commonwealth Studies (University of London); and in May 2004 at the School of Advanced International Studies (Johns Hopkins University).

Notes

1 I have analysed the implications of the existence of these competing versions of *swadeshi* in Jenkins (2003b: 584–610).
2 Ironically, Friedman introduced this term when discussing how the threat of economic competition from the likes of India (and China) would force Mexico into a new generation of reforms.
3 For an account of this rise, see Toye (1989).
4 For a useful discussion of the distinction between these two varieties of politics, see Varshney (1999).
5 This was the view of Balraj Madhok, a retired politician described as an 'old-style Hindu nationalist' who 'was Vajpayee's political mentor in the 1950s and 1960s' (*Financial Times* 2004a).
6 An interesting account of the issues arising in the BALCO case is found in Ahluwalia (2002).
7 For a good account of the balance between the liberal and representative aspects of democracy, see Zakaria (2003).

10 The NDA and Indian foreign policy

James Chiriyankandath and Andrew Wyatt

Introduction

Recent Indian foreign policy has been made in a profoundly altered context. We argue that the policies of the NDA Governments from 1998 to 2004 have to be understood as part of the larger re-orientation that has taken place since the end of the Cold War. Since 1991 India has lost its longstanding ally, the Soviet Union, and the Non-Aligned Movement has been rendered insignificant. During the same period, the US has come to dominate international politics. In assessing the foreign policy record of the NDA administrations, we will consider the impact of a number of variables that one would intuitively expect to determine policy outcomes. From a domestic point of view, these will include the impact of the BJP as the dominant party in the coalition, the effect of the coalitional character of the NDA (in particular the presence of a number of regional parties inside the coalition), prevailing ideas about India's place in the world and the institutional structure in which policy is made (in particular the dominance of the Prime Minister). From an external perspective, we will consider such variables as the policies of individual states towards India and its neighbours (with particular reference to the US and Pakistan), the role of international regimes and the changing international economy. While the focus is on developments after 1998, it is clear that some of these variables have had an impact on Indian foreign policy that predates the NDA.

In this chapter we argue that the foreign policy of the NDA has exhibited a strong degree of continuity with the conduct of its immediate predecessors. However, we do identify some significant divergences from what was India's overall trajectory in 1998. First, the BJP (rather than the NDA) took India over an important nuclear threshold in 1998. Second, Indian foreign policy more generally was more pragmatic and realist in orientation after 1998. This was true of both practice and the terms in which policy pronouncements were made. The chapter begins by considering the historical backdrop to the NDA's foreign policy making and the administrative, economic and political context within which foreign policy is made and how this has changed in the past decade and a half. It then focuses on two key aspects of post-Cold War Indian foreign policy: the adoption of nuclear weapons by the Government of Prime Minister Atal Bihari Vajpayee and relations with the US. Then we review the conduct of foreign policy in South Asia. The penultimate section evaluates the general realignment that has occurred in Indian foreign policy and the conclusion considers the role of the NDA in this process.

The NDA and longer-term trends

Jawaharlal Nehru, the country's first Prime Minister (1947–64), was the main architect of India's foreign policy. He assumed that India would become a major world power by virtue of its history, civilisational depth, size and strategic location. While other elements of the Nehruvian approach to international affairs have been rejected, this aspiration was not challenged by the NDA. The BJP restated this ambition boldly, linking India's greatness more narrowly to the superiority of Hindu culture (Harriss 2003: 7). The assertiveness of the BJP was expressed in the 1998 manifesto:

> In the recent past we have seen a tendency to bend under pressure. This arises as much out of ignorance of our rightful place and role in world affairs as also from a loss of national self-confidence and resolve. A nation as large and capable as ourselves must make its impact felt on the world arena. A BJP Government will demand a premier position for the country in all global fora.
>
> (Bharatiya Janata Party 1998)

Senior members of the BJP expressed a desire to return to the more expansive British vision of India's role in Asia. Lord Curzon, the British Viceroy from 1899 to 1905, took the view that 'the master of India, must, under modern conditions, be the greatest power in the Asiatic Continent, and therefore, it may be added, in the world' (Mohan 2003: 204). Jaswant Singh, the NDA's External Affairs Minister until 2002, identified himself with this assessment of India's status in Asia. There is, of course, a good deal of ambiguity about how the 'greatest power' in Asia might behave, though commentators sympathetic to Jaswant Singh saw him as a pragmatic realist who did not favour expansionism (Cohen 2001: 43–5).

The NDA inherited a long history of poor relations with the US, China and Pakistan. These difficulties are interrelated. Pakistan has had a close relationship with both the US and China and India's troubled relationship with Pakistan has deep roots that precede partition. Pakistan's claim to be a homeland for the Muslims of the subcontinent directly contradicted the assumption made by Nehru and the INC that India could accommodate all religious groups in a secular state. Ideological rivalry and competing territorial claims have fused in the dispute over Kashmir. India has consistently rejected Pakistan's claim to the Indian state of Jammu and Kashmir and considers that Pakistan's support for the Kashmiri militants constitutes a proxy war against India. Moreover, India remains resentful of the humiliation meted out by China in the 1962 border war. The outcome of this situation is that critical border issues remain unresolved. Further discomfort has been caused by China's sympathy towards Pakistan's view of the Kashmir dispute. Finally, China's assistance to Pakistan in the area of nuclear and missile technology has long concerned New Delhi.

India's unsteady relationship with the US foundered in the early 1970s. The US was exasperated with India's pursuit of non-alignment and the 1971 Indo-Soviet Treaty of Peace, Friendship and Cooperation confirmed India's unreliability to the US. For its part, India suspected that US Cold War objectives might conceal more sinister neo-imperial designs. The dramatic improvement in relations between China and the US in the early 1970s heightened Indian insecurity. The flow of American military aid to Pakistan was seen as a direct threat and the increase in this aid following the Soviet invasion of Afghanistan in 1979 exacerbated this tension. Little progress had been made on relations with Pakistan and China by 1998. In contrast relations with the US began to improve following the end of the Cold War and the initiation of the 1991 reforms.

The policy-making institutions

More than half a century after its inception, the Indian Foreign Service (IFS) remains exceptionally small and elitist with only 750 officers (excluding support personnel). In the first three decades of its existence entrants to the IFS had to rank in the top 0.1 per cent of the 20,000–40,000 people taking the combined Civil Services examination. While individual officers may be highly talented, the organisation of the foreign policy-making structure as a whole has been criticised by a number of commentators. One observer was moved to write that '[d]ecisions are excessively centralized, parliamentary consultation is weak, the talents of outsiders are rarely utilized, and coordination among differing ministries and bureaucracies is poor' (Cohen 2001: 302–3). In contrast to the foreign ministries of the Group of Eight (G-8) industrialised states and 18 of the 19 European Union countries, India's Ministry of External Affairs (MEA) has not undertaken significant structural reform to take account of post-Cold War changes (Rana 2002: 37). In 2000, Jaswant Singh initiated a re-examination of IFS structures. His successor as External Affairs Minister, Yashwant Sinha, called for an expansion of the service in response to new challenges (Mohan 2003: 2).

The IFS and the MEA do not have a monopoly on foreign policy making. Besides such ministries as Defence, Finance and Commerce, other bodies can also exercise influence. These include the Prime Minister's

Office, the foreign intelligence service – known as the Research and Analysis Wing (RAW) – and several influential Delhi think tanks, at least partly funded by the government, such as the Institute for Defence Studies and Analysis and the Centre for Policy Research. In exceptional circumstances, some states of India's federal system have become directly involved in the making of policy. As we shall see below, the advent of the WTO has given rise to greater assertiveness on the part of the states.

Conforming to the post-1947 norm of heavy involvement in foreign affairs by the Prime Minister (Ganguly 1994), Prime Minister Vajpayee was closely involved in the conduct of foreign policy. Ironically, one of the few Indian foreign ministers able to conduct foreign policy with little Prime Ministerial interference was Vajpayee himself, when he held the post in the Janata Party cabinet in the late 1970s. Yet Vajpayee's previous conduct in office between 1977 and 1979 was not consistent with the hardline positions on foreign policy issues taken by the erstwhile Jana Sangh (Ghosh 1999: 328–35). Twenty years later, as head of the NDA government, it was widely believed that Vajpayee relied heavily on a few men such as Jaswant Singh and Deputy Prime Minister and Home Minister L.K. Advani. Outside of the Cabinet, Principal Secretary Brajesh Mishra, a former IFS officer and former Ambassador to China, played an important role as envoy of the Prime Minister. When, in December 1998, a National Security Council headed by the Prime Minister and including the Ministers of Defence, External Affairs, Finance and Home Affairs was established, Mishra was appointed the first National Security Advisor. An annually reconstituted National Security Advisory Board – on which Mishra also served – made up of retired diplomats, military officers, civil servants, journalists and academics was also created.

A new economic context

Economic change has been associated with a number of developments in contemporary Indian foreign policy. We have identified four key themes. First, the economic reforms have altered the way in which foreign policy has been made. The MEA was considered to have little competence in the area of economic diplomacy and an early consequence of this was a limited re-organisation to address this problem (Dixit 1996: 390). Foreign economic relations have become more complex and in recognition of this, attempts have been made to coordinate policy between different ministries. Economic issues are much higher up the foreign policy agenda and this has been reflected in the foreign policy of the NDA. Prime Minister Vajpayee's numerous overseas visits routinely emphasised the economic dimension of India's overseas relationships. Economic imperatives encouraged Indian foreign policy makers to upgrade links with states that were traditionally considered politically unimportant.

Growing attention has been paid to relations with South East Asia. The vibrant economies of the region represent an important trade opportunity. They also matter politically. India needs good relations with these states if it is to be taken seriously as a world power. Moreover, they are also states with, at best, ambivalent relations with China. Thus, the NDA continued to develop the Look East Policy initiated by Prime Minister Narasimha Rao in 1994. This had resulted in India becoming a full dialogue partner of the Association of East Asian Nations (ASEAN) in 1995 and joining the ASEAN Regional Forum in the following year (Kumaraswamy 2000: 185–6). In 2002, India's rising significance in Asia was recognised in a special summit (the so-called ASEAN plus one) that brought India and the ASEAN states together (Mohan 2003: 211). However, the NDA did not achieve the larger objective of obtaining full membership of ASEAN.

Second, the perception that the 1990s was a decade marked by intensified globalisation has altered the context in which foreign policy is made. We do not subscribe to a crude hyperglobalist view that depicts territorial states as hollowed out by irresistible and impersonal global markets. Rather, the Indian case has been one in which global and domestic imperatives have been finely balanced. India's integration with the global economy is far from complete. Levels of trade remain comparatively low, FDI inflow has been modest, full capital convertibility has yet to be conceded and capital controls could be imposed should a crisis occur. While the Indian state has changed and adapted in order to assist India's integration with the global economy the state remains a significant economic actor. It quickly became clear after the first NDA Government was formed that the BJP was not going to push for the *swadeshi* policies favoured by some elements in the *Sangh Parivar*. The compulsions of electoral politics also help explain why reforms seen as having the most immediate effect in terms of jobs and wage losses, and therefore most likely to provoke a popular backlash, were, in the main, avoided (Kale 2002: 209).

Though economic policy was deemed by outside observers to fall short of neoliberal standards (Wolf and Luce 2003: 15), it was deemed impolitic for ministers to make too much of a virtue out of economic pragmatism. Likewise, although senior members of the BJP occasionally expressed heretical views, the NDA administration – like the INC administration that preceded and has followed it – was attentive to the received neo-liberal wisdom on economic issues that continues to be propagated by international financial institutions. India's new economic diplomacy required a new rhetorical approach. To the outside world, India was described as a new nodal point in the emerging global information economy (Wyatt forthcoming). At home, the 'inevitability' of globalisation obliged India to open up to the world (Advani 1998). Nevertheless, it would be misleading to suggest that globalisation, or more precisely, the perception that one acts in a globalising world, has had no impact beyond new forms of rhetoric.

There was an anxiety that India was in danger of being left behind. The popularity of regional trade blocs, widely seen as a way of cushioning the impact of globalisation, encouraged the NDA to make some belated moves towards closer cooperation in the South Asian Association for Regional Cooperation (SAARC) area. Economic interdependence was seen as necessary and largely desirable. In a twist on the classic liberal argument that shared interest creates the need for cooperation, Mehta (2003) argued that interdependence creates channels through which India could exercise power.

However, the integration with the international economy encouraged by liberalisation did not prevent the May 1998 nuclear tests. An old-fashioned realist choice was made. Political considerations overrode economic considerations (Wyatt 2003). Interestingly, INC policy makers had come to exactly the opposite conclusions a few years earlier (Perkovich 1999: 329). In sum, under the NDA Government, India acted in a changed global economic environment, but it would be a mistake to overstate the impact of that environment on foreign policy. Domestic imperatives seemed to weigh more heavily on decision makers than global pressures.

Third, the NDA administration was able to make the link between improved economic growth, willingness to reform and an improved international standing. Although it is not clear that the reforms have put the economy on a new upward trajectory (Corbridge and Harriss 2000: 171), realists increasingly saw India conforming to the economic profile required of a major power. After averaging little more than 3 per cent gross national product (GNP) growth per annum in the 1970s, India recorded rates of 4.8 per cent in 1981–86, 6.1 per cent in 1986–91, 5.5 per cent in 1991–96, and 6.2 per cent in 1996–2001 (figures from Nayar and Paul 2003: 208). Poverty and low GNP per capita had seemed to be insurmountable obstacles in the path of India's march to great power status. However, the sustained growth of the 1990s changed assumptions about India's standing in the world at home and abroad.

Fascination with the link between wealth and power reflects the realist assumption that a strong economy is a necessary but not sufficient condition for military power (Mearsheimer 2001). This realist concern with economic growth has been evident in Indian strategic thinking since the end of the Cold War. The collapse of the Soviet Union suggested to policy makers that political stability depended on a minimal level of economic success. The pre-eminence of Germany and Japan provided examples of the possibilities offered by economic dynamism (Gordon 1995: 4). In a typically realist aside, Mohan noted that the sustained growth of the 1990s created an image of a dynamic India able 'to outperform Pakistan which is seen as a failing state' (2002). India's realist ambitions have found an echo outside of India. Stephen Cohen at the Brookings Institution sees India on the cusp of great power status. He comments that a 'growing economy, coupled with an expected decline in birth rates, will add teeth to a foreign policy that has been long on rhetoric but short on resources' (2001: 103). Other Washington think tanks see India as a power that will emerge in the medium term (*The Economic Times* 2000). A changing economic dynamic is at the heart of the altered relations with the US that are discussed below.

Nonetheless, the link between economic change and India's new international status needs some qualification. Future growth cannot be predicted and significant challenges, particularly in the area of infrastructure, need to be overcome in order for growth to be sustained. India's standing also varies according to which indicators are used. Purchasing power parity measures of GDP place India as the world's fourth largest economy (after the USA, China and Japan) (*The Economist* 2001: 24). However, its share of world trade while growing, especially in sectors such as computer software, is still below 1 per cent (compared to China's share of over 4 per cent) (Baru 2002: 2591).

The fourth and final theme that we emphasise is the emergence of the states of India's federal system as foreign policy actors. This theme is taken up in the next section. Many regional parties were able to represent the concerns of their states at the centre as members of the NDA coalition. In summary, we would comment that a feature of foreign policy in the 1990s was a more challenging economic environment for foreign policy makers. In part, this stemmed from international factors and in part from domestic economic limitations. Rejecting autarchy entailed a new approach to foreign policy. Initially, only modest changes were made to Indian foreign policy after 1991. However, after 1998, the BJP-led coalition increasingly used India's relative economic success as the basis for a more assertive approach to foreign policy.

Coalition politics, federalism and foreign policy

The breakdown of the national INC and the concomitant rise of national coalition politics altered the orientation of regional parties towards politics at the centre (Wyatt 2002). Among other things, participation in national policy making is now possible for regional parties and they are beginning to adjust their expectations. The key portfolios that concern foreign policy were controlled by the BJP (namely the portfolios of Prime Minister, External Affairs and Finance), but senior members of other parties held important cabinet portfolios that have a bearing on foreign policy. For instance, NDA partners held Defence (George Fernandes (Samata Party), 1998–2001, 2001–04) and Commerce (Ramakrishna Hegde, (JD (U)), 1998–99; Murasoli Maran (DMK), 1999–2002). States in India's border regions clearly have particular concerns and links with other South Asian states that give them an interest in India's regional foreign policy. In the context of coalition politics, where the regional disaggregation of interests is usually much clearer, it is easier to track the impact of regional forces on foreign policy. The exceptional intervention of the Chief Minister of West Bengal in negotiations with Bangladesh in 1996 was not repeated under the NDA. While states are less likely to be ignored by the centre when their ruling parties are members of the central government, small regional parties were not always able to influence BJP ministers. When the Liberation Tigers of Tamil Eelam (LTTE) looked set to inflict a severe defeat on the Sri Lankan army during 2000, the BJP did consult the DMK over national policy towards Sri Lanka (Sridharan 2003: 472). However, the NDA did not achieve a consensus on the issue. Contrary to official NDA policy, the PMK and the MDMK expressed support for the cause of Tamil Eelam. In July 2002, Vaiko, the leader of the MDMK, was arrested and detained under POTA, by the state government of Tamil Nadu for expressing support for the LTTE. The case included a number of ironies. The NDA, which Vaiko supported, introduced the legislation and the MDMK remained a member of the NDA government until a few weeks before the end of Vaiko's 19-month detention. The rest of the NDA, and the BJP in particular, were keen to avoid entanglements in Sri Lanka, and ultimately did not support the LTTE.

The process of economic reform has extended the competence of the states in the federal system (Jenkins 1999: 125–51). Financial constraints have encouraged the states to look for resources outside of India. Some states have become key players in a new type of commercial diplomacy (Sridharan 2003: 476). State chief ministers have attracted a good deal of publicity as they have courted foreign direct investment. This new approach to foreign economic policy is rooted in the reforms introduced by the earlier INC and United Front Governments, but the NDA has overseen the continuation of the process. For instance, Chandrababu Naidu, the TDP Chief Minister of Andhra Pradesh (from 1995 to 2004), was particularly successful in maintaining an international profile.

The new federal arrangement helped the coastal states of the south and west, with their better social and communications infrastructure, to forge ahead. In contrast, other large, populous and poor states in the north and east have not done as well. This development has consequences for both federal politics and foreign policy. Regional parties like Naidu's TDP, a key coalition partner for the BJP, were in a position to moderate the BJP's more aggressively Hindu chauvinist instincts, though this effect, arguably, manifested itself more explicitly in domestic policy. In the longer term, it is conceivable that distinct regional interests and perspectives in foreign policy will begin to make their influence felt. For instance, southern Indian states with a growing stake in the global market in information technology, like Andhra Pradesh and neighbouring Karnataka, may set greater store by a flourishing relationship with the US. According to a report by the Confederation of Indian Industry, a majority of the US temporary work visas issued to Indians went to south Indians. The report also noted how Bangalore, the capital of Karnataka, alone accounted for around 40 per cent of India's exports in services and about 12 per cent of goods exports. The capitals of neighbouring Andhra Pradesh (Hyderabad) and Tamil Nadu (Chennai) were also identified as emerging growth poles, creating centres of excellence in IT, biotechnology and pharmaceuticals (Confederation of Indian Industry 2004). State Governments in Tamil Nadu, with its burgeoning links with Singapore and Malaysia, also had a stake in the success of the Look East Policy.

Another significant development during the NDA Government was the intensification of relations between individual states and the World Bank. A number of states, under the watchful but tolerant eye of the centre, have negotiated directly with the World Bank for loans to support a variety of projects. In some cases, such as Tamil Nadu from 2001 onwards, these packages could be construed as significant attempts to encourage structural adjustment at the state level. The implementation of the WTO agreement has created tensions that have caused the states to argue for a greater say in future negotiations with the WTO. Many of the burdens of compliance with the WTO agreement have fallen on the states that were not party to the treaty negotiations. Agriculture, constitutionally the responsibility of states, has been especially contentious (Sridharan 2003). The states have a strong case and, rather belatedly, the centre has begun to consult with the states about future WTO negotiations. However, it is far from clear that the states have actually gained a meaningful role in this area of foreign economic policy making (Jenkins 2003a).

Hindu nationalism and nuclear weapons

The nuclear tests of 11 and 13 May 1998, coming just weeks after the new BJP-led coalition government had taken office, were the most striking manifestation of the assertive militaristic nationalism of the votaries of *Hindutva*. They represented the realisation of a long held aim of the BJP and its precursor, the Jana Sangh, that India should produce nuclear weapons. The Jana Sangh first made the demand in Parliament in 1962 (Perkovich 1999: 46), immediately after the border war with China and nearly two years before the first Chinese nuclear test. M.S. Golwalkar (Guruji), the second head of the RSS and the principal ideologue of Hindu nationalism, described the manufacture of an atom bomb as an imperative (1980: 429). It subsequently featured regularly in BJP election manifestos – the 1998 manifesto committed it to 'exercise the option to induct nuclear weapons'.

Yet India's adoption of nuclear weapons was not the product of an aberrant Hindu nationalist obsession. Itty Abraham (1998) and George Perkovich (1999) have traced the genesis and development of the Indian nuclear programme, the oldest outside Europe and North America (India's first, British assisted, research reactor became operational in 1956). In the post-Cold War world of the 1990s, several developments contributed to stimulating India's nuclear programme.

The fact was that Prime Minister Vajpayee, unlike his immediate predecessors, and despite heading an unstable new coalition government, had few qualms about taking the final decisive step. Having been a leading member of the Hindu nationalist movement – that had for four decades favoured India's adoption of nuclear weapons – he did not share the moral scruples that had arguably inhibited INC leaders since Nehru. Moreover, unlike other cherished Hindu nationalist fetishes, most notably the construction of a temple to the god Rama on the site of the Babri mosque destroyed by Hindu militants in 1992, national security was relatively uncontroversial as far as the NDA was concerned. Vajpayee could afford to act decisively without risking the survival of his Government.

The other politicians privy to the nuclear test decision also harboured few misgivings on the subject. Home Minister L.K. Advani had favoured the development of nuclear weapons as president of the Jana Sangh in 1974, and of the BJP in 1987 (Perkovich 1999: 179, 282). Brajesh Mishra, Vajpayee's Principal Secretary, later said in an interview, 'I have always felt that you cannot in today's world be counted for something without going nuclear' (Swaminathan 2003: 2). Perhaps most revealing is what Jaswant Singh, who was deputed to conduct the post-tests bilateral talks with the US before being appointed Minister for External Affairs, had to say. His article in the prominent, policy oriented US international relations journal, *Foreign Affairs*, was entitled, 'Against Nuclear Apartheid' (1998). The reference to the colour discrimination institutionalised in erstwhile apartheid South Africa reflected an abiding sense among Indian leaders that the existing nuclear non-proliferation regime was influenced by a crude notion of racial superiority.

But it was not the inequity of the Non Proliferation Treaty (NPT) that most exercised BJP leaders, it was the need to assert India's claim to be considered a significant power in the world. In the immediate aftermath of the 1998 nuclear tests, Vajpayee proclaimed, in uncharacteristically crude terms, 'We have . . . a big bomb' (Bidwai and Vanaik 2000: 103n16). Later, in a statement to India's Parliament on 27 May 1998, he declared, '[i]t is India's due, the right of one-sixth of human kind' (1998).

It was the conjuncture of the shift in the distribution of power in the post-Cold War world and the advent in government of Hindu nationalists with a predilection to follow realist perspectives in making foreign policy that caused India's abandonment of four decades of nuclear ambiguity. The agenda put before the Indian electorate by the victorious BJP-led NDA in 1999 explicitly linked the adoption of a nuclear deterrent to the changed global conditions – a 'unipolar world' and the 'recently inaugurated era of global inequality and increased vulnerability' (NDA 1999).

Hitherto, India's restraint, the product of a mixture of moral reservation and strategic choice, had been unparalleled among any of the nuclear-weapon states and, despite the tests, the NDA Government too appeared to have opted for a cautious approach. Although a Draft

Nuclear Doctrine, drawn up by the new National Security Advisory Board, was released in August 1999, it was never formally adopted, and India only unveiled a Nuclear Command Authority in January 2003, more than two years after Pakistan. Ashley Tellis argues that the Vajpayee Government has chosen to keep India's nuclear weapons posture as one of a '*force-in-being*, that is, a deterrent consisting of available, but dispersed, components that are capable of being constituted into usable weapons systems' (2002: 63, emphasis by the authors).

Given that the 1998 tests and, indeed, India's entire nuclear programme, were not driven primarily by urgent security considerations, such a posture is logical. Its architects also see it as the one best serving India's purposes in an international system still in post-Cold War flux.

India and the US

India's efforts to adapt to the post-Cold War world focused particularly on relations with the US. Despite the public braggadocio, these efforts actually intensified after the 1998 nuclear tests. One of Vajpayee first actions was to write to all the leaders of the permanent members of the UN Security Council (except China), as well as those of Germany, Japan and Canada. His personal letter to President Clinton was leaked by Washington to the New York Times (*New York Times* 1998). Obliquely justifying the tests because of the supposed threat posed by China and its assistance of Pakistan, it nevertheless offered 'close cooperation' in promoting nuclear disarmament.

Although US President Clinton still imposed sanctions, describing the tests as a 'terrible mistake' (Krishnaswami 1998: 3), several analysts have argued that they provided the stimulus for a closer engagement between the US and India. For instance, Dennis Kux argued that it 'helped lance the boil of nonproliferation that had previously infected bilateral relations' (2002: 20). Both Stephen Cohen (2001: 292) and C. Raja Mohan (2003: 90) also suggested that it was a gamble that paid off, causing the US to take India seriously and engage with it in a more sustained manner than it had ever done before.

A number of factors helped to facilitate the perceptible shift away from the estrangement of the Cold War (Kux 1993). One was the greater readiness of some of the chief BJP policy makers, such as Jaswant Singh, deputed to conduct nine rounds of talks with US Deputy Secretary of State Strobe Talbott between June 1998 and early 2000, to countenance a closer relationship with the US. This was endorsed by Vajpayee who, less than four months after the US imposition of sanctions, declared in a speech – while attending the UN General Assembly session in New York in September 1998 – that India and the US were 'natural allies' (Mohan 2003: 49).

The ideological shift away from Nehruvian nonalignment, encouraged by the reality of post-Cold War American dominance, was buttressed by economic and social changes in the relationship between the world's biggest democracies. In the 1990s, Indo-US trade grew by 264 per cent (Garver 2002: 10). Thanks mainly to information technology-related sales, the balance of trade shifted greatly in India's favour; by 2002 Indian exports to the US had reached $11.7 billion, while imports stood at $3.7 billion (Bhatt 2003: 11). Though it barely makes the top 20 of the US's trading partners, the US market accounted for over a fifth of India's exports (Baru 2002: 2591) and, as in the case of the other states, this invests the relationship with Washington with a particular importance.

Another factor in promoting closer ties has been the rise over the past two or three decades of a mainly well-educated and wealthy body of Indian immigrants in the US (the 2000 US census listed 1.7 million) (Kux 2002: 21). This is likely to grow – India was, after Mexico, the second main source of legal migrants to the US in 2001–02 (*The New Indian Express* 2002). A quarter of the graduates of the elite Indian Institutes of Technology go to the US and Indian Americans own more than two-fifths of the new technology start-ups in Silicon Valley (Cohen 2001: 117). The growth of such business links has had domestic political repercussions in both countries. The bipartisan India caucus in the US Congress has nearly 160 members, while in India, the BJP numbers many US-based and educated Indians and their relatives among its leading supporters and contributors.

Such bilateral factors, as well as the lack of support from other powers like Russia, France and Britain, led to the quiet lifting of many sanctions. In the summer of 1999, US backing for India's demand that Pakistan withdraws its forces from Kargil and end border hostilities helped reassure India of Washington's commitment to rebuilding relations. The process quickened after President Clinton's successful visit to India in March 2000, postponed because of the 1998 tests and the first by a US President in over two decades, and a subsequent visit to Washington by Vajpayee. Remaining sanctions were removed by Clinton's successor, George W. Bush, on 22 September 2001 in response to the cooperation offered by both India and Pakistan following the 11 September terrorist attacks in the US.

The advent of the Bush Administration led to a marked improvement in Indo-US relations. This was helped by the new administration's effective abandonment of the Comprehensive Test Ban Treaty (CTBT), an issue that had troubled Indo-US relations since the mid-1990s, and positive statements by a succession of new US officials. Before Bush's election, National Security Advisor Condoleeza Rice had already observed that India might in the future serve as a useful counterpoise to Chinese ambitions in Asia (2000: 56), rising to the bait that Vajpayee had dangled before Clinton after the 1998 tests. The surprising receptiveness shown by the NDA Government to the plans for ballistic missile defence unveiled by President Bush in May 2001 contributed to the warming of relations. India calculated, given its concerns about Pakistan and China, that it had nothing to lose and maybe something to gain by welcoming the shift from deterrence to credible defence.

After the onset of the post-September 11th US-led global 'war on terror', the security relationship between India and the US developed further. India's rapid offer of full cooperation was useful to the US in ensuring the cooperation of Pakistan in the campaign against al-Qaeda and the Taliban in Afghanistan launched in October 2001. Despite the renewal of Washington's close military relationship with Islamabad – coupled with crises in Indo-Pakistani relations coming to a head in December 2001 and again in June 2002 over the alleged infiltration of Pakistani-based Muslim militants into India – Indo-US security cooperation continued to deepen. The National Security Strategy released by President Bush identified India, along with Russia and China, as a potential great power, and one with which US interests required a strong relationship. It added

> while in the past these concerns [over India's nuclear and missile programs, and the pace of economic reforms] may have dominated our thinking about India, today we start with a view of India as a growing world power with which we have common strategic interests.
>
> (National Security Strategy of the United States of America
> 2002, 27)

Such language played well with Indian leaders, and especially the Hindu nationalists. Like Russian leaders from the Soviet era down to Vladimir Putin, the Bush administration realised the importance of treating India with deference. A steady stream of US officials, from Secretary of State Colin Powell and Defence Secretary Donald Rumsfeld downwards, visited the country (nearly 100 in 2002 alone). President Bush and Vice President Dick Cheney made a point of cultivating personal relationships with Vajpayee and his deputy, L.K. Advani.

A revived India–US Defence Policy Group met three times between December 2001 and August 2003 (Krishnaswami 2003: 9). The two countries' armed forces held several rounds of joint exercises in both India and the US and the Indian navy escorted US naval assets through the Straits of Malacca (Mohan 2003: 236). For the first time in over three decades, India started to buy significant amounts of US weapons. In May 2003, the US also cleared Israel's transfer of Phalcon AWACS (Airborne Warning and Control Systems) to India under a $2 billion defence deal reached in 2001 (Aneja 2003: 9).

The emergence of Israel as India's second biggest weapons supplier (after Russia), and biggest Middle Eastern trading partner – less than a decade after full diplomatic relations between the two countries were established in 1992 – marked another significant turnabout in India's foreign relations since the end of the Cold War. One of only three non-Muslim states to oppose the 1947 UN resolution partitioning Palestine, India had been a stalwart supporter of the Palestinian struggle, although both the BJP and pro-Indian members of the US Congress sought to bring about a change in its position (Chiriyankandath 1989, 1991). The rapid expansion in Indo-Israeli ties after 1998 reflected the Vajpayee government's emphasis on *realpolitik* and national interest as the watchwords of its foreign policy.

South Asia

Relations with Pakistan dominated the regional foreign policy of the NDA Government. These relations were exceptionally erratic after 1998. Moments of tense confrontation contrasted with interludes of apparently promising engagement. Vajpayee made several bold attempts to improve relations with Pakistan but these were not entirely successful and engagement was not a consistent theme in Indian policy. This dualism in policy was to some extent dictated by events that were beyond India's control. However, the alternation between engagement and hardline policies also suited the political needs of the NDA and, in particular, the BJP. The BJP was quick to exploit the nuclear tests and the Kargil war against Pakistan during the 1999 general election campaign. Yet, if five years later, peace with Pakistan proved to be possible as the result of bold statesmanship, the BJP would have been able to project Vajpayee as a leader of historic importance.

The policy of the NDA has to be understood in the context of the historically poor relations with Pakistan (Ganguly 2002). The disputed territory of Kashmir has achieved totemic status in the conflict and tension between the two states. India has a jaded view of Pakistan as an unstable state that is prone to use force to resolve political problems. Pakistan is also viewed as obsessed with the question of Kashmir, pursuing it by waging a proxy war while using any available international forum to denounce India. Finally, Pakistan's inflexibility over the issue means that other negotiations and initiatives, both bilateral and multilateral ones involving all states in South Asia, are stalled. For its part, Pakistan considers India to be a state with hegemonic designs in South Asia that necessarily threatens the national security of the smaller states in the region (the 1971 war is represented as the deliberate dismemberment of the Muslim homeland in South Asia).

Towards the end of the short life of the first NDA administration (1998–99), Vajpayee made his well-publicised trip to Lahore. After several rounds of talks an agreement was signed in Lahore on 21 February 1999. Among other things, it set out the basis on which Kashmir and the issue of nuclear security could be discussed. However, the Lahore Declaration was vitiated by the Pakistani incursion in the Kargil sector in May 1999.

The diplomatic fallout of the armed conflict was favourable to India.

President Clinton personally intervened to set the conditions under which Pakistan would withdraw back over the Line of Control. China too regarded the incursion as a reckless piece of adventurism on the part of its longstanding ally. Following the Kargil conflict, India settled on a more aggressive approach towards Pakistan, and rejected diplomatic engagement. The October 1999 coup, that installed Pervez Musharraf as leader of Pakistan, provided a further advantage to the hardliners on the Indian side. An ailing economy completed the picture of Pakistan as a failing state in contrast to an image of India enjoying democratic stability and robust economic growth.

In early 2001, though, Vajpayee was in a position to take a more conciliatory line. A unilateral ceasefire was declared in Kashmir in November 2000 and extended a number of times in 2001. This prepared the way for discussions with various groups in Kashmir and opened the possibility of renewed contact with Pakistan, culminating in the Agra summit in July 2001. However, a series of personal discussions between Prime Minister Vajpayee and President Musharraf failed to produce an agreement. The Indian perception was that Musharraf wanted to keep Kashmir at the top of the agenda, refusing to give up support for the militants in Kashmir and unprepared to explore less contentious areas. The final sticking point, the status of the 1972 Simla agreement, demonstrated the importance of the historical dimension to the problem (Mohan 2003: 178–81). The NDA cabinet backed the traditional Indian preference for remaining with the Simla agreement, which keeps Kashmir a bilateral issue, while Pakistan wished to abandon it and explore a multilateral process.

India's attempt to isolate Pakistan was completely destroyed by the US response to the 11 September attacks. The US considered Pakistan to be a key ally in the 'war on terror'. As well as gaining international recognition Pakistan received substantial US aid and debt relief. India attempted to nullify this gain by picking up the theme of Pakistani support for acts of terrorism inside India. When a group of gunmen launched an audacious attack on the Indian parliament buildings on 13 December 2001, India claimed that Pakistan was culpable, and demanded strong action against militants based in Pakistan. In order to establish its resolve, India began to mobilise troops along its border with Pakistan. Further mobilisation took place in May 2002 raising serious international concern about the possibility of war between the two declared nuclear states. India reduced its military presence along the border in October 2002. However, relations between the two states were so frayed that the January 2003 SAARC summit was postponed. In a final reversion to engagement, just as the BJP had decided to call an early general election, a delicately worded agreement to resume talks between India and Pakistan was issued at the SAARC summit in January 2004 (Katyal 2004).

The NDA did not make the progress with regional cooperation that it had promised in its 1999 manifesto. The rules of the SAARC stress unanimity in decision making and act as a reassurance mechanism. India will not be outvoted if the smaller states combine and the smaller states are able to retain their autonomy in the organisation. This makes it difficult for the SAARC to produce institutional structures or reach agreements on anything but the most minor issues. Its most important function is to provide a venue for leaders to meet informally and without the burden of public expectation. The annual summit of heads of state is therefore a key feature of the organisation. On this indicator, the NDA had little to show during its combined six years in office. The tenth summit in July 1998 was held shortly after the May nuclear tests and was predictably tense as India and Pakistan eyed each other suspiciously. The smaller states expressed their discomfort about the tests. Pakistan proposed a new approach to security management in the region, but support for the original SAARC constitution, that contentious issues are to be resolved bilaterally, was reasserted by the other member states. There were no significant formal achievements at the summit and the proposed South Asian Free Trade Area (SAFTA) planned for inauguration in 2001 was postponed (*Frontline* 1998).

The eleventh summit of SAARC was scheduled to take place in November 1999 in Kathmandu. This meeting was postponed following the military coup in Pakistan in October. India refused to attend and, under SAARC rules, a summit cannot go ahead if one state does not attend. When the summit finally took place in January 2002, the issue of terrorism dominated the agenda. While deploring terrorism, President Musharraf argued that the causes of terrorism should not be overlooked. In response, Prime Minister Vajpayee complained that Pakistan continued to support groups perpetrating terrorist attacks on India. The smaller states raised questions about the efficacy of the organisation. There was no substantive progress on the SAFTA (*Frontline* 2002).

Tensions between India and Pakistan once again resulted in the postponement of the twelfth summit of SAARC scheduled for January 2003 (*The Hindu* 2002b). When the summit was finally held in Islamabad in January 2004, it coincided with a thaw in relations between India and Pakistan. As well as the announcement of bilateral talks between India and Pakistan mentioned above, the SAFTA agreement was signed. Under this agreement, tariff barriers should be substantially reduced by 2006. A protocol on the extradition of terrorists was also signed at the summit (*Frontline* 2004d).

The expansion of trade is a positive development, but the foreign policy of the NDA did not enhance the capacity of the SAARC. Nor did the NDA Government make substantial progress with its relations with the other states of South Asia. Relations with Pakistan dominated India's regional foreign policy, while relations with smaller states tended to be crisis driven (Mohan 2003: 244).

A distinctive Indian path

While the confrontation with Pakistan served to underline the importance for India of its new ties with the US, it would be erroneous to assume that India was transformed into an unquestioning ally of the world's sole superpower. The attitude it took towards the US-led invasion and occupation of Iraq in 2003 demonstrated this. Maintaining a low-key opposition to the US drive against Iraq, in the months before the war Vajpayee joined the visiting Russian President, Vladimir Putin, and French Prime Minister, Jean-Pierre Raffarin, in opposing any unilateral action undertaken without the approval of the United Nations. Yet, addressing the Non-Aligned Movement summit in Kuala Lumpur, Vajpayee called for full Iraqi compliance with UN Security Council Resolution 1441 on the elimination of alleged weapons of mass destruction facilities and said 'objectivity – and not rhetoric – should govern our actions' (*The Hindu* 2003i: 9).

After lengthy discussions between the Government and opposition parties favouring a stronger line, the Lok Sabha finally passed a unanimous resolution on 8 April 2003, on the eve of the fall of Baghdad. The resolution deplored the US-led attack on Iraq, describing the change of regime through military action as unacceptable. It further demanded a quick withdrawal of coalition forces and the reconstruction of Iraq under UN supervision ensuring the sovereignty of Iraq (*The New Indian Express* 2003). During the parliamentary debate, External Affairs Minister Yashwant Sinha, defending the Government's position, said it would continue to be guided by pragmatism and national interest and wanted its ties with the US to flourish as 'Relations between countries are not based on a single issue' (*The New Indian Express* 2003).

India continued to maintain a cautious approach. In June 2003, President Bush personally raised the US request for the dispatch of Indian troops to help police Iraq with the visiting Indian Deputy Premier, L.K. Advani. The BJP's coalition partners in the NDA agreed to leave a decision on the response to Vajpayee. However, Sonia Gandhi, the leader of the parliamentary opposition, had already communicated, in a letter to the Prime Minister, the INC's total opposition to the deployment of Indian troops without a UN Security Council mandate for a peacekeeping force. Within the NDA Government, Finance Minister Jaswant Singh was rumoured to be the only prominent voice in favour of sending Indian troops to Iraq. After a meeting of the Cabinet Committee on Security on 14 July 2003, External Affairs Minister Sinha confirmed that India could consider the deployment of troops, only with an explicit UN mandate for the purpose. He added that '[o]ur longer-term national interest ... as well as our growing dialogue and strengthened ties with the U.S. have been key elements in this consideration' (Baruah 2003: 9).

Beyond Iraq, in eschewing the strident political rhetoric of old fashioned nonalignment, India sought to cooperate with other big states of the global South in negotiating forums like the WTO. India played an important role at the 2001 ministerial meeting in Doha. Along with Brazil and South Africa it lobbied for, and achieved, a declaration that endorsed the right of member countries to produce copies of patent drugs in situations of 'extreme urgency'. India also secured a postponement of negotiations on investment and competition policy (Panagariya 2002). Ahead of the September 2003 WTO ministerial meeting in Cancun, India convened a meeting of trade representatives of developing countries in Geneva in May 2003 in order to coordinate strategy (*The Hindu* 2003a: 11). It also joined Brazil and South Africa in the June 2003 Brasilia Declaration to launch a trilateral Dialogue Forum to deepen cooperation, not just in multilateral trade negotiations, but also on a broad range of subjects from reform of the UN to defence and technology. These three countries eventually forged an alliance on agricultural issues together with 11 other leading developing countries, including China, Argentina and Thailand (*The Hindu* 2003d: 10). The alliance formed the core of a so-called Group of 20 (G-20) that opposed the retention of huge farm subsidies by the European Union and the US and successfully blocked a new round of trade liberalisation at Cancun.

The impact of the NDA

We have uncovered some evidence of state level influence on policy, but the NDA did not advance beyond the innovations of the United Front period in office in 1996 and 1997. In terms of the impact of the NDA on foreign policy making, what is surprising is that the states have not had more influence. The standard centralised model of policy making, with some subtle modifications, continued to be the pattern. An assertive Prime Minister assisted by an activist Principal Secretary was able to shape foreign policy at the centre. Though the step up in defence spending after the Kargil conflict ran against the trend of modest defence spending in the preceding decade, the policy of the NDA towards Pakistan was not strikingly different from earlier periods. While relations between the two states were frequently poor, the NDA Government did not take a more hardline position towards Pakistan.

On ideological grounds alone, one would have expected that a BJP-dominated government would have a consistently aggressive policy towards Pakistan. The views of RSS activists on foreign policy are uncompromising. Pakistan and Bangladesh are regarded as Muslim majority states that are hostile to India. A number of senior BJP cabinet ministers – though significantly not Jaswant Singh or Yashwant Sinha – continued to be RSS members throughout the tenure of the NDA. Ironically, the central role of the Prime Minister in foreign policy formulation was a crucial factor in this outcome. The evidence from the Janata Party Government (1977–79) demonstrated that Vajpayee had long favoured positive engagement in foreign policy, and when circumstances were favourable, the Prime Minister reverted to his default position. That at the local level members of the *Sangh Parivar* depicted policy in chauvinistic terms is a different matter.

In the post-Cold War world, India was 'neither bad enough, nor good enough, nor powerful enough to yet be a dominant player' (Mehta 2003: 3175). The role that the NDA sought to carve out was one more unambiguously based on a pragmatic assessment of national interest and the realities of a world in which one state (the US) commands unprecedented power. While India showed itself prepared to shed old economic and political shibboleths when necessary, the NDA foreign policy remained cautious and tempered by both past legacies and the pressure to seek a basic domestic consensus on major issues. The cultivation of the US did not prevent India from pursuing its long-term interest in seeing the eventual emergence of a multipolar world. This is an interest it shared with its old ally, Russia, which still remains its main arms supplier. The NDA Government also sought to engage with other states, such as France, China and Iran. After 2001, Prime Minister Vajpayee exchanged official visits with the leaders of all these countries. By 2002, the foreign ministers of India, China and Russia initiated the practice of holding an informal trilateral meeting during the annual session of the UN General Assembly.

The NDA continued to make the transition towards a more pragmatic, and obviously self-interested, foreign policy. However, the ease with which India can act in international politics rests on the interdependent factors of economic growth, political stability and regional peace. The NDA had only mixed success in the last two areas. Its attempt to create a gap between a democratic and stable India and a failing Pakistani state was undermined by episodes such as the appalling anti-Muslim violence in Gujarat in 2002, for which many held the BJP state government responsible. Finally, the conflict with Pakistan and the ongoing militancy in Kashmir still served to block Indian ambitions. Resolving these linked problems remains the greatest foreign policy challenge.

11 The NDA and national security

Apurba Kundu

Introduction

In 2002, India's National Security Council secretariat produced a National Security Index (NSI), which ranked the country as the tenth most powerful on earth (National Security Council Secretariat 2002). China and Pakistan, perceived as India's main security threats, were ranked third and twenty-eighth, respectively. The NSI is a composite measurement of five indices; human development, research and development, GDP, defence expenditure and population, each of which includes a number of (sometimes weighted) sub-indices based on commonly accepted reference data compiled by international organisations and/or non-partisan research institutions. Although the NSI is notable for its acknowledgement that India's national security depends on both its socio-economic and military strengths, it fails to take into consideration the country's political power, both internal and external. Any state's domestic security can only be maintained if it has a political system supported by the citizenry. Similarly, its international security is more solid if the country enjoys a moral authority – in addition to its socio-economic and military prowess – which enables it to achieve its aims by attracting others to its cause. Ultimately, the security of India is dependent not just on easily quantifiable factors such as literacy rates, GDP adjusted for purchasing power parity and ballistic missiles deployed, but also on the ideological leadership of its elected government, which lends the country a sense of identity at home and abroad.

Yet, despite the importance of the socio-economic, political and moral aspects of national security, ultimately, the state is a body of armed men and, as such, the classic indicator of India's security is the strength and ability of its armed forces. Since independence in 1947, India's armed forces have been involved in a number of challenges to the country's national security. Domestically, these have included the (sometimes-forcible) incorporation of the Princely States, left-wing terrorism in Andhra Pradesh and West Bengal and armed insurrections in the Northeast, Assam, Punjab and Kashmir. International challenges to national security have led to armed conflicts with Portugal (over Goa), China (over

Ladakh and the Northeast frontier area) and Pakistan (over Bangladesh and Kashmir). The Indian armed forces also have sent an IPKF to Sri Lanka, prevented the overthrow of the government of the Maldives and participated in almost 40 UN peacekeeping activities throughout the world. Given the ongoing violence in Assam, the Northeast and Kashmir, and disputed international borders on its north and west, the Indian armed forces will continue to serve as crucial guarantors and defenders of the country's national security.

Despite the numerous domestic and international challenges to India's security, successive national administrations have given little serious attention to military matters, especially in terms of the strategic role of the armed forces as a tool of government. With few exceptions, decisions dealing with challenges to national security have been reactive, tactical or confined to the prime minister and an informal coterie of advisors rather than proactive, strategic, and/or the result of a formal consultative process within the governing party, the armed forces and non-governmental experts. In a marked departure from previous national governments, those led by the BJP sought to address national security issues both proactively and strategically in line with the party's philosophy of achieving a strong India.

This chapter begins by examining the strategic vision of the BJP. It then analyses how this vision led the BJP to make India an overt nuclear weapons state in 1998, and how this status affected the government's actions in the Kargil conflict of 1999. This is followed by a closer examination of national security strategy under the BJP-led NDA, and how this administration responded to the near-war situation which developed between India and Pakistan in the spring–summer of 2002. The chapter then conceptualises the subsequent national security of the NDA as 'strong at home, engaged abroad' as shown by the military's continued deployment on peacekeeping duties, defence spending on external and internal security, and defence cooperation with other countries. The chapter concludes by asking if India, given the logic of maintaining a viable nuclear deterrent and the planned introduction of weapons systems qualitatively better than its strategic neighbours, may be in danger of creating a renewed arms race with Pakistan and China.

The strategic vision of the BJP

Although India's armed forces have had to combat numerous external and internal challenges to the country's national security, successive administrations have seldom given serious attention to the strategic role of the military as a tool of government. This failure may be traced to the history of Indian civil–military relations which, from colonial times onwards, has always insisted on the strict separation of civilian and soldier. Moreover, since Independence, successive governments in India always returned to the idea that development and diplomacy were better at protecting the country's national security than military force. As such, national security decision making at the highest level remained *ad hoc*, dependent more on informal personal access to the prime minister than on a formal hierarchy of strategic thought and analysis.

By the mid-1990s, the cumulative effect of Indian national security strategy, such as existed, was argued to have failed the country. In *Defending India*, a seminal work on national security by Jaswant Singh (former army captain, and later Defence and then Finance Minister in the NDA), the author asks:

> What ... has been the lasting legacy of the past 50 years? An absence of certainties in security-related issues; no established land boundaries; an absence of a secure geopolitical environment; a devaluation of India's voice in global affairs and worrisomely, not even a beginning of any institutional framework for conceptualizing and managing the country's defence.
>
> (1999: 268)

Singh's sentiments were to find prominence when many of his ideas were incorporated into the BJP manifesto for the 1998 general election.

In the 1998 general election, the BJP campaigned against the previous centre-left United Front administration and the INC using the ideology of *Hindutva* that envisaged a great India as a militarily powerful India. Their 1998 election manifesto stated that the 'frenetic pace of military expansion and modernization by some of our neighbours' (Bharatiya Janata Party 1998) had not been addressed by the country's previous administrations, argued that the defence budget had been declining in real terms, and listed numerous defence projects involving aircraft, submarines and missiles that had been delayed for lack of adequate funds. The 1998 BJP manifesto committed the party to a specific list of strategic, organisation and deployment options, including:

* the establishment of a National Security Council to 'constantly analyze security, political and economic threats and render continuous advice to the Government ... [as well as to] undertake India's first-ever Strategic Defence Review';
* a re-evaluation of India's nuclear policy with a view to 'exercise the option to induct nuclear weapons'; and
* expediting the development of the *Agni* series of ballistic missiles.

The manifesto also included a series of promises to improve the lot of the armed forces' personnel, both serving and retired (see below), as well as to allow the country's security forces 'a free hand to deal with armed insurgency and terrorism' (Bharatiya Janata Party 1998).

India goes nuclear

Within a few weeks of the NDA's victory in the 1998 elections, the new administration demonstrated the seriousness of its national security intentions when, on 11 May 1998, Prime Minister Atul Behari Vajpayee publicly announced that three nuclear devices, one of them thermonuclear, had been tested at Pokhran in the Rajasthan desert. Two days later, another series of nuclear devices were tested. Whereas the first series of devices tested included a hydrogen 'city buster' bomb, the second were quantitatively smaller, indicating, perhaps, the intention to develop battlefield nuclear weapons. A day after the second series of tests, Vajpayee declared 'India is now a nuclear weapons state' (Chengappa 2000: 433).

In fulfilling their election manifesto's pledge to induct nuclear weapons, the BJP realised long-standing Indian preparations to go overtly nuclear.[1] The strategic thinking behind Vajpayee's decision may be traced to a variety of arguments, including immediate domestic political considerations. Had the tests been timed to overshadow the domestic machinations of erstwhile BJP ally but supreme political opportunist Jayalalitha, leader of the AIADMK? No; it later emerged that Vajpayee had given the go-ahead for the Pokhran nuclear tests on 10 April 1998, just three weeks after he had been sworn in as prime minister. Nonetheless, while Vajpayee may not have foreseen the exact nature of this particular political threat, it could be argued that the BJP, mindful that their slim majority in the Lok Sabha would be vulnerable, pushed for the nuclear test so as to have a strong campaign issue in any subsequent general election. Indeed, Vajpayee had authorised a nuclear weapon test during the BJP's short-lived two-weeks in power in the spring of 1996, for much the same reason – but not been in power long enough to see it through (Chengappa 2000: 31–2, 395; Cohen 2001: 177–8).

That the BJP perceived nuclear tests to be a vote winner may be traced to its belief that demonstrable military power was an essential component in creating a great India. Nuclear weapons were argued to be a currency-of-power without which India would never be taken seriously on the world stage. Indeed, successive Indian administrations had resisted signing the nuclear NPT and CTBT as enshrining a discriminatory nuclear order. If the permanent five members of the UN Security Council insisted on retaining their nuclear weapons for national security purposes, how could they deny India the same rationale? Thus, at a meeting the day before the Lok Sabha first met after the 1998 tests, Vajpayee told BJP MPs that India was 'now among the great powers' (Dettman 2001: 41). The BJP also saw nuclear weapons as a source of pride, especially in terms of its public image. Following the tests, Vajpayee explained how 'the greatest meaning of the tests is that they have given Indian *shakti* [power], they have given India strength, and they have given India self-confidence' (Chengappa 2000: 36).

A second argument accepted by the BJP was that the overt display of nuclear weapons is essential to ensure national security. Previous strategists had argued that a policy of 'recessed deterrence' (Cohen 2001: 165) – an undeclared capability to assemble and deploy nuclear weapons at short notice – was sufficient to induce doubt in the minds of potential enemies. However, the logistical and command-and-control shortcomings of this policy were increasingly thought unworkable. On 28 January 1987, Dr Abdul Qadeer Khan, the driving force behind Pakistan's nuclear weapons programme, told an interviewer that his country had nuclear weapons and would use them to counter Indian aggression. Afterwards, recessed deterrence came to be seen as an anomaly, and perhaps it was now best if India openly declared its nuclear weapons capabilities. Further tests would enhance the effectiveness of its nuclear weapons, allow the development of effective command-and-control mechanisms, enable the armed forces to acquire suitable launch systems, and exploit the knowledge and expertise of a generation of Indian nuclear scientists and engineers nearing the end of their working lives. Most importantly, an India openly equipped with nuclear weapons would prevent further nuclear threats emanating from Pakistan, as well as other countries including China and the US. The country would 'acquire nuclear weapons in order to pressure the nuclear "haves" to disarm and to protect itself against nuclear blackmail. Indians could thus have their nuclear cake and eat it ... [too]' (Cohen 2001: 169). In early May 1998, Defence Minister George Fernandes began publicly preparing the ground for the Pokhran nuclear tests by citing China as India's 'potential threat number one' (*The Times of India* 1998a) in a television interview and a series of remarks to reporters. Only days after the tests, however, Home Minister L.K. Advani variously stated that 'India's nuclear weapons capability showed the country's resolve to deal firmly and strongly with Pakistan's hostile designs and activities in Kashmir', and it was 'Pakistan's clandestine preparations that forced us to take the path of nuclear deterrence' (Dettman 2001: 40).

Domestically, the 1998 Pokhran nuclear tests played very well. There were enthusiastic pro-nuclear test demonstrations throughout the country, and a public opinion poll conducted in India's main metropolitan cities (Bangalore, Chennai, Delhi, Hyderabad, Kolkata and Mumbai) the day following the first series of tests found that 91 per cent of respondents supported the tests, 82 per cent wanted the government to now build nuclear weapons and 67 per cent felt the BJP-led coalition was 'strong and would safeguard their security' (Dettman 2001: 41). Indian newspapers were also supportive, as were almost all India's major political parties, save the CPM and the CPI-ML which were upset that a potential threat from China was being used to justify the tests. The INC which, as stated above, had twice come close to testing in the 1980s, could hardly avoid praising the Government's actions. In a meeting of the Congress Working Committee, INC leader Sonia Gandhi stated she 'would like to place on record ... the pride we feel in the achievement of our nuclear scientists and engineers.... The nuclear question is a national matter, not a partisan one. On this every Indian stands united' (Dettman 2001: 42).

Domestic approval of the Pokhran nuclear tests was not shared internationally. Many western leaders condemned India's overt display. America's 1994 *Nuclear Proliferation Prevention Act* obliged US President Bill Clinton's administration to impose economic sanctions and all American economic aid, save that earmarked for humanitarian purposes, was halted. The Act also stipulated that the US oppose future World Bank loans to India. Japan, at the time the main source of public and private investment to India, took similar actions, and economic sanctions also were imposed by many western countries.

Most worryingly, despite huge international pressure, Pakistan declared itself an overt nuclear power by testing six such devices just weeks after India's tests. Although its economy was already in a parlous state, and the government knew the country would face international economic sanctions, domestic public opinion and heavy lobbying from the armed forces eventually convinced Prime Minister Nawaz Sharif that Pakistan must match the Indian tests.

The overt demonstration of its nuclear weapons capability meant India had to elucidate a strategy for their deployment and use. Vajpayee declared a 'no first strike policy', but little further information was forthcoming as to the exact nature of any command-and-control structure for nuclear weapons or, indeed, to what extent the Government intended to weaponise its nuclear capabilities, although there was immediate talk of a minimum deterrent to be deployed in a triad of air, land and sea weapons delivery systems.

To address these questions and other national security issues, the Government created a new National Security Council (NSC) in November 1998. This was a crucial development as, for the first time in independent India, the Government now had a civilian hierarchy of expertise to coordinate defence thinking and advise on all matters of national security. The NSC consists of several tiers. At cabinet level, it is made up of the prime minister, deputy chairman of planning, the respective ministers of Home, Finance, External Affairs and Defence, the respective military chiefs of staff and a new national security advisor (NSA) – who also serves as principle private secretary to the prime minister. The NSA, in turn, is served by a secretariat and advisory board. Indeed, it was this national security advisory board (NSAB), made up of almost 30 former officials, academics and journalists, which was charged with writing a *Draft Nuclear Doctrine.*

The Kargil conflict

Political events soon overtook debates on India's nuclear strategic doctrine. On 30 December 1998, Defence Minister Fernandes dismissed Navy

Chief Admiral Vishnu Bhagwat from his post on the grounds of insubordination. This, the first time a serving services chief had ever been forced out, was seized upon by the INC as an issue to try to force the NDA out of power. The opposition was soon joined in their efforts by BJP-coalition partner AIADMK leader Jayalalitha as a means to ensure her freedom from numerous prosecutions hanging over her head. Their joint efforts culminated in the government losing a vote of confidence by one vote on 17 April 1999. After efforts by the INC to cobble together a majority coalition failed, the President of India asked the BJP to lead a caretaker government until fresh elections could be held over August–September.

Before its fall, the direction the BJP-led coalition intended to pursue in terms of nuclear weaponisation had become obvious. On 11 April 1999, the government kept another of its 1998 manifesto pledges by testing an updated version of the *Agni* ballistic missile capable of carrying nuclear weapons to all parts of Pakistan, interior China and even Beijing and Shanghai with a reduced payload. After the successful test, Vajpayee had informal consultations with his three service chiefs who indicated that they were 'keen that the nuclear option be made a working reality' (Chengappa 2000: 3).

Before fresh elections could take place, the caretaker BJP-led coalition government found itself embroiled in yet another armed conflict with Pakistan over Kashmir. Conscious, perhaps, that a confrontation between the two nuclear weapons states could lead to millions of deaths and the radioactive poisoning of vast areas of India and Pakistan, Vajpayee had become the first Indian prime minister in over ten years to visit Pakistan when he travelled overland on 20 February 1999 to meet with Prime Minister Nawaz Sharif. This 'bus diplomacy' culminated in the *Lahore Declaration.* This reiterated the two countries' belief in 'universal nuclear disarmament and non-proliferation' and their intention to 'resolve all issues, including the issue of Jammu and Kashmir' while remaining committed to the implementation of the *Simla Agreement* (which had recognised the Line-of-Control, or LoC, in Kashmir) 'in letter and in spirit' (United States Institute of Peace 1999). India and Pakistan would also pursue other confidence-building measures designed to reduce the possibility of armed confrontation between the now overt nuclear adversaries.

However, at the same time, the Pakistan Army was engaged in a campaign of armed infiltration across the LoC into the Kargil sector of Indian-administered Kashmir. Surprised at making little or no contact with Indian forces (who, as usual practice during the winter months, had withdrawn to more hospitable positions lower down the slopes), elements of the army's Northern Light Infantry and their *mujahedeen* allies soon found themselves well entrenched in commanding heights deep inside Indian-administered Kashmir. Debate continues as to the exact tactical and strategic motives of the Pakistan Army in launching the infiltration. Was it to retaliate for India's continuing presence in Siachen, scupper the nascent Indo-Pak peace process, re-energise what appeared to be a 'flagging insurgency' (Tellis *et al.* 2001: 1) in the Kashmir valley, push Kashmir higher up the international agenda, conquer territory sufficient enough to force India to negotiate the region's sovereignty, or some combination of all these reasons?

Whatever the doubts concerning Pakistan decision making, the Kargil conflict provided a huge electoral boost to the BJP and its allies. India's 'first media war ... generated a unifying response of binding a nation together as never before' (Verma 2002: 22). The public saw Indian military personnel performing heroically while suffering heavy casualties during the fighting which lasted from late May until the end of July.[2] The NDA manifesto for the 1999 general elections played heavily on its national security credentials. It praised the caretaker administration which 'rose to the challenge and acted decisively' in Kargil, and noted the numerous national security pledges made in 1998 which had been realised in just 13 months of government (NDA 1999). These included exercising the nuclear option, testing a second-generation *Agni* ballistic missile, creating the NSC, and increasing the defence budget. In October, Vajpayee was returned to power at the head of a 24-party NDA, which won a comfortable majority in the Thirteenth Lok Sabha. In contrast, the INC suffered its worst defeat ever, winning 27 fewer seats than its 1998 total of 140 (Dettman 2001: 144–5).

The NDA in power: a strategic vision of national security

The Kargil conflict, the first armed confrontation between two states equipped with nuclear weapons, had been fought without either side having established a formal tactical or strategic doctrine for their use. In Pakistan's case, the danger posed by such a state of affairs was seen in President Clinton's warning to Prime Minister Sharif that military officers were moving nuclear weapons without his knowledge. In India's case, Vajpayee's pragmatic decision not to cross the LoC, either in hot pursuit or to attack supply lines, won the country new respect abroad – despite some of his more nationalist supporters urging that nuclear weapons be used against the enemy. Although it proved a relief when both Pakistan and India refrained from escalating the conflict beyond the immediate region, it did not prove that they would not do so in the future. Instead, contrary to the belief that nuclear weapons states would refrain from engaging in any open warfare for fear of escalating matters into a nuclear exchange, Kargil showed that there was plenty of room for low-intensity conflict.

The beginning of the end of India's lack of a formal nuclear strategic doctrine came when the NSAB concluded its Draft Nuclear Doctrine on 27 August 1999. Its findings reflected Vajpayee's elucidation of India's nuclear position in his statement to the *Lok Sabha* some days after the 1998 Pokhran nuclear tests, with some modifications. In brief, it stated that India should

- pursue a doctrine of credible minimum nuclear deterrence;
- have an adequate nuclear retaliatory capability;
- not be the first to initiate a nuclear strike;
- not use nuclear weapons against any country not in possession of such weapons and/or not aligned with nuclear powers;
- have nuclear forces consisting of a triad of land, air and sea launched systems;
- control and release nuclear weapons for use by the prime minister, president or designated successor; and
- develop an integrated operational plan predicated on established strategic objectives and targeting policy.

(Jasbir Singh 2000: 153–9)

The Draft Nuclear Doctrine also suggested that India maintain its commitment to pursuing global nuclear disarmament. Although the document was intended only as a preliminary report designed to stimulate debate rather than formally set out India's strategic nuclear doctrine, its findings formed the basis for the country's nuclear weapons strategy (until the announcement of a very similar formal nuclear strategy on 4 January 2003). The BJP's longstanding pledge to establish a national security doctrine took a further forward step in February 2001 with the submission of *Reforming the National Security System: Recommendations of the Group of Ministers*, a report reviewing all aspects of national security. Already, just over one year earlier, the government had been presented with the recommendations of the Kargil Review Committee, set up in the wake of that conflict, on how to remedy failings in intelligence, border security and defence management in the northern region.[3] The NDA subsequently charged a group of ministers consisting of Home Minister L.K. Advani, Defence Minister George Fernandes, External Affairs Minister Jaswant Singh, Finance Minister Yashwant Sinha and 'special invitee' National Security Advisor Brajesh Mishra to review all aspects of Indian security.

While *Reforming the National Security System* identifies China, on its way to 'near superpower status by 2020' as a potential threat because of its 'wide-ranging defence modernisation with a special focus on force-multipliers and high technology weapons systems' (GoI 2001b: 9), it repeatedly focuses on the danger posed by Pakistan. Pakistan, states the Report,

> will continue to pose a threat to India's security.... Its traditional hostility and single-minded aim of destabilising India, is not focused just on Kashmir but on a search for parity.... As a result of Pakistan's political and economic instability, its military regime may act *irrationally*.... Pakistan believes that nuclear weapons can compensate for conventional military inferiority; its leaders have not concealed their desire to use nuclear weapons against India.

(GoI 2001b: 9–10, author's emphasis)

The problem with addressing such threats, the Report continues, is that Pakistan chooses to employ non-state actors and non-traditional avenues in pursuit of its aims to destabilise India. Its Inter Services Intelligence (ISI) – cited over a dozen times in those pages not censored[4] – is accused of direct or indirect involvement with: 'Taliban and Jihadi elements ... [working] relentlessly for the break-up of the Indian Union' (GoI 2001b: 10, 12); drugs, arms and/or people smuggling from Bhutan, Bangladesh, Nepal, Myanmar and/or Pakistan; and 'trying to cultivate the border population on out side ... through Pakistani nationals, who visit border areas on legitimate Indian visas' (GoI 2001b: 88).

How can India hope to maintain law-and-order order internally plus defend its 14,880 kilometres of land borders and 5,422 kilometres of coastline (GoI 2001b: 58) from the multitude of threats described above? *Reforming the National Security System* suggested extensive reforms in the areas of intelligence, internal security, border management and the management of defence. The Report had a great influence on the national security apparatus of India and, with the one notable exception of the need to create a Chief of Defence Staff and Vice-Chief of Defence Staff, most of its recommendations were implemented. For instance, in the Ministry of Home Affairs there is now a Department of Border Management responsible for the management of all international and coastal borders (excluding those specifically allocated to Ministry of Defence and Ministry of External Affairs), as well as a programme aimed at developing the border areas. Also, as of March 2002, India replaced the Directorate of Military Intelligence with a Defence Intelligence Agency (DIA), which combines the intelligence networks of all three armed services. It is hoped that the DIA will significantly reduce the military's reliance on civilian intelligence agencies such as the Intelligence Bureau (IB) and Research and Analysis Wing (RAW) which have been found lacking in previous wars and conflicts.

Perhaps the most significant outcome of the *Reforming the National Security System* came with the 6 January 2003 announcement of a new Nuclear Command Authority (NCA) responsible for the management of India's tactical and strategic nuclear weapons. The NCA comprises a political council chaired by the prime minister – the only person entitled to authorise the use of nuclear weapons – served by an executive council chaired by the national security advisor. Their directives are to be operationalised by a new Strategic Forces Command under the control of a Commander-in-Chief of the rank of Air Marshal (or its equivalent) in charge of the management and administration of the tactical and strategic nuclear forces. The NCA may be seen as the first stage in the development of 'effective and robust command-and-control (C2) and indications-and-warning (I&W) systems and infrastructure for its strategic nuclear force commensurate with India's strategic requirements' (VIC 2003).

A nuclear war?

Just days after the seminal *Reforming the National Security System* was submitted to the government, it emerged that undercover reporters posing as arms dealers for the Indian news website *Tehelka.com* had secretly filmed a number of high-level political personages and serving military officers accepting bribes and/or demanding sexual favours in the hope of influencing lucrative defence contracts. The release of videotape footage of these activities forced the resignation of those directly involved, including BJP President Bangaru Laxman and Samata Party President Jaya Jaitley, and the suspension of four senior officials at the Ministry of Defence, including an army major-general responsible for evaluating defence procurements. While Prime Minister Vajpayee faced down opposition demands that he, too, resign, Samata Party founder and member Defence Minister George Fernandes, though not personally accused in the scandal, did relinquish his office on 15 March 2001. Although the scandal's reverberations rumbled on well into 2003–04, Fernandes himself was re-appointed Defence Minister just seven months later.[5]

While the *Tehelka.com* scandal exposed flaws in India's domestic security hierarchy, international events in the coming months would bring Indo-Pakistan relations to new levels of danger. In July 2001, the Agra Summit between General Musharraf and Prime Minister Vajpayee, the first face-to-face meeting of the leaders of Pakistan and India since Kargil, ended inconclusively. Indian strategists had more reason to worry when, a few months later, the attacks of 11 September 2001 brought Pakistan back into America's favour as a key ally of US President George W. Bush's new 'War on Terrorism'. The NDA's offer of Indian air bases in support of the US in its response to 9/11 helped see the lifting of all outstanding American economic sanctions imposed in the aftermath of the Pokhran nuclear tests of 1998. However, Pakistan was the bigger winner when, after some hesitation, Musharraf came down firmly on the side of the US in their fight to oust the Taliban regime from power in Afghanistan. In addition to the lifting of all remaining US economic sanctions imposed on Pakistan in the aftermath of its own nuclear tests, his cooperation led to America granting the country massive military and further economic assistance.

Pakistan's new popularity with the Bush administration also served to deflect NDA attempts to heighten global awareness of the cross-border Islamic militants India had been combating in Kashmir for over a decade. In the autumn of 2001, there was a 'dramatic increase in separatist violence' (Hussain 2001) in the region, including a suicide attack on 1 October on the Srinagar Assembly in Kashmir that killed more than 30 people. On 13 December, an unprecedented attack on the Lok Sabha in the heart of New Delhi that left 14 dead was blamed on militants who, argued the NDA, were one of many such groups aided and abetted by Pakistan. Despite denials by the Musharraf regime, relations worsened to the point where the armies of India and Pakistan began massing along their shared border. In the first few months of 2002, both countries ratcheted up tensions by successfully test-firing ballistic missiles capable of carrying nuclear weapons. Despite concerted efforts by various foreign governments to calm the growing atmosphere of hostility between India and Pakistan, the US and the UK advised their citizens to leave the region as worries rose that the world may be about to witness the first nuclear war.

Adding to concerns at the time of the heightened tensions in the spring and summer of 2002 were continued uncertainties about the respective nuclear arsenals of India and Pakistan. Neither country has openly offered details of its nuclear capabilities. However, as of early 2004, India was estimated to have approximately 60 operational nuclear weapons (up from less than ten in 1998) that could be carried on ground-to-ground Agni-1, Agni-2, Prithvi-1 and Prithvi-2 ballistic missiles, sea-launched Brahmos cruise missiles, and over 40 suitably modified MiG-27, Mirage 2000-5, Su-30MKI and/or Jaguar aircraft.[6] Pakistan was thought to have 20 operational nuclear weapons that could be deployed on Ghauri-1 ballistic missiles or over 40 Mirage aircraft (Arms Control Association ND).

Uncertainties about the command-and-control structures and nuclear doctrines of India and Pakistan further increased worries about the possibilities of their going to war. As described above, the NDA did not announce its official nuclear strategy and NCA until January 2003. In the meantime, confidence in the Government's management of its nuclear arsenals rested on their 'no first use' policy announced back in August 1999 – as well as the country's history as a democratic state which had always maintained undoubted civil supremacy-of-rule over the military (Kundu 1998). In contrast, General (later President) Musharraf, the chief architect of the 1998 Kargil conflict, remains in control of the Pakistani Government. During Kargil, elements of Pakistan's armed forces had been suspected of manoeuvring nuclear weapons independently of the country's elected civilian prime minister. Not until the day after India's announcement of its NCA did the Pakistan press carry reports that its own nuclear NCA – consisting of the president, chiefs of the three military services and the civilian prime minister – had been in control of the country's nuclear arsenal for four years, and that no one individual, not even Musharraf, had sole say as to the use of nuclear weapons.[7] However, at the time, with Pakistan (understandably) refusing to embrace a 'no first use' nuclear weapons strategy, nor publicly state what events (Indian forces encroaching its airspace and/or crossing the LoC and/or the Punjabi border and/or threatening the break-up of the country, etc.) would cause its decision makers to climb a 'ladder of escalation', the path to nuclear war remained highly volatile.

There are further notes of caution to be sounded. The first concerns the great size and populations of India and Pakistan. Even in the event of

tens of millions dead, dying and injured, the vast majority of both countries' respective populations would survive a nuclear exchange. Thus,
whereas deterrence may be argued to have worked during the Cold War
as both East and West had enough nuclear weapons and delivery systems
to ensure the complete destruction of the other side, this is not the case
for India and Pakistan. After a first and even second strike (India has
always maintained that its nuclear doctrine includes a second strike capability), the military forces of these two neighbours may well 'still be intact
to continue and even escalate the conflict' (Natural Resource Defense
Council 2002). Also, while the geographic distance between the US and
Soviet Union allowed for an approximate 30-minute gap between the
launch of a nuclear warhead and its projected impact, during which the
nature of the threat (mistaken identity, rogue launch, etc.) might be
analysed, the proximity of India and Pakistan allows no such luxury. In
such circumstances, immediate and full retaliation might be the only
option considered.

While a conventional and/or nuclear war between India and Pakistan
was averted in the spring and summer of 2002, the reasons remain contentious. Subsequently, President General Musharraf attempted to
describe India's moves as the result of Pakistan's nuclear deterrence
having worked: the NDA had peered into the abyss of a potential nuclear
exchange and climbed down. It also has been argued that the Indian
administration never seriously contemplated going to war. Instead, the
NDA used foreign fears of a nuclear exchange to push the US, the UK and
other Western powers into 'leveraging concessions from Islamabad' (VIC
2002), including the latter's assurance to the Americans that it would halt
the infiltration of militants from Pakistani territory into Kashmir. In contrast, one individual closely involved in back channel negotiations between
India and Pakistan during the height of the crisis recalls becoming

> very alarmed at the incapacity of people on both sides to focus on the
> real issues and dangers ... especially in Delhi, there was a naïve view
> of the damage that could result from an exchange of nuclear
> weapons. The blithe attitude I heard on more than one occasion
> scared me badly.[8]

Perhaps the nearness of a nuclear exchange frightened both sides. By the
autumn, both India and Pakistan had pulled back their armed forces from
their shared border.

'Strong at home, engaged abroad'

Whatever the precise matrix of factors which contributed to averting war
in the spring and summer of 2002, peering into the abyss of a nuclear
exchange caused the NDA to modify its national security strategy from

one where force was paramount into a doctrine I will call 'strong at home, engaged abroad'. The first part of this modified national security doctrine entailed a continued focus on military might as the chief guarantor of national security. The NDA continued to increase the defence budget in absolute terms; from $9.39 billion in 1998 to $12.88 billion in 2002 (see Figure 11.1), equivalent to an average 6.28 per cent per annum.

Note that these figures do not reflect the government's total spending on national security. Much of the expenditure on the research and development of nuclear weapons and their delivery systems is contained within the respective budgets of the civilian Department of Atomic Energy and Department of Space. The budgetary requirements for maintaining internal order also need to be added to the total cost of national security. The Ministry of Home Affairs meets the mounting cost of maintaining India's numerous central paramilitary forces (CPFs): from 1998 to 2001, their personnel increased by 5.2 per cent (from 567,855 to 597,492) while their cost rose by over 33 per cent (from $1.11 billion to $1.48 billion).[9] Internal order costs must also include the funding of local and state police forces paid for at the state level.

The charge that national security costs under the NDA are too high for a developing nation like India, in which almost 30 per cent of the population live below the official poverty line and over 40 per cent remain illiterate (World Bank ND), is not easy to answer. However, successive Indian administrations of whatever political ideology rarely have seen defence expenses in a 'guns or butter' light. Instead, governments have adjusted

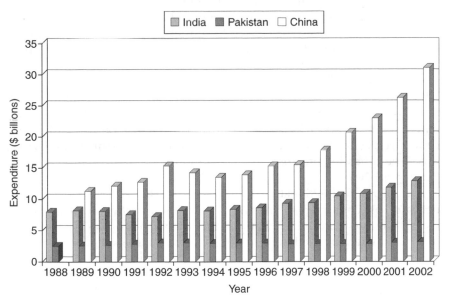

Figure 11.1 Defence expenditure in $ (billions), 1988–2002 (source: SIPRI (2003)).

defence spending in a reactive, and at times, *ad hoc* manner. Thus, one of the biggest increases (a virtual doubling) in defence expenditure came as a reaction to national security shortcomings exposed by the 1962 Sino-Indian War, another occurred in the mid-1980s when the Rajiv Gandhi administration sought to make India into a regional superpower complete with 'blue water' navy, and a third during the middle of Narasimha Rao's premiership. Even the centre-left United Front administration increased defence expenditure by almost 9 per cent in 1996.[10]

The NDA could argue that, while it had increased spending on the CPFs that help maintain internal order, this percentage annual rise never approached the levels seen in previous Janata Dal, INC or United Front administrations. *Reforming the National Security System* recommended increasing funding for the CPFs so that they might replace the Indian Army in internal security duties. Most notably, BJP-led administrations concentrated on significantly increasing the size of the Rashtriya Rifles, a paramilitary force made up of regular army soldiers and officers on rotation under the operational command of the military and funded by the Ministry of Defence (rather than Home Affairs). Up from 36 battalions in 1999 to a projected 66 in 2005 (GoI 2003j: 83), this force has succeeded in freeing many army units from internal security duties in Kashmir. Elsewhere in India, increased spending on CPFs also has been successful, even if only in crude terms of minimising casualties to government forces while increasing terrorist 'kills' (South Asia Terrorism Portal ND).

The recent BJP governments also can point out that, for all their progress on modernising the armed forces, including the induction of nuclear weapons systems, much of the defence budget continues to be eaten up by the costs of providing for the 1,325,000-strong serving personnel of the armed forces (IISS 2003: 136), their retired comrades, and the dependants of those who have died in the service of their country. These people are expensive; for 2002–03, the annual expenditure on defence pensions was $2.27 billion, and is expected to rise to an estimated $2.6 billion by 2004–05 (GoI 2004b: 20). Personnel costs, when combined with the expense of maintaining already existing weapons and infrastructure, may account for up to 90 per cent of the army's entire budget and 60 per cent of respective costs of the navy and air force (Nadkarni 2001), leaving very little funds for the costly modernisation and/or the replacement of existing hardware.

The charge that national security costs under the NDA were excessive is perhaps best countered by relating this expenditure to overall spending. As the economy continued to grow, defence expenditure as a percentage of India's GDP remained in step with its historical levels. From 1998–2001 inclusive, this figure averaged 2.33 per cent (see Figure 11.2) Even as a percentage of government expenditure, the BJP-led NDA administrations were spending no more, and often less, than their United Front, INC and Janata Dal predecessors (see Figure 11.3).

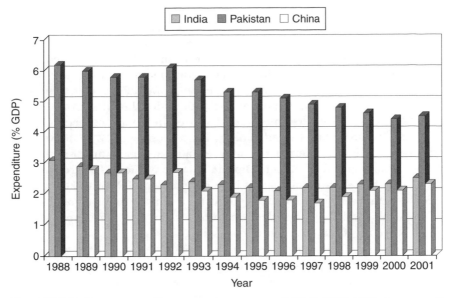

Figure 11.2 Defence expenditure as a percentage of GDP, 1988–2001 (source: all figures taken directly and/or adapted from SIPRI (2003)).

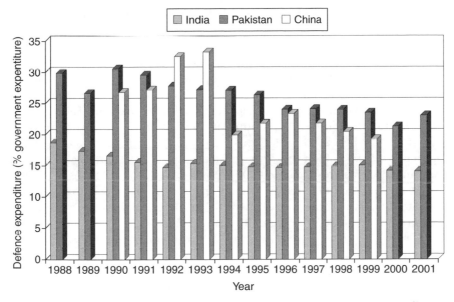

Figure 11.3 Defence expenditure as a percentage of government expenditure, 1988–2001 (source: World Bank (ND)).

One aspect of the second part of what I am describing as an NDA national security doctrine of 'strong at home, engaged abroad' is its embrace of international peacekeeping, that historically favourite expression of Indian military power. Prime Minister Nehru countered the 'with us or against us' demands of the Cold War by leading the Non-Aligned Movement, and backed up this ideological commitment by deploying Indian armed forces in support of UN peacekeeping operations. This trend continued under following administrations and, under the NDA in 2003, over 2,500 Indian military personnel were deployed in UN peacekeeping duties (GoI 2004b; IISS 2003; United Nations Peacekeeping ND). While working with their foreign counterparts in an international milieu improves the professional skills of Indian officers and the balance of the Indian treasury, the chief aim of recent administrations in participating in UN peacekeeping has been to emphasise the country's importance in the international order. Whether this will have any effect on India's claim to a permanent seat on the UN Security Council remains to be seen.

A more recent demonstration of the NDA's national security doctrine that has emerged post-2002 is its growing defence cooperation with foreign countries. In terms of traditional defence ties, Indo-Russian cooperation was once again on the upswing under the NDA. During this period, the Indian Navy benefited most. On 19 January 2003, the government agreed to lease four long-range Tu22 M3 nuclear bombers and two nuclear-capable submarines from Russia, and jointly develop the nuclear-capable Brahmos sea-launched cruise missile (Harding 2003; IISS 2003: 131). In May, the two countries' navies held joint war exercises in the Arabian Sea, and on 19 January 2004, the NDA signed a deal to purchase the ageing *Admiral Gorshkov* aircraft carrier plus numerous MiG-29 fighter jets and Kamov-31 anti-submarine helicopters (BBC 2004a; Marcelo 2004).

India's growing economy makes it an attractive buyer in the global arms market, and any number of European countries have made or are seeking to make lucrative sales of their more advanced technological weaponry either directly, or via specialised bodies like the Indo-French High Committee on Defence Cooperation, first set up just over five years ago (GoI ND; IISS 2003: 132). For instance, in September 2003, the NDA agreed to a £1 billion deal to purchase 60 Hawk training jets from Britain's BAE Systems (Marcelo 2004; Norton-Taylor and MacAskill 2002). Nor were regional defence ties being ignored by the NDA; for instance, despite the ignominious end of the IPKF in the 1980s, India and Sri Lanka began work on a defence cooperation agreement.

The NDA also explored new defence ties, most notably with Israel. Long forgotten are the days when previous administrations, in solidarity with the Palestinian cause and fearing a backlash from its Middle East oil suppliers, refused to establish diplomatic ties with Israel (formally recognised in 1992). Following Israel Prime Minister Ariel Sharon's historic visit to India in September 2003, Israeli Foreign Minister Silvan Shalom explained how, in the post-9/11 world, 'Terror is an enemy which threatens our common values and our shared way of life, and India and Israel are natural partners against it' (BBC 2004b). Indeed, while the NDA has fallen short in convincing other countries to frame (openly) the Kashmir separatist movement in terms of global terrorism, it has found a ready audience in Israel. In December 2003, the two countries set up a Joint Defence Committee and Joint Working Group on Defence Cooperation and now, after Russia, Israel has become India's largest supplier of defence materials (Bedi 2002). In moves that may well give its armed forces a qualitative advantage over those of Pakistan and China, India has finalised $1 billion-plus purchases from Israel of the Phalcon early-warning radar system and Arrow II anti-ballistic missile system.

The Phalcon and Arrow II sales also signify India's enhanced defence relations with the US. That the NDA overcame initial American objections to the deal with Israel (on the grounds that they would give India a qualitative advantage over its rivals), is in great part due to the three governments' commitment to the 'War on Terrorism'. Indian National Security Advisor Brajesh Mishra, speaking at the American Jewish Committee's annual dinner in 2003, stated how the US, India and Israel 'have to jointly face the same ugly face of terrorism. Such an alliance would have the political will and moral authority to take bold decisions in extreme cases of terrorist provocation' (Tillin 2003).

While the NDA had been aware of the importance of developing closer ties with America long before September 11, it was the 1998 nuclear tests that finally pushed the US into seriously engaging in a strategic dialogue with India (Majumder 2003). Certainly, the Bush administration held high-level meetings with Indian defence officials before the post-Pokhran economic sanctions put in place by the Clinton administration were finally lifted, and *Reforming the National Security System* advised the NDA government to continue to cultivate good relations with a US pre-eminent 'in the global strategic architecture' (GoI 2001b) now and for the foreseeable future. In military terms, this has seen India and the US conduct joint naval and special forces' anti-terrorist exercises.

Of course, not all Indian and American strategic interests were shared under the NDA administration. Despite heavy American pressure and some not inconsiderable debate at home, the NDA refused to consider the Bush administration's request to provide 17,000 Indian troops for post-war duties in Iraq unless and until there was a UN resolution authorising the US-led occupation. *Reforming the National Security System* also expressed concern that the US continued to deploy 'nuclear-powered submarines armed with long-range land-attack missiles' (GoI 2001b: 10) in the Indian Ocean, and enhance its military capabilities in Diego Garcia. Nonetheless, during the NDA administration, relations between the two countries were certainly improved. On 12 January 2004, noting the signing of an agreement the day before that will substantively increase technology cooperation between the US and India by permitting the former to export sensitive civil nuclear and civilian space equipment while committing the latter to strengthening its controls on the export of sensitive technologies to third countries, Prime Minister Vajpayee stated that the 'the India-US strategic partnership that President Bush and I share is becoming a reality.... [Our] relationship is based increasingly on common values and common interests' (Luce 2004).

Perhaps the most surprising manifestation of the 'engaged abroad' national security doctrine was the NDA's dedication to improving relations with China. After all, it was the BJP-led coalition government which reversed decades of (painfully) slow but steadily improving relations with their neighbour to the north[11] by publicly stating that the threat posed by China was the main reason for the 1998 Pokhran nuclear tests. This claim was repeated in the Indian Military of Defence *Annual Report, 2001* which also noted that China's nuclear arsenal was vastly superior to India's, all major Indian cities were within range of Chinese missiles, and China was cooperating with Pakistan in developing missiles and nuclear weapons (VIC 2001). However, Vajpayee reversed course when, following a visit to Beijing in June 2003, it was announced that India would explicitly acknowledge the Tibet Autonomous Region as Chinese territory. In return, China implicitly conceded India's sovereignty of Sikkim by signing a border trade protocol to facilitate trade through Tibet–Sikkim. India and China then conducted joint naval exercises in November (shortly after traditional allies, China and Pakistan, had completed joint exercises at sea).

The Indo-Chinese rapprochement initiated by the NDA can only go so far, however. Indeed, as both countries seek to expand their naval reach into each others' 'home' waters – India has recently conducted anti-piracy exercises in the South China Sea with South Korea and Japan, while China seeks to increase its influence in the Bay of Bengal *via* a growing defence relationship with Myanmar – the potential for future tensions remains. India's recent Russian defence purchases and its successful test of the nuclear warhead-capable Brahmos sea-launched cruise missile are further causes for concern. Also, in the Agni-2, India now has a ground-to-ground nuclear ballistic missile capable of reaching almost all of China.

In terms of conventional military capability, the situation is more ambiguous. While China's armed forces have more personnel and hardware than India's, they are increasingly concerned with the NDA's acquisition of sophisticated weapons (Banerjee 2004: 1). At the same time, China continues to spend considerably more on defence than India in terms of absolute amounts ($31.1 billion vs. $12.88 billion, respectively, in 2002; see Figure 11.1), and as a percentage of government expenditure (19.19 per cent compared to 15.03 per cent, respectively, in 1999; see Figure 11.3). China's defence spending is also rising faster than India's (a yearly average of 14.15 per cent vs. 6.28 per cent, respectively, from 1998–2001 inclusive).[12] Only as an average percentage of GDP per annum can China be said to spend less on defence than India (2.1 per cent compared to 2.33 per cent, respectively, from 1998–2001 inclusive; see Figure 11.2). In other words, the size and rate of growth of China's vibrant economy only slightly helps disguise its hugely greater defence expenditure as compared to India. This is unlikely to be a gap that any future Indian administration can afford to fill, at least in absolute terms, in the foreseeable future. Given these circumstances, the NDA decided that engaging with China – settling borders and expanding trade – while remaining strong at home – modernising the quality (destructive power and means of delivery) of its nuclear deterrent armed forces – was the best policy for ensuring India's national security.

The NDA's 'strong at home, engaged abroad' national security policy also had a great effect on India's relations with Pakistan. There was a time when more extreme Indian defence strategists believed that the fate of their neighbour was ultimately of little or no interest, and India should focus on a grander, global future (Cohen 2001: 26). After the tensions of near-war in 2002, the NDA came to the conclusion that a 'failed' Pakistan was in no one's interest, and certainly not its own. Indeed, its ambition to make India a player on the world stage could only be realised if it enjoyed a stable, peaceful and secure relationship with Pakistan. The NDA decided the best way to move relations with Pakistan forward was to concentrate on stimulating economic growth beneficial to both countries – as well as the region – while downplaying contentious security issues, especially Kashmir. Hence the sudden progress at the twelfth SAARC summit in Islamabad held from 4–6 January 2004 where a number of important agreements were signed, including the *Agreement on South Asian Free Trade Area* (SAFTA) which envisaged a virtually free trade zone in the region by 2007. At Islamabad, India and Pakistan also agreed to initiate a bilateral 'composite dialogue' beginning in February which would lay out a roadmap of talks to be held on all outstanding issues by officials of various levels. This new atmosphere of cooperation was reflected in the NDA's 'uncharacteristically reserved' (Majumder 2004) response to recent revelations that Dr Abdul Qadeer Khan, hero of Pakistan's nuclear weapons programme, had for years been selling nuclear secrets to Iran, Libya and North Korea.

An analysis of the comparative defence expenditure figures of India and Pakistan also may have played a role in the NDA's decision to lessen tensions between the two countries. The disparities are significant, if slightly confusing. India spends considerably more on defence than Pakistan in terms of absolute amounts ($12.88 billion compared to $3.18 billion, respectively, in 2002; see Figure 11.1), as well as in terms of an average percentage increase year on year (6.28 per cent compared to 2.01 per cent, respectively, over 1998–2001 inclusive).[13] However, India spends less than Pakistan on defence as a percentage of government expenditure (15.03 per cent vs. 23.43 per cent, respectively, in 1999; see Figure 11.3), and as an average percentage of GDP per annum (2.33 per cent vs. 4.58 per cent, respectively, from 1998–2001 inclusive; see Figure 11.2). In other words, while India spends almost three times as much on defence than Pakistan, the size and growth of the former's economy means it can afford this expense more easily, and can even raise it annually at a greater rate than Pakistan. As China is to India, so India is even more so to Pakistan; that is, in both relationships the latter party can little hope to compete with the defence expenditure of the former. With Pakistan unable to threaten India – except as a reaction to a perceived threat from the latter – the NDA's best means of increasing India's national security is to normalise relations with its neighbour.

Conclusion: lessons learnt and future prospects

The most momentous national security decision made by the BJP/NDA administrations was not overtly demonstrating India's nuclear weapons capabilities in 1998, but refraining from using them during the 1999 Kargil conflict and the 2002 build-up of armies along the Indo-Pakistan border. For, while the Pokhran nuclear tests brought global opprobrium and economic sanctions down on India, and caused Pakistan to become the seventh declared nuclear weapons state, they did little to change the nuclear war-fighting doctrine of either country, both of which had (limited) nuclear arsenals before 1998. Indian strategists always envisaged their country's nuclear arsenal as a purely defensive deterrent against Chinese or Pakistani adventurism. Their Pakistani counterparts also always saw their nuclear weapons as a means of negating India's superiority in conventional arms.

The 1999 Kargil conflict and the 2002 near-war scare taught different lessons. In the former confrontation, the BJP-led government resisted escalatory responses such as attacking supply lines and bases across the LoC in Pakistan. Although this prudence cost the lives of additional hundreds of Indian military personnel, it prevented the conflict from escalating into a full-blown war or even a nuclear exchange that would have killed many millions on both sides of the border. The lessons learnt?

> Lesson number one. If India could fight a relatively high-intensity but *geographically limited* war, nuclear weapons need not enter into the equation.

Yet any thoughts that limited war may still be possible between India and Pakistan were soon dispelled during the 2002 near-war situation. The Pakistan defence decision-making hierarchy, now under the direct control of General Musharraf, architect of the Kargil misadventure, was reacting to rather than controlling events. As such, it was basing its responses wholly on decisions made by the Indian leadership. Now that the burden of escalation rested with itself only, the NDA forwent the muscular response of war many were advocating as a suitable response to the unprecedented attack on the Lok Sabha and other bloody provocations. Instead, it decided that, as the chances of a nuclear exchange, however remote, could not be discounted as Pakistan's response – *under just what circumstances the Indians could not predict with any certainty* – the best option available was to use international pressure to wring promises of concessions from Musharraf regarding securing the LoC from infiltration. It seemed little reward for so much effort in the face of so much provocation. Yet the lesson learnt was vital:

> Lesson number two. Force as a means of settling *major* international disputes between South Asian states – at least between those equipped with nuclear weapons – is finished.

Realising that any sort of confrontation with a nuclear weapons-armed Pakistan was unpredictable and hence too dangerous to contemplate, the NDA also understood that a new relationship had to be forged. Put simply:

> Lesson number three. India could not take its rightful place in the world if relations with Pakistan continued to fester.

Thus, ensuring both the national security and global presence of India is best served by normalising relations with Pakistan.

From the three lessons listed above emerged the national security policy I have characterised as 'strong at home, engaged abroad'. To be strong at home means having the military means to defend the national borders, and the NDA followed a policy of military modernisation, including the induction of ballistic missiles and nuclear weapons. In terms of domestic law-and-order, national security is primarily a function of the local, state and CPFs. Again, the NDA significantly increased funding for improving the training and hardware capabilities of India's paramilitary forces. As for being engaged abroad, *Reforming the National Security System* recognised that India's national security was a function of its

> economic strength, internal cohesion, technological prowess ... [and] the ability to retain political and economic sovereignty and autonomy of decision making in an era of globalisation and increasing economic interdependence.
>
> (GoI 2001b: 6)

Thus, after the near-war scare of 2002 discounted force as a means of resolving the Kashmir issue, the NDA decided that the best way of securing peaceful relations with Pakistan was by using the economic self-interest of both countries to propel a slow but steady normalisation process. Although the NDA increased defence ties with a number of countries, it is the success of economic liberalisation measures introduced almost 15 years ago that is finally pushing India up the global radar. 'Make trade, not war' may be the best way of describing the NDA's efforts to tap the growing markets of China and Southeast Asia, as well as expand its economic dealings with the West.

Note that, despite my arguments to the contrary, it is dangerous to believe the lessons learnt from the 1999 Kargil conflict and, especially, the 2002 near-war situation have made war between India and Pakistan unthinkable or impossible. Indeed, in both confrontations, the outcome could have been different. Indian forces could have crossed the international border or the LoC to attack militant bases and supply lines, Pakistan could have launched a full-scale nuclear response resulting in millions of Indian deaths, and India could have responded with a retaliatory strike causing millions of Pakistani casualties.

All it takes is a miscalculation by the leadership of either country for a nuclear exchange to occur. For instance, on 30 December 2002, Pakistan President, General Musharraf, stated that earlier that year he had personally warned Indian Prime Minister Vajpayee to expect 'an unconventional war' (VIC 2002) if Indian forces crossed the LoC or the international border. Although an army spokesman said Musharraf had not been referring to nuclear weapons, Indian Defence Minister Fernandes warned that the 'Pakistan leadership should not get into the idea of committing suicide because we can take a bomb or two'. Pakistan Information Minister Sheikh Rashid Ahmed described Fernandes' response as the 'ravings of a crazy man. . . . We do not want war but if war is imposed on Pakistan, we have the will to give a crushing reply' (BBC 2003b). Given such rhetoric by foes who have already fought numerous wars, it is imperative that India and Pakistan continue with their current programme of installing a series of confidence building measures designed to prevent any conflict escalating into a nuclear exchange.

The almost casual manner in which the Indian and Pakistani leadership decided to conduct their respective nuclear tests in 1998 is cause for further worry. The BJP-led coalition government of Prime Minister Vajpayee conducted its tests without a nuclear war-fighting strategy or formal command-and-control hierarchy of its nuclear arsenal in place, and with no consultation with the armed forces as to the eventual deployment of nuclear weapons. It took four more years for the NDA Government to publicly announce the formation of the NCA. The decision to respond with tests of its own by the administration of Prime Minister Nawaz Sharif may be seen as a shallow populist response rather than a calculated move as it, too, went ahead with no nuclear war-fighting strategy or formal command-and-control hierarchy of its nuclear arsenal (although, in contrast to their Indian counterparts, the Pakistan armed forces had the lion's share of input in their country's decision to test). Pakistan has never definitively declared the structure of its own NCA, and worries persist over the poor quality of both countries' respective indications-and-warning and command-and-control capabilities.

Finally, now that India has nuclear weapons, where will future Indian administrations go with them? As the Cold War showed, once begun, the qualitative development and quantitative deployment of nuclear weapons is almost relentless. At present, China has over 400 nuclear warheads deliverable by ballistic missiles and aircraft. Pakistan has an estimated 20–60 nuclear warheads deliverable by ballistic missiles and aircraft. India has an estimated 60–150 nuclear warheads deliverable by ballistic missiles and aircraft (Harding 2003). The cost of maintaining and upgrading nuclear arsenals, especially for relatively poor countries like India, Pakistan and China, is substantial. There is a danger that, if continued by future administrations enjoying the country's current 8 to 10 per cent yearly economic growth, the NDA's pursuit of nuclear and/or conventional military weapons systems which make a qualitative difference to the regional security environment may lead to a costly and highly dangerous arms race in Asia.

Acknowledgements

The research for this chapter was conducted while I served as Senior Research Fellow at the European Institute for Asian Studies (EIAS) in Brussels. Various sections were presented at EIAS, the British Association for South Asian Studies annual conference 2004, and Institute for Commonwealth Studies, and I must thank the respective audiences for their knowledgeable questions. My sincere thanks also go to James Manor, Rahul Roy-Chaudhury and Thomas Thornton for their constructive comments on an earlier draft of this chapter.

Notes

1 Within days of China's 1964 nuclear test, Atomic Energy Commission Chair Homi Bhabha 'talked of India being in a position to go nuclear in about eighteen months...' (Singh 1998b: 16–35). A committee was established to study the implications. Before his death in 1965, Prime Minister Lal Bahadur Shastri instructed Bhabha to examine the possibility of a 'Subterranean Nuclear Explosion Project' (Chengappa 2000: 284–7, 382–400; Singh, Jasgit 1998: 16–35). This eventually culminated in the underground 'peaceful nuclear explosion' in 1974 under Prime Minister Indira Gandhi. Other prime ministers toyed, to a greater or lesser extent, with the idea of sanctioning a further nuclear test – Indira Gandhi in 1983, Narasimha Rao in 1995 and H.D. Deve Gowda in 1996.

2 During Operation Vijay, the Indian Army suffered 591 killed, 1,365 wounded, one missing, and the Indian Air Force five dead. An estimate as to Pakistan personnel casualties includes 737 from the army, 68 from the SSG and 13 from the ISI Directorate (Krishna 2001: 137).

3 The Kargil Review Committee was chaired by the hawkish defence analyst K. Subrahmanyam, and included Lieut.-General (Retd) K.K. Hazari, journalist B.G. Verghese and NSC Secretary Satish Chandra. The Committee submitted its report to the Government on 15 December 1999, and it was tabled in parliament on 24 February 2000 (Verma 2002: 180–215; GoI 2001b: Annexure B).

4 Although the intelligence section in *Reforming the National Security System* has been deleted from the version available to the public, scattered references are made in other parts of the text. In addition, it may be assumed that much of the intelligence section, as with other parts of the Report, would have built upon the (narrower) intelligence recommendations of the Kargil Review Committee (GoI 2001b: 121–3; Mitra 2003b: 407).

5 For more details about the *Tehelka.com* scandal, see the contribution to this volume by Gurharpal Singh (Chapter 7).

6 The Agni and Prithvi missiles are being incorporated as two missile groups into India's new NCA. The NCA also will be in direct command of the nuclear bomb-capable aircraft, as well any naval nuclear weapon-equipped delivery systems if and when they become operational (IISS 2003: 136–8, 140–2, 228–9; VIC 2001: 2, 8, 10, 15–29; Arms Control Association ND).

7 Subsequent reports have described the establishment of a Pakistani Strategic Forces Command similar to India's, though it remains unclear as to when this was formally constituted. Musharraf has stated that his country's National Command Authority consists of 'the president as the boss and there are a number of ministers – all the stakeholders – and the military men also. This is not a military body, it is the highest body of the nation'. Note that when Musharraf made this statement (and at the time of writing) he was both president of the country and chief of the army (Bokhari and Lucce 2004; BBC 2003b; VIC 2003: 2).

8 Interview with author in 2004.

9 Adapted from figures shown in GoI (2003j: 8).

10 Percentages derived from figures in SIPRI (2003).

11 Prime Minister Rajiv Gandhi visited China in 1988, Prime Minister Narasimha Rao went in 1993 and agreed to honour the Line of Actual Control (LOAC) in India's northeast frontier, and Prime Minister H.D. Deve Gowda in 1996 accepted a proposal that Chinese and Indian troops withdraw to 20 kilometres from the LOAC (Dettman 2001: 39).

12 Percentages derived from figures in SIPRI (2003).

13 Percentages derived from figures in SIPRI (2003).

12 The BJP and the 2004 general election

Dimensions, causes and implications of an unexpected defeat

Christophe Jaffrelot

Introduction

In early 2004, the BJP leaders were certain that the NDA would win the general election and that A.B. Vajpayee would remain Prime Minister of India. He was the most popular politician in India; the growth rate had just reached an unprecedented 8 per cent per annum; and Indo-Pakistan relations were characterised by a popular détente. This good fortune had been reconfirmed in December 2003 when the BJP swept the polls during the state assembly elections in Madhya Pradesh, Rajasthan and Chhattisgarh, defeating in each case the INC by huge margins in terms of seats won.

The above factors explain the decision to hold general elections earlier than expected in April–May 2004 (the latest they could have been held was in September 2004). The BJP issued positive slogans accompanying its election campaign: 'Shining India' and the 'Feel Good Factor'. This over confidence attitude, which sometimes amounted to sheer arrogance, retrospectively appeared as one of the reasons for the BJP's defeat. But there were other, deeper explanations. This chapter examines them after measuring first the real amplitude of the Party's setback and before turning to its implications for its future strategy.

The BJP's setback: uneven and relative

Most of the observers have been so overwhelmed by the BJP's defeat that, in reaction, they exaggerated its amplitude. After all, the BJP is left with only seven fewer seats than the INC –138 seats gained by the BJP compared to 145 by the INC. Nevertheless, the gap between both parties has become larger in terms of the percentage of valid votes obtained (22.16 per cent by the BJP as against 26.69 per cent by the INC). This means that the BJP, after 20 years of continuous electoral growth, has almost reverted back to the situation in 1991 when they won 120 seats and 20.1 per cent of the valid votes. However, the erosion is not as drastic as this statistic makes it

Table 12.1 Performances of the BJP over 20 years of general elections in India

Year	1984	1989	1991	1996	1998	1999	2004
Per cent of valid votes	7.4	11.4	20.1	20.3	25.6	23.8	22.2
Number of seats won	2	85	120	161	182	182	138
Number of seats contested	229	226	468	471	388	339	361

Source: Election Commission of India (ND).

appear. First of all, in 1991 the BJP won 20 per cent of the valid votes (see Table 12.1) while contesting 468 seats; whereas in 2004 it won more than 22 per cent while contesting only 361 seats. Moreover, the decline in terms of valid votes is not so dramatic compared to 1999 when it won 23.8 per cent of the valid votes, while only contesting 339 seats. This is explainable because the BJP's performances have been very unevenly distributed in geographical terms. Map 12.1 demonstrates its performance in the 2004 elections.

The new BJP electoral map

The BJP's domination has remained complete in its old strongholds dating back to the Jana Sangh's days. In Madhya Pradesh, the cradle of electoral Hindu nationalism – as I demonstrated elsewhere (1996) – the BJP displayed a remarkable degree of resilience: it won 25 out of the 29 seats it contested with 48.1 per cent of the valid votes; in Rajasthan, it won 21 out of the 25 seats it contested with 49 per cent of the valid votes, and in Chhattisgarh, it won ten of the 11 seats it contested with 47.8 per cent of the valid votes.[1] These regions are those on which Bruce Graham had focused to show the emerging area of electoral strength of the Jana Sangh in the 1960s (1990: 226). New Delhi is the only 'old' stronghold where the BJP was defeated this time, winning only one seat.

The two major states where the BJP had made recent inroads and where it recorded a setback in 2004, were Uttar Pradesh and Gujarat. Uttar Pradesh was not a stronghold of Hindu nationalism until the 1990s. In 1989, the BJP was weaker in Uttar Pradesh than in Bihar (it won 7.6 per cent of the valid votes in the former and 11.7 per cent in the latter). Of course, the Ayodhya movement catapulted the party to power in 1991 (when the BJP multiplied its share of valid votes by a factor of four in two years, with 32.8 per cent of the total) and the party was able to sustain this level of influence until the late 1990s. It peaked in 1998 with 36.5 per cent of the valid votes and 52 seats and started to decline in 1999 in terms of valid votes (30 per cent), but *not* in terms of seats since it won in a record number of electoral constituencies (57 seats). Therefore, 2004 marked a steep decline in Uttar Pradesh. The BJP secured only 22.2 per cent of the valid votes and ten seats (if the seats in the state of Uttaranchal are included, part of Uttar Pradesh until 2000, then the BJP fell to 13 seats).

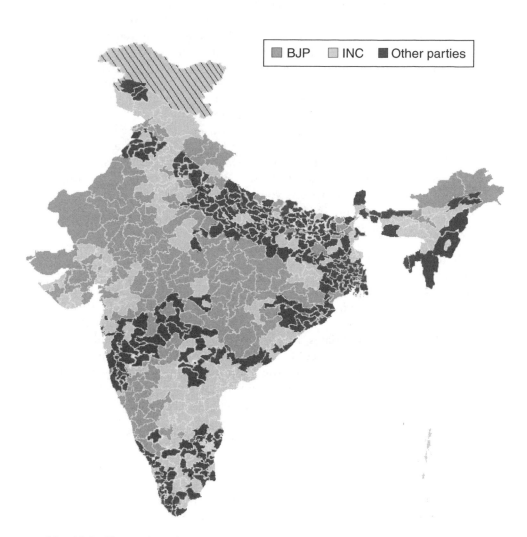

Map 12.1 Electoral results, 2004 (source: Election Commission of India).

The BJP came to power in the 1990s because of its electoral success in Uttar Pradesh – one third of its tally, at least 50 seats, came from that state in the late 1990s. Those days are over. In terms of seats, the party has reverted to its level of 1989. The decline started in 1999, but accelerated during the 2002 state assembly elections when the BJP could only secure 27.1 per cent of the valid votes. The BJP leaders, not relying on the Ayodhya issue any more – either because they did not want to raise it again or because the public was not responsive to it any more – decided to woo the OBC vote by re-inducting Kalyan Singh in the party in February 2004, only a few months before the elections. However, Singh could not compete with two parties which were the real winners of the 2004 elections in Uttar Pradesh: the Samajwadi Party which won 35 seats out of 80 and the BSP which got 19 seats. The BJP has lost the general election – and therefore power – in Uttar Pradesh this time largely because of these low caste-based parties. In addition, the BJP lost fractions of the upper caste vote by running after OBC voters. For instance, 18 per cent of the Brahmins voted for the INC this time.[2] The BJP may face future difficulties in order to overcome the impasse it has reached in Uttar Pradesh.

In 2004, its fate was also partly sealed by the electoral verdict in Gujarat. Although it was not defeated there, it lost support, and managed to merely secure two seats more than the INC. In terms of valid votes, the BJP obtained 47.4 per cent, as against 43.9 per cent for the INC. In Gujarat, the BJP's support remains around the same as in the 1990s. It peaked in 1999 with 52.5 per cent of the vote. However, in terms of seats, with 14 victorious candidates, it is as close to 1989 – when it had won 12 seats – as to 1996 – when it had won 16. In May 2004, these results stood in stark contrast with the result of the state assembly elections which had taken place only 18 months before, when the BJP had won an overwhelming majority. However, these elections had been organised by the BJP Chief Minister, Narendra Modi in the wake of unprecedented riots between Hindus and Muslims in 2002. This event had polarised the religious groups of the state in such a way as the majority community had supported the BJP almost *en bloc*. Its popularity was obviously much lower in normal conditions.

In 2004, the only states where the BJP further improved its performance after recent inroads in the 1990s were in some southern states, a region where the Hindu nationalist movement had been weak for decades, largely because of its defence of the cause of Hindi as a national language. In Andhra Pradesh and in Tamil Nadu, where the BJP operated mainly through regional allies in 2004 – the TDP and the AIADMK – the party is declining, even though it was already very low. In Kerala and in Karnataka, though, it is making some progress. In Kerala, the BJP crossed the symbolic threshold of 10 per cent of valid votes after 15 years of steady electoral gains. In this state, the party relies on the dense network of *shakhas* (local branches) that the RSS is developing with a great

Table 12.2 The share of the Hindi belt[a] MPs of the BJP in 1991–2004

Year	Hindi belt MPs of the BJP	Total BJP MPs	Col. 1:Col. 2 (ratio 1:2 as percentage)
1991	87	120	72.5
1996	119	161	73.9
1998	122	184	66.3
1999	112	183	61.0
2004	78	138	56.5

Source: Election Commission of India (ND).

Note
a The Hindi belt comprises the following states: Bihar, Chandigarh, Delhi, Haryana, Himachal Pradesh, Madhya Pradesh, Rajasthan and Uttar Pradesh.

determination to counter the Communists and the Muslim League. Of course, the main zone of influence that the BJP is carving out in the south is in Karnataka.[3] This is a major breakthrough, which shows that the BJP has travelled a long way since the Jana Sangh days. Until the early 1990s, neither the Jana Sangh nor the BJP could win more than a couple of seats in south India. In 1991, the BJP won five seats in the entire south, including four in Karnataka where it polled 28.8 per cent of the valid votes. In 2004, it won 18 seats in the south – all in Karnataka where the BJP, which had won about one fifth of the valid votes in the second half of the 1990s, secured 34.8 per cent of valid votes.

This remarkable achievement further qualifies the notion that the BJP suffered a major setback, especially because it shows that the electoral map of the party is definitely different from that of the Jana Sangh. The rise of the BJP in the 1990s has been sustained by the capacity of the party to make major inroads in the south. So much so, that the share of the north Indian MPs, which represented more than 70 per cent of the BJP MPs until 1991–96, fell to 61 per cent in 1999, and 56.5 per cent in 2004. The BJP is not only a Hindi belt party, unlike the Jana Sangh which was one during almost its entire career.

As Table 12.2 shows, the steady decline of the influence of the BJP MPs returned in the Hindi belt – also known as the cow-belt of India because of the strength of the Hindu orthodoxy in the region – may well be one of the reasons for the diminishing interest of the party on *Hindutva*-based issues, like Ayodhya.

The uneven reliability of the BJP's allies

The notion of a massive defeat of the BJP requires additional nuances, once the observation shifts from the BJP to its allies. The very idea of making alliances, instead of going it alone during election time, took a new turn in the 1990s among the BJP leaders when they started systematically to select

Table 12.3 The BJP's performance in elections 1991–2004; state-wise

State	Total no. of seats	Seats won by the BJP					Share of the valid votes				
		1991	1996	1998[a]	1999	2004	1991	1996	1998	1999	2004
Andhra Pradesh	42	1	0	4	7	0	9.6	5.6	18.3	9.1	8.4
Assam	14	2	1	1	1	3	9.6	15.9	24.5	29.6	22.9
Bihar	54	5	18	20	23	6[b]	16.0	20.5	24.0	23.3	14.2[c]
Gujarat	26	20	16	19	20	14	50.4	48.5	48.4	52.5	47.4
Haryana	10	0	4	1	5	1	10.2	19.7	18.9	28.5	17.2
Himachal Pradesh	4	2	0	3	3	1	42.8	39.6	51.4	46.2	44.2
Jammu and Kashmir	6	2	1	2	2	0	0	19.0	28.6	31.5	23.0
Karnataka	27	4	6	13	7	18	28.8	24.9	26.9	26.9	34.8
Kerala	20	0	0	0	0	0	4.6	5.6	8.0	7.9	10.4
Madhya Pradesh	40	12	27	30	29	35[d]	41.9	41.3	45.7	46.6	48.1[e]
Maharashtra	48	5	18	4	13	13	20.2	21.8	22.5	21.9	22.6
Orissa	21	0	0	7	9	18	9.5	13.4	21.2	24.6	19.3
Punjab	13	0	0	3	1	11	17.0	6.5	11.7	9.2	10.5
Rajasthan	25	12	12	5	16	21	40.9	42.4	41.7	46.9	49.0
Tamil Nadu	39	0	0	3	4	0	2.9	2.9	6.8	7.1	5.1
Uttar Pradesh	85	51	52	57	29	13[f]	32.8	33.4	36.5	27.6	22.2[g]
West Bengal	42	0	0	1	2	1	11.7	6.9	10.2	11.1	8.1
Andaman and Nicobar Islands	1	0	0	0	1	0	4.9	24.3	35.5	52.7	35.9
Arunachal Pradesh	2	0	0	0	0	2	6.1	17.4	21.8	16.3	53.8
Chandigarh	1	0	1	1	0	0	28.8	39.1	42.4	45.1	35.2
Dadar and Nagar Haveli	1	0	0	0	0	0	35.4	42.4	53.7	20.8	15.6
Daman and Diu	1	1	0	1	0	0	31.9	40.5	42.0	43.1	48.4
Delhi	7	5	5	6	7	1	40.2	49.6	50.7	51.8	40.7
Goa	2	0	0	0	2	1	15.6	13.8	30.0	51.5	46.8
Manipur	2	0	0	0	1	0	8.1	5.2	12.6	34.7	16.0
Meghalaya	2	0	0	0	0	1	6.8	9.1	9.0	9.4	8.6
Tripura	2	0	0	0	0	0	3.0	6.5	8.2	25.3	7.8
Total	537	120	161	184	183	138	20.1	20.3	25.6	23.7	22.2

Sources: Narasimha Rao and Balakrishna (1999); *Frontline* (1999a: 122–3); *The Hindu* (2004e).

Notes

a Including by-election.
b Including one in Jharkhand.
c In Jharkhand the BJP won 33 per cent of the valid votes.
d Including ten in Chhattisgarh.
e In Chhattisgarh the BJP won 47.8 per cent of the valid votes.
f Including three in Uttaranchal.
g In Uttaranchal the BJP won 41 per cent of the valid votes.

local partners to penetrate states or social groups where the BJP was weak (see Table 12.3).

This *modus operandi* continued to help the party a great deal in many cases in 2004. In Maharashtra, the Shiv Sena remains a very useful local interpreter that enabled a Hindi-belt oriented BJP to reach beyond the Vindhyas, a region with a specific identity and caste equation. The coalition won 25 out of 48 seats in 2004, with the BJP retaining most of the upper caste vote (48 per cent according to the CSDS exit poll). Meanwhile, the Shiv Sena successfully wooed substantial sections of the Maratha-Kunbi caste cluster (39 per cent) (Palshikar and Birmal 2004: AE-5). Similarly, in Punjab, the BJP–SAD (B) swept the poll, winning 11 of the 13 Lok Sabha seats. In Orissa, the BJP–Biju Janata Dal won 18 of the 21 seats. In both cases, the BJP played the role of a junior partner, even more than before. For instance, in Punjab, the party won 10.5 per cent of the valid votes, whereas the SAD (B) gained 34.5 per cent. In Orissa, the BJP won 19.3 per cent (four percentage point less than in 1999). In Bihar, the BJP declined so much, that it lagged behind its ally, the JD (U) with 14.2 per cent of the valid votes, nearly half less than its partner (22.9 per cent). The JD (U) continued to attract large numbers of low caste voters – including Kurmis, caste fellows of its local leader, Nitish Kumar – whereas the BJP is left with pockets of influence among the upper castes.

However, in most of the states, the BJP's allies brought a very limited number of seats. In Andhra Pradesh, the TDP, which was the second largest party in the NDA after the 1999 elections won only three seats compared with 29 five years before. In West Bengal, the Trinamool Congress could only win two seats compared with eight in 1999. In addition to these setbacks, the BJP made a mistake by dropping some of its allies of 1999 to make new ones in 2004. Tamil Nadu is a case in point. There, the DMK, which had switched allegiance and joined the INC coalition, won 16 seats, whereas the AIADMK, which had become the BJP's ally, did not win any. While changes in alliances since the previous general elections enabled the INC to add 47 seats to its overall tally, the BJP got 27 less seats than in 1999, largely due to the poor performance of its allies. In fact, the INC's allies contributed 74 seats to the UPA and the BJP's allies only 51 to the NDA. As a result, the BJP dominates the NDA more effectively than after the 1999 elections since its share of seats has increased from 60 to 73 per cent but the party does not need to congratulate itself for the bad results of its allies anyway.

A pro-rich party which pays the price

Immediately after the elections, BJP leaders offered their own explanation for the defeat. Outgoing Prime Minister Atal Bihari Vajpayee declared: 'It is very difficult to say what are all the reasons for the defeat in the elections [. . .] but one impact of the violence was we lost the elections', clearly an explicit reference to the adverse effect of the 2002 communal riots in

Gujarat (cited in *Central Chronicle* 2004). Ten days later, Lal Kishna Advani made the opposite comment. In a 40-minute speech to the National Executive Committee of the BJP, he considered that neglect of the Hindu nationalist themes had been one of the reasons for the party's defeat.

Has the BJP lost because of *Hindutva* or because of its neglect of *Hindutva?* Certainly Muslims resorted to strategic voting to help defeat the party whenever they could. But they have been doing so, more or less systematically, for years now in spite of the repeated attempts by the BJP at wooing them. None of the *Hindutva* themes – including the building of a Ram temple at Ayodhya – was a key issue throughout the general election campaign. However, the BJP is so closely identified with Hindu nationalist ideology that it does not need to champion it to be seen as associated with it. The defeat of the BJP candidates in the constituencies where Ayodhya, Varanasi and Mathura are situated reflected the diminishing influence of Hindu nationalism over voters. In these three places, the BJP had won repeatedly during the 1990s.[4] In Uttar Pradesh, two champions of the demand for the building of a Ram temple in Ayodhya, Vinay Katiyar – the Uttar Pradesh state BJP president – and Swami Chinmayanand – a former Union minister of state for home affairs – lost their parliamentary seats. But Ayodhya was not an issue in the 2004 elections and the defeat of the BJP, therefore, is not a vote for secularism. The CSDS exit poll shows, for instance, that there is, among the public, 'a widespread support for a ban on religious conversion' (Datar 2004), a traditional demand of the Hindu nationalist movement.

Why then, was the BJP-led coalition voted out of power? Possibly for socio-economic reasons. Following the 1999 general election, Yadav *et al.* (1999: 33) had convincingly argued that the BJP relied on a 'new social bloc' since the NDA parties secured 'the support of 60 per cent of upper caste Hindus and 52 per cent of the dominant Hindu peasant castes (which are not classified as OBCs, such as Jats, Marathas, Patidars, Reddys and Kammas)'. For five years the NDA pursued an economic policy which favoured these groups (at the very least the other ones – which formed a vast majority of Indian society – had this impression).

The 2004 exit poll conducted by the CSDS showed that 26 per cent of the 'very poor' and 18 per cent of the 'poor' considered that their economic condition had worsened under the NDA Government. Logically enough, among NDA voters, 35 per cent declared that their situation had improved compared to only 22 per cent of INC voters (Suri 2004: AE 7). One of the major allies of the BJP, the TDP, was clearly punished for what was perceived to be its 'pro-rich policy': 54 per cent of the voters interviewed by the CSDS team considered that only the rich benefited from the NDA policy; 39 per cent said that the TDP-led state government had only developed the state capital, Hyderabad, and 81 per cent were of the view that the information technology revolution – one of the priorities of the TDP Chief Minister Chandrababu Naidu – has not improved the lives of ordinary people (*The Hindu* 2004a), at a time when suicides by over indebted peasants multiplied.

The overall idea that the NDA had followed a pro-rich policy which benefited only the urban middle class is probably an exaggeration since a larger portion of society profited by the economic dynamism displayed by India during the NDA Government, but those who lagged behind resented its policy because inequalities increased. Economic liberalisation enabled the *nouveaux riches* to make progress more quickly than the others – and they showed it.

As a result, the support base of the BJP continued to rely on the same 'social bloc' as in 1999, but this bloc shrank. The CSDS data show that the richer an Indian citizen was, the more likely he was to vote for the BJP. Incidentally, a similar correlation applies in the case of education, namely college graduates and post-graduates vote much more for the BJP than non-literates.

Naturally, these variables are reflected in the caste background of BJP voters. Forty-two per cent of the upper caste people voted for the BJP (two times more than for the INC) and only 11 per cent of the *Dalits* do the same (as against 28 per cent for the INC). In spite of its repeated attempts at wooing the *Dalits* – as evidenced by its promotion of Ambedkar as one its favourite icons (Jaffrelot 2005a) – the BJP still fails to attract a substantial number of electors from the most important of the SCs such as the *Chamars* of North India (who support the BSP). In fact, it can only rely on the votes of less numerically strong groups, like the *Bhangis*, who are locked in a rivalry with the *Chamars*, and that only in some places where the INC is weak. The Hindu nationalist movement's upper caste overtone (including the militant emphasis on the ban on cow slaughter by the VHP[5]) and its courting of the OBCs – the new enemies of the Dalits in some states, like Uttar Pradesh – ultimately alienated many SCs.

Until now, the BJP could do without the *Dalit* vote and with the social bloc which supported the party. Why was this not the case in 2004? This time, the BJP was probably affected by two simultaneous developments. First, the upper caste urban middle class, though better educated, was showing less interest in the act of voting. In India, in contrast to western democracies, the turn out of postgraduates is 50 per cent lower than that of those who only went to middle school (41 per cent compared to 82.6 per cent in 1998). Similarly, voter turnout by upper castes is much lower than that of the Dalits (60.2 per cent compared to 75.1 per cent in 1998). Moreover, voter turnout of those with the highest income is ten percentage points below that of the poorest (46.6 per cent compared to 57.1 per cent in 1998). Finally, voter turnout in urban constituencies is much below that of the rural ones (in 1999, it was 53.7 per cent compared to 61.5 per cent (Yadav 2000). These trends have affected the electoral prospects of the BJP since it could not mobilise all its supporters at the time of elections. The social bloc might have remained the same, but those who cast their votes were less numerous. In Delhi, the turnout was just above 45 per cent, in Gujarat, just above 47.1 per cent, in Uttar

Pradesh just above 48 per cent. Certainly, 75 per cent of the *Patidars* and 60 per cent of the upper castes voted for the BJP in Gujarat but these big percentages represented smaller groups than before.

In any case, this explanation is only a small part of the story. A true understanding of the 2004 electoral setback of the BJP should lead us to the specificities of politics at the state level, largely because the state has become the most relevant unit of politics in India. In several states, the support of the social bloc that supported the BJP in 1999 has begun to fissure. Uttar Pradesh is a case in point. Certainly the BJP retains 77 per cent of the votes among the *Banya* community, but this is a very small community. In contrast, the Party could keep only 58 per cent of the large *Brahmin* community because 18 per cent of them have opted for the INC, as mentioned above. There may be several reasons for the erosion of the BJP's support base among the upper castes: the return of prominent OBC leader, Kalyan Singh, to the helm of the Uttar Pradesh BJP probably displeased them and the BJP's repeated alliances with a *Dalit*-based party, the BSP, had the same effect. Instead Brahmins, who had paid allegiance to the Nehru–Gandhi family till the 1980s, felt attracted by the entry of Rahul and Priyanka Gandhi into the fray. Similarly, the BJP only retains 50 per cent of the Rajput vote, whereas the SP received 28 per cent of them. This turn of events was probably caused because Mulayam Singh Yadav and his right hand man, Amar Singh (a Rajput), presented a large number of Rajput candidates. Lastly, the BJP only retained the support of 22 per cent of the peasant proprietary castes, since 54 per cent of them instead chose the SP/RLD coalition, most probably because of the attractiveness of Ajit Singh's party – the RLD – to Jat voters.

Such an intra-state analysis may be repeated in the case of Gujarat. Here, three local factors need to be taken into account to explain the mixed results of the BJP. First, the agitation – ironically led by the RSS-supported farmers' union – against the agricultural policy of Narendra Modi. Second, the factional fight between Gujarat's Chief Minister and Keshubhai Patel.[6] Third, a development in favour of the BJP, was the voting pattern of the Adivasi communities. In Gujarat, 48 per cent of them voted for the BJP (compared to 46 per cent for the INC). This remarkable achievement is largely a result of the combined ground work of the *Vanavasi Kalyan Ashram* (Ashram for the Tribal Welfare), the RSS offshoot doing social work among the tribals and the VHP whose 'missionaries' reconvert Adivasi tribals to Hinduism and then mobilise them against Christians and Muslims (Jaffrelot 2005b).

However, besides state-centred explanations for the BJP defeat, there are others with a pan-Indian relevance. The INC has certainly been responsible for the BJP's setback in two respects. First, the INC's leader, Sonia Gandhi, who had not been taken seriously by Hindu nationalist groups displayed great canvassing capabilities. Furthermore Hindu nationalist efforts to denounce her foreign origin have probably backfired, and tended to transform her into a victimised target of xenophobes. Second, the INC was quicker than the BJP in adjusting to the realities of the rise of regional parties and its corollary, the new era of coalitions. Consequently, INC leaders chose their allies much more carefully than the BJP this time.

More importantly, the BJP has been affected by the anti-incumbency reflex that the Indian electorate has developed over the years. Logically enough, this factor did not play any role in the states where the party was in command for less than six months, namely in Madhya Pradesh, Rajasthan and Chhattisgarh. In these states the party continued to benefit from the same sentiment of anti–incumbency that had removed the INC from power. The variable of anti-incumbency had some impact in Gujarat, where the BJP was in office, and in Uttar Pradesh, where it was part of the ruling coalition eight months before. Overall, the electorate's anti-incumbency reflex affected about half of the BJP's outgoing MPs, since those that had been re-nominated eventually lost in the election.

Finally, within the *Sangh Parivar*, the line of conduct pursued by the Vajpayee Government created some discontent within the VHP.[7] This organisation explicitly dissociated itself from the NDA Government when it turned out that the Prime Minister would not support the building of a temple in Ayodhya. Two other components of the *Sangh Parivar*, the BMS, the largest labour union in India today, and the SJM, the economic wing of the RSS, resented the economic liberalisation policy implemented by the NDA Government. The RSS itself shared these reservations and therefore did not wholeheartedly support the BJP during the general election campaign. For instance, soon after the general election, the spokesperson of the RSS told *The Hindu* that:

> The grassroots traditional voter and cadre of the RSS was not so enthusiastic about the BJP. There were some organisational differences. Our cadres did work [for the BJP at the time of elections], but there was resentment on several issues, *Hindutva* and also economic issues.
>
> (2004d)

The implications of a defeat: back to *Hindutva* or towards the continuation of the NDA?

The BJP – and its predecessor, the Jana Sangh – has always oscillated between two types of strategies. One based on ethno-religious mobilisations, such as the movement to build a temple at Ayodhya; the other, a more moderate strategy based on coalition-making which stresses socio-economic and patriotic issues. The first strategy is the most preferred choice of the RSS, the matrix of the Jana Sangh, as well as of the BJP cadres who have all been trained in the RSS. However, a strategy based on moderation appeared to be necessary to win power – especially to make alliances – when circumstances did not enable the Hindu nationalist forces to resort to the ethno-religious repertoire.

As I have shown in *The Hindu Nationalist Movement*, the choice between moderation or ethno-religious mobilisation is traditionally dictated by three variables: the degree of vulnerability felt by the Hindus, which prepares the ground for an aggressive articulation of an ethno-religious discourse; the attitude of other political parties, those in office as well as those sitting in the opposition; and the overall behaviour of members of the *Sangh Parivar*, particularly the RSS. Let us review these variables in the reverse order.

The 2004 defeat was considered by most of the components of the *Sangh Parivar* to be a rejection of the moderate line of conduct advocated by Vajpayee. The General Secretary of the VHP, Praveen Togadia declared soon after the elections, with his traditionally nuanced sense of rhetoric:

> The Bharatiya Janata Party betrayed the Hindus. The BJP left its core ideology of *Hindutva* and trust on the basis of which they had been voted to power. For votes they tied up with the jehadis.
>
> (*The Hindu* 2004d)

The RSS spokesperson, Ram Madhav, said almost the same thing. He admitted that 'there was a perception over the last four to five years that there had been dilution of the *Hindutva* ideology' (*The Hindu* 2004d). The RSS naturally wanted the BJP to return to a *Hindutva*-led programme in order to recapture the imagination of the people.

Among the other variables mentioned above, the role of the other political parties was crucial. In the 1990s, the Hindu nationalist party ceased to be an undesirable coalition partner. Opportunist candidates to some alliance with the BJP, which had stigmatised this party in the 1980s suddenly began to appear from all quarters as soon as the BJP emerged as a powerful political force. These partners even came from within the fold of the Socialist Party, with George Fernandes associating himself with the BJP in 1995 and Sharad Yadav doing so in 1999. At the same time, the BJP became adept at coalition making, exemplified by the formation of the NDA. However, the rules of the coalition game implied that the BJP agenda got diluted, mostly since former socialists and other self-proclaimed secularists could not support *Hindutva*-oriented objectives, such as the building of a Ram temple in Ayodhya, the proposed abolition of Article 370 of the Constitution regarding the autonomy of Jammu and Kashmir, and the calls for the introduction of a uniform civil code. With the approval of the RSS, the BJP put these issues on the backburner. Hence the contradiction in which the party found itself after the 2004 general election: on the one hand the RSS made it clear that it wanted the BJP to return to its core ideology, but on the other hand several constituents of the NDA had strong objections to this approach.

However, the 2004 general election has transformed the context substantially for the BJP's allies. First, the BJP turned out not to be an important electoral asset to some of its partners, like the JD (U) in Bihar, which
won in their own strongholds. Second, the general atmosphere has
changed in such a way as the dominant repertoire was not as much
imbued with Hindu nationalism as it used to be in previous elections.
Instead, social issues were back on the front stage – and the BJP has precisely ignored issues that concerned millions of Indians at its own cost. On
the other hand, the INC emerged as the natural spokesman for the
masses. In this changed context, coalition partners of the BJP – who swallowed the Gujarat pogrom without demurring – began to worry about
their Muslim voters. They also grew concerned about any return to a more
aggressive Hindu nationalist agitation. For instance, soon after the NDA's
defeat, the JD (U) informed the BJP that it would leave the coalition if the
party returned openly to espouse *Hindutva* issues. Right after the general
election, the National Executive Committee of the JD (U) issued a resolution to this effect. It declared that:

> We joined the National Democratic Alliance only after the three con-
> troversial issues (construction of a Ram temple at Ayodhya, Article
> 370 and Uniform Civil Code) had been removed from the agenda of
> the NDA. If any effort is now made to revive them, we shall have to
> take another road.
>
> (*The Hindu* 2004g)

The TDP, another BJP ally, has adopted a similar line of conduct to
that of the JD (U). For instance, the TDP's spokesperson announced that
'[i]f the BJP chooses to adopt the communal agenda, we will sever ties
with it' (*The Hindu* 2004h).

What could the BJP do in this changed context? Perhaps for the first
time, the party seemed to be virtually divided between moderates and radi-
cals. For long, this division had been a functional one: the party projected
a moderate face – Vajpayee – when it was in need of a widely acceptable
leader for constituting coalitions; it projected a more militant one – Advani
– when it needed to galvanise the party activists for *Hindutva*-oriented agitations. After the 2004 elections, both strategies were debated in the Party as
two full-fledged alternatives. Before the hardliners had taken up the propo-
sitions from the VHP or even the RSS, the moderates launched an unex-
pected offensive. Vajpayee, who had declined the post of leader of the
opposition – which instead was taken up by Advani – argued that the BJP
had lost partly because of the mismanagement of the Gujarat riot by Modi.
This move, at least, relocated the debate to another level, thus preventing
Vajpayee's opponents from blaming *him* for the NDA's defeat.

In August, the BJP hosted a three-day *chintan baithak* (brain storming
session) in Goa in order to take stock of the party's post-electoral situation

and to analyse the reasons for its defeat. On the one hand, Madan Das Devi, representing the RSS, declared that the Sangh expected the BJP to remain firm on *Hindutva* and propagate its ideology. On the other hand, Vajpayee stressed the need to keep the NDA intact. The ten point 'document of conclusions' resolved to focus on ideological orientation and to continue with the NDA experiment. It maintained a moderate tone, in the sense that the meeting's resolutions did not even mention the word *Hindutva*.

At the same time, it committed itself to get closer to the RSS exactly when this movement had decided to monitor more effectively the BJP's organisation and strategy. In August 2004, a new administrative position was created within the Party, that of 'regional organisation secretary' to improve the coordination between the Delhi headquarters and the state units. It is significant that the first six holders of this new position all came from the RSS, in fact, they were all *pracharaks* (full-time cadres) (*The Hindu* 2004i). On the other hand, the reshuffling of the party leadership which took place after the defeat did not make any significant change: Venkaiah Naidu remained as the BJP's party president, Pramod Mahajan kept his post of General Secretary, Arun Jaitley and Rajnath Singh made the transition from the Union Government to become the Party's secretary and spokesperson respectively.

Based on the August meeting in Goa, it seems that the BJP has either not yet made up its mind and is still hesitating between two strategies, or that it may try to combine both strategies. In terms of organisation, it would rely more on the RSS cadres, whereas in terms of electoral politics, it would continue to value the NDA and therefore retain the same leadership. This is consistent with the assessment of the situation by the RSS. The *Sangh Parivar* knows that any return to a radical brand of Hindu nationalist politics by the BJP would alienate its allies and postpone the party's return to power. During the years of the NDA Government, the RSS had been able to infiltrate the administration in key policy domains, such as education.[8] With the NDA out of power, the RSS would not be able to exert that sort of influence. A few weeks before the 2004 elections, Madan Das, the joint general secretary of the RSS, has declared to *Organiser*, the mouthpiece of the Sangh: 'the government's responsibility is to create such an atmosphere that India can become great. I feel this atmosphere is being created' (2004: 18). Though the BJP cadres were not happy with the dilution of its *Hindutva* agenda by the BJP, the RSS leaders were happier with the NDA experiment.

The attempt at combining the pursuit of the NDA experiment and a closer association with the RSS also reflects the thinking of Advani, who should have been the natural candidate for a radical reorientation of the party. In March 2004, Advani articulated very clearly the party's dilemma:

> A country as vast and pluralistic as India cannot be ruled only by an ideological party such as the Jana Sangh. It has to be an aggregative

party [. . .] I propounded that either we limit our objectives as an ideological party and fight election in some states or corporations, but if we aspire to become a ruling party in India, we cannot be limited as an ideological party [. . .] To rule India, we have to be inclusive.

(*The Hindu* 2004c)

But is the combination of the NDA and the RSS tenable for the BJP? It depends whether such a tactic delivers or not. The outcome of the state assembly elections in Maharashtra and in Bihar – where the BJP is in the opposition – will give the first indication of the success of this tactic. If the general assessment is favourable, the party may pursue this line of conduct with the discrete approval of the RSS. If not, the radical alternative may offer a more promising scenario. Then the party would have to persuade Vajpayee that the NDA has become a spent force and that it is counterproductive for the BJP. The Hindu nationalist movement may also consider that, in contrast to many other political parties, the BJP is not based on one leader only and that it would be a good thing to depersonalise the BJP's image by sidelining Vajpayee. However, this would be a risky strategy – according to the 2004 CSDS exit poll, the BJP would have won 5.7 percentage points less than it did, had Vajpayee not been at the helm (*The Hindu* 2004e).

Another development that will have to be watched carefully by the BJP is the possible creation of a political outfit by the VHP. In July 2004, Ashok Singhal threatened that 'a political forum to challenge the BJP would soon be formed' (*The Hindu* 2004g). If so, it would immediately re-launch the Ayodhya movement. What could be, then, the response of the new INC-led UPA Government as well as that of the Hindu public – the two variables of our model that we have not studied yet?

Government policy has always been an important parameter in the shaping of the Jana Sangh's strategy, and then of the BJP. Whenever the BJP thought that the state would not strictly enforce the secular principles of the Constitution, they opted to agitate and unleash communal violence. When they feared repression, their strategy was more circumspect. Although the INC under Indira and then Rajiv Gandhi indulged in a new form of communalisation of politics, and the BJP seized this opportunity to impose its own ethos, the INC in 2004 fought the general election on a secularist plank and the UPA has been formed on a secularist platform. In fact, the strongest cementing force in the coalition is the opposition to Hindu nationalism. The INC needs the Communists, the DMK, and will possibly need the SP, all which are committed to secularism. We can expect that such a coalition will mean a return to the secular line of conduct that INC governments had adopted until the 1980s.

How would the Hindu society react to a re-launch of the Ayodhya movement anyway? So far, no ethno-religious mobilisation has been successful when Hindu society was not experiencing feelings of vulnerability.

Though the Hindus are in a large majority, Hindu feelings of vulnerability vis-à-vis internal threats (such as the perceived 'separatism' of Untouchables converting to other religions), and more importantly, vis-à-vis external threats (such as the pan-Islamic allegiance of the Muslim minority) have played an important role in the formation and development of Hindu nationalism over the last 80 years. This is evident from the impact of emblematic historical episodes, like the Khilafat movement, Partition, the Meenakshipuram conversions, or the *Shah Bano* case. Obviously, what I mean by 'vulnerability' may only be related to the perceived bias of the government in favour of minorities – like in the *Shah Bano* case. In these situations, the *Sangh Parivar* has become adept at crystallising anxieties and anger. But the *Sangh Parivar* requires fears to exist before it can exploit them to create a wave in its favour. Today, neither the internal nor external context of Hindu vulnerability exists. Muslims have not been favoured as a community for years, and externally, Pakistan is negotiating with India. Nevertheless, these anxieties could be reactivated if terrorist attacks by *jihadists* multiplied in Kashmir or elsewhere in India. It could also re-emerge if the UPA Government implemented pro-minority programmes, such as the granting of reservations to Muslims.

Conclusion

The electoral setback that the BJP registered in 2004 has put an end to 20 years of continuous electoral gains, but the set back is not as important as some of the commentators who relied too much on the pre-elections polls and were taken by surprise by the outcome, had suggested. Despite this, it is worrying for the BJP leaders, because the only state where the BJP's losses were really severe is the largest one in the Indian Union, Uttar Pradesh. In Uttar Pradesh, the BJP has been caught in a basic dilemma for the last ten years. When it reaches power by making alliances with the BSP, it alienates its upper caste support base; when it attempts to woo OBC voters, for instance by projecting Kalyan Singh as its candidate for Chief Ministership, it also alienates some of its upper caste supporters. On the other hand, if it promotes upper caste leaders only, it takes the risk of being cut off from the lower caste voters. After the 2004 debacle, the BJP replaced the state president with a Brahmin, Kesari Nath Tripathi. At the same time, in order to balance this decision, Kalyan Singh became the all-India leader in charge of Uttar Pradesh in New Delhi. The case of Uttar Pradesh suggests that the BJP needs to find a different solution to its electoral problem in each state. But of course Uttar Pradesh is a key state: if the BJP does not recover there, it might not be able to return to power.

Postscript (written in March, 2005)

Though limited, the BJP's defeat has put its strategy into question. The state assembly elections, which have taken place in Maharashtra in October 2004 and in Bihar and Jharkhand in February 2005, have not strengthened the adepts of *Hindutva* who would like to see the BJP returning to its strategy of ethno-religious mobilisation. The BJP has not been able to dislodge the INC from power in Maharashtra. In alliance with the Shiv Sena, the coalition won only 116 assembly seats, as opposed to 140 seats for the NCP/INC alliance. This failure resulted in the resignation of BJP President V. Naidu who was replaced by L.K. Advani in October 2004. In contrast, the BJP has performed well in Jharkhand, where it won the election with 30 assembly seats and 24 per cent of the valid votes. It seemed that the BJP was unaffected by the anti-incumbency factor in Jharkhand. The BJP also did well in Bihar, where Laloo Prasad Yadav's RJD was not able to form the government. In both Jharkhand and Bihar, the BJP had formed a pre-poll alliance with the JD(U), which benefited both parties. In Bihar, the JD(U) won 55 seats – only 20 less than the RJD – whereas the BJP won 37 seats. Such electoral scenarios demonstrate that the BJP benefits from its policy of coalition-making, all the more so when its partners are secular and OBC-oriented, like the JD(U).

Notes

1 Incidentally these were the three states where the party had won the assembly elections in 2003 – the polls from which the BJP wrongly came to the conclusion that it was bound to win the general election: the party was much less popular elsewhere.
2 This is what the CSDS exit poll survey shows (Singh and Verma 2004: AE-5).
3 For a better understanding of this phenomenon, see Manor (1998: 163–201).
4 Another component of the *Sangh Parivar*, the VHP, claimed that the sites of local mosques should be returned to Hindus for rebuilding temples allegedly destroyed by Muslim invaders.
5 After the killing of four Dalits who had been accused of cow slaughter in Haryana in 2002, Acharya Giriraj Kishore, an important VHP leader, reportedly declared that 'cows are more important than the Dalits'. This statement was widely commented upon in Dalit circles.
6 Former Gujarat Chief Minister Patel still resents the way he was removed from power in October 2001 to make way for Modi.
7 For additional perspectives on the internal dissension within the *Sangh Parivar*, see the contributions by John Zavos and James Manor (Chapters 2 and 3) in this volume.
8 For more details on this influence, see Chapter 8.

13 *Hindutva*'s march halted? Choices for the BJP after the 2004 defeat

Meghnad Desai

Introduction

Two things are true about the 2004 general election in India. First, that they attracted worldwide attention, perhaps for the first time spontaneously and not because of some violent incidents that could have occurred. Second, because just about no one anticipated the results.[1] The day before the results were announced, the *New York Times* summed up the feelings of many forecasting that the NDA would come in but with a reduced majority (Wildman 2004). This was the way most newspapers in India interpreted the successive rounds. As the exit polls came out, they were greeted with scepticism when they showed a large shortfall in the NDA's strength. Many had written off the INC, and 'India Shining' looked like the winning formula it was meant to be. A range of pre-budget sweeteners had been announced by the Finance Minister Jaswant Singh from early January onwards. When the INC denounced them as doing nothing for the common man, few thought it had landed a blow.

The NDA's surprise defeat and the INC's return to power raise a number of questions. One of them is about the nature of social science and its usefulness. If everyone gets the forecast wrong, why should we trust social scientists/India experts such as are gathered together in this volume? In what follows, I shall first address that question. The second, much larger question, concerns the choices facing the BJP in light of its defeat. In the title to this chapter I deliberately echo the question that Eric Hobsbawm asked of the British Labour Party after its election defeat in 1979 – rephrasing thus – '*Hindutva*'s march halted?' Had the BJP/NDA coalition won, there was little doubt that the BJP would have become the natural party of power, much like the INC used to be in the first 40 years after independence. It would have moved into a hegemonic position in a Gramscian sense and controlled the discourse along its own ideological tramlines. School textbooks would have forever changed children's views of Indian history and minorities would have had to come to terms with a precarious state of existence, henceforth under suspicion of their loyalty. When this did not happen, the question about BJP's future choices becomes urgent as much for the party activists as for students of Indian politics. The latter part of this chapter addresses that issue.

Uses of social science

What use are all the articles written about India, all the polls and surveys conducted, if virtually no one could predict the 2004 election outcome? Here I would like to make an econometrician's distinction between predictions and forecasts. Forecasts concern what would happen tomorrow or at some specific date in the future. The model at hand is cranked out, relevant values of the exogenous variables are fed in, and out comes the forecast values of the endogenous variables. An exit poll or an opinion poll tells us such a tale. Prediction is about questions of 'What if?'. If you alter some particular exogenous variable, what are the likely effects on the endogenous variables of interest? Prediction uses the structural information in the model to lay out the various likely effects, only some of which may actually come about. This is said not to evade the problem of failure of forecast. There still remains the question do experts know anything useful?

To answer that question I shall review the essays included in this volume. The initial drafts were written in early 2004, before the results of the elections were announced. Their objective analysis of the NDA's performance did not concern itself with the issue of its re-electability. However, the analyses yielded insights about the NDA's policy-making challenges, largely at national level. Likewise, the post-election discussions of the results interpreted them at first as people's protest about the limited rewards of economic reform for the poor, of the need to manage globalisation more equitably. After more reflection some people instead interpreted the results as revealing no national message, but as an outcome of state level forces which led to a surprise national outcome. This emerged clearly in articles written by Yogendra Yadav and colleagues from the CSDS which appeared on one of India's leading newspapers, *The Hindu*, on 20 May 2004 (2004e). There, the defeat was attributed to a fatal choice of dropping DMK and siding with AIADMK in Tamil Nadu and the reversal in the fortunes of TDP in Andhra Pradesh that accounted for a substantial part of the loss of the NDA's fortunes. The Trinamul Congress was humiliated as the Left's fortunes brightened in West Bengal and then losses in Gujarat were a severe blow to the BJP.

Now this set of events tell us that the nature of the NDA coalition was itself a force in the election, over and above the individual electoral fortunes of the parties. This is discussed in Alistair McMillan's analysis of coalitions, both at a theoretical and at an applied level. As he remarks '[r]ather than simply analysing coalition formation, coalition theory must also address the strategic incentives in maintaining or terminating coalitions in the light of the developing political context'. Quite so, since the

BJP made a mistake in breaking with a local opposition party in Tamil Nadu and aligning with a governing party late in the life of the coalition. Given the strong anti-incumbency tendency of Indian electorates – some things are constant in Indian politics – this was a predictable own goal. Nevertheless, McMillan, as well as Jenkins, Zavos and Adeney bring out the federal nature of India's polity whereby people primarily choose a state government, but coalition politics determines what the national ruling coalition will be like. This interplay of state and federal politics, at both the executive and the party levels, is similar to a nested game, which McMillan cites as a possible analytical tool for studying coalitions.[2]

There are also insights in this volume about the BJP's conduct prior to the 2004 general election. While it relied on sophisticated TV commercials and Short Message Service (SMS) text messaging, the BJP appears to have ignored the rural and the poorer urban voter. James Manor's chapter shows how the BJP's organisation is not at all strong, but quite thin, especially in rural areas. The INC was able to exploit this weakness by directing its leader, Sonia Gandhi, to large rural meetings. After the election, it was reported by many papers that the BJP had been sanguine about its chances and had failed to get its troops out for election work. In addition, there had been a reluctance of the RSS cadre to come out. Manor warns us against assuming that RSS always does the BJP's bidding or vice versa. This is an insight that will be useful in asking questions about the choices facing the BJP.

Nevertheless, between the RSS and the BJP, there are also differences about ideology. As Zavos and Manor point out, for the RSS *Hindutva* matters and its agenda is one of Hindu nationalism. The BJP, on the other hand, wants to win power and hold on to it. This requires coming out of the ghetto and making alliances. Thus, it was the alliance of the Jana Sangh with Jaya Prakash Narayan's *andolan* (movement) in Gujarat in 1974 that made the party respectable for the first time since the assassination of Mahatma Gandhi (for which the RSS and vaguely Hindu nationalist forces were blamed). Efforts of this type, as Jaffrelot points out,[3] were the incipient attempts by the Jana Sangh at coalition building. It means tackling bread and butter issues, not just the ideological ones. In the statewide elections held in late 2003, the BJP tried a *roti/kapda/makan* (food/clothing/shelter) strategy, and reaped dividends. This encouraged it to play the same card in the 2004 general election. This not only kept its coalition partners happy, but it was a way of casting its appeal wider. Indeed by attracting many ex-INC members to its fold on the eve of the election, including Muslim members (Najma Heptulla, for instance), the BJP was launching itself as the true successor of Nehru's Congress Party. But this action alienated its core ideological support, which wanted a commitment on *mandir* (temple) issues. It is no surprise that the post-election reactions by the VHP have been not entirely sympathetic. But this is precisely where the party lost its ideologically minded cadres. The

British Labour Party, for instance, is undergoing a very similar experience. If and when an ideological party widens its appeal to garner more votes, it stands to lose the support of its more fanatical supporters. This is a classic democratic compulsion. The BJP has tried to become an inclusive party, like the INC, and thus weakened its hold over the Hindu nationalist core.

Governing also involves dealing with day-to-day challenges. Since the balance of payments crisis of 1991 successive governments have had to rethink what they said about the economic reforms while in opposition, mostly since reforms are no longer a matter of choice. The only choice is the pace of reforms and an occasional twist one way or another. India needs to display a willingness to attract FDI and for that end demonstrate good governance. Thus, privatisation is urgent and reforms of the labour market necessary. This is a story, which again meshes in with the federalist theme as Rob Jenkins points out. Of course, reforms do not please the ideologues of the RSS and the BJP; hence the dilemma of governing and keeping faithful to one's beliefs raises its head again. The success of the BJP/NDA in managing the economy (by the end of its tenure the growth rate of GDP was over 8 per cent) alienated its core support, since it was soft on liberalisation and the entry of foreign capital.[4] By pointing out in its 'India Shining' commercials what it had done, the NDA Government also reminded its supporters of facts which were not to their liking. Hence, the 'India Shining' campaign did not only alienate rural voters.

The story of the BJP/NDA Government, as it unfolds in the various essays in this volume, is that of continuity rather than change. Whatever its rhetoric, the BJP is as much of a centralist political party as the INC. It wants a militarily strong India with a high status on the world stage. Thus Kundu, as well as Chiriyakandath and Wyatt, point out that the nuclear decision and the alliances with the US and Israel are driven by the *realpolitik* of India's ambitions to be taken seriously as a regional power. But at the same time, no 'national' party can ignore regional and caste forces in its policies. In a coalition with such parties that rely on caste, region and religion for their appeal, this is doubly so. Therefore, while an analysis of foreign policy and national security reveals continuity, it is in the domestic policy arena where we would expect local and contemporaneous pressures to differentiate the NDA's Government's policy from other governments.

However, here again the brute facts of coalition building point to the limits of what any dominant party in a coalition can do. The facts of life in India compel any coalition to accommodate regional and caste parties. These parties are, by and large, non-ideological, their principal focus being rent seeking for sharing with their clientele. So provisions for minorities and for particular states, the need to direct more revenues to the states with each successive Finance Commission are the common concerns of every coalition. Now that the INC is in power, it will have to play to the same tune as BJP had to as head of the NDA coalition. Subrata Mitra deals with the issue of minorities, while Katharine Adeney discusses in detail the BJP's attitude about the federal constitution. They each show how the BJP had to come to terms with minorities and states, despite its centralist and monist view of Hindu society.

The reality is that neither of the two largest national parties – INC or BJP – can by itself come to power. Indeed in the 2004 general election, their combined strength in the Lok Sabha fell from 293 seats in 1999 – 182 for the BJP plus 111 for the INC – to 283 seats in 2004 – 138 for the BJP and 145 seats for the INC – as did their vote share. India's politics is becoming more fragmented, more devolved and less majoritarian. This requires living with federalism. Katharine Adeney shows that, despite the BJP's ambivalence about linguistic states and its preference for a strong unitary India, the BJP has had to come to terms with regionalism and cope with the challenges of adapting and reforming the structure of the federation. One strategy to strengthen the centre against the regions is to break up the larger states into smaller units. Nevertheless, as big states are divided into smaller states, the number of small parties with a strictly local focus is going to rise, and the fragmentation of politics will increase. But, if this is the case, then a larger question is raised. Can the BJP ever realise its dream of a *Hindutva*-based government in India?

The halted march of *Hindutva*?

The defeat in 2004 is not just sad for the BJP; it is tragic for the party. Through the 1980s and 1990s, it has struggled to acquire a national status. Far from being a minority, extremist pariah party, it has commanded national attention and international respect. From the irresponsible behaviour of some of its leaders as part of a howling mob bringing down the Babri mosque in 1992, it rose to come to power (briefly) in 1996 and again in 1998 and 1999. Its strength was confirmed at 182 parliamentary seats in two general elections (1996 and 1998). This was a contrast from the Jana Sangh polling approximately 50 seats (much as the CPI/CPM used to). In 2004, it had the chance to move up 182 seats to the sunlit uplands of 200 seats and above. Had the BJP broken through to 225 seats, then it could have dominated the next coalition, or even ruled alone with outside support (much as Narasimha Rao managed to do between 1991 and 1996). Winning another five-year term would have been an immensely significant step for the BJP's programme of gaining cultural hegemony. What Murli Manohar Joshi wanted to do, as Marie Lall has argued in her piece, was to change the Indian view of history so as to demonise Muslim rule forever more. Five more years would have given the BJP ideologues a real stranglehold on history and social science disciplines. The new Congress-led Government has shown the importance of this by moving on the school history textbooks issue immediately.

However, the setback from 182 to 138 parliamentary seats is serious, despite the fact that in terms of share of the vote the BJP did better than the INC. The question is, 'Will this mean the end of the road for BJP's dream of ruling India as a single party and of installing a *Hindutva* Raj forever or is this just a blip, *reculer pour mieux sauter* (to back up so as to better leap over), and the BJP will bounce back next time?'

Through the 1990s, the BJP had a difficult trapeze act to perform. It wanted to be known as the party for Hindus and this required them to be strongly anti-Muslim, not simply anti-Pakistani. It also had to convince the voters that it could be a responsible party capable of competently ruling India. For the latter it needed to not only manage the economic reforms but also to build a coalition with disparate forces. Its Hindu phase led to Advani's *Rath Yatra* (chariot procession) of 1992 and the demolition of the Masjid at Ayodhya. Its more extreme supporters have moved from anti-Muslimism to sheer xenophobia, so that all non-Hindu religions are demonised. Attacks on Christian missionaries were the latest expression and weapon in the struggle. While Narendra Modi did not foment the post Godhra riots in 2002, he did nothing to curb them and was re-elected later that year. This told one section of the BJP that coming to power via mob riot was, if unattractive, at least an effective option. There was much talk of a 'Modi strategy' for winning mid-term state elections in Himachal Pradesh and elsewhere after Modi's triumphal re-election. This section of the party is the traditionalist core of the BJP whose favourite ideologue is Hedgewar and whose custodian is Advani.

The other face of the BJP is not as a Hindu party, but as a nationalist party, believing in India emerging as a strong nuclear power able to strut on the world stage with its weapons rather than any message of *ahimsa* (non-violence). It wants to show competence in government. This BJP wants a high status in world politics for India; it wants rapid economic growth with the latest technological gizmos. It wants India to rival China and contain Pakistan. Its favourite ideologue is Savarkar and Vajpayee is its face.

In possessing this Janus face, the BJP is not unusual. Ideological parties of the Left or the Right also face such a perpetual problem. The core supporters want to change the world, the pragmatic office seekers merely want to manage the world better than other parties have done. The ideologues want to take to the streets, mobilise the masses, bring down the old order, and usher in a new era. The pragmatists want to move in the corridors of power, raise real resources and achieve set targets. The very success of the pragmatists ruins the chances of the ideologues since the world is not ruined but improved.

Thus far, the BJP has managed to keep the two factions together since it wanted to achieve power. Having tasted power and made inroads in the cultural sphere, it badly wanted to continue in power. Indeed, the ideologues let the pragmatists have the front line roles in the election in the hope that their strategy would win another term to sharpen the ideological struggle. Now with a defeat, recriminations are breaking out as to who was responsible. There has already been a skirmish around the issue of Narendra Modi. Vajpayee was quoted as having said that Modi needed to be removed if the BJP was to win national confidence. The ideologues shot this down pretty quickly. Instead, they were quick to blame Arun Shourie who as the Minister for (under another name) privatisation was outstandingly successful. However, Shourie was not ideological enough for the RSS. On the other hand, the ideologues overreacted to the prospect of Sonia Gandhi becoming Prime Minister. BJP leaders, such as Uma Bharti and Sushma Swaraj, took this almost as a personal affront and instead of behaving like rulers of states; they behaved like the mob that destroyed the Masjid 12 years ago. In the event they were wrong footed by Sonia Gandhi who stepped back from taking the position of Prime Minister.

In opposition, the BJP will have difficulty keeping the ideologues down, unless there is a real prospect of a return to power soon. The party faces a problem of competing generations. The 'old guard', composed of Vajpayee, Advani and Joshi is moving on, and the 'new generation' of Pramod Mahajan, Arun Jaitley, Narendra Modi and Uma Bharti are waiting to take over. The ideology/pragmatism divide stretches across the generations. Unlike the INC, the BJP does not currently rule in many states, though it gained a few in the 2003 state assembly elections. Narendra Modi and Uma Bharti are ideologues, rather than pragmatics. However, the pragmatists were not totally marginalised since they were able to secure Arun Shourie a seat in the Rajya Sabha.

The BJP and its choices

The critical problem, however, will not be solely one of managing factions or the transition from one generation to the next. The structural problem facing the BJP is whether a party based on *Hindutva* can command a large enough vote share to come to power on its own?

The choice is between a sharp ideological and Hindu focus, which will test the hypothesis that since the majority of the voters are Hindus then a party based on Hinduism should eventually command majority support. The example, often cited by BJP ideologues, is that of Israel which bases itself on the strong racial/religious identity of Jews. Hinduism is, however, nothing like Judaism. It is pantheistic, lacks a single church or even a single book. It has no priesthood that is universally accepted. Hindus worship different gods and have various practices all of which pass as correct. There is no confession and no necessity to go to the temple everyday or even once a week.

Hinduism is not a single religion. It is neither unitary nor indeed unifying. Intra-faith rivalries between devotees of Vishnu as against Shiva are frequent, though not lethal like Shia–Sunni battles. During an attempt in 2003 by the Shankaracharya of Kanchi to settle the Ayodhya *mandir/masjid* (temple/mosque) dispute, the secretary of the VHP questioned his bona fides saying that the Shankaracharya was a Shivaite and the temple was dedicated to an avatar of Vishnu! If the VHP itself takes such a fragmented view of Hinduism what hope is there for ordinary citizens of uniting under the banner of Hinduism?

The founders of the RSS were aware of this problem. Indeed every effort at reforming Hinduism in the wake of the ideological challenge of British and indeed Western Imperialism has been at recasting the old religion in the image of a monotheistic creed such as Christianity. The movements of Brahmo Samaj, Arya Samaj and indeed Vivekanand, were efforts at sanitising if not semitising Hinduism, so that it would have one God, one Book. The exalted status that the nationalist leaders, such as Aurobindo, Tilak and Gandhi conferred on the *Bhagavad-Gita* by writing commentaries was one such effort. Nevertheless, that approach proved too highbrow for the masses. Initially the RSS eschewed religion and emphasised social regeneration of Hindu society.

But Hindu society is also not a unity. Even in its idealistic conception, it is a structured hierarchy that rejects egalitarianism. The caste structure has evolved from a four-fold *varnashrama* (castes) to multifarious *jatis* (subcastes) but it still retains not only the distinction between the upper (twice born) castes and the lower castes, but also the untouchables-*harijans* or *dalits* who are outside the pale and yet part of Hindu society. What would be regeneration of Hindu society for an upper caste RSS man would not be the same for a lower caste or a *dalit*. For the *dalit*, it would be the abolition of the hierarchy, which would constitute reform or regeneration. Hence, Ambedkar's decision to leave the Hindu fold altogether after a lifetime of fighting for reform and embracing Buddhism.

The upper castes are not numerous enough to hold power in a democracy by themselves. As westernised urban elites, they had a head start soon after Independence, but they were also members of the INC which meant that they were able to retain power. The pressures of democratic elections soon valorised the caste divisions and made jatis into vote banks. A party hoping to come to power had to recruit lower castes and dalits as well as Muslims. The INC did this effectively until the late 1980s. Then the Mandal Commission split the Hindu vote along upper and lower caste lines. The BJP's moment came then.

The agitation for the Ram temple in Ayodhya was a stroke of genius. Instead of the abstruse philosophy of the *Bhagavad-Gita*, the unifying symbol of Ram was upheld; known from the epic mythologies as an ideal person and popularised by Gandhi no less in his favourite *bhajan* (prayer), Raghupati Raghav Raja Ram. Here was a unifying symbol for Hindus, of upper as well as lower castes. If the *Hindutva* programme could be recast along the Ram bhakti lines, there was indeed a rainbow at the end of that dream.

The destruction of the *masjid* damaged the BJP's reputation, but it recovered by putting Vajpayee forward as its sober face and it was able to come to power as the leading member of a coalition. However, the provocative act of destroying a mosque had antagonised many smaller parties and thus the temple issue had to be put on ice. Had its ideologues displayed patience until single party rule by BJP became a reality, it may have been possible for the BJP to build a temple at Ayodhya. As it was, the BJP could not deliver what its impatient ideologues wanted and there was a distinct cooling between the various parts of the *Sangh Parivar*. In light of this history, both the VHP and the RSS were less than enthusiastic when the general elections were held in April 2004.

The structural question is, thus, as urgent as ever. Can *Hindutva* be Hindu based and still win a majority or does it have to be reshaped as nationalism first with less of an emphasis on Hinduism? Of course, there have been attempts to say that *Hindutva* is not about Hinduism, but about India and Indianness. The destruction of the Babri Masjid devalued that defence forever. As all can see, *Hindutva* is anti-Muslim even before it is pro-Hindu. So while the temple issue excites the ideologues of BJP, there is no hope of convincing the electorate that *Hindutva* is an inclusive philosophy.

Thus, Hinduism is a risky gambit for majority power. At best it can make BJP the largest party in a coalition, but not strong enough to meet the ideologues' demands. That was the lesson of the last government. Mere competence in governing and raising the growth rate of GDP – policies which would be almost 'secular' also did not help. How can BJP then shape its strategy so that it can win a majority on its own?

Hindutva or Hindu democracy?

In choosing Israel as their ideal country, the ideologues of *Hindutva* have missed a vital ingredient. Judaism is a non-proselytising religion, like Hinduism, but it is also exclusive and guards its frontiers fiercely. It has also the recent experience of the worst tragedy of modern times in the Holocaust. Its need for a protective approach to its identity is well understood. Hinduism is inclusive but, by and large, it has suffered no grave tragedy. The Partition of India was a traumatic event, but it was an Indian tragedy not a solely Hindu one despite efforts on the part of RSS and others to claim so. Muslims remain in India as do Sikhs, Christians and others. India is not so much a secular society as a multi-religious one. The Indian state in colonial times ran a regime that did not interfere in religious practices and discouraged, much to its chagrin, the Anglican Church from proselytising. The Indian state continued that after Independence, though secularism was added in the title of the Republic only in the mid-1970s by Indira Gandhi.[5]

The Partition of India, as well as Nehru's own attitudes, made religious affiliations in political parties a disadvantage. Speculations about the possibility of a Hindu Socialism, which flourished in the 1940s and early 1950s, were soon laughed off the court. Yet at the same time as India's independence, the recovery in Europe was aided by the revival of Christian Democratic

Parties. In Germany and Italy, Christian Democracy played a crucial role in stabilising and consolidating democracy after years of Fascism. Christian Socialism is a hardy plant in British politics (Stafford Cripps was a Christian Socialist, for example). Zionism at its origin was a socialist movement. The idea that religion and politics cannot or should not mix is a very peculiarly Indian idea shared by 'progressive' elements. The BJP has not countered this idea by pointing to the European experience with Christian Democracy. It has not even shown any awareness of Christian Democracy.

This is not the occasion to give a full account of Christian Democracy, but suffice it to say that it has adapted Christian ideals for the Cold War era of liberal democracy. Christian Democracy was always anti-Communist, but also very much in favour of business treating workers fairly and in a spirit of communal harmony rather than class struggle. Christian Democracy was a social as well as a political movement. It adapted itself to the secularising forces in European life by underplaying the formal religious elements in its make up and bringing out the social relevance of religious values. It was a conservative but socially inclusive movement. For around 40 years after 1945, it was the bulwark of Italian democracy and it is still alive as a powerful force in German politics.

It may be that the BJP may yet learn from the Christian Democratic experience or it may fall foul to its own contradictions. It is not my purpose to solve the BJP's problems. The only point of discussing Christian Democracy is to expose a successful model of combining religion with politics. If Christian Democracy can flourish in a secular Europe there is no reason, in theory at least, why a Hindu Democracy cannot flourish in India.

Conclusion

The defeat in the 2004 general election puts the BJP at a crossroads. It has to reconcile itself to never coming to power as a single party and hence implementing its *Hindutva* dream by stealth or not at all. In either case, a *Hindutva*-based India remains a distant prospect. It could, however, build a vote winning strategy by following the example of Christian Democratic parties that downplayed religion as such but took its ethical message into the social sphere. Will it be *Hindutva* or Hindu-Lite for the BJP?

Notes

1 During the conference on 'Coalition Politics and Hindu Nationalism' held at the Institute of Commonwealth Studies, James Manor cautioned against automatically assuming that the NDA would win the 2004 general election.
2 See Alistair McMillan's contribution to this volume (Chapter 1).
3 See Christophe Jaffrelot's discussion of this issue in Chapter 12.
4 See Rob Jenkins' discussion of this issue in Chapter 9.
5 Article 25 of the Indian Constitution provides for the free profession, practice and propagation of religion.

Bibliography

Official documents

AIR (1996) (Bombay) p. E.S.1115 Supreme Court, R. Prabhoo vs. P. Kunte, J. Verma, N. Singh and K. Veknatswami, JJ.

Bommai, S. (1994) *S.R. Bommai* v. *Union of India* 3 SCC 1.

Election Commission of India (1998) *Statistical Report on General Elections 1998 to the XII Lok Sabha*, New Delhi: Election Commission.

Election Commission of India (1999) *Statistical Report on General Elections 1999 to the XIII Lok Sabha*, New Delhi: Election Commission.

Election Commission of India (ND). Online. Available at: http://www.eci.gov.in (accessed 1 June 2004).

GoI (1990) 'The Constitution (Sixty-Fifth Amendment) Act'. Online. Available at: http://indiacode.nic.in/coiweb/amend/amend65.htm (accessed 15 February 2004).

GoI (2000a) 'The Constitution (Seventy-Ninth Amendment) Act, 2000'. Online. Available at: http://indiacode.nic.in/coiweb/amend/amend79.htm (accessed 16 February 2004).

GoI (2000b) 'The Constitution (Eightieth Amendment) Act, 2000'. Online. Available at: http://indiacode.nic.in/coiweb/amend/amend80.htm (accessed 16 February 2004).

GoI (2000c) 'The Constitution (Eighty-First Amendment) Act'. Online. Available at: http://indiacode.nic.in/coiweb/amend/amend81.htm (accessed 16 February 2004).

GoI (2000d) 'The Constitution (Eighty-Second Amendment) Act'. Online. Available at: http://indiacode.nic.in/coiweb/amend/amend82.htm (accessed 16 February 2004).

GoI (2000e) 'The Constitution (Eighty-Third Amendment) Act'. Online. Available at: http://indiacode.nic.in/coiweb/amend/amend83.htm (accessed 16 February 2004).

GoI (2001a) *National Policy for the Empowerment of Women*, Ministry of Human Resource Development, New Delhi.

GoI (2001b) GoI Ministry of Defence, *Reforming the National Security System: Recommendations of the Group of Ministers*. Online. Available at: http://mod.nic.in/newadditions/welcome.html (accessed 1 February 2004).

GoI (2002a) 'The Constitution (Eighty-Fourth Amendment) Act, 2002'. Online. Available at: http://indiacode.nic.in/coiweb/amend/amend84.htm (accessed 16 February 2004).

GoI (2002b) 'The Constitution (Eighty-Fifth Amendment) Act, 2001'. Online. Available at: http://indiacode.nic.in/coiweb/amend/amend85.htm (accessed 16 February 2004).

GoI (2002c) 'The Constitution (Eighty-Sixth Amendment) Act, 2002'. Online. Available at: http://indiacode.nic.in/coiweb/amend/amend86.htm (accessed 16 February 2004).

GoI (2003a) 'The Constitution (Eighty-Seventh Amendment) Act, 2003'. Online. Available at: http://www.hindu.com/thehindu/2003/05/09/stories/2003050907451300.htm (accessed 16 February 2004).

GoI (2003b) 'The Constitution (Eighty-Ninth Amendment) Act, 2003'. Online. Available at: http://indiacode.nic.in/incodis/whatsnew/Const94.htm and http://www.deccanherald.com/deccanherald/aug20/n4.asp (accessed 16 February 2004.

GoI (2003c) 'The Constitution (Ninetieth Amendment) Act, 2003'. Online. Available at: http://www.deccanherald.com/deccanherald/aug20/n4.asp (accessed 16 February 2004).

GoI (2003d) 'The Constitution (Ninety-First Amendment) Act, 2003'. Online. Available at: http://lawmin.nic.in/legislative/press-release.htm (accessed 16 February 2004).

GoI (2003e) 'The Constitution (Ninety-Second Amendment) Act, 2003'. Online. Available at: http://mpa.nic.in/postw03I.htm and http://manupatra.com/latest/latest.asp (accessed 16 February 2004).

GoI (2003f) 'The Constitution (Ninety-Fifth Amendment) Bill, 2003'. Online. Available at: http://www.stpam.org/law_updates/acts/mar03/ninetyf_amend_bill03.htm (accessed 16 February 2004).

GoI (2003g) *Annual Report 2002–2003*, New Delhi: Department of Women and Child Development, Ministry of Human Resource Development.

GoI (2003h) *Annual Report 2002–2003*, New Delhi: Ministry of Tribal Affairs.

GoI (2003i) *Annual Report 2002–2003*, New Delhi: Ministry of Social Justice and Empowerment.

GoI (2003j) GoI Ministry of Home Affairs *Annual Report, 2002–2003*. Online. Available at: http://mha.nic.in/annual-2002–2003/annual_rep.htm (accessed 2 January 2004).

GoI (2004a) *India's Foreign Trade Update*, New Delhi: Ministry of Commerce and Industry, GoI: Section II.1.a.

GoI (2004b) GoI Ministry of Defence, *Major Activities and Achievements*. Online. Available at: http://mod.nic.in/reports/achievements/majoractivities.doc (accessed 4 February 2004).

GoI (ND) GoI Ministry of Defence, *Associated Institutions*. Online. Available at: http://mod.nic.in/ainstitutions/welcome.html (accessed 16 February 2004).

Judgement by Justice M.B. Shah, D.M Dharmadhikari and H.K. Sema in Writ Petition (Civil) No. 98 of 2002, *Ms. Aruna Roy and others* v. *Union of India and others*.

Ministry of Tribal Affairs (ND). Online. Available at: http://tribal.nic.in/index1.htm (accessed on 27 January 2004).

National Security Council Secretariat (2002) 'National Security Index', in S. Kumar (ed.) *India's National Security: Annual Review 2002*, New Delhi: India Research Press.

National Security Strategy of the United States of America (2002). Online. Available at: http://www.whitehouse.gov/nsc/nss.html (accessed 10 October 2002).

Natural Resource Defense Council (2002) *The Consequences of Nuclear Conflict between India and Pakistan.* Online. Available at: http://www.nrdc.org/nuclear/southasia.asp (accessed 1 February 2004).

NCRWC (2002) *Report of the National Commission to Review the Working of the Constitution,* Delhi: Universal Law Publishing.

NEP (National Education Policy) (1986) Reproduced in P. Shukla (1988) *The New Education Policy,* Delhi: Sterling Publishers Private Ltd.

Planning Commission (2002) 'Commitments of the tenth plan to empower women', New Delhi: GoI.

Prime Minister's Office (2003) 'Inter state council meeting concludes', GoI: 28 August 2003. Online. Available at: http://pib.nic.in/archieve/lreleng/lyr2003/raug2003/28082003/r280820037.html (accessed 10 February 2004).

PROBE (1999) *The Public Report on Basic Education in India,* New Delhi: Oxford University Press.

SRC (States Reorganisation Commission) (1955) *Report of the States Reorganisation Commission,* compiled by S. Fazl Ali, H. Kunzru and K. Panikkar. New Delhi, GoI.

WTO (World Trade Organisation) (1999) Appellate Body Report: *India-Quantitative Restrictions on Imports of Agricultural, Textile and Industrial Products,* AB-1999-3, WT/DS90/AB/R (99-1329), adopted by Dispute Settlement Body, 22 September.

Zahira Habibulla H. Sheikh v. *State of Gujarat* (Best Bakery Case) (2004) Supreme Court of India, Judgment 12 April.

Books and articles

Abraham, I. (1998) *The Making of the Indian Atomic Bomb. Science, Secrecy and the Postcolonial State,* London: Zed Books.

Adeney, K. (2002) 'Constitutional centring: nation formation and consociational federalism in India and Pakistan', *Commonwealth and Comparative Politics,* 40(3): 8–33.

Adeney, K. (2003) 'Federal formation and consociational stabilisation: the politics of national identity articulation and ethnic conflict regulation in India and Pakistan', unpublished thesis, University of London.

Adeney, K. and Lall, M. (forthcoming) 'Institutional attempts to build national identity in India: internal and external dimensions'.

Adeney, K. and Wyatt, A. (2004) 'Democracy in South Asia: getting beyond the structure-agency dichotomy', *Political Studies,* 52(1): 1–18.

Advani, L. (1998) 'Globalisation on the solid foundation of Swadeshi', *Lecture to the 71st Annual Session of the Federation of Indian Chambers of Commerce and Industry,* 25 October. Online. Available at: http://www.rediff.com/business/1998/nov/02spl.htm (accessed 26 August 2003).

Ahluwalia, M. (2002) 'Privatization: from policy formulation to implementation. The view from the inside', Fifth Annual Fellow's Lecture 17 April 2002, Centre for the Advanced Study of India, University of Pennsylvania.

Ali Engineer, A. (2003) 'Communal riots in 2002: a survey', *Economic and Political Weekly,* 25 January. Online. Available at: http://www.epw.org.in (accessed 7 February 2004).

Anandan, S. (1995) 'BJP to bring out Koran in Sanskrit', *Indian Express,* 21 April.

Andersen, W. and Damle, S. (1987) *The Brotherhood in Saffron: The Rashtriya Swayamsevak Sangh and Hindu Revivalism,* New Delhi: Vistaar.

Aneja, A. (2003) 'U.S. drops objections to Phalcon transfer to India', *The Hindu International Edition*, 31 May: 9.

Ansari, J. (2001) 'Govt. move to "saffronise" education rejected', *The Hindu*, 3 September. Online. Available at: http://www.thehindu.com/thehindu/2001/09/03/stories/01030001.htm (accessed 7 February 2004).

Arora, B. (2000) 'Negotiating differences: federal coalitions and national cohesion', in F. Frankel, Z. Hasan, R. Bhargava and B. Arora (eds) *Transforming India: Social and Political Dynamics of Democracy*, Oxford: Oxford University Press: 176–206.

Ausaf Saied Vasfi, S. (1998) 'Women's Bill: introduction for introduction's sake', *Radiance*, 26 July.

Austin, G. (1999) *Working a Democratic Constitution: The Indian Experience*, Oxford: Oxford University Press.

Banerjee, D. (2004) *China, India and Pakistan: A Nuclear Arms Race in Asia?* European Institute for Asian Studies (Brussels) Policy Brief, 04/01, January.

Barry, B. (1975) 'The consociational model and its dangers', *European Journal of Political Research*, 3: 393–412.

Baru, S. (2002) 'Strategic consequences of India's economic performance', *Economic and Political Weekly*, 37(26), 29 June: 2583–92.

Baruah, A. (2003) 'No troops for Iraq without explicit U.N. mandate: India', *The Hindu International Edition*, 26 July: 9.

Basu, A. (1995) 'Feminism inverted: the gender imagery and real women of Hindu nationalism', in T. Sarkar and U. Butalia (eds) *Women and the Hindu Right: A Collection of Essays*, New Delhi: Kali for Women: 158–80.

Basu, A. (1999) 'Resisting the sacred and the secular', in P. Jeffery and A. Basu (eds) *Resisting the Sacred and the Secular: Women's Activism and Politicized Religion in South Asia*, New Delhi: Kali for Women.

Basu, A. (2001) 'The dialectics of Hindu nationalism', in A. Kohli (ed.) *The Success of India's Democracy*, Cambridge: Cambridge University Press: 163–90.

Basu, D. (2000) *Introduction to the Constitution of India*, 18th edn, Delhi: Wadhwa and Company Law Publishers.

Batliwala, S. (1993) 'Empowerment of women in South Asia: concepts and practices', *Report for Asian–South Pacific Bureau of Adult Education and FAO's Freedom from Hunger Campaign*, Bangalore: Action for Development.

Baviskar, A. (1997) 'Tribal politics and discourses of environmentalism', *Contributions to Indian Sociology*, 31(2): 195–223.

Baweja, H. (1998) 'Failing the test: Joshi's *Hindutva* agenda on education backfires on the Government', *India Today*, 2 November.

Bedi, R. (2002) 'The Tel Aviv connection grows', *Indiatogether.org*, July 2002. Online. Available at: http://www.indiatogether.org/govt/military/articles/isrlbuy02.htm (accessed 12 February 2004).

Benei, V. (2001) 'Teaching nationalism in Maharashtra schools', in C. Fuller and V. Benei (eds) *The Everyday State and Society in Modern India*, London: Hurst & Company.

Bhatt, A. (2003) 'Blackwill's concern over trade imbalance', *The Hindu International Edition*, 7 June: 11.

Bhatt, C. (2001) *Hindu Nationalism: Origins, Ideologies and Modern Myths*, Oxford: Berg.

Bhushan, P. (2002) 'India approves freedom of information law'. Online. Available at: http://www.freedominfo.org/news/india/ (accessed 12 January 2004).

Bidwai, P. and Vanaik, A. (2000) *New Nukes. India, Pakistan and Global Disarmament*, Oxford: Signal Books.

Bogdanor, V. (1988) 'Introduction', in V. Bogdanor (ed.) *Constitutions in Democratic Politics*, Aldershot, Gower: 1–16.

Bokhari, F. and Luce, E. (2004) 'General defiant in face of scandal over scientist's nuclear secrets', *Financial Times*, 18 February 2004.

Brass, P. (1982) 'Pluralism, regionalism and decentralising tendencies in contemporary Indian politics', in A. Wilson and D. Dalton (eds) *The States of South Asia: Problems of National Integration*, London: Hurst & Company: 223–64.

Brass, P. (2003) *The Production of Hindu–Muslim Violence in Contemporary India*, New Delhi: Oxford University Press.

Browne, E. and Franklin, M. (1973) 'Aspects of coalition payoffs in European parliamentary democracies', *American Political Science Review*, 67: 453–64.

Browne, E., Frendreis, J. and Gleiber, D. (1984) 'An "events" approach to the problem of cabinet stability', *Comparative Political Studies*, 17(2): 167–97.

Bueno de Mesquita, B. (1975) *Strategy, Risk and Personality in Coalition Politics: The Case of India*, Cambridge: Cambridge University Press.

Buvinic, M. (1986) 'Projects for women in the Third World: Explaining their misbehaviour', *World Development*, 14(5): 653–64.

Chandra, B. (2002) 'Texts were rewritten in Nazi Germany, Pak', *Indian Express*, 6 October 2002.

Chandrasekhar, C. and Ghosh, J. (2000) 'Maccal devolution in the era of globalisation', *MacroScan: An alternative economics webcentre*, 22 August 2000. Online. Available at: http://www.macroscan.com/the/macro/aug00/mac220800Fiscal_ Devolution_1.htm (accessed 17 February 2004).

Chatterjee, P. (1993) *The Nation and its Fragments: Colonial and Post-colonial Histories*, Princeton: Princeton University Press.

Chatterjee, P. (1999) 'Modernity, democracy and a political negotiation of death', *South Asia Research*, 19(1): 103–19.

Chengappa, R. (2000) *Weapons of Peace: The Secret Story of India's Quest to be a Nuclear Power*, New Delhi: Harper Collins Publishers India.

Chhibber, P. and Kollman, K. (2004) *The Formation of National Party Systems: Federalism and Party Competition in Britain, Canada, India, and the US*, Princeton: Princeton University Press.

Chhibber, P. and Nooruddin, I. (2004) 'Do party systems count? The number of parties and government performance in the Indian states', *Comparative Political Studies*, 37(2): 152–87.

Chiriyankandath, J. (1989) 'The US and Indo-Israeli relations', *Israeli Foreign Affairs*, 5(6) June: 1, 5–7.

Chiriyankandath, J. (1991) 'Indian opposition demands full ties', *Israeli Foreign Affairs*, 7(9) November: 5.

Cohen, S. (2001) *India: Emerging Power*, New Delhi: Oxford University Press.

Cook, T. (2002) *Nested Political Coalitions: Nation, Regime, Program, Cabinet*, London: Praeger.

Corbridge, S. (2000) 'Competing inequalities: The Scheduled Tribes and the reservations system in India's Jharkhand', *Journal of Asian Studies*, 59(1): 62–85.

Corbridge, S. and Harriss, S.J. (2000) *Reinventing India. Liberalization, Hindu Nationalism and Popular Democracy*, Cambridge: Polity.

Cox, A., Furlong, P. and Page, E. (1985) *Power in Capitalist Society: Theory, Explanations and Cases*, Brighton: Wheatsheaf.

Das Gupta, J. (1998) 'Community, authenticity and autonomy: insurgence and institutional development in India's Northeast', in A. Basu and A. Kohli (eds) *Community Conflicts and the State in India*, Delhi: Oxford University Press: 183–214.

Das, S. (2001) *Public Office, Private Interest: Bureaucracy and Corruption in India*, New Delhi: Oxford University Press.

Datar, A. (2004) 'A vote for secular politics', *The Hindu*, 20 May: AE–2.

de Swaan, A. (1973) *Coalition Theories and Cabinet Formations: A Study of Formal Theories of Coalition Formation Applied to Nine European Parliaments After 1918*, London: Elsevier.

Deshpande, C. (2001) 'Empowering women of the Hindu right: a case study of Shiv Sena's Mahila Aghadi', unpublished MPhil thesis, University of Oxford.

Dettman, R. (2001) *India Changes Course: Golden Jubilee to Millennium*, Westport: Praeger.

Dev, M. (2003) '*Rural Employment: Trends and Policies*', paper presented at the All India Conference on Agriculture and Rural Society in Contemporary India, Bardhaman, West Bengal, 17–20 December.

Dixit, J. (1996) *My South Block Years: Memoirs of a Foreign Secretary*, New Delhi: UBPSD.

Dodd, L. (1976) *Coalitions in Parliamentary Government*, Princeton: Princeton University Press.

Downs, A. (1957) *An Economic Theory of Democracy*, New York: Harper and Row.

Drèze, J. and Sen, A. (2003) 'Basic education as a political issue', in B. Tilak (ed.) *Education, Society and Development*, New Delhi: NIEPA: 3–48.

Duverger, M. (1963) *Political Parties: Their Organisation and Activity in the Modern State*, New York: Wiley.

Echeverri-Gent, J. (2002) 'Politics in India's decentred polity', in A. Ayres and P. Oldenburg (eds) *India Briefing: Quickening the Pace of Change*, New York: East Gate Book: 19–53.

Echeverri-Gent, J. (2004) 'Financial globalization and India's equity market reforms', in R. Jenkins and S. Khilnani (eds) *The Politics of India's Next Generation of Economic Reforms*, Special Issue of *India Review*, 3(4): 306–32.

Evans, G. and O'Leary, B. (2000) 'Northern Irish voters and the British–Irish agreement: foundations of a stable consociational settlement?', *Political Quarterly*, 71(1): 78–101.

Friedman, T. (2004) 'What's that sound?', *New York Times*, 1 April 2004.

Galanter, M. (1997) 'Pursuing equality: an assessment of India's policy of compensatory discrimination for disadvantaged groups', in S. Kaviraj (ed.) *Politics in India*, Delhi: Oxford University Press: 187–99.

Gallie, W. (1955–56) 'Essentially contested concepts', *Proceedings of the Aristotelian Society*, vol. 56.

Ganguly, S. (1994) 'The Prime Minister and foreign and defence policies', in J. Manor (ed.) *Nehru to the Nineties: The Changing Office of Prime Minister in India*, London: Hurst & Company: 138–60.

Ganguly, S. (2002) *Conflict Unending? India–Pakistan Relations Since 1947*, Oxford: Oxford University Press.

Garver, J. (2002) *The China–India–U.S. Triangle: Strategic Relations in the Post-Cold War Era*, Seattle: National Bureau of Asian Research.

Ghosh, A. and Sengupta, N. (1982) 'The nationality question in Jharkhand', in N. Sengupta (ed.) *Fourth World Dynamics: Jharkhand*, Delhi: Authors Guild Publications: 231–54.

Ghosh, P. (1999) *BJP and the Evolution of Hindu Nationalism: from Periphery to Centre*, New Delhi: Manohar.

Ghosh, P. (2003) 'The Congress and the BJP: Struggle for the heartland', in A. Mehra, D. Khanna and G. Kueck (eds) *Political Parties and Political Systems*, New Delhi: Sage: 224–43.

Gillan, M. (1998) 'BJP in 1998 Lok Sabha elections in West Bengal: Transformation of opposition politics', *Economic and Political Weekly*, 5–12 September: 2391–5.

Golwalkar, M.S. (1939) *We or Our Nation Defined*, Nagpur: Bharat Publications.

Golwalkar, M.S. (1944) *We or Our Nation Defined*, Nagpur: Bharat Prakashan.

Golwalkar, M.S. (1966) *Bunch of Thoughts*, Bangalore: Vikram Prakashan.

Golwalkar, M.S. (1980) *Bunch of Thoughts*, Bangalore: Jagarana Prakashana.

Gordon, S. (1995) *India's Rise to Power in the Twentieth Century and Beyond*, Basingstoke: Macmillan.

Graham, B.D. (1987) 'The challenge of Hindu nationalism: the Bharatiya Janata Party in contemporary politics', *Hull Papers in Politics*, October: 15.

Graham, B.D. (1990) *Hindu Nationalism and Indian Politics: the Origins and Development of the Bharatiya Jana Sangh*, Cambridge: Cambridge University Press.

Gupta, D. (1997a) 'Positive discrimination and the question of fraternity: contrasting Ambedkar and Mandal on reservations', *Economic and Political Weekly*, 32(31), 2 August: 1971–78.

Gupta, D. (1997b) 'Ethnicity and Politics', in S. Kaviraj (ed.) *Politics in India*, Delhi: Oxford University Press: 228–40.

Gupta, S. (2004) 'Interview of P.V. Narasimha Rao, broadcast on NDTV program "Walk the Talk"', *The Indian Express*, 11 May. Online. Available at: http://www.indianexpress.com/full_story.php?content_id=46723&spf=true (accessed 1 June 2004).

Hall, S. (1996) 'The problem of ideology: Marxism without guarantees', in D. Morley and K. Chen (eds) *Stuart Hall: Critical Dialogues in Cultural Studies*, Routledge: London: 25–46.

Hansen, T. (1998) 'The ethics of *Hindutva* and the spirit of capitalism', in T. Hansen and C. Jaffrelot (eds) *The BJP and the Compulsions of Politics in India*, Delhi: Oxford University Press: 291–314.

Hansen, T. (1999) *The Saffron Wave: Democracy and Hindu Nationalism in Modern India*, Princeton: Princeton University Press.

Hansen, T. (2001) *The Wages of Violence: Naming and Identity in Post-colonial Bombay*, Princeton: Princeton University Press.

Hansen, T. and Jaffrelot, C. (eds) (1998a) *The BJP and the Compulsions of Politics in India*, Delhi: Oxford University Press.

Hansen, T. and Jaffrelot, C. (1998b) 'Introduction: The BJP after the 1996 elections', in T. Hansen and C. Jaffrelot (eds) *The BJP and the Compulsions of Politics in India*, Delhi: Oxford University Press: 1–21.

Hansen, T., Hasan, Z. and Jaffrelot, C. (1998) 'Short cuts to power: From Lucknow to Delhi', in T. Hansen and C. Jaffrelot (eds) *The BJP and the Compulsions of Politics in India*, Delhi: Oxford University Press: 315–32.

Hardgrave, R. and Kochanek, S. (1993) *India: Government and Politics in a Developing Nation*, 5th edn, London: Harcourt Brace College Publishers.

Hardiman, D. (2000) *Christianity and the Adivasis of Western India: 1880–1930*, paper presented at the 16th European Modern South Asian Studies Conference, Edinburgh.

Hardiman, D. (2002) 'Passing blame on Godhra Muslims', *Economic and Political Weekly*, 37(19), 11 May: 1785.

Harding, L. (2003) 'Russia leases nuclear bombers to India', the *Guardian*, 20 January.

Harriss, J. (2003) *India: The Bitter Fruits of Grandiose Ambition*, LSE DESTIN Working Paper 03-45.

Harriss-White, B. (2003) *India Working: Essays on Society and Economy*, Cambridge: Cambridge University Press.

Hasan, Z. (1999) 'Gender politics, legal reform, and the Muslim community in India', in P. Jeffery and A. Basu (eds) *Resisting the Sacred and the Secular: Women's Activism and Politicized Religion in South Asia*, New Delhi: Kali for Women: 71–88.

Heath, A. and Yadav, Y. (1999) 'The united colours of Congress: Social profile of Congress voters, 1996 and 1998', *Economic and Political Weekly*, 34(34/35), 28 August–3 September: 2518–28.

Heath, O. (1999) 'Anatomy of BJP's rise to power: social, regional and political expansion in the 1990s', *Economic and Political Weekly*, 21–28 August: 2511–17.

Hewitt, V. (2000) 'A wolf at the door? Politics, ideology, and the BJP's rise to national power 1989–99', paper presented at the annual conference of the Political Studies Association, London, April.

Horowitz, D. (1985) *Ethnic Groups in Conflict*, Berkeley: University of California Press.

Horowitz, D. (1991) 'Electoral systems for a divided society', in D. Horowitz (ed.) *A Democratic South Africa? Constitutional Engineering in a Divided Society*, Berkeley: University of California Press: 163–95.

Huang, Y. and Khanna, T. (2003) 'Can India overtake China?', *Foreign Policy*, July/August: 74–81.

Hussain, A. (2001) 'Dramatic rise in Kashmir violence', *BBC News*, 8 November. Online. Available at: http://news.bbc.co.uk/1/hi/world/south_asia/1645302.stm (accessed 19 March 2004).

Jacobsohn, G. (2003) *The Wheel of Law: India's Secularism in Comparative Perspective*, Princeton: Princeton University Press.

Jaffrelot, C. (1996) *The Hindu Nationalist Movement and Indian Politics, 1925 to the 1990s: Strategies of Identity-Building, Implantation and Mobilisation (with Special Reference to Central India)*, London: Hurst & Company.

Jaffrelot, C. (1998a) 'BJP and the challenge of factionalism in Madhya Pradesh', in T. Hansen and C. Jaffrelot (eds) *The BJP and the Compulsions of Politics in India*, Delhi: Oxford University Press: 267–90.

Jaffrelot, C. (1998b) 'The Sangh Parivar between Sanskritization and social engineering', in T.B. Hansen and C. Jaffrelot (eds) *The BJP and the Compulsions of Politics in India*, Delhi: Oxford University Press: 22–72.

Jaffrelot, C. (2000) 'Hindu nationalism and democracy', in F. Frankel (ed.) *Transforming India: Social and Political Dynamics of Democracy*, Delhi and Oxford: Oxford University Press: 353–78.

Jaffrelot, C. (2003) 'Communal riots in Gujarat: the state at risk?', *Heidelberg Papers in South Asian and Comparative Politics*, 17 (July). Online. Available at: http://www.hpsacp.uni-hd.de (accessed on 31 August 2004).

Jaffrelot, C. (2004) 'From Indian territory to Hindu *Bhoomi*: the ethnicisation of nation-state mapping in India', in J. Zavos, A. Wyatt and V. Hewitt (eds) *Politics of Cultural Mobilization in India*, New Delhi, Oxford University Press: 197–215.

Jaffrelot, C. (2005a) *Dr Ambedkar and Untouchability: Analysing and Fighting Caste*, London: Hurst.

Jaffrelot, C. (ed.) (2005b) *The Sangh Parivar: A Reader*, Delhi: OUP.

Jasbir Singh, R. (ed.) (2000) *Indian Defence Yearbook 2000*, Dehra Dun: Natraj Publishers.

Jayapalan, N. (2001) *Problems of Indian Education*, Delhi: Atlantic Publishers and Distributors.

Jeffery, P. and Jeffery, R. (1999) 'Gender, community, and the local state in Bijnor, India', in P. Jeffery and A. Basu (eds) *Resisting the Sacred and the Secular: Women's Activism and Politicized Religion in South Asia*, New Delhi: Kali for Women: 123–42.

Jeffrey, R. (1994) *What's Happening to India: Punjab, Ethnic Conflict, Mrs Gandhi's Death and the Test for Federalism*, Basingstoke: Macmillan.

Jenkins, R. (1999) *Democratic Politics and Economic Reform in India*, Cambridge: Cambridge University Press.

Jenkins, R. (2003a) 'How federalism influences India's domestic politics of WTO engagement (and is itself affected in the process)', *Asian Survey*, 43(4): 598–621.

Jenkins, R. (2003b) 'International development institutions and national economic contexts: Neoliberalism encounters India's indigenous political traditions', *Economy and Society*, 32(4): 584–610.

Joshi, G. (2003) 'The story of the Central Vigilance Commission Bill, 2003', *Commonwealth Human Rights Initiative 2003*. Online. Available at: http://www.human-rightsinitiative.org/programs/aj/police/india/initiatives/story_of_the_central_vigilance_commission_story_2003.pdf (accessed 14 January 2004).

Joshi, P. (2003) 'From chalk to cheese', *Outlook*, 18 August.

Kabeer, N. (1999) 'Resources, agency, achievements: reflections on the measurement of women's empowerment', *Development and Change*, 30(3): 435–64.

Kakuta, E. (2002) 'Hindu nationalist movement and rural development: a case study of Deendayal Research Institute: Chitrakoot Project', unpublished MPhil thesis, University of Oxford.

Kale, S. (2002) 'The political economy of India's second-generation reforms', *The Journal of Strategic Studies*, 25(4) December: 207–25.

Kapur, A. (1993) 'From deity to crusader: the changing iconography of Ram', in G. Pandey (ed.) *Hindus and Others: the Question of Identity in India Today*, New Delhi: Viking: 74–109.

Katju, M. (2003) *Vishwa Hindu Parishad and Indian Politics*, Hyderabad: Orient Longman.

Katyal, K. (2004) 'After the breakthrough', *The Hindu*, 14 January.

Keesing's (1998–2003) *Keesing's Record of World Events*, London: Longman, Vols. 44–9.

Khare, H. (2003) 'Transforming the BJP', *The Hindu*, 18 September.

Khare, H. (2004) 'Waiting for the Atal decade', *Seminar* 533. Online. Available at: http://www.india-seminar.com (accessed 30 March 2004).

Kothari, R. (1964) 'The Congress "system" in India', *Asian Survey*, 4(12): 1161–73.

Krishna, A. (2001) 'The Kargil war', in A. Krishna and P. Chari (eds) *Kargil: The Tables Turned*, New Delhi: Manohar: 77–138.

Krishnaswami, S. (1998) 'A terrible mistake: Clinton', *The Hindu International Edition*, 23 May: 3.

Krishnaswami, S. (2003) 'India–US to step up defence cooperation', *The Hindu International Edition*, 16 August: 9.

Kuczynski, P. and Williamson, J. (eds) (2003) *After the Washington Consensus: Restarting Growth and Reform in Latin America*, Washington, DC: Institute for International Economics.

Kumar Singh, U. (2004) 'POTA and federalism', *Economic and Political Weekly*, 1 May. Online. Available at: http://www.epw.org.in (accessed 31 May 2004).

Kumar, S. and McMillan, A. (2004) 'Caste matters, but so do a whole lot of other things', *The Hindu*, 20 May. Online. Available at: http://www.hindu.com/elections2004/verdict2004/stories/2004052000310700.htm (accessed 30 May 2004).

Kumaraswamy, P. (2000) 'South Asia after the Cold War. Adjusting to new realities', in L. Fawcett and Y. Sayigh (eds) *The Third World Beyond the Cold War: Continuity and Change*, Oxford: Oxford University Press: 171–99.

Kundu, A. (1998) *Militarism in India: The Army and Civil Society in Consensus*, London: I.B. Tauris.

Kux, D. (1993) *Estranged Democracies: India and the United States 1941–1991*, New Delhi: Sage.

Kux, D. (2002) 'A remarkable turnaround: U.S.–India relations', *Foreign Service Journal*, October: 18–23.

Lal, S. (2003) 'Can good economics ever be good politics? Case study of the power sector in India', mimeo, revised version of a paper presented to a consultation organised by the World Development Report 2004 team, The World Bank, 31 July, Washington, DC.

Lall, M. (2001) *India's Missed Opportunity*, Aldershot: Ashgate.

Laver, M. and Budge, I. (eds) (1992) *Party Policy and Government Coalitions*, New York: St Martin's Press.

Laver, M. and Schofield, N. (1990) *Multiparty Government: The Politics of Coalition in Europe*, Oxford: Oxford University Press.

Laver, M. and Schofield, N. (1991) *Multiparty Government*, Oxford: Oxford University Press.

Lijphart, A. (1969) 'Consociational democracy', *World Politics*, 21(2): 207–25.

Lijphart, A. (1977) *Democracy in Plural Societies: A Comparative Exploration*, New Haven, Yale University Press.

Lijphart, A. (1984) *Democracies: Patterns of Majoritarian and Consensus Government in Twenty-One Countries*, New Haven and London: Yale University Press.

Lijphart, A. (1990) 'Electoral systems, party systems and conflict management in divided societies', in R. Schrire (ed.) *Critical Choices for South Africa*, Cape Town: Oxford University Press: 2–13.

Linz, J. (1978) *The Breakdown of Democratic Regimes*, Baltimore: Johns Hopkins University Press.

Linz, J., Stepan, A. and Yadav, Y. (2004) '"Nation State" or "State Nation"? Comparative reflections on Indian democracy', paper presented at the third NETSAPPE meeting in Paris, 28–30 June.

Louis, P. (2003) 'Scheduled castes and tribes: the reservation debate', *Economic and Political Weekly*, 38(25): 2475–8.

Luce, E. (2004) 'India hails new "partnership" with the US', *Financial Times*, 13 January.

Luebbert, G. (1986) *Comparative Democracy: Policymaking and Governing Coalitions in Europe and Israel*, New York: Columbia University Press.

Mahmood, C. (1996) *Fighting for Faith and Nation: Dialogues with Sikh Militants*, Philadelphia: University of Pennsylvania Press.

Majumder, S. (2003) 'Did nuclear status boost India's clout?', *BBC News*, 5 December. Online. Available at: http://www.bbc.co.uk/go/pr/fr/-/1/hi/world/south_asia/3016775.stm (accessed 12 February 2004).

Majumder, S. (2004) 'India steers clear of nuclear row', *BBC News*, 9 February. Online. Available at: http://news.bbc.co.uk/go/pr/fr/-/2/hi/south_asia. 3472061.stm (accessed 13 February 2004).

Manasa (2000) 'Karnataka and the Women's Reservation Bill', *Economic and Political Weekly*, 28 October: 2475–8.

Manor, J. (1994) 'Organisational weakness and the rise of Sinhalese Buddhist extremism', in M. Marty and R. Appleby (eds) *Accounting for Fundamentalisms: The Dynamic Character of Movements*, Chicago and London: University of Chicago Press: 770–84.

Manor, J. (1995) 'Regional parties in federal systems', in D. Verney and B. Arora (eds) *Multiple Identities in a Single State: Indian Federalism in Comparative Perspective*, Delhi: Konark Publishers: 105–35.

Manor, J. (1996) 'Ethnicity and politics in India', *International Affairs*, 72(1): 459–75.

Manor, J. (1998) 'Southern discomfort: the BJP in Karnataka', in T. Hansen and C. Jaffrelot (eds) *The BJP and the Compulsions of Politics in India*, Delhi: Oxford University Press: 163–201.

Manor, J. (2000) 'Small-time political fixers in Indian states: "towel over armpit"', *Asian Survey* (September–October): 816–35.

Manor, J. (2001) 'Centre-state relations', in A. Kohli, *The Success of India's Democracy*, Cambridge: Cambridge University Press: 78–102.

Manor, J. (2004) 'The Congress defeat in Madhya Pradesh', *Seminar*, 534, February: 18–24.

Marcelo, R. (2004) 'India to close Russian aircraft carrier deal', *Financial Times*, 19 January.

Mawdsley, E. (2002) 'Redrawing the body politic: federalism, regionalism and the creation of new states in India', *Commonwealth and Comparative Politics*, 40(3): 34–54.

McGarry, J. and O'Leary, B. (1995) *Explaining Northern Ireland: Broken Images*, Oxford: Blackwell.

McMillan, A. (2000) 'Delimitation, democracy, and the end of the constitutional freeze', *Economic and Political Weekly*, 8 April: 1271–6.

McMillan, A. (2001a) 'Population change and the democratic structure', *Seminar*, 506: 50–6.

McMillan, A. (2001b) 'Constitution 91st Amendment Bill: a constitutional fraud?', *Economic and Political Weekly*, 14 April: 1171–4.

Mearsheimer, J. (2001) *The Tragedy of Great Power Politics*, New York: W.W. Norton.

Mehra, R. (1997) 'Women, empowerment and economic development', *The Annals of the American Academy of Political and Social Science*, 554: 136–49.

Mehta, P. (2003) 'A new foreign policy?', *Economic and Political Weekly*, 38(30), 26 July: 3173–5.

Mehta, P. (2004) 'The education wars', *The Hindu*, 8 January.

Menon, N. (1998) 'State/gender/community: citizenship in contemporary India', *Economic and Political Weekly*, 33(5), 31 January: PE 3–10.

Menon, N. (2000) 'Elusive "woman": Feminism and Women's Reservation Bill', *Economic and Political Weekly*, 35(44), 28 October: 3835–44.

Mershon, C. (2002) *The Costs of Coalition*, Stanford, California: Stanford University Press.

Mill, J. (1817) *The History of British India*, London: Baldwin Cradock and Joy.

Misra, S. and Fazili, E. (2003) 'Article 356 to be used only with safeguards: Inter-State Council arrives at consensus', *The Tribune*, 29 August. Online. Available at: http://www.tribuneindia.com/2003/20030829/main1.htm (accessed 10 February 2004).

Mitra, S. (2003a) 'The morality of communal politics: Paul Brass, Hindu–Muslim conflict and the Indian State', *India Review*, 2(4): 15–30.

Mitra, S. (2003b) 'The reluctant hegemon: India's self-perception and the South Asian strategic environment', *Contemporary South Asia*, 12(3): September: 399–417.

Mitra, S. and Fischer, A. (2002) 'Sacred laws and the secular state: an analytical narrative of the controversy over personal laws in India', *India Review*, 1: 99–130.

Mitra, S. and Singh, V.B. (1999) *Democracy and Social Change in India: A Cross-Sectional Analysis of the Indian Electorate*, Delhi: Sage.

Mody, A. (2003) 'Bodos sign peace accord with centre', *The Hindu*, 11 February. Online. Available at: http://www.thehindu.com/2003/02/11/stories/2003021105560100.htm (accessed 11 February 2004).

Mohan, C. (2002) 'Budget and security strategy', *The Hindu*, 28 February.

Mohan, C. (2003) *Crossing the Rubicon. The Shaping of India's New Foreign Policy*, New Delhi: Viking.

Mohanty, C. (1991) 'Under Western eyes: feminist scholarship and colonial discourses', in C. Mohanty, A. Russo and L. Torres (eds) *Third World Women and the Politics of Feminism*, Bloomington: Indiana University Press: 51–80.

Morris-Jones, W. (1971) *The Government and Politics of India*, London: Hutchinson.

Mukherji, R. (2004) 'Managing competition: politics and the building of independent regulatory institutions', in R. Jenkins and S. Khilnani (eds) *The Politics of India's Next Generation of Economic Reforms*, Special Issue of *India Review*, 3(4): 278–305.

Mukhopadhya, N. (2004) 'Taming of the shrew', *Hindustan Times*, 2 March: 10.

Müller, W. and Strøm, K. (eds) (2000) *Coalition Governments in Western Europe*, Oxford: Oxford University Press.

Munda, R. (1988) 'The Jharkhand movement: retrospect and prospect', *Social Change*, 48(2): 28–58.

Muralidharan, S. (2000) 'A conclave of eight', *Frontline*, 2 September.

Nadkarni, J. (2001) 'The defence budget: lost opportunities', *Rediff.com*, 14 March. Online. Available at: http://www.rediff.com/news/2001/mar/14nad.htm (accessed 23 November 2003).

Nandy, A. (1983) *The Intimate Enemy: Loss and Recovery of Self Under Colonialism*, Delhi: Oxford University Press.

Narasimha Rao, G. and Balakrishna, K. (1999) *Indian Elections: The Nineties*, Delhi: Har-Anand.

Narayan, J. (2003) 'A vital step in cleaning our polity: an analysis of the new Campaign Funding Reform Law'. Online. Available at: http://www.frdi.org/documents/ (accessed 30 January 2004).

Nayar, B. and Paul, T. (2003) *India in the World Order. Searching for Major-Power Status*, Cambridge: Cambridge University Press.

Nehru, J. (1985) *Discovery of India*, New Delhi: Oxford University Press.

Norton-Taylor, R. and MacAskill, E. (2002) '£1bn arms push to India', *The Guardian*, 12 January.

O'Leary, B. (2003) 'Multi-national federalism, federacy, power-sharing and the Kurds of Iraq', paper presented at Multi-Nationalism, Power-Sharing and the Kurds in a New Iraq, Cafritz Foundation Conference Center, George Washington University 12 September.

Osborne, E. (2001) 'Culture, development, and government: reservations in India', *Economic Development and Social Change*, 49(3): 659–85.

Pai, Y. and Adler, S. (2001) *Cultural Foundations of Education*, 3rd edn, Upper Saddle River: Merrill Prentice Hall.

Palshikar, S. and Birmal, N. (2004) 'Shifting loyalties don't augur well for Congress, NCP', *The Hindu*, 20 May: AE-5.

Panagariya, A. (2002) 'India at Doha: retrospect and prospect', *Economic and Political Weekly*, 37(4), 26 January: 279–84.

Pandey, G. (1990), *The Construction of Communalism in Colonial North India*, New Delhi: Oxford University Press.

Parsai, G. (2003) 'RS passes bill on service tax', *The Hindu*, 9 May. Online. Available at: http://www.hindu.com/thehindu/2003/05/09/stories/2003050905181100.htm (accessed 16 February 2004).

Patil, S. (2001) 'India's experiment with coalition government at the federal level', *Indian Journal of Political Science*, 62(4): 586–93.

Perkovich, G. (1999) *India's Nuclear Bomb. The Impact on Global Proliferation*, Berkeley: University of California Press.

Powell, G. (1981), 'Party systems and political system performance: voting participation, government stability and mass violence in contemporary democracies', *American Political Science Review*, 75(4): 861–79.

Pridham, G. (ed.) (1986) *Coalitional Behaviour in Theory and Practice: An Inductive Model for Western Europe*, Cambridge: Cambridge University Press.

Rabushka, A. and Shepsle, K. (1972) *Politics in Plural Societies: A Theory of Democratic Instability*, Columbus, Ohio: Merrill.

Raghavan, J. (2003) 'Educational planning in India', in B. Tilak (ed.) *Education, Society and Development*, New Delhi: NIEPA: 49–62.

Rajalakshmi, T. (2003) 'Politics of cow slaughter', *Frontline*, 20(18). Online. Available at: http://www.flonnet.com/fl2018/stories/20030912005002700.htm (accessed 12 February 2004).

Ram, D. and Gehlot, N. (2000) 'Coalition politics in India (search for political stability)', *Indian Journal of Public Administration*, XLVI(4): 733–5.

Ramachandran, V. and Sahjee, A. (2002) 'The new segregation: Reflections on gender and equity in primary education', *Economic and Political Weekly*, 27 April: 1600–13.

Raman, V. (2001) 'The women's question in contemporary Indian politics', *Asian Journal of Women's Studies*, 7(2): 39–71.

Rana, K. (2002) 'Inside the Indian Foreign Service', *Foreign Service Journal*, October: 35–41.

Rangarajan, M. (2004) 'Advantage Vajpayee', *Seminar*, 533. Online. Available at: http://www.india-seminar.com (accessed 5 June 2004).

Rao, N. (2003a) 'Jharkhand: life and livelihood in Santal Parganas – does the right to livelihood really exist?', *Economic and Political Weekly*, 38(39): 4081–4.

Rao, N. (2003b) 'Vision 2010: chasing mirages', *Economic and Political Weekly*, 38(18): 1755–8.

Rawls, J. (1971) *A Theory of Justice*, Cambridge, Massachusetts: Harvard University Press.

Reilly, B. (2001) *Democracy in Divided Societies: Electoral Engineering for Conflict Management*, Cambridge: Cambridge University Press.

Reynolds, A. and Reilly, B., for the International Institute for Democracy and Electoral Assistance (1997) *The International IDEA Handbook of Electoral System Design*, Stockholm: International IDEA.

Rice, C. (2000) 'Promoting the national interest', *Foreign Affairs*, 79(1) January/February: 45–62.

Riker, W. (1962) *The Theory of Political Coalitions*, New Haven: Yale University Press.

Riker, W. and Ordeshook, P. (1973) *An Introduction to Positive Political Theory*, Englewood Cliffs: Prentice Hall.

Rowlands, J. (1998) 'A word of the times, but what does it mean? Empowerment in the discourse and practice of development', in H. Afshar (ed.) *Women and Empowerment: Illustrations from the Third World*, London: Macmillan: 11–33.

Rudolph, L. and Rudolph, S. (1987) *In Pursuit of Lakshmi: The Political Economy of the Indian State*, Chicago: University of Chicago Press.

Rudolph, S. (2004) 'Is civil society the answer?', in S. Prakash and P. Selle (eds) *Investigating Social Capital: Comparative Perspectives on Civil Society, Participation and Governance*, New Delhi: Sage Publications: 64–87.

Saberwal, S. (1986) *India: The Roots of Crisis*, Delhi: Oxford University Press.

Sachar, R. (2000) 'Issue of constitution review: examining the parameters', *The Tribune*, 4 September. Online. Available at: http://www.tribuneindia.com/2000/20000904/edit.htm#3 (accessed 9 February 2004).

Sáez, L. (2002) *Federalism Without a Centre: The Impact of Political and Economic Reform on India's Federal System*, New Delhi, London: Sage Publications.

Sarkar, T. (1995) 'Heroic women, mother goddesses: Family and organisation in *Hindutva* politics', in T. Sarkar and U. Butalia (eds) *Women and the Hindu Right: A Collection of Essays*, New Delhi: Kali for Women: 181–215.

Sathiya Moorthy, N. (2002) 'Anti-conversion bill passed by Tamil Nadu Assembly'. *Rediff.com* 31 October. Online. Available at: http://www.rediff.com/news/2002/oct/31tn.htm (accessed 15 December 2003).

Savarkar, V. (1947) *The Indian War of Independence 1857*, Bombay: Phoenix.

Savarkar, V. (1989) *Hindutva/Who is a Hindu?* Bombay: S.S. Savarkar.

Sen, G. and Grown, C. (1987) *Development, Crises and Alternative Visions: Third World Women's Perspectives*, New York: Monthly Review Press.

Sengupta, N. (1982) 'Background of the Jharkhand question', in N. Sengupta (ed.) *Fourth World Dynamics: Jharkhand*, Delhi: Authors Guild Publications: 3–39.

Sengupta, U. (1998) 'Much ado about nothing in UP', *Times of India*, 20 November.

Shah, G. (1998) 'The BJP's riddle in Gujarat: caste, factionalism and *Hindutva*', in T. Hansen and C. Jaffrelot (eds) *The BJP and the Compulsions of Politics in India*, New Delhi: Oxford University Press: 243–66.

Shankar, S. (2003) 'India's secularism in comparative perspective', *India Review*, 2(4): 43–58.

Sharma, J. (2003) *Hindutva: Exploring the Idea of Hindu Nationalism*, Delhi: Penguin.

Sharma, K. (1998) 'Power and representation: feminist dilemmas, ambivalent state and the debate on reservation for women in India', Occasional Paper No. 28,

New Delhi: Centre for Women's Development Studies (also published in *Asian Journal of Women's Studies*, 2000, 6(1): 47–87).

Sharma, R. (2002) *Indian Education at the Crossroads*, Delhi: Shubhi Publications.

Sharma, S. (2003) 'Creation of new states: need for constitutional parameters', *Economic and Political Weekly*, 38(38), 20 September: 3973–5.

Sharma, V. (2003) 'High-fives: we'll have two more women CMs', *Hindustan Times*, 4 December.

Shourie, A. (2004) 'When spirit is willing, flesh has a way', *Indian Express*, 4 February.

Shukla, P. (1988) *The New Education Policy*, Delhi: Sterling Publishers Private Ltd.

Singh, G. (1997a) 'The coalition experience', *Indian Journal of Political Science*, LVIII(1–4): 39–54.

Singh, G. (1997b) 'Understanding political corruption in contemporary Indian politics', in P. Heywood (ed.) *Political Corruption*, Oxford: Blackwell: 210–22.

Singh, G. (1998) 'The Akalis and the BJP in Punjab: from Ayodhya to the 1997 Legislative Assembly Elections', in T. Hansen and C. Jaffrelot (eds) *The BJP and the Compulsions of Politics in India*, New Delhi: Oxford University Press: 228–42.

Singh, G. (2000) *Ethnic Conflict in India: A Case Study of Punjab*, London: St Martin's Press.

Singh, G. (2002) 'Still democratic in spite of itself', *The Times Higher Education Supplement*, 24 May.

Singh, G. (2003) 'South Asia', in R. Hodess (ed.) *Global Corruption Report 2003. Transparency International*, London: Profile Books: 153–64.

Singh, G. (2004) 'Corruption, transparency and the good governance agenda in India', paper presented at a conference on EU–India: Beyond the New Delhi Summit, European Institute for Asian Studies. Online. Available at: http://www.eias.org/conferences/euindia412/singh.pdf (accessed 2 February 2004).

Singh, Jasgit (1998) *Nuclear India*, New Delhi: Knowledge World.

Singh, Jaswant (1998) 'Against nuclear apartheid', *Foreign Affairs*, 77(5) September/October: 41–52.

Singh, Jaswant (1999) *Defending India*, New Delhi: Macmillan India.

Singh, M.P. (2001) 'India's National Front and United Front coalition governments: a phase in federalized governance', *Asian Survey*, XLI(2): 328–50.

Singh, O. (2001) 'Advani denies move for Greater Nagaland', *Rediff.com*, 18 June 2001. Online. Available at: http://www.rediff.com/news/2001/jun/18mani3.htm (accessed 9 February 2004).

Singh, V. and Verma, A. (2004) 'BJP the real loser, Congress the real winner', *The Hindu*, 20 May: AE-5.

Sleeter, C. (forthcoming) 'State standards and a curriculum for imperialism', paper presented at AERA, San Diego, April 2004.

Sonalkar, W. (1999) 'An agenda for gender politics', *Economic and Political Weekly*, 34(1–2), 2–9 January: 24–9.

Sontheimer, G. (1989) 'Hinduism: the five components and their interaction', in G. Sontheimer and H. Kulke (eds) *Hinduism Reconsidered*, Delhi: Manohar: 197–212.

Sridharan, E. (2002) 'The fragmentation of the Indian party system, 1952–1999: seven competing explanations', in Z. Hasan (ed.) *Parties and Party Politics in India*, Oxford: Oxford University Press: 475–503.

Sridharan, K. (2003) 'Federalism and foreign relations: the nascent role of the Indian states', *Asian Studies Review*, 27(4): 463–89.

Stepan, A. (2001) *Arguing Comparative Politics*, Oxford: Oxford University Press.

Stockwell, R. (2003) 'Democracy and ethnic conflict: A comparative analysis of Mauritius, Trinidad, Guyana and Fiji', paper presented at Comparativists' Day Conference, UCLA Centre for Comparative Social Analysis.

Strøm, K. (1985) 'Party goals and government performance in parliamentary democracies', *American Political Science Review*, 79(3): 738–54.

Subhas Mishra, S. (2000) 'Family face off', *India Today*, 3 April.

Subramanian, T. (2004) 'Vaiko on bail', *Frontline*, 14 February. Online. Available at: http://www.flonnet.com/fl2104/stories/20040227007713300.htm (accessed 15 March 2004).

Sundar, N. (forthcoming) 'Teaching to hate: the Hindu right's pedagogical program'.

Suri, K. (2004) 'Reform: The elites want it, the masses don't', *The Hindu*, 20 May: AE-7.

Suryamurthy, R. (2003) 'NDA allies may form forum to "check" BJP', *The Tribune*, 3 October. Online. Available at: http://www.tribuneindia.com/2003/20031003/nation.htm (accessed 9 February 2004).

Swami, P. (2004) 'A shot in the dark', *Frontline*, 21 February. Online. Available at: http://www.flonnet.com/fl2104/stories/20040227004102500.htm (accessed 3 March 2004).

Swaminathan, R. (2003) 'Pokhran-II: five years later', *South Asia Analysis Group*, Paper 690, 19 May. Online. Available at: http://saag.org/papers7/paper690.htm (accessed 28 July 2003).

Taneja, N. (2003) *BJP Assault on Education and Educational Institutions*. Online. Available at: http://www.cpiml.org/liberation/year_2001/september/saffron-imp.htm (accessed 2 February 2004).

Tellis, A. (2002) 'Toward a "force-in-being": The logic, structure, and utility of India's emerging nuclear posture', *The Journal of Strategic Studies*, 25(4) December: 61–113.

Tellis, A. , Fair, C. and Medby, J. (2001) *Limited Conflicts Under the Nuclear Umbrella: Indian and Pakistani Lessons from the Kargil Crisis*, Santa Monica: RAND.

Tillin, L. (2003) 'US–Israel–India: strategic axis?', *BBC News*, 9 September. Online. Available at: http://news.bbc.co.uk/2/hi/south_asia/3092726.stm (accessed 17 October 2003).

Toye, J. (1989) *The Dilemmas of Development. Reflections on the Counter-Revolution in Development Economics*, Oxford: Blackwell.

Tripathi, P. (2003) 'Uneasy unity', *Frontline*, 20(8) 12 April. Online. Available at: http://www.flonnet.com/fl2008/stories/20030425004403000.htm (accessed 9 February 2004).

Tsebelis, G. (1990) *Nested Games: Rational Choice in Comparative Politics*, Berkeley: University of California Press.

Tsebelis, G. (2002) *Veto Players: How Political Institutions Work*, New York, Princeton: Russell Sage Foundation, Princeton University Press.

Tully, M. (2000) 'India: a democracy or kleptocracy?', paper presented at a conference on Political Reform in India: Ways Ahead, September, Oxford University: 1–11.

Upadhyaya, D. (1965) *Integral Humanism*. Online. Available at: http://www.bjp.org/philo.htm (accessed 7 September 2004).

Vajpayee, A. (1998) 'Statement to the Lok Sabha 27 May 1998'. Online. Available at: http://www.indiatoday.com/ntoday/cabinet.html (accessed 28 May 1998).

Varshney, A. (1999) 'Mass politics or elite politics? India's economic reforms in comparative perspective', in J. Sachs, A. Varshney and N. Bajpai (eds) *India in the Era of Economic Reforms*, Delhi: Oxford University Press: 222–60.

Varshney, A. (2002) *Ethnic Conflict and Civic Life: Hindus and Muslims in India*, New Haven: Yale University Press.

Varshney, A. and Sridharan, E. (2001) 'Towards moderate pluralism: political parties in India', in L. Diamond and R. Gunther (eds) *Political Parties and Democracy*, Baltimore: Johns Hopkins University Press: 207–37.

Venkatesan, V. (2000) 'Contradictions and pressures', *Frontline*, 17(26) 23 December–5 January.

Venkatesan, V. (2003) 'Inter-State Council: A blow for federalism', *Frontline*, 13 September. Online. Available at: http://www.frontlineonnet.com/fl2019/stories/20030926005003000.htm (accessed 15 February 2004).

Verma, A.K. (2002) *Kargil: Blood on the Snow: Tactical Victory Strategic Failure: A Critical Analysis of the War*, New Delhi: Manohar.

Vittal, N. (2001) 'Corruption in India – a strategic perspective', (unpublished): 1–9.

von Stietencron, H. (1989) 'Hinduism: on the proper use of a deceptive term', in G.D. Sontheimer and H. Kulke (eds) *Hinduism Reconsidered*, Delhi: Manohar: 11–27.

Wade, R. (1985) 'The market for public office: why the Indian State is no better at development', *World Development*, 13(4): 467–95.

Weiner, M. (1978) *Sons of the Soil: Migration and Ethnic Conflict in India*, Delhi: Oxford University Press.

Weiner, M. (1986) 'India's minorities: Who are they? What do they want?', in J. Roach (ed.) *India 2000: The Next Fifteen Years*, New Delhi: Allied.

Wildman, A. (2004) *The New York Times*, 13 May.

Wilkinson, S. (2000) 'India, consociational theory, and ethnic violence', *Asian Survey*, 40(5): 767–91.

Wolf, M. and Luce, E. (2003) 'India's slowing growth: why a hobbled economy cannot meet the country's needs', *Financial Times*, 4 April.

Wolfensohn, J. (1999) 'Keynote Address at the IMF Institute Conference on Second Generation Reforms', Washington, DC, 8 November.

Wright, T. (1983) 'The ethnic numbers game in South Asia: Hindu–Muslim conflicts over family planning, conversion, migration and census', in W. McCready (ed.) *Culture, Ethnicity and Identity*, New York: The Academic Press: 405–27.

Wright, T. (1997) 'A demand for Muslim reservations in India', *Asian Survey*, XXXVII(9): 852–8.

Wright, T. (2001) 'The impact of coalition politics in India on Indian minorities: the case of Muslims and Christians', *Indian Journal of Secularism*, 5(2) July/September: 1–7.

Wyatt, A. (1999) 'The limitations on coalition politics in India: the case of electoral alliances in Uttar Pradesh', *Commonwealth and Comparative Politics*, 37(2): 1–21.

Wyatt, A. (2001) 'Elections in India, 1999–2000', *The Round Table*, 306: 379–90.

Wyatt, A. (2002) 'The federal dimension of party politics in Tamil Nadu', *The Indian Journal of Federal Studies*, 3(2): 127–44.

Wyatt, A. (2003) 'Recasting India's economic nationalism', paper presented at the ECPR General Conference, Marburg, September.

Wyatt, A. (forthcoming) '(Re)imagining the Indian (inter)national economy'.

Wyatt, A. (2004) 'Religious nationalism in a regional context: Hindu nationalism in South India', paper presented at the Political Studies Association Annual Conference, Lincoln, April.

Yadav, Y. (1999) 'Electoral politics in the time of change: India's third electoral system, 1989–99', *Economic and Political Weekly*, 21–28 August: 2393–9.

Yadav, Y. (2000) 'Understanding the second democratic upsurge', in F. Frankel *et al.* (eds) *Transforming India: Social and Political Dynamics of Democracy*, Delhi: OUP.

Yadav, Y. (2004) 'BJP's consolidation will be hard to break in Chhattisgarh', *Countercurrents.org*, 21 March. Online. Available at: http://www.countercurrents.org/ie-yadav210304.htm (accessed 25 May 2004).

Yadav, Y. and Palshikar, S. (2003) 'From hegemony to convergence: party system and electoral politics in the Indian States, 1952–2002', *Journal of Indian School of Political Economy*, 15(1–2): 5–44.

Yadav, Y., Kumar, S. and Heath, O. (1999) 'The BJP's new social bloc', *Frontline*, 19 November: 33.

Zakaria, F. (2003) *The Future of Freedom: Illiberal Democracy at Home and Abroad*, New York: W.W. Norton.

Zavos, J. (2000) *The Emergence of Hindu Nationalism in India*, New Delhi: Oxford University Press.

Zavos, J. (2001) 'Conversion and the assertive margins: an analysis of Hindu nationalist discourse and the recent attacks on Indian Christians', *South Asia*, 24(2): 73–89.

Zavos, J., Wyatt, A. and Hewitt, V. (2004) 'Deconstructing the nation: politics and cultural mobilization in India', in J. Zavos, A. Wyatt and V. Hewitt (eds) *Politics of Cultural Mobilization in India*, New Delhi: Oxford University Press: 1–16.

Zerinini-Brotel, J. (1998) 'The BJP in Uttar Pradesh: From *Hindutva* to consensual politics?', in T. Hansen and C. Jaffrelot (eds) *The BJP and the Compulsions of Politics in India*, Delhi: Oxford University Press: 71–100.

Editorials and other media sources without a named author

BBC (2002) 'Kashmir elections "fair but not free"', *BBC News*, 9 October. Online. Available at: http://news.bbc.co.uk/2/hi/south_asia/2313347.stm (accessed 10 October 2002).

BBC (2003a) 'Vajpayee demands murder inquiry'. Online. Available at: http://news.bbc.co.uk (accessed 10 December 2003: 1–3).

BBC (2003b) 'Pakistan hands nuclear arms to army', *BBC News*, 8 January. Online. Available at: http://news.bbc.co.uk/1/hi/world/south_asia/2638679.stm (accessed 19 February 2004).

BBC (2004a) 'India, Russia sign defence deal', *BBC News*, 20 January. Online. Available at: http://news.bbc.co.uk/go/pr/fr/-/2/hi/south_asia/3408437.stm (accessed 12 February 2004).

BBC (2004b) 'Israeli FM in India terrorism plea', *BBC News*, 10 February. Online. Available at: http://news.bbc.co.uk/go/pr/fr/-/2/hi/south_asia.stm (accessed 17 February 2004).

Business Standard (2003) 'Who wants reforms?', *Business Standard*, 22 August.

Central Chronicle (2004) *Central Chronicle*, 13 June. Online. Available at: http://www.centralchronicle.com (accessed June 14 2004).

Dawn (2000a) 'Amnesty International slams India over anti-terrorism law', *Dawn*, 29 June.

Dawn (2000b) 'Delhi Muslims protest religious restrictions', *Dawn*, 4 March.

Deccan Herald (2003) 'Elections: disclosures now mandatory', *Deccan Herald*, 23 March: 1–2. Online. Available at: http://www.indiatogether.org/2003/mar/law-ncerscverd.htm (accessed on 1 February 2004).

EPW (2000a) 'Centre-state transfers: a step back', *Economic and Political Weekly*, 11 March. Online. Available at: http://www.epw.org.in (accessed 9 February 2004).

EPW (2000b) 'Federal finance: Central intrusion', *Economic and Political Weekly*, 6 May. Online. Available at: http://www.epw.org.in (accessed 9 February 2004).

EPW (2000c) 'TADA: hard law for soft state, report of the People's Union of Democratic Rights', *Economic and Political Weekly*, 25 March: 1066–71.

EPW (2003) 'POTA: well-founded fears', *Economic and Political Weekly*, 5 April. Online. Available at: http://www.epw.org.in (accessed 9 February 2004).

EPW Research Foundation (2004) 'Finances of state governments: deteriorating fiscal management', *Economic and Political Weekly*, 1 May.

Financial Times (2002) 'India: Country struggles to break cycle of corruption', *Financial Times*, 8 August.

Financial Times (2003) 'BJP gains raise chances of early elections', *Financial Times*, 4 December.

Financial Times (2004a) 'Master of ambiguity', *Financial Times*, 2 April.

Financial Times (2004b) 'Victorious BJP restarts reform drive in India', *Financial Times*, 6 December.

Free Press Journal (2003) 'Vajpayee, Advani have backstabbed the VHP: Ashok Singhal', *Free Press Journal*, 9 May.

Frontline (1998) 'A Low-key summit', *Frontline*, 15 August.

Frontline (1999a) *Frontline*, 5 November: 122–3.

Frontline (1999b) 'Ayodhya agenda', *Frontline*, 25 December.

Frontline (2001) 'Belated response', *Frontline*, 4–17 August: 1. Online. Available at: http://www.flonnet.com/fl1816/18160870.htm (accessed 23 January 2004).

Frontline (2002) 'Unity against terror', *Frontline*, 19 January.

Frontline (2003a) 'Delays and doubts', *Frontline*, 11–24 October. Online. Available at: http://www.flonnet.com/fl2021/stories/20031024003403000.htm (accessed 23 January 2004).

Frontline (2003b) 'An image of corruption', *Frontline*, 6–19 December. Online. Available at: http://www.flonnet.com/fl2025/stories/20031219004803200.htm (accessed 23 January 2004).

Frontline (2003c) 'Badals in the dock', *Frontline*, 6–9 December. Online. Available at: http://www.flonnet.com/fl2025/stories/20031219003104600.htm (accessed 23 January 2004).

Frontline (2004a) 'Advani roadshow', *Frontline*, 9 April.

Frontline (2004b) 'Saffonising the tribal heartland', *Frontline*, 26 March.

Frontline (2004c) 'The blame game in Mumbai', *Frontline*, 16 July.

Frontline (2004d) *Frontline*, 17 January.

Hindu Business Line (2003) 'Labour reforms not to shrink job market, assures Jaitley', *Hindu Business Line*, 26 November.

India Business World (2003) 'Govt. includes four new languages in the Constitution', *India Business World*, December. Online. Available at: http://news.helplinelaw.com/1203/d_eco_4-lang-constitution-1203.php (accessed 13 March 2004).

India Today (2002a) 'Overseas robbery', *India Today*, 21 January: 26–7.

India Today (2002b) 'Politics of trust', *India Today*, 13 August: 20–1.

India Today (2002c) 'Trading in trust', *India Today*, 16 July: 31–7.

India Today (2002d) 'Is reliance the red herring?', *India Today*, 20 August: 30–1.

India Today (2003) *India Today*, 29 December: 7.

Mid–Day (1996) 'Full protection to Muslims: Vajpayee', *Mid–Day*, 19 May.

New York Times (1998) 'Nuclear anxiety: India's letter to Clinton on nuclear testing', *New York Times*, 13 May: A12.

Newsinsight.net (2002) 'Scams and JPC reports', *Newsinsight.net*, 24 August. Online. Available at: http://www.indiareacts.com/archivedebates/nat2.asp?recno=431&ctg=business (accessed 5 February 2004).

Newsinsight.net (2003) 'Community', *Newsinsight.net*, 13 November. Online. Available at: http://www.indiareacts.com/archivedebates/nat2.asp?recno=762&ctg=community (accessed 5 February 2004).

Organiser (2004) 'Varsha Pratipada special', *Organiser*, 21 March: 18.

Outlook (2003) 'We don't consider anyone Atalji's successor', *Outlook*, 30 June.

Rediff.com (2003) 'Phukan to head Tehelka inquiry commission', *Rediff.com*, 4 January: 1. Online. Available at: http://www.rediff.com/news/2003/jan/04def.htm (accessed 8 January 2004).

Rediff.com (2004) 'CII urges timely VAT launch in pre-budget memorandum', 28 June. Online. Available at: http://www.rediff.com/money/2004/jun/28bud2.htm (accessed 20 July 2004).

Telegraph (Calcutta) (2003) 'Atal and Aruns in Swadeshi line of fire', *Telegraph (Calcutta)*, 5 February.

The Asian Age (1998) *The Asian Age*, 1 January.

The Asian Age (2000) 'BJP trying to woo Muslims for more votes: Sher Khan', *The Asian Age*, 11 September.

The Economic Times (1994) *The Economic Times*, 15 April: 7.

The Economic Times (2000) 'India may emerge as economic, military power', *The Economic Times*, 17 December.

The Economic Times (2003) 'Labour laws: a fresh breath of life', *The Economic Times*, 12 October.

The Economist (2001) *Pocket World in Figures*, London: The Economist.

The Economist (2003a) 'Goodbye to all VAT', *The Economist*, 22 May.

The Economist (2003b) 'The right connections', *The Economist*, 18 December.

The Hindu (1955a) *The Hindu*, 5 November.

The Hindu (1955b) *The Hindu*, 7 November.

The Hindu (1990) *The Hindu*, 15 February.

The Hindu (2002a) 'BJP preparing to return to *Hindutva* agenda?', *The Hindu*, 24 June.

The Hindu (2002b) 'Pak Seeks to defer SAARC summit', *The Hindu*, 10 December.

The Hindu (2002c) 'Petrol, patronage, probe', *The Hindu*, 23 December: 1. Online. Available at: http://www.hinduonnet.com/thehindu/2002/12/23/stories/2002122300441000.htm (accessed 4 January 2004).

The Hindu (2003a) 'Developing countries seek to build coalition', *The Hindu International Edition*, 17 May: 11.

The Hindu (2003b) 'Government to bring comprehensive legislation of languages', *The Hindu*, 24 December. Online. Available at: http://www.thehindu.com/2003/12/24/stories/2003122406841100.htm (accessed 15 March 2004).

The Hindu (2003c) 'Haj subsidy will continue', *The Hindu*, 23 October.

The Hindu (2003d) 'India forms new alliance on farm sector at WTO', *The Hindu International Edition*, 30 August: 10.

The Hindu (2003e) 'Nod for Bill on increased donations to parties', *The Hindu*, 5 August: 1–2. Online. Available at: http://www.hinduonnet.com/thehindu/2003/08/05/stories/2003080504831200.htm (accessed 12 January 2004).

The Hindu (2003f) 'PM's stand on "Greater Nagaland" hailed in Manipur', *The Hindu*, 31 October. Online. Available at: http://www.hindu.com/the-hindu/2003/10/31/stories/2003103104361100.htm (accessed 15 March 2004).

The Hindu (2003g) 'Protecting the bureaucracy', *The Hindu*, 2 July: 1–3. Online. Available at: Http://www.hinduonnet.com/thehindu/2003/03/07stories/20033030700761000.htm (accessed 1 January 2004).

The Hindu (2003h) *The Hindu*, 12 October.

The Hindu (2003i) *The Hindu International Edition*, 8 March: 9.

The Hindu (2004a) 'Poll graphics'. Online. Available at: http://www.hinduonnet.com/elections2004/index.htm (accessed 30 September 2004).

The Hindu (2004b) *The Hindu*, 6 January.

The Hindu (2004c) *The Hindu*, 23 March. Online. Available at: http://www.hindu.com (accessed 24 March 2004).

The Hindu (2004d) *The Hindu*, 15 May. Online. Available at: http://www.hindu.com (accessed 16 May 2004).

The Hindu (2004e) 'How India voted: Supplement', *The Hindu*, 20 May. Online. Available at: http://www.hindu.com (accessed 21 May 2004).

The Hindu (2004f) *The Hindu*, 31 July. Online. Available at: http://www.hindu.com (accessed 1 August 2004).

The Hindu (2004g) *The Hindu*, 2 August. Online. Available at: http://www.hindu.com (accessed 3 August 2004).

The Hindu (2004h) The *Hindu*, 5 August. Online. Available at: http://www.hindu.com (accessed 6 August 2004).

The Hindu (2004i) *The Hindu*, 7 August. Online. Available at: http://www.hindu.com (accessed 8 August 2004).

The Hindustan Times (1999) 'BJP's image as anti-Muslim party blunted: Vajpayee', *The Hindustan Times*, 3 May.

The Indian Express (1993) 'Advani promises Muslim welfare', *The Indian Express*, 24 January.

The Indian Express (2001) 'Book historians under POTO? Listen to Joshi', *The Indian Express*, 20 December.

The New Indian Express (2002) 'India second highest source of migrants to the US', *The New Indian Express*, 6 September.

The New Indian Express (2003) 'LS adopts resolution "deploring" the war', *The New Indian Express*, 9 April.

The Statesman (1995) 'Muslims have nothing to fear under BJP rule: Keshubhai', *The Statesman*, 29 March.

The Telegraph (1996) 'Advani "guarantees" justice to Muslims', *The Telegraph*, 2 May.

The Times of India (1997) 'Advani uses every trick to woo Muslim voter', *The Times of India*, 16 June.

The Times of India (1998a) 'George and the dragon', 5 May, as cited in G. Perkovich (1999) *India's Nuclear Bomb: The Impact of Global Proliferation*, Berkeley: University of California Press: 415.

The Times of India (1998b) 'No scrapping of SC, ST quotas, says Vajpayee', *Times of India*, 10 July.

The Times of India (1998c) 'Volte faced by Joshi on "saffronising" education', *Times of India*, 22 October.

The Times of India (1999) 'Ominous growth of madrasas, farm houses on Nepal border', *Times of India*, 7 May.

The Times of India (2000a) 'BJP freezes UP religious bill', *Times of India*, 27 May.

The Times of India (2000b) 'Govt. puts anti-terrorism law on hold', *Times of India*, 6 August.

The Times of India (2004a) 'Feelgood 2003, feelbetter 2004?', *The Times of India*, 1 January. Online. Available at: http://timesofindia.indiatimes.com/articleshow/msid-398692,prtpage-1.cms (accessed 1 January 2004).

The Times of India (2004b) 'Jethmalani to form anti-NDA alliance', *The Times of India*, 21 January. Online. Available at: http://www1.timesofindia.indiatimes.com/articleshow/msid-435974,prtpage-1.cms (accessed on 25 October 2004).

The Times of India (2004c) 'SC to look into CVC Act on probing higher ups', *The Times of India*, 21 January: 1–2. Online. Available at: http://timesofindia.indiatimes.com/articleshow/433727.cms (accessed 21 January 2004).

The Times of India (2002) 'Labour reform stumbles on cabinet divide', *Times of India*, 24 February.

The Tribune (2002a) 'Big challenge ahead in Punjab', *The Tribune*, 1 March. Online. Available at: http://www.tribuneindia.com/2002/20020301/edit.htm#3 (accessed 24 February 2003).

The Tribune (2002b) 'It's IAS v Vigilance Bureau now', *The Tribune*, 19 May. Online. Available at: http://www.tribuneindia.com/2002/20020519/punjab1.htm#3 (accessed 26 March 2004).

The Tribune (2002c) 'Justice A.S. Garg resigns', *The Tribune*, 15 May. Online. Available at: http://www.tribuneindia.com/2002/20020515/main6.htm (accessed 30 March 2004).

The Tribune (2002d) 'Right to information cannot be curtailed', *The Tribune*, 9 May. Online. Available at: http://www.tribuneindia.com/2002/20020509/main1.htm (accessed 30 March 2003).

The Tribune (2002e) 'Waiting for Lok Pal', *The Tribune*, 21 August: 1. Online. Available at: http://www.tribuneindia.com/2002/20020821/edit.htm#1 (accessed 21 April 2004).

The Tribune (2003a) 'Attack on SAD is attack on NDA: George', *The Tribune*, 13 August. Online. Available at: http://www.tribuneindia.com/2003/20030813/punjab1.htm (accessed 15 December 2004).

The Tribune (2003b) 'Dogri in Eighth Schedule: Parties claim credit', *The Tribune*, 23 December. Online. Available at: http://www.tribuneindia.com/2003/20031224/j&k.htm (accessed 15 March 2004).

The Tribune (2003c) 'Judeo issue: PM assures fair probe', *The Tribune*, 11 December. Online. Available at: http://www.tribuneindia.com/2003/20031211/main5.htm (accessed 11 December 2003).

The Tribune (2003d) 'No complaints against ministers, says PM', *The Tribune*, 12

November. Online. Available at: http://www.tribuneindia.com/2003/20031112/
nation.htm#6 (accessed 26 December 2004).

The Tribune (2003e) 'Opinions', *The Tribune*, 25 November: 1. Online. Available at:
http://www.tribuneindia.com/2003/20031124/edit.htm (accessed 25 November 2003).

The Tribune (2003f) 'Parliament approves anti-defection Bill', *The Tribune*, 19
December: 1. Online. Available at: http://www.tribuneindia.com/2003/
20031219/main2.htm (accessed 19 December 2003).

The Tribune (2003g) 'Probe ordered into intranet deal', *The Tribune*, 31 December.
Online. Available at: http://www.tribuneindia.com/2003/20031231/main1.
htm#2 (accessed 31 December 2003).

The Tribune (2004a) 'Case against Bhattal to stay, says CM', *The Tribune*, 8 January.
Online. Available at: http://www.tribuneindia.com/2004/20040108/main3.htm
(accessed 8 January 2004).

The Tribune (2004b) 'Magistrate suspended', *The Tribune*, 30 January: 1. Online.
Available at: http://www.tribuneindia.com/2004/20040130/main1.htm
(accessed 30 January 2004).

The Tribune (2004c) 'No withdrawal of case against Bhattal: CM', *The Tribune*, 2
January. Online. Available at: http://www.tribuneindia.com/2004/20040102/
punjab1.htm#2 (accessed 2 January 2004).

The Tribune (2004d) 'No clean chit to Fernandes, says Justice Phukan, *The Tribune*,
5 February: 1. Online. Available at: http://www.tribuneindia.com/2004/
20040205/main3.htm (accessed 5 February 2004).

The Tribune (2004e) 'Swadeshi Jagran Manch hits out at NDA, welcomes CMP', *The
Tribune* 2 June. Online. Available at: http://www.tribuneindia.com/2004/
20040602/nation.htm#2 (accessed 7 September 2004).

THES (2004) 'OUP Withdraws book after violent protest', *The Times Higher Education Supplement*, 23 January: 18.

Publications of organisations

Arms Control Association (ND), *Worldwide Ballistic Missile Inventories*. Online. Available at: http://www.armscontrol.org/factsheets/missiles.asp (accessed 12 February 2004).

Awaaz (2004) 'In bad faith? British charity and Hindu extremism', *Awaaz*. Online.
Available at: http://www.awaazsaw.org/ibf/ (accessed 2 February 2004).

Bharatiya Janata Party (1998) *Vote for a Stable Government and an Able Prime Minister*.
Online. Available at: http://www.bjp.org/manifes/manife99.htm (accessed 9
February 2004).

Bharatiya Janata Party (2004) *Vision Document 2004*. Online. Available at:
http://www.bjp.org (accessed 25 October 2004).

CII (Confederation of Indian Industry) (2004) *Key Factors Making India a Major
Global Player: The Southern Stake*, New Delhi: CII.

CPI (ML) (2004) *CPI (ML) Manifesto for the 14th Lok Sabha Elections*. Online.
Available at: http://www.cpiml.org/liberation/year_2004/april/manifesto.htm
(accessed 1st April 2004).

CSDS (Centre for the Study of Developing Societies) (1996) *National Election
Survey 1996*, Delhi: CSDS.

CSDS (Centre for the Study of Developing Societies) (1999) *National Election Survey 1999*, Delhi: CSDS.

CSDS (Centre for the Study of Developing Societies) (2003) ' "Statistical supplement", Special issue on Political Parties and Elections in Indian States', *Journal of Indian School of Political Economy*, 15(1–2): 279–614.

CWDS (Centre for Women's Development Studies) (1997) *National Population Policy: Perspectives from the Women's Movement*, New Delhi: CWDS.

CWDS (Centre for Women's Development Studies) (2003) *Human Rights and Human Development*, New Delhi: CWDS.

Hindu Mahasabha (1954) *Full Text of Resolutions and the Report of the Mahasabha, 31st Session, Hyderabad*, New Delhi: Hindu Mahasabha Bhavan.

Human Rights Watch (2002) ' "We have no orders to save you". State participation and complicity in communal violence in Gujarat', *Human Rights Watch*, 14(3C): 1–68.

IISS (International Institute for Strategic Studies) (2003) *The Military Balance, 2003–2004*, London: IISS.

Indian Council of Social Science Research (1975) *Status of Women in India: A Synopsis of the Report of the National Committee*, New Delhi: Allied Publishers.

NABARD (National Bank for Agriculture and Rural Development) (2002) *SHG-bank Linkage Programme*. Online. Available at: http://www.narbard./org/roles/mcid/highlights.htm (accessed 11 March 2005).

NDA (National Democratic Alliance) (1999) *For a Proud, Prosperous India: An Agenda*. Online. Available at: http://www.bjp.org (accessed 10 February 2004).

NDA (National Democratic Alliance) (2004) *An Agenda for Development, Good Governance, Peace, and Harmony: Manifesto for Elections to the 14th Lok Sabha April–May 2004*. Online. Available at: http://www.bjp.org (accessed 20 August 2004).

SIPRI (Stockholm International Peace Research Institute) (2003), *The SIPRI Military Expenditure Database 2003*. Online. Available at: http://first.sipri.org/ (accessed 5 February 2004).

South Asia Terrorism Portal (ND). Online. Available at: http://www.satp.org/ (accessed 14 February 2004).

The National Security Strategy of the United States of America (2002). Online. Available at: http://www.whitehouse.gov/nsc/nss.html (accessed 10 October 2002).

United Nations Peacekeeping (ND). Online. Available at: http://www.un.org/Depts/dpko/dpko/index.asp (accessed 9 February 2004).

United States Institute of Peace (1999) *Lahore Declaration. Online*. Available at: http://www.usip.org/library/pa/ip/ip_lahore19990221.html (accessed 15 February 2004).

VIC (Virtual Information Center) (2001) *India's Nuclear Strike Force: A Special Report*, 18 June. Online. Available at: http://www.vic-info.org/soasia/indiapage.htm (accessed 5 February 2004).

VIC (Virtual Information Center) (2002) *India–Pakistan: Loose Talk About Nukes*, 30 December. Online. Available at: http://www.vic-info.org/SOAsia/Pakistan-page.htm (accessed 17 February 2004).

VIC (Virtual Information Center) (2003) *Special Press Summary: India: New Nuclear Command Authority*, 7 January. Online. Available at: http://www.vic-info.org/soasia/indiapage.htm (accessed 12 February 2004).

World Bank (2003) *India: Sustaining Reform, Reducing Poverty*, Poverty Reduction and Economic Management Sector Unit, South Asia Region (Report No. 25797-IN), 14 July.

World Bank (ND) 'International Bank for Reconstruction and Development', *World Development Indicators* (Washington DC, various years) database held at the University of Bradford Library. Online. Available at: http://www.brad.ac.uk/lss/library/index.php (accessed 16 February 2004).

Index

eBooks – at www.eBookstore.tandf.co.uk

A library at your fingertips!

eBooks are electronic versions of printed books. You can store them on your PC/laptop or browse them online.

They have advantages for anyone needing rapid access to a wide variety of published, copyright information.

eBooks can help your research by enabling you to bookmark chapters, annotate text and use instant searches to find specific words or phrases. Several eBook files would fit on even a small laptop or PDA.

NEW: Save money by eSubscribing: cheap, online access to any eBook for as long as you need it.

Annual subscription packages

We now offer special low-cost bulk subscriptions to packages of eBooks in certain subject areas. These are available to libraries or to individuals.

For more information please contact webmaster.ebooks@tandf.co.uk

We're continually developing the eBook concept, so keep up to date by visiting the website.

www.eBookstore.tandf.co.uk